ANALECTA BIBLICA
INVESTIGATIONES SCIENTIFICAE IN RES BIBLICAS

—— 149 ——

T0153864

CHRISTOPHER T. BAGLOW

"MODUS ET FORMA":

A New Approach to the Exegesis of
Saint Thomas Aquinas with an Application
to the *Lectura super Epistolam ad Ephesios*

EDITRICE PONTIFICIO ISTITUTO BIBLICO - ROMA 2002

IMPRIMI POTEST

Romae, die 17 ianuarii 2002

R.P. ROBERT F. O'TOOLE, S.J.
Rector Pontificii Instituti Biblici

IMPRIMATUR

Dal Vicariato di Roma, 17 gennaio 2002

✠ LUIGI MORETTI
Vescovo tit. di Mopta
Segretario Generale

EDITRICE PONTIFICIO ISTITUTO BIBLICO
Piazza della Pilotta, 35 - 00187 Roma, Italia

For Christine Kelly Baglow

ACKNOWLEDGMENTS

Many individuals were of assistance in the writing of this study; without their aid and encouragement, it could not have been completed.

Many thanks are due to Michael J. Cahill, Ph.D., who as director was ever-present with direction, correction, and a promptness of response rarely found among academic guides. In particular, I am grateful for Dr. Cahill's willingness to direct a dissertation written in its entirety from afar. I also wish to extend my gratitude to Michael Slusser, D. Phil., who as first reader offered many helpful editorial comments and challenges as well.

I would also like to thank the two other members of the dissertation committee who approved what must have seemed an all-but-exhausted topic at the time of its proposal. Both deserve to be mentioned by name: Anne M. Clifford, C.S.J., Ph.D.; and Rev. Sean P. Kealy, C.S.Sp., Ph.D.

Others outside of the Duquesne University academic community have been of great assistance in the completion of this work. Above all, Gregory Vall, Ph.D., of Notre Dame Seminary, who not only proofread the entire text for errors but also offered keen insights and challenges without which Part I of the study would have lacked a necessary precision regarding its most crucial assertions. Recognition must be offered as well to Rev. David Balas, O. Cist., S.T.D., and Rev. Roch Kereszty, O. Cist., S.T.D., of the University of Dallas, who as readers of my M.A. Thesis were the first to encourage me to continue my research in the area of Thomas' exegesis. Thanks to Sr. Barbara Dupuis, Librarian, of Notre Dame Seminary, who allowed me the greatest possible leeway in my use of the Seminary Library, most notably the privileges of interlibrary borrowing and after-hours access. I would also like to recognize Mrs. Susan F. Dane for her financial sponsorship of my graduate studies, and Mr. Michael G. Gaffney and Mr. Thomas G. Krentel, custodians of The Gloria Shearin Smith and Ivy A. Smith Jr. Charitable Trust, a grant from which made this volume possible.

Thanks also to my family, near and extended, especially Richard and Melanie Baglow, my parents, who first encouraged me to pursue graduate studies and have always been supportive of my interest in Theology.

3 December, 2001   Christopher Trevor Baglow
Feast of St. Francis Xavier   Covington, Louisiana

Contents

PART I. THE EXEGETICAL CORPUS OF AQUINAS:
A NEW VANTAGE POINT AND A NEW APPROACH

PART II. "BUILT INTO A HOLY TEMPLE": THE CHURCH
IN THE *LECTURA SUPER EPISTOLAM AD EPHESIOS*

INTRODUCTION

Thomistic scholarship in the 20th century has witnessed a surge in two previously neglected areas of inquiry - the study of Thomas Aquinas as an exegete and biblical theologian on the one hand, and the study of his vision of the Church on the other. It is indisputably in these two areas that Thomistic scholarship has demonstrated the fastest rate of growth, from which a body of literature has developed and slowly has taken on a comparable status to more frequented avenues of research. Both areas correspond quite naturally to larger developments in the Catholic theology of this century, and find their places within two growth centers of which the better contemporary theologians are aware - the renewal of biblical studies and the renewal of ecclesiology. Yet in the case of these two areas of Thomistic scholarship (and unlike the larger movements of which they are a part), the growing interest and literature regarding them have grown up more or less separately. It is necessary to examine both more closely in order to understand this separation.

A) *Thomas Aquinas as Biblical Exegete and Theologian*

In the renewed awareness of Thomas as biblical exegete and theologian one locates a field which has become almost mandatory for any survey of Thomas' works or general inquiry into his theology. Ever since the discovery by Heinrich Denifle in 1894 of the all-important fact that the Bible was Thomas' official textbook in his various positions as a teacher,[1] it has become commonplace for scholars to recognize certain facts considered essential to Thomas' study of the Bible, such as his theory of interpretation, his understanding of the senses, and the nature of his masterpiece, the *Summa Theologiae*, as being intrinsically and even primarily biblical. One could say that the major shift of this century in our comprehensive understanding of Thomas Aquinas is this new awareness of the pervading presence and

---

[1] Heinrich DENIFLE, "Quel livre servait de base à l'enseignement des Maîtres en Théologie dans l'Université de Paris?," *Revue Thomiste* 2 (1894) : 129-161.

influence of Scripture on his thought. One need only survey the works of such pioneering Thomistic scholars as M.D. Chenu, Yves Congar and J.P. Torrell to see that the relationship between Thomas and the Bible is at the cutting edge of development in this field.

These are not new observations for anyone who has kept an eye on the literature. What is surprising, however, is the attitude which pervades this literature itself, one which almost seems to be an absence of recognition of the growing mountain of monographs, books and dissertations focused precisely on the Thomas/Bible connection. Hence C. Clifton Black can say that "the biblical exegesis of Thomas Aquinas defines a field of inquiry whose richness is exceeded only by its relative neglect in contemporary scholarship."[2] Donal J. O'Connor must point out to his readers that Thomas' exegetical writings are "lesser known" but "very important."[3] T. Gilby, in the face of a century of intensive discussion among numerous scholars regarding Thomas as a biblical theologian,[4] must remind his readers that "only in recent years have we recovered the sense of how profoundly biblical St. Thomas' theology is."[5] These and countless other scholars seem almost apologetic in discussing the issue, a sign that perhaps all is not well with the substantive research that they instinctively dismiss, or of the possibility that their own research does not tread much new ground.

It is this latter possibility which seems the more likely of the two. In his excellent, groundbreaking and yet generally neglected doctoral dissertation, Wilhelmus Valkenberg goes a long way towards uncovering this very real problem in contemporary Thomas/Bible scholarship. In his own words,

> A survey of the literature on Aquinas and Holy Scripture gives the impression of a well-examined field. But on closer inspection it can be argued that there are some well-trodden paths in this field, whereas other spots remain totally unvisited. Issues such as the exegetical principles of Aquinas, Scripture as a source of his

---

[2] C. Clifton BLACK, "St. Thomas' Commentary on the Johannine Prologue: Some Reflections on its Character and Implications," *Catholic Biblical Quarterly* 48 (October 1986) : 681.

[3] Donal J. O'CONNOR, "The Concept of Mystery in Aquinas' Exegesis," *The Irish Theological Quarterly* 36 (July 1969) : 183.

[4] Cf. Frank Powell HAGGARD, "An Interpretation of Thomas Aquinas as a Biblical Theologian with Special Reference to his Systematizing of the Economy of Salvation" (Ph.D. Thesis, Drew University, 1972) : 55-153, for an excellent analysis of these thinkers.

[5] T. GILBY, appendix to *Summa Theologiae* (New York: Blackfriars / McGraw -Hill, 1964), 138.

theology and his opinion on the senses of Scripture, in short: his theories on Scripture, are thoroughly investigated. But as far as I know, surprisingly little attention is paid to the question, as to what exactly Thomas does when he uses Scripture...”[6]

Valkenberg locates the problem precisely when he focuses on practice as the "great beyond" in this field - the place where Thomas, whose theoretical genius no one disputes, actually begins his work as an exegete and interpreter of Sacred Scripture.

If this observation is correct, then it is not surprising that the biblical commentaries of St. Thomas Aquinas remain largely unexamined even while existing in an atmosphere in which they are often recalled, extolled and recommended. This is the current situation even though contemporary scholarship could not be more poised for undertaking a thorough examination of them.[7] Yet only in the past thirty years have any significant advances been made into these works, and of these advances, many have been limited by the presuppositions and general approach with which they were made. This has resulted more often than not in the mere rediscovery of ideas and data already to be found in Thomas' systematic writings. In fact, the discovery that Thomas' basic theological ideas and principles remain more or less the same throughout all of his later works, exegetical and systematic, has been the most important and simultaneously the most discouraging discovery (from the point-of-view of potential inquiry into the exegetical works as primary sources) that has arisen from these various attempts to analyze the content of the commentaries. (A second more disputable "discovery," which has never

---

[6] Wilhelmus G.B.M. VALKENBERG, "'Did not our Heart Burn?' Place and Function of Holy Scripture in the Theology of St. Thomas" (Ph.D. diss., Katholieke Theologische Universiteit Utrecht, 1990), 2-3. Perhaps the most illustrative example of Valkenberg's point is the otherwise excellent doctoral dissertation by Robert G. KENNEDY, "Thomas Aquinas and the Literal Sense of Sacred Scripture" (Ph.D. diss., University of Notre Dame, 1985). Although his in-depth analysis of Thomas' theories regarding the literal sense of Scripture is peerless, never once does Kennedy produce an example of Thomas' dealing with an actual text of Scripture and its literal sense.

[7] This century has witnessed a flourishing of inquiry into the provenance of the biblical commentaries of St. Thomas Aquinas along with his other works. For instance, the 1920's and 1930's witnessed a running debate regarding the dating of the biblical commentaries in which a number of important scholars were involved: Synave, Glorieux and Grabmann among them. Yet in the midst of this debate (which still continues) on the order of the commentaries and their respective provenances, not a single scholar gives anything more than a passing glance at the content of these works. This is typical of the way the commentaries are treated by many even to this day.

been explicitly stated but is often assumed, is that greater depth and development cannot be found in the biblical commentaries than is already found in the *Summa* and the other systematic works.)

These attempts and their rather unpromising results have been, at least implicitly, the source of a number of criticisms levied against Thomas' exegesis[8] in recent decades. These criticisms, particularly those of T.F. Torrance,[9] O.H. Pesch,[10] and C. Clifton Black,[11] have been by no means entirely pessimistic. Yet they do highlight the quandary facing scholars in this field, and clearly question whether or not the biblical commentaries can be considered as anything more than supplements to the other, more comprehensive works of Aquinas. These authors demonstrate (if nothing else) where the large part of the scholarship in this field has stalled.

If one examines these criticisms closely, one finds that far from dismissing the commentaries entirely (or relegating them back to the status of secondary sources, which they have been treated as for centuries), they actually provide a new direction for inquiry into these works. For while Thomas' "homogenizing"[12] approach (which is owed as much to his frequent citation of other biblical sources as it is to his penchant for systematization) does result in the general repetition of ideas found elsewhere, what is not generally recognized is that he is enough aware of his primary text to find a new direction and new applications for these ideas in the occasion of his commenting on the text. This is overlooked frequently because of the tendency of modern scholarship to be intimidated by his precritical style of interpretation and to dismiss it too readily. It is true that exegesis as we now understand it is far more capable of uncovering the original meaning and context of scriptural sources than Thomas would ever have been. Yet to

---

[8] By using the terms "exegete," "exegesis," etc. in reference to Thomas Aquinas, I obviously do not mean biblical exegesis as it is understood by modern scholars - Thomas is certainly not a critical exegete in this sense. However, this observation must be qualified by the currently renewed realization that exegesis is not exclusive of theological interpretation and actually errs when it attempts to be. See PONTIFICAL BIBLICAL COMMISSION, "The Interpretation of the Bible in the Church" (April 23, 1993), Pt III, "Characteristics of Catholic Interpretation," for an excellent and very positive analysis of this position.

[9] T.F. TORRANCE, "Scientific Hermeneutics according to St. Thomas Aquinas," *Journal of Theological Studies* 13 (October 1962) : 259-289.

[10] Otto Herman PESCH, "Paul as Professor of Theology: The Image of the Apostle in St. Thomas' Theology," *Thomist* 38 (1974) : 584-605.

[11] BLACK, 681-698.

[12] Ibid., 696.

throw out the possibility that Thomas was profoundly influenced by his text *as a text* is to miss what is most original to his biblical commentaries.

In particular, too little attention has been given to the possibility that Thomas' interpretation of Sacred Scripture changes with the text at hand, even while his basic principles remain the same. No one has yet to consider, for instance, the peculiar characteristics of Thomas as a specifically Pauline or Johannine exegete, although the modern critical methods have proven that these are two very different kinds of literature which affect their readers as such, regardless of where these readers are located in history. Thomas was aware of the different literary genres of the Bible.[13]   Might he not also have been aware of, or at least influenced by, the way these different genres mediate their messages?

A final neglected point deals more with the question of context. Is it possible that, in the midst of his admittedly eisegetical approach on the one hand, and his universalizing, homogenizing tendency on the other, Thomas was forced at times by the text to add emphases and directions to ideas which he would otherwise have left in the abstract? For instance, is it possible that in dealing with the Epistle to the Ephesians, Thomas was influenced by elements such as tone and specific concerns implicit in the text in such a way that his interpretation yields not a different theology but one accommodated to concerns and issues not raised in the *Summa Theologiae*? It would seem that this is most likely, considering that the *Summa* stands at the beginning of theological studies in Thomas' *ordo disciplinae*, whereas direct and formal study of the text of Scripture is considered to be only for the *profecti*.[14]   One would expect the creative range of interpretation to undergo development of some sort from the former to the latter, which it does.

In short, I propose to consider Thomas Aquinas not as a theoretical exegete primarily, but as a Pauline exegete; specifically a Pauline exegete of the text of Ephesians.[15]   In so doing I hope to demonstrate what has already been observed by others, namely that Aquinas' theories of interpretation often

---

[13] *Super Psalmos,* Proemium.   See also *"De commendatione et partitione sacrae scripturae"* in *Opuscula Theologica.*

[14] *ST, Prol.* Cf. John SHEETS, "The Scriptural Dimension of St. Thomas," *American Ecclesiastical Review* 144 (1961) : 155-158.

[15] The term "Pauline exegete" is not an implicit judgment on the authorship of Ephesians. It is rather a recognition of two facts which are essential to the topic at hand: a) that Aquinas considers Ephesians to be a Letter written by St. Paul (as everyone did in his day), and b) that regardless of direct authorship, Ephesians is certainly influenced by Paul and his theology.

fall significantly behind his practice[16]; when forced into uncharted hermeneutical realms by the task at hand he affords certain surprises, and this is where the unique value of his biblical works is to be located. This approach is not entirely new; others have already made similar inquiries into the biblical commentaries and have produced excellent results. However, no comprehensive approach to Thomas' exegesis has ever been developed. Nor has any scholar undertaken a sustained, in-depth inquiry into the *Lectura super epistolam ad Ephesios* (a commentary of particular import for understanding Thomas' ecclesiology[17]) with any emphasis on the fact that it is a work of exegesis.

B) *Thomas Aquinas' Vision of the Church*

As mentioned previously, Thomas' vision of the Church has been explored numerous times in this century, beginning with the work of Grabmann[18] and reaching its highpoint with the work of Congar.[19] Not only the contours but also many of the minute details of Thomas' ecclesiology have been demonstrated, and the bibliography of the present study gives a thorough list of books and monographs on the subject. A few of these demand further consideration when it comes to their relevance for the present study.

George Sabra's fine book on Thomas' ecclesiology is the best recent treatment of the subject.[20] He succeeds in developing a comprehensive exposition which has been conspicuously absent among the many monographs dealing with this or that aspect or application of Aquinas' vision of the Church. In his work he also draws out certain aspects of Thomas' ecclesiology "which reveal its ecumenical nature and potential and which

---

[16] Among others, see M.D. CHENU, *La Théologie comme science au XIII*[e] *siècle, troisième édition*, Bibliothèque Thomiste 33 (Paris: J. Vrin, 1957), 79-89; M. CORBIN, *Le chemin de la théologie chez Thomas d'Aquin,* Bibliothèque des Archives de Philosophie, Nouv. Ser.16 (Paris, 1974), 899; W. VALKENBERG, 3.

[17] Thomas points out in his general prologue to the *corpus paulinum* that Ephesians is primarily concerned with "the origination of ecclesial unity." Here one sees that the Church is at the heart of Thomas' interpretation of this Epistle.

[18] M. GRABMANN, *Die lehre des heiligen Thomas von Aquin von der Kirche als Gotteswerk. Ihre Stellung im thomistischen System und in der Geschichte der mitteralterlichen Theologie* (Regensburg : C.J. Manz, 1903).

[19] Cf. Yves CONGAR, *Thomas d'Aquin: sa vision de la théologie et de l'Eglise* (London: Variorum Reprints, 1984), for the only collection of his work on this topic.

[20] George SABRA, *Thomas Aquinas' Vision of the Church: Fundamentals of an Ecumenical Ecclesiology* (Mainz: Matthias Grünewald, 1987).

dispel the faulty view that Thomas' ecclesiology is the exclusive domain of Roman Catholic theology..."[21] His willingness to incorporate the brilliant insights of Congar and others make it the best work of synthesis that exists on the subject today.

However, two things are missing from Sabra's treatment. Most conspicuous is the absence of a survey of the influences on Thomas' ecclesiological vision, an inquiry which would help to pinpoint certain theological trends by which Thomas was drawn to the formulations and conclusions specific to his ecclesiology. Such an analysis would be helpful to identify the *auctoritates* to which Thomas is most indebted. But its greatest pay-off would be to reveal which biblical sources show up most frequently and forcefully in his vision of the Church. This aspect of Thomas' ecclesiology, the very root of it, still awaits in-depth analysis.

Finally, Sabra does not consider the possibility that the biblical commentaries of Aquinas may have a value as theological works which allows them to be considered in a primary way. They remain mere sources in a uniform collection of works more or less indistinguishable from each other theologically. In other words, Sabra maintains at least implicitly that Thomas does not come away from his engagement with specific texts of Scripture with anything more than perhaps a deeper familiarity with those texts and an opportunity to once again announce his own themes. It is clear that he recognizes the biblical influence on Thomas' ecclesiology, but it is an influence that is homogeneous and affected only by biblical ideas, not by encounters with specific texts.

Surprisingly, this is also true of the work of M.P. Cuéllar,[22] whose published doctoral dissertation (along with Grabmann's) merits recognition by Sabra as being the closest among his predecessors to giving "a systematic and comprehensive presentation of Thomas' ecclesiology."[23] Cuéllar sets out to consider Thomas' understanding of the nature of the Church as it is found in his Pauline commentaries, which he basically succeeds in doing. Yet like Sabra he considers these commentaries as equal sources without a further consideration of the differences in the Epistles on which Thomas is commenting. As such his work offers little more than a re-presentation of

---

[21] Ibid., 18.

[22] Miguel Ponce CUÉLLAR, *La Naturaleza de la Iglesia según Santo Tomás. Estudio del Tema en el Comentario al "Corpus Paulinum"* (Pamplona: Ediciones Universidad de Navarra, 1979).

[23] SABRA, 15.

Thomas' larger vision of the Church, one that is not specific to the commentaries on the *corpus paulinum* and which could have been better ascertained through a consideration of all of his theological writings.

Sabra criticizes Cuéllar on this very point:

> Cuéllar's (work)... offers a good discussion of the nature of the church in Thomas' theology, but it limits itself to Thomas' commentaries on the Pauline corpus. Thus, all of Thomas' other works figure in only marginally, and Cuéllar is more interested in what Thomas had to say about the church than in the place of Thomas' ecclesiology in the structure of his theological syntheses.[24]

This latter point demonstrates Sabra's own emphasis on the necessity of recognizing the *place* of ecclesiology in Thomas' theological syntheses for understanding his vision of the Church. In contrast, Cuéllar fails to incorporate a sufficient consideration of place in his work; he does not consider that the ecclesiological themes which arise in the Pauline commentaries do so in works of exegesis, and so neglects to consider how the biblical texts profoundly influence that ecclesiological vision.

One characteristic of his work demonstrates this point. Cuéllar establishes a structure of inquiry that is foreign to the commentaries themselves, an obvious necessity (in the sense that he is about cataloguing ecclesiological topics found therein), but one that limits his ability to draw out the organic structure of which Thomas' ecclesiological themes are but a part. This process of distillation takes ecclesiology out of the context of the many other theological topics contained within these works. This is clear in the way Cuéllar uses the prologues (both general and specific) to the commentaries; they are considered for their "ecclesiological implications"[25] (that is, how they demonstrate that Thomas had the Church in mind as he set out to comment on the Epistles). Yet this is secondary to Thomas' purpose in providing prologues, which is clearly to establish his understanding of the texts at hand and their interrelation.[26] By not allowing the texts of the commentaries themselves to govern his inquiry, Cuéllar sets off from a place that Thomas did not, and never raises the question of whether his starting point is the most profitable place from which to launch his inquiry. It is not surprising that he

---

[24] Ibid., 16.

[25] CUÉLLAR, 21-35.

[26] *Super Epistolas Pauli Apostoli*, Prologue, 10-11.

makes no significant notice of the fact that in Thomas' schema different primary topics are recognized for each Epistle, with some being more ecclesiological than others.[27]

The following example demonstrates this weakness. In his chapter on "the marks and properties of the Church," Cuéllar devotes eleven pages to the apostolicity of the Church, and in so doing gives much attention to the Ephesians *lectura*, especially the commentary on Ephesians 1-3.[28] To his credit, he has located the place where Thomas provides his most in-depth consideration of this topic. Yet he fails to note that this discussion takes place in the larger context of Thomas' consideration of the defining characteristics of what an apostle is, with a particular emphasis on pastoral activity and preaching the Gospel rather than on the apostolicity of the Church. While it is certainly legitimate for Cuéllar to limit himself to direct references by Thomas to apostolicity, is there any doubt that such an exposition cannot serve as the final word when this larger framework remains unconsidered? At the very least, what can be said is that while Cuéllar succeeds in uncovering ecclesiology in the *Lectura super epistolam ad Ephesios*, he fails to uncover the ecclesiology that is specific to it. In fact, it receives no attention as a distinct commentary, but only as one source among many.

The work of J. Ti-Ti Chen,[29] even more than that of Cuéllar, closely resembles the second part of the present study in its specific attention to a single commentary. However, she shares the fundamental weaknesses of both Sabra and Cuéllar in missing the importance of considering Thomas' Pauline commentaries (in her case, specifically and solely the *Lectura super Epistolam ad Ephesios*) as works of exegesis. Ti-Ti Chen does not attempt to consider the possible implications of this essential fact - instead, she concentrates on ecclesiological themes (particularly, the five images of the Church found in the commentary), some sacramental considerations (such as the nature of baptism) and the ecclesiological implications of the notion of charity as it is described by Thomas in the Ephesians *lectura*. In only three or four instances does she directly consider the relationship between the

---

[27] Ibid., 11.

[28] CUÉLLAR, 250-261.

[29] J. TI-TI CHEN, "La unidad de la Iglesia según el Comentario de Santo Tomás a la Epístola a los Efesios," *Scripta Theologica* 8 (1976) : 111-230.

commentary and the text of Ephesians;[30] in the rest of her article it remains unexplored.

It is not surprising, then, to find that Ti-Ti Chen does not follow the chronological (and organic) order of the commentary; rather, she cites examples according to her own order of treatment, which is that of the five images. This causes her to overlook a fundamental characteristic of the Ephesians *lectura* which is also overlooked by Sabra and Cuéllar - that, contrary to the title of her article, the theme of the commentary (which is the same as that of Ephesians itself, at least in the mind of Aquinas) is not "the unity of the Church," but rather the origination of ecclesial unity.[31] This may seem like hair-splitting, but it is not - the former is a static concept, one that is present in the commentary and important to it, but not as its central topic. In contrast, the latter is a dynamic concept, implying a movement from division to oneness which is much closer to the real flavor of the Epistle itself.[32]

These approaches to Thomas' ecclesiological vision in the Pauline commentaries demonstrate an intersection with the aforementioned unexplored features of Thomas' biblical exegesis. That is, they leave uncon-sidered the possibility that Thomas' confrontations with specific works of Scripture were capable of giving unique casts or directions to his theology, ones that are worth noticing. As a result, currently we know much about Thomas' general ecclesiology, but little of how he might have applied it. A closer look, and one from a new angle, is necessary if our understanding of Thomas' vision of the Church is to progress.

C) *Outline*

In regard to the topics and concerns detailed above, the present study has two parts. Part I will focus entirely on Thomas as exegete and interpreter of Sacred Scripture, relying on the wealth of scholarship which already exists on this subject. Chapter I will consider Thomas' understanding of prophecy and biblical inspiration, the nature of revelation and biblical interpretation. Such an analysis will establish how Thomas understood the various texts of the Bible in terms of their value for theology and doctrine. This foundational

---

[30] See Ibid., 127-128, contrasting Thomas' more frequent use of the image of the Church as city (*civitas*) vs. its infrequent use by the author of Ephesians (who uses it only once).

[31] "*Agit ergo Apostolus, primo quidem, de institutione Ecclesiasticae unitatis in epistola ad Ephesios...*" [*Super Epist.*, Prol., 11].

[32] Cf. Eph. 2:11-22 for an example of this important theme of Ephesians.

chapter will be invaluable for establishing how Thomas would approach biblical texts, and what he would garner from them.

Chapter II will examine criticisms of Thomas' exegetical practices which pose unavoidable challenges to any serious inquiry into the biblical commentaries of Thomas Aquinas. This consideration will lead to the question of what (if any) value the biblical exegesis of Aquinas has for modern biblical scholars and theologians. Also, some initial distinctions will be made in light of the discoveries of the first two chapters.

One essential aspect of this second chapter will be the hitherto unrecognized fact that Thomas is most adept at exegesis when he is dealing with texts which are not primarily involved in the narration of events but rather reflection, moral exhortation and theological exposition. I will argue that Thomas successfully straddles a hermeneutical gap which he inherits from the Christian exegetical tradition by focusing on non-narrative texts. In fact, it will be demonstrated (in both the first and second chapters) that the "shortcomings" which are attributed to Thomas as exegete are actually ones which particularly suit him for dealing with specifically non-narrative texts. The title of the present study, "*Modus et Forma*," itself a paraphrase of Thomas' designation of diverse literary genres in Scripture as found in the *proemium* of his *Postilla super Psalmos*, reflects my contention that he was aware of these genres and adapted himself to them in his various works of exegesis.

Chapter III will represent the most innovative aspect of Part I. In it I will propose a new approach to Thomas' biblical commentaries, one from an angle taken by only a few and, until now, systematically developed by none. Through an analysis of the best existing scholarship on these commentaries an approach to them will be developed that surpasses a mere examination of Thomas' exegetical theories to focus specifically on his practice. This will involve a consideration of the type of text that Thomas is dealing with and how the nature of the text governs Thomas' approach. To put this more simply, this chapter will involve an attempt to deal with Thomas not primarily as a theorist or even as a mere biblical exegete, but rather as an exegete in action, dealing with specific texts.

Part II will consist of an in-depth analysis of the Ephesians *lectura* itself, applying the approach outlined in Chapter III. Chapter IV will consist of a pre-analysis, establishing the facts about the commentary in relation to Thomas' life, the chronology of his work, and the rest of the commentaries on the *corpus paulinum*. Particular consideration will be given to the text itself, including a survey of the editions currently available (as to their reliability and integrity) and the critical rationale for choosing the Marietti edition, the English translation by Matthew Lamb and the 1992 CD-ROM edition of the *Thomae Aquinatis Opera Omnia cum hypertextibus* as primary sources (attention will also be devoted to the electronic search possibilities of the latter source). Another consideration will be of the nature of the text as a *reportatio* (the notes of a student on Thomas' lecture rather than an actual work from his hand), and the question of whether or not such a text is a reliable source for Thomas' thought. Finally, the approach developed in Part I will be applied in its primary elements to the commentary, including a heuristic analysis of the place and function of both Scripture and *auctoritates* within the work.[33] Some preliminary conclusions will be drawn regarding this data in preparation for the analysis of the commentary.

Chapters V-VI will consist of this analysis and will consider, respectively, Chapters 1-3 and Chapters 4-6 of the Ephesians *lectura* which follows (as all of Thomas' commentaries do) the chapter divisions of the Paris Vulgate.[34] This analysis will focus on the specifically ecclesiological themes which are developed in the commentary, with particular reference to how these themes are related to the text of the Epistle itself. This will be a critical analysis in that how Thomas interacts with the text will be of primary concern, and so obviously involves the presupposition that more is known about the text of Ephesians and that its content is better understood now than it was by Aquinas, his predecessors and his contemporaries. The analysis will involve understanding the ecclesiological themes and structure of the Epistle itself, the ecclesiological themes and structure of the commentary, and the relationship between the two. Of particular interest will be Thomas' theologizing within the commentary - where does the Epistle "send" him theologically? Or, to use the felicitous expression of Pesch, does Thomas allow Paul to "challenge" him,[35] or does he just take over the Epistle and subordinate it to his own alien categories?

Chapter VII will be evaluatory - it will summarize the findings of Chapters V-VI and make some comparisons with Thomas' more general

---

[33] VALKENBERG has developed an excellent heuristic device for this purpose, and a modified version will be used in this work. See pp 17-71.

[34] This division into two chapters of the analysis of the *In Ephesios* follows Aquinas' own division: the first three chapters recall "the divine blessings through which the Church's unity has originated and been preserved," the last three admonish the Ephesians to remain within the Church's unity. See *In Eph.*, 4.1.187.

[35] PESCH, "Paul as Professor of Theology," 593.

vision of the Church. In particular, the focus of this chapter will be on the difference between the general ecclesiology of Thomas and the one found in the commentary. This comparison will demonstrate by contrast what is u-nique to the commentary and also what it has in common with what one could call Thomas' "base ecclesiology."

In this final chapter the findings of the first two parts will also be considered as to their relevance for contemporary theology. This will include a reflection on the findings of the inquiry itself, but also a consideration of what possibilities the general approach developed and utilised has for future inquiries into Thomas' biblical commentaries, focusing on specific discoveries made in the analysis of Ephesians *lectura*. This chapter with a short conclusion will form the ending of this study.

As noted above, the present study will marry two aspects of Thomas' thought that are often considered in separation - while it includes a focus on Thomas' Ephesians *lectura* and his ecclesiology as it is found in his Ephesians *lectura*, no less than three of the seven chapters are to be devoted to the question of Thomas' biblical exegesis considered in itself and the formulation of an approach to the same. As shall become clear in Part I, such a structure cannot be avoided, and is in fact the strength of the present study. If we are to explore Thomas' Ephesians commentary as a biblical commentary, and not merely as a doctrinal mine from which ideas can be gathered, then the issue of approach becomes one of priority. Therefore, it is my contention that a study such as this is a proper and even advantageous context for developing an approach to Thomas' biblical exegesis, including as it does an extensive consideration of an actual specimen of that exegesis. This reflects two fundamental assertions of the present study: a) that a truly systematic and comprehensive approach to Thomas' biblical commentaries is necessary for a fruitful encounter with his biblical corpus, and b) that such an approach must be united to the analysis of his actual practice as an exegete. Both are required for the greatest possible access to his biblical commentaries.

PART I

THOMAS AQUINAS' EXEGETICAL CORPUS: A NEW VANTAGE POINT AND A NEW APPROACH

CHAPTER I

THOMAS' EXEGETICAL PRESUPPOSITIONS
IN LIGHT OF HIS EXEGETICAL PRACTICE

A) *Hugh Pope and the Standard Paradigm of Inquiry into Thomas' Biblical Exegesis*

As noted in the introduction, there has been no shortage of discussion in our century regarding St. Thomas' exegetical principles. Looking back on it from the vantage point of its dawning, one discerns a steady stream of treatises over the past 100 years, beginning in the 1890's and taking a first major turn into English speaking territory with the contribution of Hugh Pope in the early 1920's.[1] In these works one finds discussion of nearly every conceivable facet of Thomas' relationship to the Bible. This stream has not ceased (though at times has waxed and waned) through to the present day. If a century represents anything resembling a trend in Catholic scholarship, we can expect further discussion well into the next century and perhaps even beyond it.

Given so many contributions it can very well be asked what justification can be offered for adding one more discussion as a part of this dissertation. A consideration of the whole genre will demonstrate that its inclusion is a necessity, especially since we will be considering one of Thomas' biblical commentaries as the primary object of analysis for the present study. Such an analysis can reasonably begin with Hugh Pope, who (though not without some minor predecessors) was a pioneer in retrieving Thomas' scriptural doctrine from a growing neglect, one caused most notably by the steady growth of critical biblical analysis among Catholic scholars. It is clear that Pope understood his work in this light; he endeavors from the very beginning to dispel the idea that a medieval scholastic such as Thomas could not possibly be held up as "an example of what a Biblical expositor

---

[1] Hugh POPE, *St. Thomas as Interpreter of Holy Scripture* (Oxford: Basil Blackwell, 1924).

should be."[2] Pope's work is not often regarded with any particular interest, as he was so quickly eclipsed in both scope and scholarship by a great pioneer of the historical study of exegesis, Beryl Smalley. Yet the fact that, Denifle notwithstanding, he is the first to give a comprehensive account of Thomas' relationship to the Bible is not a negligible item.[3] Indeed, one finds in Pope's work the concerns and categories which will predominate for generations of scholars who will follow in his footsteps. It is this setting of the standards by Pope which gives his work its greatest value for the present study; his concerns and categories reveal certain oversights which will also affect those who take up the question after him. Using the helpful methodological distinction employed by Lamb,[4] it is easy to summarize Pope's contribution in both its positive and negative aspects. On the one hand, he demonstrates strong insight into Thomas' "exegetical presuppositions" (which he calls "principles of exegesis" as well as "principles of biblical interpretation"[5]); he also demonstrates a firm grasp of Thomas' "exegetical techniques" (for which he has no exact designation). On the other hand (adding a category to Lamb's distinction), Pope does not even raise the issue of Aquinas' *exegetical practice*, with this being defined as what Thomas produces when he deals with actual biblical passages and texts, such as is found in his many biblical commentaries.

What Pope offers us instead are general observations of exegetical characteristics illustrated by a few examples. We find in his work the familiar pattern of introductory pedagogy, in which the student is invited into further penetration of the subject matter by a few outstanding examples.[6] However,

---

[2] Ibid, 7-8.

[3] As mentioned above Pope does have some predecessors, although their brevity and limited scope limit their significance in comparison. See A. THOLUCK, *De Thoma Aquino et Abaelardo S. Scripturae interpretibus* (Halle: E. Anton, 1842); D. SAUL, "Thomas von Aquino als Ausleger des A.T," *Zeitschrift für wissenschaftliche Theologie* (1895) : 603-626; A. GARDEIL, "Les procédés exégétiques de S. Thomas," *Revue Thomiste* 11 (1903) : 428-457; F.-A. BLANCHE, "Le sens littéral des Écritures d'après saint Thomas d'Aquin," *Revue Thomiste* 14 (1906) : 192-212; A. FERNANDEZ, "Système exégétique de saint Thomas," *España y America* 10 (1909); P. SYNAVE, "Les Commentaires scripturaires de saint Thomas d'Aquin," *Vie Spirituelle* 8 (1923) : 455-469.

[4] Matthew LAMB, intro. to *Commentary on St. Paul's Epistle to the Ephesians*, by St. Thomas Aquinas (Albany, NY: Magi Books, 1966), 4.

[5] POPE, 5, 21.

[6] It should be noted that Pope's short book was originally a long lecture, one in celebration of Aquinas' sexcentenary, and it is therefore not surprising that it should carry the overtones of an introduction.

it is a pattern that scholars of Thomas' relationship to the Bible never seem to surpass; even the very examples used by Pope will be recycled by numerous scholars to follow him. For instance, Pope points out that Thomas "is singularly broad in his actual interpretation of the Bible,"[7] using the example of Thomas' interpretation of the firmament in the Creation account to demonstrate this point.[8] Since then this characteristic of Thomas' exegesis has been demonstrated repeatedly (and often solely) with his interpretation of the Creation account.[9] (In a similar way, Chenu and Congar will point out Thomas' restraint in spiritual exegesis as demonstrated by his treatment of the Old Law {ST I-II.102.2}.[10] Here we see the same pattern repeated - numerous later authors will rely on the same example.[11])

It would be a grave misrepresentation of subsequent scholarship if one were to maintain that we have gone nowhere substantial in our understanding of Thomas as an exegete since Pope. Other characteristics than the ones he puts forth will be uncovered by later scholars, and many will be enumerated as time progresses. Yet these will often only be expounded in the general framework of Pope, in which the specimens of Thomas' exegetical practice will be examined only for the purposes of demonstrating Thomas' general presuppositions and techniques, not out of any regard for their own value. Ironically, this is almost always done in an atmosphere of praise for Thomas' ingenuity.

The many commendations of Thomas' novelty and ingenuity as an exegete do serve to pique the interest of the student of exegetical history. The

---

[7] POPE, 36-37.

[8] ST I.68.3.

[9] For some examples, see LAMB, 25; C. Clifton BLACK, "St. Thomas' Commentary on the Johannine Prologue," 691; Charles J. SCALISE, "The 'Sensus Litteralis' : A Hermeneutical Key to Biblical Exegesis," Scottish Journal of Theology 42 (1989) : 57-58.

[10] M.-D. CHENU, La Théologie comme science au XIIIᵉ siècle, 208; "La loi ancienne selon S. Thomas," Revue Thomiste 61 (1961) : 485-497. Yves CONGAR, "Le sens de l'économie salutaire dans la théologie de S. Thomas," in Festgabe Joseph Lortz , vol. I (Baden-Baden: B. Grimm, 1957), 91-96

[11] For two examples, see M. DUBOIS, "Mystical and Realistic Elements in the Exegesis and Hermeneutics of St. Thomas Aquinas," in Creative Biblical Exegesis: Christian and Jewish Hermeneutics through the Centuries, ed. Benjamin Uffenheimer and H.G. Reventlow, vol. 59, Journal for the Study of the Old Testament Supplement Series (Sheffield, England: JSOT Press, 1988), 46-49; Leo ELDERS, "Aquinas on Holy Scripture as the Medium of Divine Revelation," in La doctrine de la révélation divine de saint Thomas d'Aquin. Actes du Symposium sur la pensée de saint Thomas d'Aquin tenu à Rolduc, les 4 et 5 Novembre1989, ed. Leo Elders (Città del Vaticano: Libreria Editrice Vaticana, 1990), 145-146.

consensus of scholars seems to be virtually unanimous on the value of Thomas' exegesis for understanding his theology and for seeing how truly biblical it is. Although no one would any longer maintain with Pope that Thomas largely anticipated the modern critical inquiry into the Bible,[12] few would disagree with the viewpoint of a very recent scholar in his praise for Thomas' exegetical work: "The biblical commentaries of St. Thomas, even with their limitations, have a fruitful exegetical and theological offering to place before contemporary scholarship."[13]

How disconcerting it is to search, on the basis of this high praise, for the real proof of this enthusiasm, which could be nothing less than sustained and comprehensive inquiries into the various works of exegesis which the Thomistic corpus offers us. Instead, one finds only a few dissertations, a handful of short articles, and only one or two books.[14] The disparity is so radical that one almost feels deceived, the victim of theological pillow-talk.

In the face of this anomaly, it seems clear that what is lacking is a new approach, one which jumps the deep groove (and long trend) of Pope's approach on the very basis of the fruits and insights that this trend has produced. Thanks to Pope and many others, we now know a great deal about both Thomas' exegetical presuppositions and his techniques. The fact that Thomas put both of these to good purpose cannot be made any clearer. The logical next step is certainly to use our superior knowledge (thanks to a myriad of scholars) of these presuppositions and techniques to pierce the invisible barrier that has arisen around Thomas' exegesis itself.

The first and most essential question in such an inquiry will necessarily be this one: Are there any particular insights and vantage points of Aquinas that facilitate successful biblical interpretation on his part? That is, does he find certain avenues (even if he does so only implicitly or even by accident) which give him an unusually penetrating access to the biblical corpus, and if so, does this interface with scripture affect him theologically?

---

[12] Pope, 38.

[13] Terence McGuckin, "St. Thomas Aquinas and Theological Exegesis of Sacred Scripture," *New Blackfriars* 74 (1993) : 210; for another example, see Charles J. Callan, "The Bible in the Summa Theologica of St. Thomas Aquinas," *Catholic Biblical Quarterly* 9 (1947) : 33-47.

[14] My own experience may be instructive. In researching the topic of my M.A. Thesis ["The Doctrine of the Eucharist in St. Thomas Aquinas' *Commentary on the Gospel of St. John*" (Univ. of Dallas, 1996)], I was able to locate only four works in the English language on any aspect of this commentary, and none of them on the Eucharistic doctrine which Thomas expounds so beautifully in his commentary on John 6.

This basic question demands an even greater precision if it is to make its mark. It would be naive to try to answer the above question of Thomas' relationship to the Bible as if the Bible itself were a homogeneous whole and not made up of very diverse parts. Thomas wrote commentaries on works as different as psalmody, wisdom literature, classical prophecy, a synoptic gospel, the Fourth Gospel and the Pauline corpus.[15] Was he more or less suited for any particular one of these, better at being this, rather than that, kind of exegete? This is obviously a much more specific question than that of his suitability for exegesis in general, and a much more valuable one as well. For Thomas' ability to access a text will certainly mean that its effect on the theology he builds with that text will have natural points of connection with the theology of our own day. To be succinct, Thomas' ability to effectively access particular works of Scripture holds promises for our ability to access Thomas. Just as human relationships can be enhanced by dwelling in the same house together, so our understanding of Thomas can be enhanced by locating those places that he and we are most able to coinhabit.

B) *The Three "Great Works" of Thomistic Exegesis*

It is the author's opinion that one of the most coinhabitable scriptural "abodes" for Thomas and the modern scholar is the Pauline corpus. Yet this is not an unsubstantiated opinion. A survey of scholarly appraisal of Thomas' biblical commentaries demonstrates a very particular preference for certain of his works rather than others, including (though by no means limited to) the *Lectura super Epistolas Pauli Apostoli*. In fact, it can be confidently asserted that a strong scholarly consensus has been formed for the superiority of three of Thomas' biblical commentaries: the *Lectura super Iohannem*, the *Lectura*

---

[15] The biblical commentaries of St. Thomas are as follows (and in no particular order): the *Lectura super Matthaeum* , the *Expositio super Iob,* the *Glossa Continua super Evangelia* (popularly known as the *Catena Aurea in Quatuor Evangelia,* a "golden chain" of commentary from the Latin and Greek Fathers on the four Gospels), the *Lectura super Iohannem,* the *Postilla super Isaiam,* the *Postilla super Jeremiam,* the *Postilla super Threnos,* the *Postilla super Psalmos,* the *Lectura super Epistolas Pauli Apostoli* and possibly a commentary on the Song of Songs, the *Super Cantica Canticorum.* The earliest possible date for any of these is 1248/52 for the *Expositio super Isaiam ad litteram,* the *Postilla super Jeremiam* and the *Postilla super Threnos,* a period in which Thomas served as *cursor biblicus* under Albert the Great [TORRELL, *Saint Thomas,* 337]; the latest date would be February - March 1274, on his death-bed (for the non-extant *Super Cantica Canticorum*). Cf. Karl FROEHLICH, "Aquinas, Thomas," in *Historical Handbook of Major Biblical Interpreters,* ed. Donald K. McKim (Downers Grove, IL/Leicester, England: InterVarsity Press, 1998), 86-87.

super Epistolas Pauli Apostoli, and the *Expositio super Iob*. This consensus is enlightening, and deserves further consideration.

We have two early testimonies to the superior quality of two of these three. The earliest extant example of a preference being given to a work of biblical commentary by Aquinas is the judgment of Bartholomew of Capua, and comes to us in the primitive catalogue of Thomas' writings which Bartholomew composed circa 1320. It is here that he singles out the *Lectura super Iohannem* as a work "better than which none can be found."[16] Although he gives no other comments regarding any of the other commentaries, it is clearly doubtful that he would give the honor of the highest value to any of the other exegetical works. But why Bartholomew prefers this commentary to the rest remains unknown - he does not specify his praise. The second example is just as emphatic (though no more explanatory) and comes to us from John of Colonna, who (in his list of Thomas' works dated ca. 1323-1325) refers to the commentary on Job as a *mirabile opus*.[17]

Modern scholars have been more explanatory than these two medieval scholars concerning their high regard for these works and the Pauline commentaries. This is especially true of the *Lectura super Johannem*. No one has given more or higher praise to it than Weisheipl; in his classic biography of Thomas he refers to this *lectura* as "sublime in theological profundity...":

> Modern biblical studies have, of course, surpassed the work of earlier generations, and there are a number of excellent modern commentaries on the Gospel according to John. Nevertheless no modern work has surpassed or replaced the sublime theological dimensions of Thomas' *lectura*. It is a mature work for theologians as well as for students of Scripture.[18]

---

[16] *"qua non invenitur melior"* [TOLOMEO OF LUCCA, *Ptolomaei Lucensis Historia ecclesiastica nova*, Lib. XXII17-XXIII16, bk.23,chap.15, in L.A. MURATORI, *Rerum italicarum scriptores*, vol. 11 (Milan: 1724), as found in the partial critical edition by A. DONDAINE, "Les *Opuscula fratris Thomae* chez Ptolémée de Lucques," *Archivum fratrum praedicatorum* 31 (1961) : 142-203].

[17] B. de RUBEIS, "Dissertatio II: De Vetustis opera sancti Thomae Indicibus: deque genuinis commentariis eius in Iobum, in Psalmos, in Cantica Canticorum: suppositisque in Genesim, in totum Pentateuchum, in Ecclesiasticem," in *Thomae Aquinatis, Opera Omnia*, Vol. I, Leonine edition (Rome: 1932), lxxvii. John of Colonna is quoted approvingly in John F. JOHNSON, "Biblical Authority and Scholastic Theology," in *Inerrancy and the Church*, ed. John D. Hannah (Chicago: Moody Press, 1984), 83.

[18] James A. WEISHEIPL, *Friar Thomas D'Aquino: His Life, Thought, and Works* (Washington, D.C.: Catholic University of America Press, 1974), 246. Weisheipl does not

He continues his praise in his introduction to the English translation of the *lectura*, where he refers to it as "a real masterpiece of its kind in medieval literature."[19] Elsewhere he deems it "the most satisfying of all the [Thomistic] commentaries on Scripture."[20]

Others give similar praise to this work. Glorieux approvingly quotes the early annotation of its value by Bartholomew (although he does not explicitly attribute it to him).[21] Chenu also notes this annotation and points out that "posterity has ratified this judgment."[22] C. Clifton Black affirms this particular stream in the tradition as well by noting that "from among his prestigious exegetical writings, Thomas' lectures on the Gospel of St. John have long been esteemed as being of the highest caliber."[23] In the opinion of Stump, the *lectura* is "a rich and subtle exposition of the narrative together with compendious theological reflections"[24]; M.-D. Philippe even goes so far as to call it "the theological work *par excellence* of St. Thomas."[25]

The scholars who give the highest preference to the *Lectura super Epistolas Pauli Apostoli* are not as numerous. In fact, there are only two, but both of these individuals carry considerable weight, enough to give them a certain leverage in regard to the superiority question. The first is Spicq, who gives his input in the context of his excellent (indeed classic) treatment of Thomas as an exegete: "...one is justified in seeing in the commentaries of St. Thomas on St. John *and especially on St. Paul* [emphasis mine] the most

---

neglect the commentaries on the Pauline Epistles, which receive honorable mention as a group. See Ibid., 246-247, 248-249.

[19] Idem, Introduction to *Commentary on the Gospel of St. John* by Thomas Aquinas, vol. 1, trans. by Fabian R. Larcher (Albany: Magi Books, 1980), 16.

[20] Idem, "The Johannine Commentary of Friar Thomas," *Church History* 45 (1976), 195.

[21] P. GLORIEUX, "Essai sur les Commentaires scripturaires de saint Thomas et leur chronologie," *Recherches de théologie ancienne et médiévale* 17 (1950) : 245.

[22] M.-D. CHENU, *Toward Understanding St. Thomas*, trans. by A.-M. Landry and D. Hughes (Chicago: Henry Regnery Press, 1964), 247.

[23] BLACK, 682.

[24] Eleonore STUMP, "[Aquinas'] Biblical Commentary and Philosophy," in *The Cambridge Companion to Aquinas*, ed. Norman Kretzmann and Eleonore Stump (Cambridge: Cambridge University Press, 1993), 260. This is not her final word on the subject, as we shall see.

[25] M.-D. PHILIPPE, Preface to *Commentaire sur l'Evangile de saint Jean* by Thomas Aquinas, vol. 1-3, trans. under the direction of M.-D. Philippe (Versailles: Buxy, 1981, 1982, 1987), as quoted approvingly by McGUCKIN, "St. Thomas Aquinas and Theological Exegesis of Sacred Scripture," 200.

mature fruit and the most perfect realization of medieval scholastic exegesis."[26] The second is none other than Pope Pius XII, who approvingly offers "the opinion of men of the finest judgment" when he states that "the commentaries that St. Thomas wrote on the books of the Old and of the New Testament, *and especially on the Epistles of St. Paul the Apostle* [emphasis mine], reflect such authority, such keen insight and such diligence that they can be counted among his greatest theological works..."[27]

Other scholars rank the *lectura* on Paul very highly, even if they do not give it pride of place. Haggard points out that "it is especially, although not exclusively, in his commentaries on Job, the Gospel of John and the Pauline Epistles where Thomas practices most rigorously his theological exegesis using the dialectical subtlety perfected in the scholastic method."[28] Stump (who is quoted earlier in favor of the *lectura* on John) makes the following positive commendation: "With the possible exception of the cursory commentaries on the prophets and the Psalms, all of Aquinas' biblical commentaries repay careful study, but three are worth singling out, the commentaries on Romans, the Gospel of John and Job"[29] McGuckin has praise for all three of these commentaries as well.[30] For T. Gilby, it is the commentaries on John and the Pauline Epistles which are to be deemed as "great" works, noting as he does that they are "directly theological in intention."[31] Torrell also refers to these as the "two great works" of Thomistic biblical commentary,[32] though he does remark that one could classify the *lectura* on John "along with the commentary on Job or on the Epistle to the Romans as among the most fully finished and most profound that he has left

---

[26] Ceslas SPICQ, "Saint Thomas d'Aquin Exégète," in vol. 15, *Dictionnaire de Théologie Catholique,* ed. A. Vacant, E. Mangenot and E. Amann (Paris: Librairie Letouzey et Ané, 1946), col. 695.

[27] PIUS XII, "An Address to the Faculty and Students of the Roman Athenaeum Angelicum," (January 14, 1958) *The Pope Speaks* 5 (1958) : 93.

[28] Frank Powell HAGGARD, "An Interpretation of Thomas Aquinas as a Biblical Theologian with Special Reference to his Systematizing of the Economy of Salvation" (Ph.D. Thesis, Drew University, 1972), 248. Haggard's insight here is particularly relevant to the present work, and we shall return to it shortly.

[29] STUMP, 260.

[30] McGUCKIN, 206-207.

[31] T. GILBY, appendix to *Summa Theologica,* 134.

[32] J.-P. TORRELL, *Saint Thomas Aquinas : The Person and His Work,* vol. 1, trans. Robert Royal (Washington, D.C.: Catholic University of America Press, 1996), 197.

us."[33] In the case of the commentary on Job, only one scholar ranks it as the best; according to A. Dondaine, it is "*le sommet de l'exégèse médiévale.*"[34]

The acclaim evidenced for these three commentaries is enhanced by the virtually complete silence regarding the other biblical commentaries of Aquinas. Nowhere does the *Lectura super Matthaeum* receive any particular honor - along with the commentaries on Isaiah, Jeremiah and Lamentations it is among the least noticed items in the Thomistic corpus.[35] Chenu goes so far as to point out the inadequacy of the *lectura* on Matthew as a work of exegesis - the "solutions of difficulties" contained within it are "not very elaborate."[36]

Those familiar with the generally accepted chronology of Thomas' works may find an objection to the judgments in favor of superiority for the three commentaries documented above, particularly an objection to using them as evidence of anything other than Thomas' growth as an exegete. All three do represent later works of Thomas, and only for this reason, it may be surmised, do they contain a certain excellence which is lacking in the works he produced first as a *cursor biblicus* and then as a young *magister*. This would militate against the possibility that there is something intrinsic to these three biblical texts which they share in common to "bring out the best" in Thomas as an exegete. Such an objection would be unanswerable except for one piece of evidence - the *Postilla super Psalmos.* Here we have a work which, like the earlier commentaries, has never been singled out for its superiority (and has, at least in one case, been set aside as inferior[37]). Yet it is certainly the latest of his commentaries; along with the second course on the Pauline corpus, it is always dated as post-1270.[38] Add to this the fact that the

---

[33] Ibid., 200.

[34] A. DONDAINE, preface to *Expositio super Job, tom. XXVI, Opera Omnia*, by Thomas Aquinas, 420-430. Dondaine is quoted approvingly by DUBOIS, 52, who remarks that the commentary on Job "appeared as witness to a new exegesis."

[35] Of these four, only two have drawn the attention of scholars, and in only two monographs. See H. WIESMAN, "Der Kommentar des hl. Thomas von Aquin zu den Klageliedern des Jeremias," *Scholastik* 4 (1929) : 82-86; J.-P. TORRELL and D. BOUTHILLIER, "Quand saint Thomas méditait sur le prophète Isaïe," *Revue Thomiste* 90 (1990) : 5-47.

[36] CHENU, *Toward Understanding*, 247.

[37] See STUMP as quoted above.

[38] GLORIEUX, 251; I.T. ESCHMANN, "A Catalogue of St. Thomas' Works," in Etienne GILSON, *The Christian Philosophy of St. Thomas Aquinas,* trans. L.K. Shook (London: Victor Gollancz, 1957), 393-399; WEISHEIPL, *Friar Thomas*, 368; TORRELL, *Saint Thomas*, 257-258.

commentary on Job is at least three years older than the *Lectura super Matthaeum*,[39] and the argument breaks down - to maintain it one would have to expect the Matthew *lectura* to supersede the *Expositio super Iob*, and the *postilla* on the Psalms to supersede all the rest. Yet this is certainly not the case.

Other points must be considered before the reasons why these three commentaries stand out from among the rest can be fully established - a significant part of this chapter will be dedicated to doing just that. But before we are able to progress into a consideration of Thomas' exegetical presuppositions and techniques from the point of view of his exegetical practice, at least a summary analysis of the preeminence of these works needs to be undertaken. In particular, two points are essential for embarking on a deeper consideration of Thomas' exegetical presuppositions.

The first point that must be noted is a negative one, namely that the difference between these three commentaries and the rest of Thomas' exegetical corpus is not to be located in Thomas' approach. An entire chapter could be dedicated merely to demonstrating this fact - suffice it to say that the unanimous scholarly consensus is that Thomas' basic methodology remains remarkably consistent throughout his career as an exegete. The classic expositions of Thomas' exegetical methods and characteristics found in Spicq, Chenu and Weisheipl, plus the innumerable works on his theories of revelation and his hermeneutic do not demonstrate any significant change from work to work in terms of how Thomas deals with Scripture in general. One could perhaps point to his stated intention to expound only on the literal sense of Job as Thomas opting for one approach or method over another,[40] but a closer examination shows indisputably that Thomas is merely distinguishing his work from the *Moralia in Iob* of Gregory the Great in order to justify his supplementation of this highly respected patristic authority.[41] One is forced to acknowledge that, in regard to shifts in method and approach, Thomas' work is virtually seamless.

The second point arises from this first one, namely that the difference between these three works and the rest of Thomas' exegetical corpus lies in the texts he is commenting on. Chenu notes this in regard to the *Lectura*

---

[39] TORRELL, *Saint Thomas*, 327-329.

[40] *Super Iob*, Proemium.

[41] Mary L. O'HARA, "Truth in Spirit and in Letter: Gregory the Great, Thomas Aquinas and Maimonides on the Book of Job," in *From Cloister to Classroom : Monastic and Scholastic Approaches to Truth,* ed. E. Rozanne Elder, vol. III, The Spirituality of Western Christendom (Kalamazoo, MI: Cistercian, 1986), 63-64.

super Epistolas Pauli Apostoli; he sees it as a particularly significant work "not only because the text of it represents a third of all the exegetical writings of Saint Thomas, but especially because it deals with a book of Scripture *that by its subject matter is the most propitious to theological exegesis* [emphasis mine]."[42]   We have already seen above that Haggard makes a similar judgment about all three of these commentaries.   Both of these scholars capture, in a basic and undeveloped way, what these three works have in common - to use a distinction employed by Leland Ryken, they are all commentaries on texts which contain large portions of theological and/or moral "exposition," in contrast to biblical texts that are primarily "historical" or "literary."[43] In fact, in all three cases each of these biblical texts relies in a primary way on its expository elements, in contrast to other biblical texts which merely contain such elements. This fact will be analyzed more fully in the next chapter. In the present consideration, however, it is enough to be able to ask a basic question of Thomas' exegetical presuppositions and methods relying on this insight - what aspects of Thomas' understanding of and approach to Scripture make him amenable to exegeting texts "most propitious to theological exegesis?" In particular, we must ask this question in a primary way regarding his exegesis of the Pauline Epistles, one of which (Ephesians) is of primary importance to the present study.

Three aspects of Thomas' understanding of scripture will be analyzed from this perspective: his theory of prophecy and biblical authorship, his understanding of the Bible as revelation, and his basic hermeneutic.

C) *Prophecy and Biblical Authorship*

Contemporary scholarship has demonstrated clearly that Thomas' understanding of inspiration and revelation is closely linked to his understanding of the gratuitous grace of prophecy,[44] one which he adopts from his immediate predecessors (Philip the Chancellor, Hugh of St. Cher and St. Albert the Great) but also, under the influence of Aristotle, develops in some

---

[42] CHENU, *Toward Understanding*, 248.

[43] Leland RYKEN, *Words of Delight : A Literary Introduction to the Bible* (Grand Rapids: Baker Book House, 1992), 12-13. We have already noted a similar distinction by Valkenberg in the introduction.

[44] POPE notes that it is under prophecy that Thomas "groups all divine manifestations;" he cites the entire section of the *Summa* on prophecy to illustrate this, but especially *ST* II-II.173.2 (*Interpreter*, p.19)

new and significant ways.[45] In particular, Thomas is the first to place an in-
depth analysis of prophecy into a work (the *Summa Theologiae*) of vastly
greater proportions than the narrowly formulated disputed questions by means
of which it had been treated by scholastic theologians up until his day.[46] In
giving it its own place in his major theological synthesis Thomas puts the
notion of prophecy into a proportionate relationship with (and vital connection to) other theological topics, including the topic of biblical authorship.
It is his treatment in the *Summa* (II-II.171-174) which is the most important of
the many references he makes to the gift of prophecy in his works, with the
De Veritate (q.12) running a close second.[47]

   One of the most unique developments in Thomas' understanding of
prophecy is that he is one of the first to surpass the restrictive specification of
prophecy to the knowledge of future events.[48]   Like his teacher Albert,[49]
Thomas grapples with the definition of prophecy (first formulated by
Cassiodorus and passed on approvingly by Peter Lombard) as "a divine inspiration or revelation which proclaims the outcome of events with unspeak-
able truth."[50] He responds that prophecy, which is caused by an enlightening
of the mind with the divine light, extends to all realities, be they "human or
divine, spiritual or corporeal" (just as physical light makes one able to to
exercise the *visio corporalis* to see the whole spectrum of colors).[51]
Elsewhere he specifies his definition with reference to knowledge pertinent to
salvation; according to Thomas, "...all those things the knowledge of which
can be useful for salvation are the matter of prophecy, whether they are past,
or future, or even eternal, or necessary, or contingent. But those things which
cannot pertain to the matter of salvation are outside the matter of prophecy."[52]

---

[45] J.-P. TORRELL, "Le traité de la prophétie de s. Thomas d'Aquin et la théologie de la
révélation," in *La doctrine de la révélation divine de saint Thomas d'Aquin. Actes du
Symposium sur la pensée de saint Thomas d'Aquin tenu à Rolduc, les 4 et 5 Novembre 1989*,
ed. Leo Elders (Città del Vaticano: Libreria Editrice Vaticana, 1990), 173-174.

[46] Ibid., 171-172.

[47] To this list one might also add: *S.c.G.*, III.154; *In I Cor.*, 14.1.807-819

[48] TORRELL, "Le traité de la prophétie," 174.

[49] J.-P. TORRELL, "La question disputée De prophétie de saint Albert le Grand. Edition
critique et commentaire," *Revue des sciences philosophiques et théologiques* 65 (1981) :
203.

[50] "...*prophetia est inspiratio vel revelatio divina, rerum eventus immobili veritate
denuntians*" [*ST* II-II.171.3]. Cf. CASSIODORUS, *Exposition on Psalms*, Prol. (*CCSL* 97, pg. 7)
for the original definition.

[51] "... *tam divina quam humana, tam spiritualia quam corporalia*" [Ibid., II-II.171.3].

[52] *De Ver.*, 12.2.

As such, prophecy is not only a social but also an ecclesial charism,[53] a gift for the purpose of revealing to human beings everything which God desires them to know regarding the life of faith.

Although the gift of prophecy has the final goal of revealing and informing, Thomas does not see it as a charism of action, but rather as one of knowledge.[54] He goes so far as to call it the highest form of knowledge, comparing it to charity which he considers to be the perfection of the will.[55] Yet in noting this it must also be noted that Thomas would qualify various modes and even grades of prophetic knowledge. Here Thomas unknowingly uses a false etymology, though he does so with a great deal of utility; all prophecy is the "appearing" to the mind (from "*phanos*," "appear") of what is distant from it (from "*procul*;" hence *prophanos*, "prophecy").[56] Yet as indicated above, this distance is more than just a spatial or temporal one; it is also a distance in terms of the object of prophecy "exceeding the natural reason."[57] This leads us to the first differentiation that Thomas asserts regarding prophecy, in which he grades the levels of perfection in the gift according to its potential objects - "because prophecy relates to what is far from our range of knowledge, then the more a reality is distant from human knowledge, the more properly will that reality belong to prophecy."[58] Thomas specifies three "degrees of remoteness" (*triplex gradus*) from ordinary human knowing in prophetic knowledge - what is hidden from this or that person but not from all (the lowest type), what universally surpasses human knowledge because of a defect in it, and that which surpasses human knowledge because the truths concerned "are not knowable" (*non sunt cognoscibilia*). He illustrates this third and highest grade by referring to the prophetic knowledge of future

---

[53] The fact that prophecy is not merely a "social," but also an "ecclesial," charism is not often sufficiently recognized; cf. POPE, 21; HAGGARD, 157; by contrast, cf. LAMB, 7, for a view that is much closer to the original intention of Aquinas.

[54] *ST* II-II.171.1 obj. 4.

[55] "...*caritas secundum quam fit homo amicus Dei, est perfectio voluntatis... sed prophetia est perfectio intellectus...*" (Ibid., II-II.172.2 ad 1). This comparison has profound ramifications, especially when one considers that love and knowledge are closely related in Thomas' anthropology. However, it is not the prophet alone who knows in prophecy, but all who receive his message in faith.

[56] Ibid., II-II.171.1; *De Ver.*, 12.1c; *In 1 Cor.*, 14.1.812.

[57] "*Cum ergo prophetia pertineat ad cognitionem quae supra naturalem rationem existit...*" [Ibid., II-II.171.2].

[58] "...*quia prophetia est de his quae procul a nostra cognitione sunt, tanto aliqua magis ad prophetiam pertinent quanto longius ab humana cognitione existunt*" [Ibid., II-II171.3].

events; this he designates as what is most properly called prophecy.[59] In this distinction Thomas is clearly indebted to the tradition and its preoccupation with this particular aspect of prophetic knowledge;[60] his distinctions can be characterized as prophetic modality from the point of view of God's acting in and upon the prophet.

Yet this is not the only (nor is it the most innovative) enumeration of prophetic modes for Thomas. He also distinguishes the various forms of prophecy by reference to the two distinct aspects of human knowledge[61] - the *lumen intelligible*, which he defines as "the interior power which illuminates the object and causes one to form a judgment about it..."; and the *species*, "the representations which furnish the subject matter of the judgment."[62] In these considerations Thomas discusses prophecy according to whether or not one or both of these elements is given by God to the prophet, in the form of either "a supernatural light, or infused representations, or even both."[63] Here Thomas' approach is much more anthropocentric - although God's action in the prophet is still essential to his treatment, this action is considered in its relation to the structure of human knowing.

The more indispensable of these two is the supernatural *lumen*. Since it is judgment that specifies knowledge as knowledge, therefore the formal element in prophetic knowledge is the divine light[64] which enables one to judge things according to divine truth (*secundum divinam veritatem*).[65] Thomas does (in deference to the tradition, I believe) speak of the perfection of prophecy as the reception of both *lumen* and *species*,[66] but this is an almost non-functional distinction which is itself qualified by him.[67] Where Thomas really places his emphasis is on the ability given by the divine light to judge what is true: "So essential is the light which causes the judgment that it can

---

[59] Ibid., II-II.171.3

[60] See GREGORY THE GREAT, *Homiliae in Hiezechihelem prophetam,* I.I (*CCSL* 142, pp. 5-6), upon whom Thomas relies for this distinction

[61] Brian MCCARTHY, "El modo del conocimiento profético y escriturístico según Sto. Tomás de Aquino," *Scripta Theologica* 9 (1977) : 432.

[62] P. SYNAVE and Pierre BENOIT, *Prophecy and Revelation. A Commentary on the Summa Theologica II-II, Questions 171-178,* trans. by Avery Dulles and Thomas L. Sheridan (New York: Desclée, 1961), 64. The entire treatment of the modes of prophecy contained in this work is peerless; see idem, 64-68.

[63] Ibid., 64.

[64] *ST* II-II.171.3 ad 3.

[65] Ibid., II-II.173.2.

[66] Ibid., II-II.174.2 ad 1 and 3; III.30.3 ad 1.

[67] Ibid., II-II.174.2.

suffice by itself to characterize the true prophet and distinguish prophetic knowledge from all other types."[68] In Thomas' view, if one were to receive only the *species* without the *lumen*, then one would be a prophet either only in an imperfect sense,[69] or (in some cases) not at all.[70] This distinction allows Thomas a great deal of leeway in identifying prophetic activity; for instance he refers to Solomon as a prophet because, even though he foresaw no future events, his sapiential writings demonstrate the gift of supernatural light in the judgment of everyday human affairs.[71]

Yet such an intellectual elevation is not a passive instrumentality on the part of the human prophet (or author). Thomas, who at least twice describes the prophetic gift as a transient and imperfect one,[72] nevertheless sees a certain intrinsicality to it, such that it is perfective of the intellect which receives it. As Synave and Benoit remark, "The prophet actually receives this light in his intellect; it reinforces the natural light of his reason and becomes for him an active principle of knowledge. Once he has received it, and insofar as he makes use of it, he formulates with its help judgments which truly issue from him."[73]

This can be seen most clearly in an often neglected element of Thomas' teaching on prophecy; the idea of the prophetic *habilitas*. In both the *Summa* (II-II.171.2) and in the *De Veritate* (12.1) Thomas refers to the reception of the prophetic light as leaving behind an aptitude or propensity for receiving it again. The magnificent analogy he uses is that of a piece of wood which, once it has been made to burn incompletely and then been extin-

---

[68] SYNAVE and BENOIT, 64. The authors cite *ScG* III.154 as an example of Thomas' strong insistence on the primacy of the *lumen divinum*.

[69] *ST* II-II.173.2.

[70] *De Ver.*, 12.7.

[71] "*Secundus vero gradus [prophetiae] erit in eo qui habet visionem intellectualem tantum secundum iudicium, ut in Salomone*" [*De Ver.*, 12.13c]. Cf. *De Ver.*, 12.12; *In 1 Cor.*, 14.1.813. Thomas's identification of Solomon as a prophet is an ambivalent one, departing as it does from the received wisdom which considers prophecy primarily in terms of future contingencies. Elsewhere Thomas treats Solomon differently: "*Primum est revelatio eorum quae excedunt humanum cognitionem, alias non dicitur propheta, sed sapiens, sicut Salomon, cuius mens illuminata est ad ea quae sunt secundum rationem humanam*" [*In Heb.*, 1.1.16]. It should be noted that the case of Solomon is the clearest example of Thomas' oscillation between the tradition and his own opinion; in this way it is instructive for interpreting the various statements Thomas makes regarding prophecy. See MCCARTHY, 450-452, for a more extended treatment of Solomon's prophetic status in Thomas' thought.

[72] *ST* II-II.171.2, 171. 4.

[73] SYNAVE and BENOIT, 74.

guished, is made to burn much more easily a second time. In the same way, "in the mind of the prophet, there still remains a certain *habilitas* to be enlightened once again from above."[74] In other words, the prophet has been changed by his experience of the divine light in the very ability he has to grasp divine things. Here we see Thomas in a dilemma - he is trying to emphasize (with Hugh of St. Cher[75]) that prophecy is not a *habitus;* more specifically, that it is not under the control of the prophet to decide when he will make use of it.[76] Yet in introducing this new term Thomas is attempting to avoid discarding an element normally associated with habit - ability. He is asserting that the prophet's ability is sharpened by the prophetic light, even if he does not have the liberty to decide when he exercises that ability.

Thomas has made a barely imperceptible shift here, yet it is one that is of crucial significance. It is clear that prophecy understood as the seeing of future events has receded into the background - Thomas is referring primarily to judgment.

To be precise, what Thomas is referring to is the transformation of the prophet from one who knows to one who thinks, from seer to (dare we say it?) theologian. Here we must recall that for Thomas prophecy is a charism of knowledge - he places its effect not in the will but in the intellect.[77] Therefore this *habilitas* is "in the mind of the prophet." It could be objected that this refers to some mysterious sharpening of the prophet's ability to receive supernatural representations. But given the already noted emphasis on prophecy as judgement, one that allows even Solomon to be a prophet, we are certainly dealing with an idea of the prophet as a thinker, as one who grasps truth, both divine and natural, in his/her mind. A number of insights follow from this realization.

First of all, Thomas is obviously developing a very particular way of thinking about prophecy which less and less resembles the seeing of future events and more and more resembles insight into what is already present. His emphasis is no longer on seeing, but rather on enlightening and being enlightened, not on viewing what will happen primarily but piercing through it to its meaning. In fact, he even states this directly; when considering Augustine's claim that prophecy which is intellective and imaginative is su-

---

[74] "... *remanet quaedam habilitas ad hoc quod facilius iterato illustretur...*" [*ST* II-II.171.2 ad 2].

[75] TORRELL, "Le traité de la prophétie," 178.

[76] *ST* II-II.171.2; *De Ver.*, 12.7.

[77] Ibid., II-II.171.1 sed contra. Cf. *ST* II-II.172.2 ad 1; *De Ver.*, 12.2.

perior to that which is intellective only, Thomas replies, "When some supernatural truth is to be revealed through bodily images, then more of a prophet
is he who has both, namely intellectual light and imaginative vision, than he
who has one only of the two... *Yet that prophecy in which intellectual truth is
revealed without adornment is superior to all* [emphasis mine]."[78]

That Thomas' understanding of the prophetic gift needs to be
considered from the aspect of his exegetical practice should be clear on the
basis of the above considerations. The type of prophetic gift which Thomas
focuses on the most, in which the divine light is given without infused rep-
resentation(s), is of particular relevance to the present study because it ac-
curately describes many cases of the authorship of Scripture,[79] and
particularly describes the authorship of Job, the Fourth Gospel and the
Epistles of St. Paul as they would have been understood by St. Thomas. In all
three cases the human authors of these biblical works were apparently writing
not primarily about future events but rather about past and present realities
which they had been enlightened by God to understand in a privileged way.[80]
In the case of supernatural truths, they were given the ability to comprehend
them; in the case of natural realities, they were enabled by the divine light in
such a way as to extract from them lessons of supernatural value.[81]   In
contrast, Thomas would not have understood the author of Judges in the same
way (or at least not to the same degree) - such a work is descriptive and
mediates its message not through insight but through narration.[82]

It is also clear that Thomas' doctrine represents a primarily
theological/expository way of conceiving of prophecy and therefore of human
biblical authorship.   When he refers to *habilitas*, Thomas is clearly not

---

[78] "*Ad primum ergo dicendum quod quando aliqua supernaturalis veritas revelanda est per
similitudines corporales, tunc magis est prophetia qui utrumque habet, scilicet lumen
intellectuale et imaginarium visionem, quam ille qui habet alterum tantum, quia perfectior est
prophetia... Sed illa prophetia in qua revelatur nude intelligibilis veritas, est omnibus potior*"
[Ibid., II-II.174.2 ad 1].

[79] Pierre BENOIT, *Inspiration and the Bible*, trans. by Jerome Murphy-O'Connor and M.
Keverne (London; Melbourne; New York: Sheed and Ward, 1965), 13.

[80] A possible exception might be the Fourth Gospel, as Thomas would have understood
John as narrating both the actions and the words of Jesus. But because so much of the text
consists of Jesus' teaching, it easily fits the non-narrative framework. And as we shall see
below, Thomas does give John a certain role in the transmission of divine truth when he
emphasizes that John was a contemplative.

[81] BENOIT, 14.

[82] Exactly how Thomas deals with narration will be considered in the next chapter.

referring to the prophet's ability to imagine things - nowhere in his epistemological writings does he mention anything resembling grades of perfection
in the human ability to form mental images. As we have already seen,
Thomas asserts that he who receives representations without divine light is
not a prophet.[83]

In summary, Thomas' understanding of prophecy and its implications
for his understanding of human biblical authorship shows a keen perception
on the part of Aquinas for envisioning biblical authorship as focused not on
narrative primarily, but rather on meaning transmitted by concepts. He sees
the most superior form of prophecy to be intellectual truth unadorned by
image. This is not surprising when one considers that Thomas lived in a
world which gave speculative knowledge pride of place - "he [Thomas]...
conceives his [the prophet's] role as a sublime act of knowledge, receiving
from God truths otherwise unknowable and transmitting them to men."[84] In
such a milieu an exegete would naturally have a certain affinity to texts that
most closely resemble conceptual speculation, as well as possess more
advanced skill in dealing with such texts. Hence we see that even in Thomas'
conceptualization of prophecy and biblical authorship, the deck is stacked in
favor of theological/philosophical exposition. This emphasis will be confirmed by Thomas' understanding of biblical truth itself, and the proper
interpretation of it.

D) *The Bible and Revelation*

Commenting on Jn 14:6, Thomas notes that the Divine Person of the
Son, being both man and God, is himself both the way for humanity and its
end (*terminus*), being signified as such in the passage by the words "*veritas*"
and "*vita.*"[85] This pattern described by John and wonderfully interpreted by
Thomas is the analogy *par excellence* for the Thomistic notion of Scriptural
revelation; the fact that the words of Scripture are human words makes the
Bible a way which the human mind can traverse; the fact that these human

---

[83] See n. 66.

[84] BENOIT, *Inspiration*, 25-26. Obviously "truths" here refers to concepts, not mere
physical descriptions.

[85] *In Io.* 14.2.1865-1872. For an analysis of revelation as it is treated in this passage and
elsewhere, see A. BLANCO, "Word and Truth in Divine Revelation. A study of the
Commentary of St. Thomas Aquinas on John 14,6," in *La doctrine de la révélation divine de
saint Thomas d'Aquin. Actes du Symposium sur la pensée de saint Thomas d'Aquin tenu à
Rolduc, les 4 et 5 Novembre 1989*, 27-48, ed. Leo Elders, 27-48 (Città del Vaticano: Libreria
Editrice Vaticana, 1990).

words somehow contain divine revelation makes it the medium of divine truth as well as salvation.

In a key passage of the *Compendium Theologiae*, Thomas beautifully describes Scripture with reference to the Incarnation: "the Word of the Father, comprehending everything by his own immensity, has willed to become little through the assumption of our littleness, yet without resigning his majesty, in order that he may recall man who had been laid low through sin, to the height of his divine glory."[86] Indeed, if any one term is most central to Thomas' understanding of revelation, it is almost certainly "word;"[87] for him, "the outward word of Scripture is the visible, material representation of an interior word formed in the intellect of the writer, impressed upon it by divine revelation."[88] Yet it must also be noted that this term, "Word," is qualified in the above quotation (albeit indirectly) by another term, "majesty." The Word of God becoming little and yet remaining majestic is an image which characterizes the fundamental paradox which brackets Thomas' entire consideration of the Bible as divine revelation, and offers us another clue concerning his exegetical practice.

As Thomas often points out, truth is the conformity of the mind with the thing known.[89] Yet this conformity comes about through the formulation of an inner word (which he describes variously as *"verbum interius," "verbum cordis,"* and *"verbum mentis"*).[90] In a process which can itself be termed revelatory, the human authorship of Scripture is the formulation of outer words that are caused by the inner words impressed by God upon the writer's intellect[91] and which signify them in a direct and immediate fashion.[92] It is Thomas' notion of the intricacies of this process that is of most interest to the present study.

The starting point of the revelatory process is God; in particular, the Word of God or the Son. In unanimity with the Christian tradition, Thomas ascribes perfect oneness to this Divine Word:

---

[86] *Comp. Theol.*, I.1.

[87] Leo ELDERS, "Aquinas on Holy Scripture as the Medium of Divine Revelation," 135-136. Elders notes that "word" is also the "favorite term" of the Bible for describing revelation.

[88] T.F. TORRANCE, "Scientific Hermeneutics according to St. Thomas Aquinas," 277.

[89] *ST* I.16.1; *De Ver.*, 1.1; *In I Sent.*, 19.5.1.

[90] Bernard LONERGAN, *Verbum: Word and Idea in Aquinas,* ed. by David B. Burrell (Notre Dame: University of Notre Dame Press, 1967), 7.

[91] *In I Sent.*, 19.5.1.

[92] LONERGAN, 2.

The difference between our word and God's is that ours is imperfect, but God's word is most perfect, for we cannot express all the things that are in our soul by one word, and so there must be many imperfect words through which we express separately all the things that are in our soul by one word, and so there must be many imperfect words through which we express separately all the things that are in our knowledge. But in God it is not so. For since he understands... by his own essence, by one act, so one unique word of God is expressive of all that is in God, not only of the Father but of creatures as well; otherwise it would be imperfect.[93]

The content of this divine Word is none other than the plenitude of divine knowledge. As Torrance notes,

With us human beings our words convey less than we know and are defective instruments, but that is not the case with God's word for the whole of his wisdom is contained in it. Hence there is an element of impropriety in speaking about the words of God, for that is a way of speaking assimilated to our human imperfection. Thus behind all the words of holy scripture, behind all the commands and utterances of God in them, there stands the reality of the *unum unicum verbum Dei*."[94]

If such a radical disparity exists between the words of scripture and the one Word of God, then there must be a process by which this one Word of God is prismated into the great multitude of words which comprise Sacred Scripture. We have seen one aspect of this process in the consideration of Thomas' notion of prophecy; in particular, the aspect of the human instrument. But what is of present concern is how the divine Word takes on the "littleness" of the biblical writings. In this we do not witness a change in God; Thomas is clear that in impressing a likeness of Himself upon the human intellect, no change is caused in the immutable divine essence, nor is this essence completely revealed, "since he [God] infinitely transcends every created form, consequently God cannot be made accessible to the mind through created forms."[95] This "created form" is the effect of God's action (for it is itself a creation of God like the intellect upon which it is impressed, and to this degree compatible with it), and this is what the author of Scripture

---

[93] *De differentia divini verbi et humani*, Opusc. XIII; cf. *ST* I.34.3.

[94] T.F. TORRANCE, 274.

[95] *In Boeth. De Trin.*, I.2.

comprehends; Thomas calls it "the word of the Word."[96]   Yet this is "the word of God only in a figurative or metaphorical sense... The word in scripture is a creature of the Word and is not the proper word of God, but only an instrument expressing it."[97]

Thus Thomas' concept of revelation is "highly intellectualistic"[98]; it focuses on Scripture in terms of its relation to the infinite all-encompassing divine Word. It is no wonder, therefore, that Torrance comments that it lacks the emphasis on the "historical and concrete event" that is so evident in the biblical notion of revelation.[99]   Such immediacy, it is true, is not at the forefront of Thomas' mind; he would emphasize revelation's completeness rather than its concreteness - the finality and perfection of revelation due to its intimate connection and similitude to the divine Word which it reflects.

This is not to say (as Torrance seems to) that Thomas' conception is at odds with a more historical, event-oriented understanding of revelation. As Torrance notes himself, the Aristotelian view of knowledge had a "sobering effect" on Thomas' exegetical practice, "for it disparaged the cultivation of a world of meanings that could be correlated on its own without scientific reference to the historical sense of Scripture and careful examination of words and concepts..."[100] Nor is Thomas' emphasis alien to the Bible itself, where one finds both ideas of revelation; in certain passages (for instance, Jn 1:1-18) the oneness and completion of revelation is emphasized, while in others the concrete and historical aspect takes center stage (Acts 2:14-41).

An understanding of biblical revelation such as Thomas' would obviously favor theological exposition on the part of the biblical author over the description of events that one finds in works of primarily historical and/or narrative dimensions. As one surveys the Thomistic doctrine regarding Scripture itself, two examples present themselves which clearly demonstrate that Thomas conceives of Scripture primarily as a complex of expressions that seek resemblance to the single self-expression of God in all truth, a self-expression which is his Word.

---

[96] "...non solum divini intellectus conceptio dicitur Verbum, quod est Filius, sed etiam explicatio divini conceptus per opera exteriora verbum Verbi nominatur" [S.c.G., IV.13]. Cf. T.F. TORRANCE, 278-279

[97] T.F. TORRANCE, 279; cf. In I Sent., 27.2.2 s. 2 ad. 3.

[98] Ibid., 281.

[99] Ibid., 281.

[100] Ibid., 259.

For instance, Thomas refers to the Bible as *sacra doctrina*, or "holy teaching";[101] in one place he offers the two terms as synonyms of each other (*sacra scriptura seu doctrina*).[102] In the section of the *Summa* on prophecy, Thomas refers to revelation as being given "*per modum cuiusdam doctrinae.*"[103] And when he speaks of apostolic doctrine he is clearly referring to the writings by which these teachings are transmitted to us.[104] Hence his concern for the relation of Scripture to argumentation in *ST* I.1.8-10; Thomas is clearly attempting to conceive of Scripture in terms of contemporary Aristotelian methods of instruction.

Yet this identification poses a serious difficulty. How can Thomas assert that Scripture is sacred doctrine when it so often takes forms that are not properly argumentative? It is a leap he takes much too easily, especially in the light of his affirmation once again in article 10 (ad 1) that the literal sense is the only sufficient basis for theological argumentation.[105] How can Scripture remain authoritative in its literal sense,[106] and yet that literal sense be in forms alien to argumentation? Persson would have us believe that Thomas achieves this by giving preference to certain biblical works over others because they are more obviously doctrinal: "even within the canon of scripture Thomas gives precedence to certain writings on the grounds that they contain everything that is essential as regards doctrine."[107] Is there any evidence that his judgment is correct?

Thomas never addresses this issue directly. However, he does reveal his mind on the issue when he asserts that "those things which are taught metaphorically in one part of Scripture are taught more openly in other

---

[101] J. VAN DER PLOEG, "The Place of Holy Scripture in the Theology of St. Thomas," *The Thomist* 10 (1947) : 411.

[102] *ST* I.1.1. It should be noted that this is not an absolute identification, such that the terms become mutually exclusive, "...in this context, *sacra Doctrina* seems to have a rather flexible sense, which allows it to designate the teaching received by divine revelation..." [Etienne MÉNARD, *La Tradition: révélation, écriture, Église selon s. Thomas d'Aquin* (Bruges: Desclée, 1964), 115].

[103] Ibid., II-II.171.6.

[104] Ibid., II-II.1.10 ad 1.

[105] Cf. *De pot.*, 4.1; *Quodl.*, VII.6.3.

[106] John F. BOYLE, "St. Thomas Aquinas and Sacred Scripture," *Pro Ecclesia* 4 (1996) : 97.

[107] Erik PERSSON, *Sacra Doctrina: Reason and Revelation in Aquinas*, trans. by Ross Mackenzie (Philadelphia, Fortress Press, 1970), 53; cf. *Super Epist.*, Prol.; *Super Psalm.*, Proemium.

parts."[108] This passage has massive ramifications for our present study and for understanding Thomas' notion of scriptural revelation as a whole. For what he is doing here is no less than establishing a relationship of dependence between various parts of the Bible upon other parts; namely, a dependence of those parts which are metaphorical upon those which are not. Might this be a small part of a larger pattern, in which a dependence is posited by Thomas of what is more literary upon what is more expository and argumentative? There is concrete evidence of such a pattern - Thomas singles out the Pauline corpus as one body of writing in the New Testament that contains *"fere tota theologiae... doctrina"* ("almost the entire teaching of theology").[109] Is this not the most argumentative group of texts which Thomas encounters in Scripture? Indeed he places it (along with Job) into the literary genre of "disputative" writing;[110] in other words, it comes ready-made for being expressed pedagogically and for developing theological positions. Therefore in a very real (though not absolute) sense, Job and the Pauline Epistles functionally resemble Thomas' conception of Scripture as *sacra doctrina* much more than other parts of Scripture, which in his mind depend upon the former to teach "more openly" than they do.

This evidence is strongly reinforced by Thomas' conception of the apostle himself. In his study of Thomas' treatment of the Resurrection of Christ, Valkenberg notes that Thomas uses the Gospels and Acts mainly as sources of data - his tendency is to consider these sources as "objective information." But in his use of the Pauline letters these are considered not as sources of testimonial data but rather are utilized for Paul's theological insights. "Consequently, Paul is the main source for Aquinas when considering the soteriological value of the resurrection of Christ. *He considers Paul as the first and foremost of all theologians* [emphasis mine], someone who indicates the significance of the salvation Christ brought us..."[111]

This insight is directly corroborated by Thomas. He refers to Paul in two places as one who argues scientifically.[112]   In both cases Thomas refers to 1 Cor 15:12 ("If Christ is raised, the dead will also rise") and, interestingly enough, in both cases his purpose is to demonstrate that sacred doctrine is a matter of argument. In *ST* I.1.8, for instance, Thomas asserts that:

---

[108] *ST* I.1.9 ad 2.

[109] *Super Epist.*, Prol.

[110] *Super Psalm.*, Proemium.

[111] VALKENBERG, 196-197.

[112] *In I Sent.*, Prol., 5 ad 4; *ST* I.1.8. These passages are nearly identical.

> As other sciences do not argue in proof of their principles, but argue
> from their principles to demonstrate other truths in these sciences:
> so this doctrine does not argue in proof of its principles, which are
> the articles of faith, but from them it goes on to prove something
> else; *as the Apostle argues from the resurrection of Christ in proof
> of the general resurrection* (1 Cor 15).[113]

What is significant here is that Thomas uses Paul and not any other
biblical author to demonstrate this aspect of his teaching on *sacra doctrina*.
That is, Thomas relies upon a specimen (1 Cor 15) of the non-narrative,
expository genre which we have argued best fits his conception of *sacra
scriptura* as *sacra doctrina*.

This dilemma regarding the relationship between *sacra doctrina* and
sacra scriptura is closely related to another aspect of Thomas' scriptural
doctrine - his teaching on the literal and spiritual senses. It has been noted
that Thomas' remarkable (indeed paradoxical) pluralism in his biblical
exegesis has precipitated the astonishing fact that "no one has successfully
categorized his approach to the Bible. Advocates of allegory claim him as
their own and defenders of strictly literal interpretation praise him for
asserting the sufficiency of the letter."[114] That Thomas has an extremely
eclectic approach cannot be disputed. However, there may be more to this
diversity of opinion regarding his position on the senses than first meets the
eye.

To recognize this it is necessary to remember the quote from the
Compendium cited above; Thomas affirms both the littleness as well as the
majesty of the presence of revelation in Scripture. This wonderful expression
of the incarnational nature of revelation takes on its fullest significance when
one considers that Thomas approaches the biblical text with many centuries of
exegetical patrimony standing behind him,[115] a patrimony which can be
characterized by a strong urge to find the proper balance between revelatory
littleness and revelatory majesty. In particular, the insistence of this tradition
on the spiritual senses to be found in Scripture is an integral element of this

---

[113] *ST* I.1.8.

[114] LAMB, 3. He goes on to give two examples of this remarkable diversity of opinion; cf.
Beryl SMALLEY, *The Study of the Bible in the Middle Ages*, 2d rev. ed. (Oxford: Basil
Blackwell, 1952), 292-294, 300ff, for advocacy of the former opinion; cf. Henri de LUBAC,
Exégèse Médiévale: Les Quatre Sens de l'Écriture, vol. II. (Paris: Aubier, 1964), 272-302,
for a defense of Thomas' "traditionalism."

[115] KENNEDY, 10-97, for an excellent analysis of the development of the Christian
approach to the Bible precisely in relation to Thomas' own place in this history.

attempt to preserve an understanding of Scripture as precious and peerless writing, coming as it does from God himself. Origen of Alexandria, one of the great exegetical pioneers of the tradition that Thomas inherits, will initiate a long and influential current in it by insisting that some passages of Scripture do not contain a plain sense that is worthy of God, but only a "spiritual" one;[116] a hidden meaning that underlies the obvious meaning of the text.[117] His notion will affect the practice of many exegetes to follow him, including even those who will give the literal sense their greatest attention, such as St. Jerome.[118] St. Augustine will himself affirm this position by asserting that the literal sense must be abandoned if it is absurd.[119]

Just as it would be an exaggeration to maintain that Thomas' strong insistence on the literal sense originated with him,[120] so would it also be a misstatement if one were to maintain that Thomas' exegetical practice was devoid of a certain leftover hesitancy regarding the absolute sufficiency of the literal sense. We have already seen above that for Thomas even literary forms such as metaphor in Scripture rely on other, more explicitly theological texts for clarity. What of those instances when we find references to ordinary places and events, even objects in Scripture? It is in these cases that Thomas demonstrates an instinctive reliance upon deeper, hidden meanings for preserving the majesty of the text he is dealing with.

Therefore we see him pursuing spiritual senses energetically even while he engages in his pursuit of the literal sense; after all perceived literal meanings are exhausted, Thomas will invariably move on to posit additional significances, demonstrating parallels between the Old and New Testaments, finding additional symbolisms, etc.[121] This practice obviously has its dangers from the perspective of modern critical inquiry into the Bible. What it does for Thomas is allow him to doctrinalize Scripture, to weave each part into a seamless unity with every other. Yet on further investigation it becomes clear

---

[116] ORIGEN, *De Principiis*, IV.2.5.

[117] KENNEDY, 16.

[118] Louis N. HARTMANN, 'Jerome as an Exegete," in *A Monument to St. Jerome*, ed. Francis Xavier Murphy (New York: Sheed and Ward, 1952), 46.

[119] AUGUSTINE, *De Doctrina Christiana*, III.29.41 (*CCSL* 32, pg. 102).

[120] Cf. KENNEDY, 144-149; see FROEHLICH, 88, for the opinion that Thomas' teaching on the literal sense derives from the Victorine school of exegesis.

[121] M.D. MALHOIT, "La pensée de saint Thomas sur le sens spirituel," *Revue Thomiste* 59 (1959) : 613-663.

that Thomas is doing more than this; he is drawing the narrative and historical parts of the Bible into a unity with the parts which are more expository.

The example of Thomas' exegesis of John 6 is particularly helpful in demonstrating this aspect of his understanding of revelation, mainly because it contains both narrative and non-narrative sections that are related to each other. In the narrative section (Jn 6: 1-26)[122] which describes the multiplication of the loaves, Thomas offers no less than twenty different mystical interpretations in twenty-seven verses. Yet when he treats the Bread of Life discourse (Jn 6:26-72),[123] which is comprised of forty-two verses, Thomas offers not a single mystical interpretation; he is too busy expounding on the literal meaning, which is already being presented as teaching and therefore easily fits into his conception of Scripture as *sacra doctrina*. From a contemporary perspective, it is obvious which of these two closely connected specimens of Thomas' exegetical practice is of more interest - the latter can obviously cohere more closely to the original meaning because it leaves behind the soaring flights of allegory, keeping firmly rooted in the text itself.[124]

In both of these cases what we see illustrated is an understanding of scriptural revelation which, while being progressive for its day, has an obvious bias in favor of those parts of the Bible that have argumentative and speculative forms. Metaphorical and narrative texts are certainly not debased

---

[122] *In Io.*, 6.1-3.

[123] Ibid. 6.3-8

[124] Perhaps this helps to explain why Thomas' approach to Scripture can be so confusing at times; when insufficient account is taken of the differences in the texts Thomas is dealing with, he can seem to be two entirely different commentators living in the same skin. Smalley's bewildered remarks capture the almost schizophrenic nature of what one finds in Thomas' exegetical corpus, "His [Aquinas'] ideas on the four senses *as applied to the Gospels* [emphasis mine] are hard to fathom. At least he bespeaks as keen an interest in actual historical detail as any of his predecessors." She continues, "It is fashionable now to credit Thomas with a sense of history... The truths perceived by our minds change. The only eternal truth belongs to the divine mind. Such truths as we can reach are achieved in time and through history... *I can only note that the texts supporting it hardly ever come from his exegesis* [emphasis mine]" [Beryl SMALLEY, *The Gospels in the Schools: c.1100-c.1280*, vol. 41, Hambledon History Series (London: The Hambledon Press, 1985), 270]. In light of the considerations above, is this surprising coming from an author who states elsewhere that in her study of medieval exegesis, "the Pauline Epistles... have been set aside by design" [Idem, *Study*, xxi]? Had she not set them aside, perhaps she would have seen Thomas' work as an exegete from an entirely different angle. Although it is true that in the former case her stated intention is to focus on the Gospels alone, at the very least her criticism there of Thomas' *exegesis* (a noun not qualified by a reference to his specific exegesis of the Gospels) is an unwarranted generalization.

by Thomas; in fact it can be argued that Thomas' Aristotelianism goes a long way towards establishing an atmosphere in which the concrete historical nature of God's salvific activity can be fully appreciated. Torrance notes that Thomas inclusion of the parabolic and metaphoric as part of the literal sense shows a desire on Thomas' part to allow a certain depth to the literal sense that many of his predecessors did not;[125] and one must not forget that even as he relied on the spiritual senses, he relativized them by teaching that nothing which is taught in the mystical sense is not taught elsewhere in the literal,[126] and also that the mystical senses do not carry the weight of proof in theological argumentation.[127] Yet it is also true that for Thomas, texts which reflect concrete historicity and narrative do not speak for themselves in the way that "disputative" texts do. When he turns his attention to the Pauline Epistles, therefore, one can rightly assert that his attention had never actually left them. Indeed, everything he sees is seen through a Pauline lens.

E) *Thomas' Basic Hermeneutic*
Even as it is acknowledged with Henri de Lubac that Thomas Aquinas was in many ways a traditionalist when it comes to the spiritual interpretation of Scripture, it must not be forgotten that the effect of Aristotelianism immunized Thomas against the danger of becoming beholden to such an approach. It is one which he definitely surpasses even as he uses it, and Smalley's characterization of the exegete of the Schools applies to no one more surely than him: "Transferring his view of body and soul to 'letter' and 'spirit' the Aristotelian would perceive the 'spirit' of Scripture as something not hidden behind or added on to, but expressed by the text. We cannot disembody a man in order to investigate his soul; neither can we understand the Bible by distinguishing letter from spirit and making a separate study of each."[128] Following her lead, we can say with safety that although Thomas often does resort to an extrinsic and veiled sense when the text itself seems to lose its conceptual sparkle, even more often he focuses on the text's literal meaning as it is incarnated and manifested by the letter in every passage. It is this latter which is Thomas' major preoccupation as an exegete, and on which his theory of interpretation focuses.

---

[125] T.F. TORRANCE, 282.

[126] *ST* I.1.9 ad 2; I.1.10 ad 1; *Quodl.*, VII.6.1 ad 3.

[127] *In I Sent.*, Prol.; *In Boeth. de Trin.*, II.3 ad 5; *Quodl.*, VII.6.1 ad 4.

[128] SMALLEY, *Study*, 293.

We are fortunate to have a unique guide to Thomas' hermeneutical principles in his commentary on the *Peri Hermeneias* of Aristotle, which closely follows Aristotle's text up to Book II.2.[129] We will follow the text (without limiting ourselves to it) in an attempt to discern the essential features of Thomas' theory of interpretation and his corresponding application of it to scriptural exegesis.

In any task of interpretation, there is a definite goal which is involved, and this is one of understanding (*intelligere*), "...in which the mind pierces through to see the *quid* of a thing, that is, to read the truth in the very essence of it."[130]   Although neither Thomas nor Aristotle is primarily concerned with grammar here,[131] both go to lengths to establish the various modes of linguistic signification involved in speech, since it is the items of speech which the act of interpretation labors to understand. Therefore Thomas points out that certain vocal sounds ("conjunctions" and "prepositions," specifically) do not signify anything taken by themselves, and that other kinds of vocal sounds (i.e., "names" and "verbs") do so only partially. It is only "enunciative speech" (the rational ordered usage of the various parts of speech to declare upon the truth or falsity of something) that can claim to be interpretive, for only in this kind of speech is located the proper objects of understanding. Other forms of speech (such as the optative and imperative forms) cannot claim to be interpretive because they are ordered toward expressing the will and not the intellect.[132] So the interpretation of any text, including Scripture, will involve analyzing propositions, "for the interpretation of language is the interpretation of thought."[133]

Thomas turns often to the etymology of the word *intelligere* in his theory of interpretation; it is *intus legere*, "to read within,"[134] "to penetrate beneath the sensible surface (*sensus*) and discern the rational meaning (*intellectus*)."[135] This penetration is one to "the very essence [or substance] of

---

[129] TORRELL, *Saint Thomas*, 342-343.

[130] T.F. TORRANCE, 261.

[131] Jean T. OESTERLE, commentary on St. Thomas Aquinas, *Aristotle: On Interpretation* (Milwaukee: Marquette University Press, 1962), 19 n.3.

[132] *Periherm.*, I, Intro.

[133] T.F. TORRANCE, 260.

[134] *ST* I-II.108.1. ad 3, II-II.8.1, II-II.49.5 ad 3; *De Ver.*, 1.12.

[135] T.F. TORRANCE, 261.

a thing" (what Thomas often refers to as "*quod quid est*"[136]), "the goal and
term of all positive inquiry."[137]   This is not a cryptic activity that is exclusive
to the domain of the philosopher, but is rather the basic activity one pursues in
every attempt to understand anything.[138]   In interpretation it occurs specifically through an apprehension of the speaker's (or in the case of Scripture,
the author's) intention - Thomas agrees with Aristotle that words do not
signify things immediately (as the Platonists believed) but signify instead the
author's intellectual conception of things.[139]   "This means that the interpreter
of a particular author must first of all concentrate his attention on the author's
use of language before he determines what truth the author is attempting to
signify...";[140] successful interpretation will involve understanding how the
author contrived his language, interpreting it first as "the expression of a
particular mind in a particular historical situation," and only then as "the
expression of some universal truth."[141]   In the case of Scripture, this process
remains essential, although it requires augmentation on the part of God and
his grace if the interpreter is to pierce through to divine truth.[142]   Thomas
succeeds in developing a concept of the human author as a relatively free
secondary cause under the Principal Author who is God, so that what the
human author produces must be analyzed as a truly human composition
(though not a *merely* human one).

Yet the act of interpretation is not complete until all of the various
propositions of a speech or text have been grasped not only in their individual
truth, but also in a system of mutual interconnections with other truths.
Multiple insights combine with each other, or develop so as to include each
other, into what both Aristotelian and Thomistic philosophy refer to as a
science;[143] as such these truths are gathered around a center (the first

---

[136] See LONERGAN, 16-25, for an excellent analysis of Thomas' use of this phrase and its
roots in Greek philosophy. Thomas makes this term synonymous with *substantia*: "*quod quid
est, idest substantia rei*" [*ScG.*, III.56.5].

[137] Ibid., 24.

[138] T.F. TORRANCE, 262.

[139] *Periherm.*, I.2.5.

[140] HAGGARD, 182. "This understanding of language as the mediation of reality through
the thought of a particular author would favor a greater attachment to the literal sense before
moving on to further speculation about the spiritual sense."

[141] Ibid., 183.

[142] *ST* I.1.10 ad 1, II-II.173.2; *Quodl.*, VI.1.

[143] LONERGAN, 51.

principles) in order for the whole to be grasped as a whole. As T.F. Torrance explains it,

> No science can prove its first principles, for it is in light of them that it knows what is less knowable, but in ordering its matter in the light of the first principles it does succeed in connecting the contents rationally together and so directs attention back again to the first principles. They on their part can now be discerned more clearly and the intellect is the more convinced of their truth because through the light they cast other things become knowable and evident.[144]

With this characterization of Aristotelian (and Thomistic) science, we are only one step away from Thomas' characterization of *sacra doctrina* itself as a science.[145] This is preeminently a science of Scripture, which serves as the locus of greatest proof in theological argumentation.

To understand the significance of this for our topic we must return briefly to Thomas' notion of *doctrina* or instruction, which we have so far considered only in relation to Scripture. This notion is one which he ex--pounds on frequently in his writings. He defines it as an activity in which a person leads another to the knowledge of something.[146] More specifically, the teacher actually causes *science* [147] in the pupil through the operation of the pupil's nature; as Aristotle puts it, demonstration is a syllogism causing science.[148] Although *doctrina* can refer to the acquisition of any knowledge, it is most precisely the generation of the knowledge of conclusions through their principles that is instruction properly defined.[149]

Given Thomas' understanding of interpretation as leading to scientific knowledge, what can be deduced regarding his exegetical practice? The answer becomes clear as soon as we question how Thomas could achieve movement from text to science, from *sacra scriptura* to *sacra doctrina*. It is necessary to remember that for Thomas, Scripture is one work, coming to us as it does from God who is one - "sacred doctrine bears, as it were, the stamp

---

[144] T.F. TORRANCE, 285. Cf. *ST* I.7.8, I.79.3-4, I.85.1, I-II.54.2, I-II.57.2, II-II.1.5; *In Boeth. De Trin.*, I.3, II.1-3; *De Ver.*, 1.9, 10.5, 11.1.

[145] *ST* I.1.2.

[146] *In II Sent.*, IX.1.2 ad 4.

[147] *In V Phys.*, 2.3.

[148] Gerald F. VAN ACKEREN, *Sacra Doctrina: The Subject of the First Question of the Summa Theologica of St. Thomas Aquinas* (Rome: Catholic Book Agency, 1952), 61.

[149] Ibid., 72-74.

of the divine science, which is one and simple, yet extends to everything."[150] Although Thomas does give a value to the individual sacred writings, he does so as parts of a whole, a whole which has a superior unity as it is the revelation of perfect truth. As he attempts to penetrate the sacred text in order to understand it and then to expound it as a science, where in Scripture does Thomas find his firmest foothold? Would it not be in texts that are already expository, that do not primarily narrate the events of salvation history but attempt some interpretation of these events? Two examples in particular come to mind, and we have already considered them in relation to Thomas' exegetical practice - the Fourth Gospel, which contains a great deal of reflection upon itself (that is, upon the narrative contained within it), the other Gospels, and to a lesser degree, the Old Testament; and the Pauline Epistles, where the full extent of salvation history comes under continuous scrutiny and is interpreted thoroughly. Is there any evidence to confirm that Thomas relies on these two groups of texts as guides with which to interpret the rest of the Bible?

Although he draws no specific conclusions regarding this conclusion, Valkenberg gives us a strong piece of evidence in favor of it. In analyzing the place and function of Scripture in Thomas' theology, he places under analysis two texts dealing with Christ the Savior: *In III Sent.* 1-22 and *ST* III.1-59. He then calculates the percentage of total references to authors by Thomas in these two selections, listing the twenty most frequently referred to in each. In both cases, Thomas refers to Pauline and Johannine texts more often than any other (Paul is referred to in 9.87% of the total cases, while John is referred to in 6.02% of the total cases). References to these two make up 15.89% of all references to *auctoritates*, while all other references to Scripture are only 18.39% *combined*.[151]

What about Job? Shouldn't this work show up here as well if Thomas is relying on "disputative" texts to draw the whole of his interpretation of Scripture into a scientific synthesis? It is true that Job does not even chart in the above experiment by Valkenberg. Yet we have other evidence concerning Job, as it demonstrates a peculiarity that is found in none of the other biblical commentaries - copious intra-referencing. That is, just as in the above case (and throughout Thomas' work) the preponderance of scriptural citations come from Johannine and Pauline texts, in the *Expositio super Iob* one text is

---

[150] *ST* I.1.3 ad 2.
[151] VALKENBERG, 44-46, 388-392.

cited significantly more often than any other, and this is Job itself (401 references, with the closest runner-up being Psalms with a mere forty-five).[152] This is significant because in his other scriptural commentaries Thomas seldom cross-references within the text; he is too busy referencing other texts. The reason for this anomaly is clear; Job is a self-contained work, which carries its own exposition and garners very little reflection outside of itself. It contains its own argumentative foothold, and so Thomas does not need to seek another one outside of it. So even here we see that the same principle applies - exposition is used to interpret the text, though in the case of Job the interpretive guide and the text itself are one and the same.[153]

This brings us to a final and crucial observation. If it is true that Thomas uses John and Paul as guides to interpret other parts of Scripture, *what does he use to interpret their writings*? Here Thomas comes to the edge of a hermeneutical gap in his theory of interpretation. Other parts of Scripture (in the form of citations) can reinforce or confirm these texts, but in the preponderant number of cases it would be expected that the former certainly cannot clarify the latter, at least not until the former is allegorized or forced to fit a new context. Given this dilemma, we would expect that Thomas would do one of three things: a) he would be forced to go to other authorities outside of Scripture to aid him in clarifying the text; b) he would use his ingenuity to forge his own interpretation; or c) he would develop an interpretation that is a combination of (a) and (b). The most important consequence of his dilemma is clear - it is in commenting on these texts (as well as specimens like them as they are found scattered throughout the Bible) that Thomas would be pushed to his most original contributions as an exegete.

These observations are by no means complete, nor have they solved every difficulty.[154] Yet the decision to consider these three of Thomas' exegetical principles (i.e. the nature of prophecy, the nature of the Bible as revelation and Thomas' basic hermeneutic) from the vantage point of his

---

[152] St. Thomas AQUINAS, *The Literal Exposition on Job: A Scriptural Commentary Concerning Providence*, trans. by Anthony Damico, Interpretive Essay and Notes by Martin D. Yaffe, Classics in Religious Studies, ed.Carl A. Raschke (Atlanta: Scholars Press, 1989), 487-493.

[153] In the case of his exegesis of other non-narrative texts (such as Ephesians), Thomas uses a different approach, but one which follows the same pattern and illustrates it even more emphatically, as will be demonstrated in the third chapter of this study.

[154] For instance, Thomas cites the Psalms almost as often as he cites Paul and John, and like the Pauline Epistles he refers to them as *"fere tota theologiae... doctrina"* [*Super Epist., Prol.*]. Yet the Psalms are certainly not expository texts, and very little resembling argumentation can be found in them.

exegetical practice (particularly from the vantage point of his most "successful" commentaries) has yielded some significant insights regarding Thomas' exegetical practice that the standard approach could not. Here it is of value to consider again the novelty of this approach. Rather than the usual paradigm of inquiry (from presuppositions to practice), we began with the unexplored observation of many scholars that certain works in the exegetical corpus are of a greater quality than the rest. Noting their similarity, we searched Thomas' exegetical principles for an explanation as to why this kind of text is more accessible to Thomas than others. This search reaffirmed the judgment that the commentaries on Job, John and Paul are of a higher quality than the rest, revealing a certain presuppositional bias on Thomas' part for conceiving of Scripture in a non-narrative way. This leaves us in an excellent place to approach Thomas' biblical works profitably, because it gives a reasonable basis upon which to judge the quality of the various commentaries, which will serve as a foundation for other insights. In short, we have located a more advantageous place from which to approach Thomas' relationship to the Bible, using the standard paradigm of inquiry as an indispensable springboard.

CHAPTER II

CONTEMPORARY CRITICISM
OF THOMAS' EXEGESIS:
A CALL FOR A NEW APPROACH?

When one considers the contemporary state-of-affairs in the study of Thomas' relationship to the Bible, a situation in which, in the opinion of one scholar, "almost all of the theology... which is founded on Thomas omits from consideration what he provides in his biblical commentaries;"[1] when one makes the observation that this virtually complete omission of the biblical commentaries occurs within an atmosphere of the highest enthusiasm for Thomas as an exegete and a biblical theologian, then it is difficult to be surprised when evidence begins to mount of scholars throwing up their hands and adopting dismissive or at least strongly critical attitudes regarding these works and Thomas' abilities as an exegete.[2] And this is exactly what we witness when we survey the last 30-40 years, in which some blows have been launched against scholarship into Thomas' relationship to the Bible, blows which have neither been returned nor parried. These need to be considered before any honest inquiry can be made into the biblical commentaries, or at least before any more significance can be attributed to them.

It would be futile to attempt a consideration of every critical remark, since most of these are minor, repetitive and undeveloped. Rather, our concentration will be focused on those examples which carry the greatest weight in terms of either severity, profundity or both. This will be an attempt to not only answer these objections but also to learn from them, recognizing that they represent some of the most original and honest insights that we currently have into Thomas' relationship to the Bible. As this is undertaken, ingre-

---

[1] Waclaw SWIERZAWSKI, "L' exégèse biblique et la théologie spéculative de s. Thomas d'Aquin," *Divinitas* 18 (1974) : 138.

[2] This criticism is not always exclusive to Thomas' exegesis; see Roland MURPHY, "Patristic and Medieval Exegesis - Help or Hindrance?," *Catholic Biblical Quarterly* 43 (1981) : 505-510, for an example of a more far-reaching pessimism regarding the Christian exegetical tradition.

dients of a new approach will emerge, contributing to the formulation of a distinction regarding the biblical texts themselves (as has already been initiated in Chapter I) for the sake of properly positioning this new approach. This will prepare for Chapter III, in which this new approach will be formulated and demonstrated.

A final note of caution is necessary regarding this endeavor, and actually serves as a guiding principle for it. One does well to remember the now famous observation of Beryl Smalley regarding St. Thomas' exegesis: "Reading these [Thomas' lectures on Scripture] against a background of modern exegesis, one naturally finds the medieval element in them startling; approaching them from the twelfth and thirteenth centuries, one is more startled by their modernity."[3] What follows will not be an attempt to dispel or discard the insight of Smalley that Thomas' biblical commentaries are not modern - only a flight of fancy could ever make them seem to be modern. Yet it is in noting and affirming with her the latter part of her statement, that we do find in Thomas certain real advances and even affinities with modern exegesis, that this chapter and indeed this whole dissertation finds its inspiration. To answer the modern criticisms of Thomas' medieval biblical commentaries is not to ignore that the latter are truly medieval, but rather to tackle the question of their accessibility as works of biblical commentary which have value as such - as works by a truly great biblical theologian whose significance no one can question.

These criticisms will be considered according to the order of their relevance to our topic, starting with the most general and moving to the most specific. I have narrowed this consideration down to three authors whose work is representative of the criticisms of others while being at the same time the most precise and developed examples of this contemporary scrutiny of Thomistic exegesis: T.F. Torrance, C. Clifton Black, and Otto Hermann Pesch.

A) *T.F. Torrance*

The first critic which will be considered is T.F. Torrance, a Protestant scholar whose massive contributions to theological scholarship span not only a half-century of continuous production, but also a remarkable array of topics, from Reformation theology to patristic hermeneutics.[4] His genius is attested

---

[3] SMALLEY, *Study*, 301.

[4] For an account of Torrance's output, see Iain R. TORRANCE, "A Bibliography of the Writings of T.F. Torrance : 1941-1989," *Scottish Journal of Theology* 43 (1990) : 225-262.

to by the fact that his sole contribution to Thomistic studies stands on a par with the work of Lonergan in terms of its indispensability for understanding Thomas' theory of biblical interpretation. A quick glance at the notes of Chapter I reveal Torrance's value in this regard, as well as my own dependence on his insights.

When reading his monograph one first notices the tremendous praise which Torrance has for Thomas as a biblical interpreter. He attributes to scholastic exegesis in general the triumph of detaching biblical interpretation from the complex of mystical meanings rationally unrelated to the text itself, bringing exegesis and theology into a closer relationship with each other.[5] In his own words, "It is above all to Thomas Aquinas that we must turn to see how these developments affected the interpretation of holy scripture...;" and this is because Thomas' exegesis has a "sober and judicious quality" in comparison to his predecessors, and also because his views on Scripture synthesized all that was outstanding in the tradition he inherited.[6]

Yet Torrance's praise of Thomas is mitigated by his claim that in Thomas' work "the meaning [of Scripture] is inevitably schematized to the philosophical thought-forms brought to its understanding."[7] This leads him to a stark conclusion:

> St. Thomas had a giant mind, to which there have been few equals, but his own immense intellectual powers laid him open to great temptations. His prior understanding of human experience, of the intellect and the soul, his masterful interpretation of Aristotelian physics, metaphysics and psychology, proved too strong and rigid a mould into which to pour the Christian faith. It is philosophy that tends to be the master, while theology tends to lose its unique nature as a science in its own right in spite of the claims advanced for it. In so far as the contents of theology surpass the powers of scientific investigation they are to be accepted as revealed truth but in the end the authority of ecclesiastical tradition outweighs in practice the authority of sacred scripture so that interpretation of revealed truth is schematized to the mind of the church.[8]

---

[5] T.F. TORRANCE, "Scientific Hermeneutics according to St. Thomas Aquinas," 260-261.

[6] Ibid., 261.

[7] Ibid., 281.

[8] Ibid., 289.

Torrance's indictment is so strong that it leads one to wonder whether
or not he can find any value left in Aquinas' approach to Scripture, other than
that it is "judicious," "rational" and "carefully scientific."[9]

It would be too easy to dismiss Torrance's critique of Thomas' scientific hermeneutics as a specific application to his thought of the general critique made by classical and neo-Protestant thinkers of the Catholic understanding of the relationship between reason and revelation. It is true that Torrance's critique is closely related to this general critique, and seems to arise
from it;[10] however, to relegate his comments to the category of a different
issue would be to fail to recognize their timeliness in regard to the present
topic. It is necessary to consider whether there are other reasons that give rise
to his pessimistic view of Thomistic biblical interpretation; and on closer
inspection it seems that there are.

For one thing, Torrance seems to envision Thomas as first and
foremost a writer of scientific, systematic works of theology. This is clear
from his citations, which are taken almost entirely from works that are only
secondarily biblical in nature, and in some cases are not biblical at all.[11]
Torrance falls prey to the general trend we have already illustrated; that is, he
talks at length about Thomas' theories about Scripture without even once
considering his exegetical practice, the actual application of these theories.
This leaves him in a difficult place; while his observations are ones that can
be logically deduced from what Thomas posits theoretically, no concrete
evidence of these deductions is offered to the reader to give his criticism the
weight of proof.

A closer look at Thomas' exegetical practice may have given
Torrance a different view. If one considers Thomas' more scientific theological works (such as the *Scriptum super Sententiarum* and the *Summa
Theologiae*) it is easy to be struck by the number of times Thomas refers not
only to Aristotle but also to Plato, the *Platonici* and other philosophers - 3098

---

[9] Ibid., 289.

[10] Torrance is not alone in his neo-Lutheran critique of Catholic rationalism as it is
supposedly present in the work of Thomas Aquinas; cf. Jonathan SELDEN, "Aquinas, Luther,
Melancthon and Biblical Apologetics," *Grace Theological Journal* 5 (1984) : 181-186, for
another example of this critique; cf. VALKENBURG, 61-63, for an answer to this general
opinion.

[11] Torrance cites Thomas over 200 times in his article; only seven of these citations are
from biblical commentaries.

times in the former, 3777 times in the latter.[12] Yet in his works of biblical interpretation a completely different pattern emerges. In the *Lectura super epistolam ad Ephesios*, for instance, Thomas cites philosophical authorities only four times (Aristotle three times and Ovid once), yet he cites biblical sources no less than 1030 times. This massive disparity demonstrates that Thomas' work is not easily characterized in terms of the place and function of philosophy or Scripture within it, and also that Torrance has jumped the gun in his characterization of Thomas as a philosopher in theological clothing.

Also, Torrance seems to equivocate the terms "scientific" and "philosophical" too easily in his exposition of Thomas' thought; in fact his usage of these terms demonstrates an uncertainty and even ambivalence regarding them. At one point Thomas is praised for being scientific;[13] and yet at another his inclusion of human thought-forms developed outside of biblical revelation in our understanding of divine things is castigated as adulterating the purity of revelation.[14] Is this not too rigid a separation of revelation and human reason? In fact, one wonders if the fullest logical extension of Torrance's criticisms would allow for any scientific ordering of the truths of revelation, even though he seems to advocate the necessity of doing so at certain points in his treatment. And if there is no scientific ordering of revealed truth, can there be any interpretation of it in its unity? Torrance seems to want Thomas' interpretation of Scripture to cease being interpretive.

The *lectura* on Ephesians is illustrative of the fact that Torrance overestimates the place and function of philosophy in Thomas' work. As mentioned above, Thomas cites philosophical sources four times in this work.[15] This paucity of references allows us to ask a question of the *In Ephesios*: how does Thomas use these philosophical sources?

In the first philosophical citation in this work Thomas is not even commenting on the main text yet, at least not directly. Rather, he is commenting on the *accessus* which he provides his students in order to

---

[12] VALKENBERG, 28-29. It would still be difficult to prove from this that "it is philosophy that tends to be the master" [T.F. TORRANCE, 289]; Valkenberg enumerates a greater number of Scripture quotations than philosophical ones in both works - 3226 in the *Scriptum*, and 8250 in the *Summa*. While the difference in the *Scriptum* is negligible, is there any doubt that the mature Thomas has surpassed any tendency he may have had towards allowing philosophy the dominant place in his work?

[13] T.F. TORRANCE, 260-261.

[14] Ibid., 288-289.

[15] *In Eph.*, Prol., 1, 5.8.316, 6.1.339, 6.3.358.

prepare them for the commentary (in this case Ps 74:4). He cites Ovid's *De Arte Amatoria*, II.13: "No less energy is spent in retaining possessions than in acquiring them," as a pithy way of introducing the authorship of Paul as an admirable achievement of strengthening a people (the Ephesians) in the faith even though he had not been the one to initiate them into it. Here Thomas does not substitute philosophy for Scripture, but simply uses a maxim in much the same way as a modern author might do so to persuade his readers of a point. In this way his usage of Ovid is very similar to his usage of scriptural proverbs in other places, as we might expect when we consider that Ovid's maxim is itself proverbial.[16]

In the three cases in which Thomas cites Aristotle in the Ephesians *lectura* we see a little more variety in his use of philosophical sources. In 5.8, Thomas is commenting on Eph. 5:22-28, the famous (perhaps infamous?) passage regarding the relationship of wives to husbands and husbands to wives. He notes that in the *Politics* the Philosopher asserts that a home needs three relationships if it is to be complete, "that of the husband and wife, of the father and the children, and that between the master and his servants."[17] On the basis of this Thomas asserts that "therefore, these three [relationships] following, he [Paul] teaches," and proceeds to demonstrate that the next three topics (including the topic of the text he is commenting on) will be these relationships: "*Primo mulierem et virum; secundo, patrem et filium, cap. VI ibi **Filii, obedite**, etc.; tertio, servos et dominos, ibi **Servi, obedite**, etc. ...*"[18] Aristotle's division of the perfect home corresponds exactly to the stated recipients of the Letter's domestic teaching, and so Thomas uses the former to characterize it. But he doesn't use it to illustrate Paul's dependence on Aristotle, nor does he explicate the content of the domestic teaching of Ephesians with the teaching of the *Politics*. Rather, Thomas uses the citation to help explain the division of the text and his own commentary on it. But this division is not the text - he uses Aristotle only once to explain the division, but in commenting on the text itself he has another source - namely the Bible, which he quotes almost 100 times to demonstrate the passage's content.[19]

---

[16] For some examples of Thomas' use of scriptural proverbs, see his citations of Proverbs and Sirach in *In Eph.*, 5.8.317-323

[17] "... *scilicet viri et mulieris, patris et filii, domini et servi...*" [*In Eph.*, 5.8.316]. For the original, see ARISTOTLE, *Politics*, I.11; I.24.

[18] Ibid., 5.8.

[19] This should demonstrate that the use of awkward words such as *quia* in conjunction with philosophical and extra-biblical sources in Thomas' commentary on biblical passages is not

In the second case of Thomas' use of Aristotle, he paraphrases the *Ethics* [20] in explicating Eph 6:2; in his words this work of Aristotle "points out that we have three things from our parents: existence, life and education."[21] Here Thomas asserts that just as the commandments were given on two tablets, one which contained the first three commandments in reference to God, the second tablet containing those referring to one's neighbors and starting with the commandment to honor one's parents, so it is fitting that this one should be the first of the latter category of commandments, as parents do give so much to their children (as demonstrated by the citation from Aristotle). Thomas' interpretation of 6:2 is obviously a poor one; he even offers a second and more adequate interpretation immediately following it. What it is important to note here is that his poor interpretation is not caused by his use of a philosophical source - in fact, this use actually draws him back closer to the true sense of the passage he is commenting on, which does give a singular importance to this particular commandment. Here the quotation from Aristotle is interpretive, but not in such a way as to master or alter the meaning of the passage. Its function is one of demonstration, but it is a demonstration that does not throw off his interpretation of the passage, nor does it subordinate it to an alien framework.

The final citation of Aristotle comes in the lecture on Eph 6:10-12, the exhortation to put on the armor of God. In commenting on 6:12 ("For our wrestling is not against flesh and blood..."), Thomas gives characteristics of these "Principalities and Powers;" they are "powerful and great" (hence they are called "rulers"), they are also "cunning" (hence "spirits"). According to Thomas, the term "spirits of wickedness," "is an emphatic way of saying 'spiritual wickedness,' by which is understood the fullness of evil."[22] In keeping with the functional contrast of the passage (these evil realities compared to flesh and blood), Thomas points out that "the higher one's nature is, the more

---

intended to demonstrate a relationship of dependency of the latter on the former - if it did, we should expect many more philosophical citations than the very few we do find.

[20] Cf. ARISTOTLE, *Nichomachean Ethics*, VIII.12.1162a.4-8. This is misquoted by Thomas (or possibly by his secretary); the paraphrased passage is referred to as coming from Book VI of the *Ethics*, rather than Book VIII.

[21] "... ut dicitur VI Ethic., tria habemus a parentibus, scilicet esse, vivere, et disciplinam..." [In Eph., 6.1.339].

[22] "...*spirituales nequitias, emphatice loquendo, per quod intelligitur plenitudo nequitiae*" [Ibid., 6.3.358].

terrible and pernicious it is when it turns to evil;"[23] he uses Aristotle's assertion that an evil man is worse than all the animals because he is higher than them to illustrate this.[24] Here Aristotle is used solely in an illustrative function - the interpretation has already been made previous to Thomas' reference to the philosopher.

It is clear that in none of these four cases does the presence of philosophical citations thwart Thomas' exegetical enterprise, and in one case (*In Eph.* 6.1) actually corrects his interpretation slightly. Thomas' real dependence is on other biblical works, which are used to interpret the text in the preponderant number of cases. This practice involves other problems, but one of them is certainly not the domination of Thomas' exegesis and theology by philosophy.

Yet Torrance is still correct in his central point regarding Thomas' hermeneutical approach to Scripture in asserting that it is a preeminently scientific one. However, it is not philosophical sources which have the upper hand in the translation of *sacra scriptura* into *sacra doctrina*. We have seen above that Thomas relies heavily on the expository biblical writings for his ordering of the data of revelation scientifically. At this point we can specify this insight - it is specifically interpretive New Testament passages which are used to order the rest of the revealed data, particularly the Pauline and Johannine materials (which are primarily expository in nature, at least in major portions). The *Lectura super ad Ephesios* can be used to illustrate this point as well - of the 1046 biblical citations in the *Lectura*, 535 come from non-narrative, expository New Testament texts (390 from the Pauline corpus and Hebrews, 73 from the Johannine corpus, 31 from the Petrine corpus and 16 from James). This is the case even though the non-narrative texts are only 21 of the 60 biblical books that are cited.[25] We conclude from this that Torrance's basic insight (that Thomas is scientific) is correct - however, he succumbs too easily to a stereotype of scholasticism when he posits that this aspect of Thomas' work is an example of his excessively rationalistic character. A quick glance at his biblical commentaries would have demonstrated to Torrance that, at least in their case, Thomas is no more rationalistic than the great New Testament theologians he quotes so often in all of his theological works.

---

[23] "...*quia quanto est altior secundam naturam, tanto, quando convertitur ad malum, est peior et nequior*" [Ibid., 6.3.358).

[24] ARISTOTLE, *Politics* I.2.1253a.30ff.

[25] This enumeration was undertaken by employing the electronic search capacities of the CD-ROM version of the *Thomae Aquinatis Opera Omnia* by Roberto Busa, S.J.

B) *C. Clifton Black*

As we consider the insights of C. Clifton Black it is important to note that in his work we encounter a criticism of Thomas less focused on Thomas' general relationship to the Bible and more specifically focused on Thomas' work as an exegete as demonstrated by his exegetical corpus. In this he takes the same approach as the present study, which is based on the presupposition that this is precisely where our attention should be focused if we are to retrieve the richest possible understanding of Thomas' exegesis, not only in his presuppositions and techniques but also in his practice. Black's decision to study the implications of Thomas' interpretation of the Johannine prologue puts him in the best position to plumb the depths of Thomas' relationship to the Bible; it is in the light of his analysis of the former that his understanding of Thomas' general approach emerges. Therefore it is not surprising that Black's study represents one of the most comprehensive and insightful critiques currently available.

To consider Black as a critic of Thomistic exegesis is not to conclude that his criticisms are overly negative or even as strongly pessimistic as Torrance's. Rather, he sees Thomas' biblical interpretation as defining "a field of inquiry whose richness is exceeded only by its relative neglect in contemporary scholarship."[26] In Black's view, Thomas displays "a scrupulous attention to detail"[27]; he is aware of "a rich depth of meaning in Scripture"[28]; in one example his "expository restraint is striking."[29] Black is even cautious about criticizing Thomas, as "it might encourage the lamentable modern tendency to use medieval exegetes as whipping boys."[30] In the end, he even goes so far as to elaborate not only his criticisms of Thomistic exegesis but also Thomas' "particular contributions" to the exegetical enterprise,[31] which we shall consider below.

In Black's analysis, Thomas' exegetical practice is found to be lacking in some very important ways. In particular, he enumerates five

---

[26] BLACK, "St. Thomas' Commentary on the Johannine Prologue: Some Reflections on its Character and Implications," 681.

[27] Ibid., 685.

[28] Ibid., 688.

[29] Ibid., 690.

[30] Ibid., 694.

[31] Ibid., 696.

"negative aspects" of Thomas' approach to Scripture; we shall consider them in the order in which he gives them.[32]

His first criticism concerns Thomas' use of scripture to interpret Scripture; as he puts it, "so undeviating is Thomas' perception of the unity of the Scriptures that he tends to fuse a number of diverse biblical perspectives."[33] The particular example that Black refers to is the prologue of the *Lectura super Ioannem*; he notes that in this case Thomas is guilty of fusing the Johannine and Isaian perspectives (Thomas uses Is 6:1 as the *accessus* for John's Gospel). In Black's opinion such activity robs Scripture of the "richness in diversity" which is provided it by the differences between the various biblical perspectives. He uses a term that I have adopted and use in the introduction to the present study to characterize Thomas' biblical interpretation; it is an "homogenizing" exegesis,[34] one which treats the Bible as a monolithic source. Thomas engages in this homogenization of the text on the basis of his faith in God as the one divine Author of the Bible. But to the modern exegetical sensibility it is a confounding habit, as it seems to rob us of the perspective of the human author and to abort an essential aspect of the interpretive enterprise. Indeed, it almost seems as if Thomas is playing a game with the text in which he tries to quote every item in the biblical corpus in the course of a single commentary!

Black tries to help Thomas out of this pitfall by invoking "the current resurgence of interest in canonical criticism," of which a holistic reading like Thomas' might be informative. He even goes so far as to imply that Thomas' approach "resonates with" an approach like that of Brevard Childs.[35] At this point one wishes Black would say more. Is this an identification of the two (i.e., medieval exegesis and canonical criticism)? If so, Black is oversimplifying canonical criticism; he is not recognizing that the latter is a postcritical approach which actually presupposes modern critical methods and the proper differentiation of the various biblical texts according to their uniqueness and diverse authorship. It is true that canonical criticism is more prepared to dialogue with an often homogenizing and basically pre-critical

---

[32] For an excellent reformulation of Black's enumeration of the negative (and positive) aspects of Thomas' approach to Scripture, see Sean P. KEALY, *Matthew's Gospel and the History of Biblical Interpretation*, Mellen Biblical Press Series 55A (Lewiston: Edwin Mellen Press, 1997) : 170-172.

[33] BLACK, 695.

[34] Ibid., 696.

[35] Ibid., 696. Cf. Brevard S. CHILDS, *The New Testament as Canon: An Introduction* (Philadelphia: Fortress, 1985).

approach such as Thomas', but its critique of the narrowness of modern criticism is not a return to this kind of approach. Given this, what can be said about Thomas' use of Scripture to interpret Scripture? Can his exegetical practice be rescued from this dangerous tendency?

It is Black himself who gives the answer; his own analysis of the prologue to the *In Ioannem* is not nearly as pessimistic as he characterizes it in review. Returning to the specific example Black criticizes, we see that Thomas gives Is 6:1 as an *accessus* for two reasons: a) it crystallizes the quality of contemplation exemplified by John, particularly in John's prologue; and b) it adumbrates the order of John's prologue.[36] In regard to the former, Black points out that to dismiss this use of the Isaian passage as "improbable allegorical exegesis" is to miss the "hermeneutical point"; "namely, that there is, for Thomas, a rich depth of meaning in Scripture..."[37] In regard to the second use of Is 6:1, Black notes that "Thomas' aim is not to impose upon the biblical text an order that is foreign to it; on the contrary, his intention is to tailor his commentary to the highly refined order unfolded in the Gospel by the fourth evangelist himself."[38] So the situation is not so bleak as one might suppose; in fact on further analysis we see that Black's criticism needs to be further qualified.

A closer look at the text shows that although Black makes a valid point here, he misses another point which is demonstrated by the text of Thomas' commentary. According to Thomas, the words of Is 6:1:

> ...are the words of a contemplative, and if we regard them as spoken by John the Evangelist they apply quite well to showing the nature of this Gospel. For as Augustine says in his work, *On the Agreement of the Evangelists*: "The other Evangelists instruct us in their Gospels on the active life; but John in his Gospel instructs us also on the contemplative life."[39]

---

[36] Ibid., 682-683.

[37] Ibid., 687-688.

[38] Ibid., 683-684.

[39] "*Verba proposita sunt contemplantis, et si capiantur quasi ex ore Ioannis Evangelistae prolata, satis pertinent ad declarationem huius Evangelii. Ut enim dicit Augustinus in libro De Consensu Evangelistarum, 'caeteri Evangelistae informant nos in eorum Evangeliis quantum ad vitam activam; sed Ioannes suo Evangelio informat nos etiam quantum ad vitam comtemplativam*" [*In Io.*, Prol., 1]. Black misinterprets this passage as Thomas' attempt to "read back into Isaiah the intentions of John the Evangelist..." (BLACK, 688); he mistakenly identifies Thomas' interpretation as allowing that the words of Is 6:1 were somehow actually

With this quote from Augustine, Thomas is far from the homogenization Black accuses him of; in fact, the identification of John in terms of
the Isaian text is actually part of Thomas' endeavor to distinguish his gospel
from the synoptic gospels, thus demonstrating its uniqueness.[40]   And this
identification of John by Thomas as a contemplative using Is 6:1 is not problematic from this point forward; in fact, Thomas' use of the various parts of
the passage to illustrate the nature of John as a contemplative is both beautiful
and illuminating. It serves the purpose of preparing the reader (or listener) for
a work quite different from the other Gospels, and in fact shows that Thomas
was aware of a certain authorial independence on John's behalf - John is not
just reporting Jesus' words without understanding, but is somehow involved
in their transmission - that is, he transmits them as a contemplative. At the
very least Thomas' use of Is 6:1 is non-threatening; it demonstrates how
Thomas sees the Apostle and his Gospel and does not surface in any significant way again in the course of the commentary.

Black could point to other examples of this "negative approach" of
Thomas to reinforce his point. What the above analysis serves to show is that
the reality of Thomas' use of Scripture is not as simple as Black characterizes
it to be. Even in those cases where Thomas does "fuse" biblical perspectives
(and there are as many cases in which he does this as not), it is most often the
case that it is the cited text, not the text under scrutiny, which loses its
identity. This is exactly what we see in the case of Is 6:1; it retains only its
barest possible meaning while it is used to frame John's Gospel, to give a
background for it and to illuminate it.[41]   So Thomas' constant, unrelenting citations of Scripture passages are not so homogenizing as they might seem to
the untrained eye; indeed, Thomas begins to emerge as a genius whose ability
to access the Bible by memory gives him the ability to search the mental
database for just the right quote to bring out the emphasis he desires. This is a

---

spoken by John (686). Black does not take the "*quasi*" in the passage very seriously; if he had
he may not have been as quick to accuse Thomas of fusing the Johannine and Isaian
perspectives.

[40] In light of the last chapter there is much more that could be said about this passage's
implications for the present study. Let it be noted simply that Thomas' emphasis on John's
contemplation as his defining quality, the positive terms which he uses to describe this
contemplation, and his distinguishing of the other Gospels from this more expository, reflective
Gospel points once again to the preeminence in Thomas' mind of a certain conceptualization of
Scripture that is significant to his exegetical practice.

[41] In this sense it could be said that Thomas interprets Scripture with *scripture*; the small
case "s" denoting the transformation of reinforcing passages into subordinate and self-
contained elements outside of their original context.

dangerous practice in exegesis, and Thomas does succumb to homogenization at times. But even more often Thomas escapes this and does what he does in the present case; the text under examination is accentuated, not masked, by his practice. As Martin Yaffe notes in regard to the same phenomenon as it appears in the *Expositio super Iob*:

> What unifies the parts of the book [of Job] for Thomas... is not their putative accretion over a period of time, but the notion that, taken as a whole, they convey a more or less coherent message to their intended addressee. In this respect, Thomas follows the procedures of Aristotelian "science" rather than those of modern philology. Viewing the completed text as an artisan views an artifact, Thomas would understand the materials, format, and genesis of the book in accordance with its intended purpose or function... Thomas' otherwise anachronistic recourse to the notions of later Christian theology, as well as to pagan Greek philosophy, may be explained accordingly. In comparing the figure of Job with that of Christ, for example, *and in comparing Old Testament citations with those of the New Testament* [emphasis mine]... Thomas' own intention is not to blur the differences among his sources, *but to articulate the theological meaning of the received text with the help of authorities which may be more familiar and approachable to his Christian reader* [emphasis mine].[42]

In other words, Thomas' usage of scripture to interpret Scripture conforms to his own approach to the text and is helpful in the articulation of theological meaning. This latter articulation is admittedly a step past what we now consider to be exegesis, but it is a step which we must take with Thomas if his exegetical works are to be allowed to speak to us.

Black's second criticism is that Thomas "uncritically accepts a number of patristic interpretations of a text without any attempt to evaluate their relative cogency."[43] He cites Lamb in this regard, in whose opinion "this appears to be not so much the expression of a serious hermeneutical decision made by Thomas as a pragmatic norm designed to accommodate the wide variety of patristic opinion in cases where there could be little hope of arriving

---

[42] YAFFE, intro. to St. Thomas Aquinas, *The Literal Exposition on Job: A Scriptural Commentary Concerning Providence*, 11.

[43] BLACK, 695.

at a consensus on the author's meaning."[44] This reference to Lamb softens
Black's criticism of Thomas. Indeed, in the passage Black cites, Lamb is actually praising Thomas' restraint: "They [Thomas' exegetical presup-
positions] were not delivered in the clear-cut, settled once and for all categories which theological manuals associate with Thomistic thought. He was
grappling with problems the implications of which are not yet fully
comprehended today."[45] If this is the case, then it is hard to understand what
Black's criticism actually boils down to. Would he prefer Thomas to settle on
an interpretation, or not to use patristic authorities at all? Seen from this
perspective, Black's criticism seems almost trifling; in other places he praises
Thomas for his recognition that "it is the coalescence of their [the Fathers']
slightly different insights that... eventuate in a properly inflected reading of an
already inflected text"[46]; he also praises Thomas' for his "conversational"
approach to the text that is "a model of disciplined, systematic, dialectical
exposition."[47]

     Yet his criticism does have a relevance for the present study, even if
this relevance will not be fully apparent until the next of Black's criticisms is
considered. What he seems to be alluding to is the awkward appearance of
patristic authorities as biblical experts when, in many cases, they were no
closer (from a modern perspective) to giving an adequate account of the text
than Thomas was. Thomas quotes Basil, Hilary and Chrysostom in commenting on the Johannine prologue as often as a modern commentator might
quote Brown, Schnackenburg and Feuillet. Yet obviously such quotations are
not the same, precisely because the exegetical presuppositions of Thomas and
the modern commentator are very different. We will return to this point.

     The third of Black's criticisms is the most important of all. In spite of
the fact that Thomas has a "reasoned hermeneutic," his tendency is not only to
explain but also to "generate" the literal sense.[48]   Black is not the first to
make this point regarding Thomas' exegesis; Lamb also notices this dangerous tendency "to *develop* the literal sense rather than *explain* it."[49]   For his
example, Black points to Thomas' interpretation of John 1:6-7, regarding "the

---

[44] Ibid., 695. Cf. LAMB, 17.

[45] LAMB, 17.

[46] BLACK, 691.

[47] Ibid., 696.

[48] Ibid., 695.

[49] LAMB, 27.

Baptist's fourfold qualities"[50]: "He describes the precursor in four ways. First, according to his nature, **There was a man**. Secondly, as to his authority, **sent by God**. Thirdly, as to his suitability for the office, **whose name was John**. Fourthly, as to the dignity of his office, **he came as a witness**."[51] Black sees this attribution of meaning to every minute detail of the verse as lending its elements more stress than they merit.

In my opinion, this is the real obstacle for modern scholars when they attempt to find any value in Thomas' exegesis. One is left in a serious quandary when faced with such an interpretive anomaly; at certain points it can threaten to subvert the entire exegetical enterprise which at other times seems so promising. One need only consider what immediately follows the error described above in the Johannine commentary to grasp this; here we see Thomas giving a subtle and insightful linguistic analysis of Jn 1:6 that still resonates today:

> We should note with respect to the first that, as soon as the Evangelist begins speaking of something temporal, he changes his manner of speech. When speaking above of eternal things, he uses the word "was" (*erat*), which is the past imperfect tense; and this indicates that eternal things are without end. But now, when he is speaking of temporal things, he uses "was" (*fuit*, i.e., "has been"); this indicates temporal things as having taken place in the past and coming to an end there.[52]

In the close proximity of these two specimens of Thomas' exegesis we see how quickly Thomas can move from generation of the literal sense to accurate exposition of it, and vice-versa. To separate out the non-generative elements destroys the continuity of his exegesis; to leave them in seems to eliminate the possibility of taking Thomas seriously. Does he foil our attempts to access his exegesis here?

---

[50] BLACK, 695.

[51] "*Praecursorem autem describit quadrupliciter. Primo a naturae conditione, cum dicit* **Fuit homo**; *secundo ab auctoritate, cum dicit* **Missus a Deo**; *tertio ab officii idoneitate, cum dicit* **Cui nomen erat Ioannes**; *quarto ab officii dignitate, ibi* **hic venit**" [*In Io.*, 1.4.108].

[52] "*Considerandum autem est circa primum, quod statim cum Evangelista incipit de aliquo temporali, mutat modum loquendi. Cum enim supra loqueretur de aeternis, utebatur hoc verbo erat, quod est praeteriti imperfecti, ostendens per hoc, aeterna interminata esse; nunc vero, cum loquitur de temporalibus, utitur hoc verbo, fuit, ad ostendendum quod temporalia sic praeterierunt quod tamen terminatur*" [*In Io.* 1.4.109].

It must be admitted that he does, at least if exegesis in the limited sense we understand it now is all that we are looking for. But what is not permissible in modern exegesis is licit in theology, and here is where we must situate ourselves in regard to Thomas. If we are willing to let him wear both hats, to be both exegete and theologian at the same time, the occasional production of the literal sense will manifest itself for what it also is - the production of theological ideas and patterns of ideas that are woven into a great edifice of thought that is as much biblical as it is systematic, and that is in much closer proximity to the text of Scripture than any of the other works in the Thomistic corpus.

This is the great insight of Yaffe, whose interpretive essay on the *Expositio super Iob* is a masterpiece of insight into Thomas' exegesis. Rather than allow his own interpretation of Thomas to be confounded by Thomas' production of the literal sense, he gives us a way of conceiving of this activity that allows it its own sphere of relevance:

> ...Thomas' "literal" approach resembles that of an architect or builder. His finished exposition may be compared to a Gothic cathedral, whose massive earthbound structure points heavenward. What is most awesome here is not its massiveness, however, but its artfulness. The whole sublime facade may be seen to consist of units carefully fitted and bonded together in accordance with the artisan's design. In the case of Thomas' exposition the design is no ordinary product of art, but is dictated by that of the Book of Job itself, as Thomas reads it.[53]

Yaffe's brilliant analogy contains two insights that help to situate the modern student of Thomas' exegetical works in the proper vantage point. The first of these is his recognition that Thomas is not merely an explainer of the text, but also a reconstructor of it - his design is as decisive as the author's design. The second is his recognition that this reconstruction is one that is closely bound to the biblical work itself. Following from these insights, another analogy is conceivable that helps to distinguish Thomas from the modern commentator. For the modern exegete, the commentary on the text is like a microscope which reveals hidden aspects of the text (its genesis, redaction, literary elements, original audience, etc.), aspects which are hidden from the unaided eye. But Thomas is doing something different in his inter-

---

[53] YAFFE, Interpretive Essay to St. Thomas Aquinas, The Literal Exposition on Job: A Scriptural Commentary Concerning Providence, 12.

pretation - he is more like a molder who works with a pre-existing frame or mesh upon which final materials (such as plaster or *papier-mâché*) are applied. In his efforts he labors to make his applications fill out the underlying frame, drawing out its contours and maintaining its peculiar symmetry. Therefore the finished product, although inseparable from the underlying frame, gives us something new even as it shows the excellence of the frame itself. A new model (in the case of Thomas, a new theological model) has emerged from the molder's labors, one which arises out of the fusion of the work of the two artisans. We can therefore speak of the theology of a particular Thomistic commentary as distinct from Thomas' theology in general, much as we can speak of the molder's final product as distinct from his general style, choice of subjects and choice of tools. However, in both cases we learn much about the one by studying the other.

With regard to the above observations, one must take issue with the characterization of the usefulness of Thomas' exegetical corpus offered by McGuckin,

> What is of value... is the thought of St. Thomas, which lies, as it were, beneath the texts of Scripture as he meditates on them, and then breaks out from place to place, a succession of profound reflections, but lacking in orderly thematic structure. For the reader, there are, therefore, many encounters with profoundly rich considerations which appear unexpectedly. Consequently, much scholarly labor is required in order to compile from the extensive commentaries of St. Thomas, a pattern of ideas which then can be applied or offered to contemporary discussion. An immediate reading of the expositions in their 'natural form' will not assist the seeker of specific theological themes. Study, research, organization and synthesis are required. It is necessary to weave into a system, the undoubtedly significant thought which is to be discovered within the exegesis. Then, the usefulness of it is striking.[54]

McGuckin is offering advice specifically to "the seeker of specific theological themes," so it is not surprising that he is loathe to advise an "immediate reading" of any of the exegetical works. But it must also be asked if such a lifting of themes from their context is an advisable activity for the analysis of any work. A parallel can be made with the doctrinal exegesis of

---

[54] McGuckin, "St. Thomas Aquinas and Theological Exegesis of Sacred Scripture," 210-211.

Scripture itself - just as the searching of Scripture for specific teachings can easily degenerate into the damaging of those specific teachings by the violence with which they are wrenched from their context, so too does Thomas' exegesis lose its specific character when it is mined for themes without regard for its organic unity.[55]

Returning to Yaffe's insights, we can corroborate them with the observations of Pesch (the author whose criticisms we will consider in the next section), who gives an even more precise picture of Thomas' constructive artistry as it arises on the basis of the biblical text. He lays out a three-step pattern that characterizes Thomas' approach. The first step is an analysis of the text consisting in dividing and subdividing the text "in order to clarify its inner structure, the exact sequence and connection of the ideas."[56] The next step is to understand (or give reasons for) what is found in the text,[57] and it is here that we encounter the primary locus of theological construction - in giving "reasons," Thomas takes liberties such as the one Black identifies in Thomas' exegesis of Jn 1:6 (which we have analyzed above). Yet it is also here that Thomas makes his most fruitful and decisive interpretations as well, examples of which we will analyze in the following section. Finally, on the basis of the first two steps, a third, fully theological step follows; "the integration of small systematical chapters into the context of the biblical commentary."[58] It is thus that Thomas rises to a doctrinal reformulation of the text,[59] and so produces a work just as much his as it is the biblical author's.

Returning to Black's criticism, it must be affirmed that it is an absolutely precise observation regarding the limits of Thomas' exegetical practice when it is examined in terms of modern critical study of the Bible. Yet it would be a mistake to dismiss it on the basis of this observation - M.-D. Phillippe's description of the *Lectura super Ioannem* as the theological work

---

[55] It should be noted that if any works submit themselves most readily to McGuckin's approach, it is the synthetic works. The latter contain divisions and subdivisions which Thomas himself formulated (vs. the exegetical works, which contain divisions which Thomas discerns and sometimes imposes).

[56] PESCH, 589-591. This step is the most frequently observed of Thomas' exegetical method; cf. J.-M. VOSTÉ "S. Thomas epistularum S. Pauli interpres," *Angelicum* 19 (1942) : 268-269; SPICQ, *D.T.C.*, col. 715; CHENU, *Toward Understanding*, 250-251; LAMB, 26; Jose M. REVUELTA, "Los Comentarios Bíblicos de Santo Tómas," *Scripta Theologica* 3 (1971) : 572-573.

[57] Ibid., 591-592.

[58] Ibid., 592-593.

[59] Ibid., 591.

par excellence of Aquinas immediately comes to mind in this regard. This may be an exaggerated estimation of this particular exegetical work. But the theology produced there by Thomas as he explores the text of the Fourth Gospel certainly does carry a value for us today, a value which it receives from both Thomas and the Fourth Gospel, in particular from the encounter of the former with the latter.

In short, to dismiss Thomas' exegesis because of his development of the literal sense is to treat the very thing that is unique to Thomas' encounter with specific biblical texts as an unwanted accretion. Another more constructive possibility is to treat the various developments of the literal sense for what they are - unique theological models which have significant value for us today. Our ability to do so is facilitated by Thomas himself, who always identifies for the reader what he believes is the theme of each of the biblical texts he is commenting on.

Such a conception of the biblical commentaries relativizes the last two of Black's criticisms. In fact, Black himself counterbalances each of them with positive aspects of Thomas' exegetical practice. For instance, when he questions Thomas' use of the Bible as the final arbiter which settles "later disputes over orthodox and heretical positions," therefore identifying it as "an all-purpose doctrinal sourcebook" and anachronistically ascribing to it "some clearly defined orthodox position to which the biblical writers putatively conformed,"[60] he also takes a different tack: "...Thomas reminds us that the Bible... is God's Word for all seasons," and Black concludes that "*Theological reflection* [emphasis mine], in conversation with the community of faith, remains a necessary step in the enterprise of biblical hermeneutics."[61] And his final criticism of Thomas' "identification of exegesis and dogmatics" as being unworthy of "repristination" today[62] is tempered by his recognition that Thomas' willingness to find a fecund depth of meaning in the biblical text finds resonances in the thought of Ricoeur, who identifies an "inexhaustible surplus of meaning that lies in front of a text," and also in the thought of Gadamer, because Thomas engages, "some seven centuries before Gadamer gave the endeavor a name - in a 'fusion of the horizon' (*Horizonver-schmelzung*) of the text with the horizon of meaning of his [Thomas'] own

---

[60] BLACK, 695.
[61] Ibid., 697.
[62] Ibid., 695.

day."[63] In both cases Black implicitly recognizes that to hold Thomas to an understanding of biblical exegesis that did not exist in the Middle Ages would be just as anachronistic as some of Thomas' own exegetical maneuvers; also, he sees that another angle is necessary if we are truly to appreciate what Thomas has to offer modern scholarship.

We will return to Black (and Yaffe) in the next chapter, when an attempt is made to formulate an approach to Thomas' biblical commentaries. However, the former has already contributed significantly to the present study in aiding us to specify what we are dealing with in Thomas' exegetical corpus. In Black's eyes, Thomas' exegesis of Scripture is a theological exegesis, one that is as much constructive at it is explanatory. He would certainly agree with Lamb's observation that "the dominant note in his [Thomas'] exegesis is its theological import,"[64] and the more developed observation of Spicq:

> If he [Thomas] exercises in some works rudiments of philological knowledge, and submits at times to the exigencies of the textual critic, above all if he applies himself in drawing out the true literal sense, this is only to the degree that these efforts are necessary and fruitful *in order to elaborate a biblical theology as a source for his scholastic theology* [emphasis mine] [translation mine]. [65]

C) *O.H. Pesch*

Our last critic, O.H. Pesch, touches our subject more directly than any other author. Like Black, he chooses an actual specimen of Thomas' biblical exegesis to serve as his primary object of analysis; thus he is well-situated for contributing new insights into Thomas' exegetical practice. But more importantly, the specimen he chooses to analyze is the *Lectura super epistolas Pauli*, which has already been identified as the source of the primary object of analysis of the present study. This being the case, it is not surprising that Pesch has much to add to our considerations - no other critic of Thomas' approach is situated more closely than he is to our own vantage point.

Ironically, it is also Pesch who deals the hardest blows to Thomas' exegetical practice. In particular, he sees Thomas as the most anachronistic of exegetes; his title, "Paul as Professor of Theology," gives the singular

---

[63] Ibid., 697. Cf. Paul RICOUER, *Interpretation Theory: Discourse and the Surplus of Meaning* (Fort Worth, TX: Texas Christian University Press, 1976), 76-91; H.-G. GADAMER, *Truth and Method* (New York: Seabury, 1975), 269-274, 337-341.

[64] LAMB, 26.

[65] SPICQ, *D.T.C.*, col. 718. Cf. REVUELTA, 574-575.

impression that this criticism is the primary message of the article (which it is not). As he says in his introduction:

> The modern reader cannot believe his eyes: the medieval commentator [Thomas] stresses a picture according to which the most spirited and least systematic author of the New Testament sits at his writing table, far from the world, and meditates on the suitable division of a dogmatical monograph about the grace of Christ. The results were fourteen chapters which treat the whole topic in an exhaustive way and in a definite sequence. Only an unimportant accident diffused this monograph over the whole world in the form of fourteen letters.
> But that is Paul in the eyes of Thomas Aquinas! The Apostle is for him the greatest systematician of the New Testament, the professor among the Apostles. How could such an image of Paul arise, in which the features of the Apostle obviously assimilate the traits of Aquinas and of his time?[66]

This is not the only evidence that Thomas hopelessly mischaracterizes Paul; according to Pesch, Thomas also sees him as a philosopher trained in Aristotelian logic.[67] Under the weight of such remarks, one wonders if Thomas' exegesis of the Pauline corpus can hope to avoid collapse. However, we can be thankful that Pesch answers his own heavy-handed criticisms; in fact the rest of his monograph not only qualifies his critique of Thomas but actually does battle with it. Before we consider this, it is necessary to analyze some rhetorical imprecisions in Pesch's critique itself.[68]

Some of his characterizations can be misleading. Thomas never mentions Paul at a "writing table," nor is the picture of him being "far from the world" one that Thomas espouses - the picture offered by our primary text, for instance, is of Paul "strengthening the pillars" of the Ephesian church, "lest they falter in their faith, as the workman will buttress a building against a fall."[69] Consider the sentences that follow:

---

[66] PESCH, "Paul as Professor of Theology," 585.

[67] Ibid., 592.

[68] "Rhetoric" is not an improper designation for this critique; the article is "the revised and enlarged English text of a German radio-lecture" [Ibid., 584].

[69] "...ne a fide vacillarent, sicut artifex confirmat aedificium, ne cadat" [In Eph., Prol., 1].

'And thou, being once converted, confirm thy brethren' (Lk 22:32), was spoken to Peter *and accomplished by Paul* [emphasis mine]. A verse in Job (4:4) applies to him: 'Thy words have confirmed them that were staggering.' Paul strengthened the Ephesians not to fear unreasonably, as a bishop confirms a boy to fortify him [against timidity].[70]

It is clear from this that Thomas sees Paul as a pastor, as one actively involved in the concerns of the Church of his day. To assert that Thomas sees the sending of this Letter as "an unimportant accident" is a definite mischaracterization. A similar mischaracterization is Pesch's assertion that Thomas believes the Pauline corpus to be a single monograph. In his prologue to the entire commentary on the Pauline Epistles, Thomas addresses the question of which of the letters was written first, and concludes that 1 Corinthians is earlier than Romans,[71] demonstrating that he is aware that the composition of the Epistles does not follow their order of placement. We have Thomas' direct testimony on this: "The letters of Paul are not arranged chronologically... [Romans] is placed first because of its matter, which is worthier."[72]

But Thomas does characterize the Pauline Epistles as bearing "entirely on the grace of Christ."[73] Is this not an alien and restrictive format for the Epistles, considering how broad a scope they have (not to mention that Thomas includes Hebrews in his count)? The answer is affirmative only until we realize that Thomas' definition of grace is almost as broad as the Epistles themselves, in fact is clearly dictated not only by the Pauline teaching on grace but also by the general content of these fourteen texts as Thomas reads them. Hence Thomas includes under grace: christology (Hebrews), grace itself (Romans), the sacraments (1-2 Corinthians), the relationship between the two testaments (Galatians), the origination of Church unity (Ephesians), its confirmation and progress (Philippians), the refutation of errors

---

[70] "*Unde dictum est Petro Lc. XXII, v. 32: 'Et tu aliquando conversus confirma fratres tuos,' quod fecit Paulus. Unde ei competit illud Iob IV,4: 'Vacillantes confirmaverunt sermones tui.' Confirmavit item ne pseudo timerent, sicut Episcopus confirmat puerum ad robur contra pusillanimitatem...*" [Ibid., Prol., 1]. LAMB, 40 translates "*contra pusillanimitatem*" as "against becoming spiritless." I have changed it to "against timidity"above, as this is a more precise rendering of the phrase.

[71] *Super Epist.*, Prol., 11.

[72] "*Et epistolae Pauli non ordinantur secundum tempus... Et praemittitur illa propter materiam, quia de digniori*" [*In Philemonem*, 2.30].

[73] "*Est enim haec doctrina tota de gratia Christi...*" [*Super Epist.*, Prol., 11].

(Colossians), the problem of present persecution (1 Thessalonians), the Antichrist (2 Thessalonians), Church government (1 Timothy), persecution once again (2 Timothy), error once again (Titus), and the Christian conduct of temporal lords (Philemon).[74]   Would Pesch venture that Thomas would naturally include a *quaestio* on the Antichrist as part of a treatise on grace? It is clear that "grace" acts here as a thematic *accessus* (much as the introductory Scripture verses do), and not as a controlling concept.

We venture onto more shaky grounds when we object to Pesch's characterization of Paul as "the most spirited and least systematic" of the authors of the New Testament. It is true that Paul's writings are occasional - they address particular situations that arise in specific Christian communities. And he truly is the most spirited of the NT authors, although it is hard to understand why this is necessarily opposed to systematization.[75]   But are there any qualities of the Pauline corpus as understood by Thomas that might reveal them to be more amenable to, or at least more compatible with, systematization?

It would seem that the answer is yes, precisely because Paul develops his theological ideas by way of direct reflection on the Christian mystery: on the life, death and resurrection of Christ, on the Old Testament as predictive of Christ and fulfilled by him. It is indisputable that Paul develops certain ideas that become central to his thought in the light of which he judges other realities. In so doing he is not being systematic in the way that Thomas is in the *Summa Theologiae*, but he is certainly closer to such a systematization than the synoptic gospels and other parts of the Bible which mediate ideas and judgments through narrative means. In fact, we have already discussed that Paul and other expository writings act as a bridge between the former and the latter, and that the style of Paul, the medium of his teaching, comes ready-made for Thomas' attempts to build a systematic theology (or more precisely, systematic theolog*ies*). If Thomas is to let the Bible interpret itself, then the Pauline corpus (among other writings) is an obvious foothold for him.

---

[74] Ibid., Prol., 11.

[75] In fact, it would seem that the emphatic nature of Paul's assertions, especially those that he absolutely insists on, can be seen as placing these assertions at the center of his theology. Might not we say that this centrality of certain assertions is such that Paul solves problems, gives commands, and even interprets reality in the light of these assertions? If so, then spiritedness can be a standard by which to judge those truths which are most important to Paul, and to a minimal degree reveal what can be called a "system" of thought.

When we turn to Pesch's direct consideration of Thomas' Pauline exegesis, we see that he emphasizes Thomas' ability to access Paul in spite of his pessimism about Thomas' anachronisms. He offers an excellent measuring rod with which to judge Thomas' exegesis: "Paul remains Paul even in the mind of Thomas, if we but perceive that the latter agrees even to be challenged by Paulinian thought, both in its technical procedure and in his theological ideas. Does Thomas permit Paul to challenge him? Is it Paul or is it Thomas who has the last word?"[76] He concludes that Thomas is truly faithful to Paul, that his exegesis of Romans in particular shows a willingness on his part to be challenged by him.

To this effect he analyzes five test cases: Thomas' interpretation of Paul's doctrine of justification (in his exegesis of Rom 1:17 and 4:5), his treatment of Paul's "technical procedure" (in his exegesis of Heb 11:1), and three specific instances where Paul's ideas are an obvious challenge to Thomas: a) 1 Cor 1:23 on the stumbling-block and folly of the Cross as it is interpreted in *In 1 Cor* 1.3; b) Rom 4:15, 7:9-13, Gal 3:9 on the Law as killing and working wrath in *ST* I-II.98; and c) Rom 8:2 on "the Law of Freedom" as it is interpreted in *ST* I-II.106.1.[77]

In the first case, which Pesch considers as entailing "two relatively harmless challenges to which Thomas exposes himself," he observes that Thomas interprets Rom 1:17 in precisely the same manner as Luther does much later. In his restatement of Thomas' interpretation, that v.17 shows "that the Gospel words have salvific power,"[78] Pesch notes:

> The justice of God is therefore not that righteousness by which God is righteous in himself and rewards or punishes men according to their merit... but the righteousness by which God makes us righteous. And if one nevertheless prefers to interpret this verse in relation to the inner righteousness of God, then it is always to be understood that God is righteous in keeping his promises.[79]

This openness to Paul's thought is corroborated by a second example; Thomas goes so far as to say that the sinner is justified "by faith alone,

---

[76] PESCH, 593.

[77] Ibid., 593-603.

[78] "...*quomodo evangelium sit in salutem...*" [*In Rom.*, 1.6.102].

[79] PESCH, 594. Cf. *In Rom.*, 1.6.

without works."[80] He sees this not as a paradox but as God acting according to his essence, which is love.[81] Such a conception is thoroughly Pauline and shows that Thomas allows Paul to influence him in a significant way. Indeed, in at least this case Thomas' thought is as Pauline as Luther's.

The second example shows how Thomas is ready to bend his usually strict adherence to the rules of Aristotelian logic in order to stay closely connected to Paul's own manner of proceeding. In Heb 11:1, "Paul" defines faith: "Faith is that which gives substance to our hopes, which convinces us of things we cannot see." Thomas notes that this definition does not fulfill the Aristotelian criteria of a formal definition. "But we can excuse the Apostle for - as Thomas remarks - things like that happen sometimes even in the writings of the philosophers."[82] In other words, Thomas does not rule out the legitimacy of "Paul's" definition of faith, but shows a willingness to allow what he himself would never do in order to continue to unfold the substance of the text.

The last three test cases are the most decisive. In these Pesch focuses on instances that would certainly force Thomas to reconsider some of his most foundational assumptions. According to Pesch, Thomas responds to such challenges in "a threefold way":

> Either he allows such a text to remain and renounces any attempt to elucidate it by means of speculation. Or he contents himself with an improvised, almost sophisticated distinction in order to exclude the threat of misunderstanding as he sees it. Or he adjusts his entire thinking to the text and feels stimulated by it to a completely new speculative conception in which he cannot hope for support either from philosophical statements or from theological tradition.[83]

It should be noted that Pesch does not consider Thomas to have failed in his interpretation in either of these three cases – in each case he answers to varying degrees the challenges set before him by the Pauline text. At the very least, he shows a great deal of restraint; at most, he rises to a new and

---

[80] Ibid., 594-595. "...*scilicet sola (fides) sine operibus exterioribus...*" [*In Rom.*, 4.1.330]. PESCH also cites *ST* II-II.113.4 as an example of "the incomparable importance of faith for the justification of the godless... in the framework of the general systematic concept" [Idem, 595 n. 23].

[81] Ibid., 596.

[82] Ibid., 596-597. Cf. *ST* II-II.4.1; *In Heb.*, 11.1.552.

[83] Ibid., 597.

thoroughly biblical perspective which trumps his pre-understanding as it is mediated to him by his philosophical and traditional *auctoritates*.

In the first example Thomas, who sees God as "a God of wise order" (he often gives arguments of convenience showing the fittingness or even necessity of the events which occur in God's creation, and often quotes the Vulgate translation of Wis 8:1: "He arranges everything in a smooth manner"),[84] is confronted with Paul's assertion that the Cross is a folly and a stumbling block. His analysis of this text deserves full quotation, because no example demonstrates more clearly that Thomas' exegesis must be considered for itself and not merely in support of his systematic works:

> Where Thomas is not bound immediately by the Paulinian text, he becomes the victim of his basic inspiration and procedure. In a long chapter of his *Summa Theologiae* he questions every perspective and viewpoint of Christ's death on the Cross...
>
> But all that is seemingly forgotten when Thomas interprets 1 Cor 1:23 in the context of his commentary on Paul. *He allows Paul to challenge him* [emphasis mine]. In a concise commentary and without discovering a "deeper" meaning he explains why the Cross is a stumbling block for the Jews and folly (that is to say: a meaning*less* thing!) for the Gentiles: The Jews "demanded power which works miracles, and what they saw was weakness bearing the cross (*desiderabant virtutem miracula facientem et videbant infirmitatem crucem patientem*)" To the Gentiles however, "it seemed according to human wisdom impossible that God die and that a righteous and wise man deliver himself voluntarily to the most ignominious death (*contra rationem humanae sapientiae videtur quod Deus moriatur et quod homo iustus et sapiens se voluntarie turpissimae morti exponat*)." Some phrases later on, indeed, the "convenience" of the Cross comes back into the argumentation. But it is the convenience precisely of *God's* mysterious acting, therefore no human reason (including theological reason) and faith alone can maintain this divine convenience of the Cross against all appearances.[85]

---

[84] Ibid., 597-598. Pesch mistakenly identifies this as a quote from the Song of Solomon, and perhaps a better translation of the Vulgate than Pesch's is "*She* orders all things smoothly," which corresponds much more closely to the original text. He cites several examples of Thomas' citation of this passage: *ST* I.22.2 sed contra, 103.8, 109.2; I-II.110.2; II-II.23.2, 165.1; III.44.4 sed contra, 46.9, 55.6 sed contra, 60.4.

[85] Ibid., 599

Thomas preempts the "argument of convenience" method in preference for the Pauline idea of the Cross being only accessible and acceptable through faith. In doing so he relativizes a crucial axis for his thought and adopts a new one. From an exegetical perspective, he trumps the arguments of *ST* III.46 with a viewpoint that gives pride of place not to reason but to incomprehensibility and awe.

In the second example, Thomas gives Paul the last word again. Although he does do some violence to the idea of the Law as being something which kills (namely, by allowing an escape hatch for those OT personages who understood the cult as prophetic and so came to faith in the "coming mediator," thus living in the New Covenant in the time of the Old[86]), he still maintains with Paul that the Law does entangle man in sin: "only by means of God's grace is man able to fulfill the Old Law and its supreme commandment of love of God and neighbor. The Law however did not endow man with this strength of grace. Thus the demand of the Law becomes strained."[87] But doesn't this fly in the face of a foundational Thomistic precept that God does not directly cause sin? To deal with this difficulty, Thomas makes a distinction: "The Law does not kill in an 'effective' way, '*effective*,' impelling directly to sin; it kills rather by giving the 'occasion' for sin, '*occasionaliter*.'"[88] Once again, Pesch's analysis is excellent:

> No one will imagine that the distinction given by Thomas is sufficient to solve his own problems regarding this text... But Thomas is content to have made his reservation in favor of a correct idea of God. As for the rest, the paradox of the Paulinian text dominates, and Thomas remains on its track by the assertion that God really *wanted* to permit sin coming through the Law with the purpose that men, thereby humbled, did then desire Christ's grace.[89]

The third example is for Pesch the most decisive of all. In his exegesis of Rom 8:2, "The law of the spirit of life in Christ has set me free from the law of sin and death," "Thomas does not only admit to a challenge, but he develops a conception which is without equivalent in the Middle

---

[86] Ibid., 601. Cf. *ST* I-II.98.2 ad 4, 101.2, 103.2 c., 107.1 ad 2.

[87] Ibid., 600-601. Cf. *ST* I-II.98.6, 100.10 ad 3, 100.12.

[88] Ibid., 601. Cf. *ST* I-II.98.1 ad 2.

[89] Ibid., 602. Cf. *ST* I-II.98.2 ad 3, 106.3 c.

Ages."[90] He cross-references this verse with Jer 31:31-33 to conclude that the Law which confronts the Christian is one which comes from inside, not burdening him/her but providing a spontaneity and strength to do God's will. The letter only manifests this interior law, and it kills in the same way the Old Law did if separated from the grace of the Holy Spirit in the heart of the believer.[91] Thomas even enunciates a duty (and a very Paulinian one at that) of Church leaders to be reserved in the making of laws, or run the risk of making life under the New Law even more intolerable than under the Old.[92]

Pesch thus gives us ample proof of his final conclusion that, although in other places Thomas does not allow Paul to challenge him (he quickly notes in this regard that this is to some degree "the fate of every interpretation of Paul and of the whole of Scripture, even in a strict historical explication of modern style"), the former is not guilty of perverting the theology of Paul.[93] Even Thomas' alleged domestication of him as a professor is superseded by his close adherence to and respect for the text of the Pauline corpus. Combining his insight with that of Yaffe's, it is safe to conclude that the theology Thomas builds in his exegesis of Paul conforms to the text; we can also say with Black that this fusion of horizons is a fruitful one, one well worth paying attention to.

D) *A Summary*

In combining the conclusions of this chapter and the one preceding it, it can be easily demonstrated by the accumulated evidence that both the new vantage point which has been adopted as well as a new approach such as the one about to be proposed are necessary if any new insights are to emerge from the field of inquiry into Thomas' relationship to the Bible.

By approaching Thomas' exegetical presuppositions not as primary subjects but rather in relation to his exegetical work itself, we have discovered that Thomas conceives of Scripture as primarily argumentative and/or speculative. Indeed, Thomas sees the inspired writer as one who, even more than a seer, is a reflector, a contemplative who meditates on God's truth. His notion of Sacred Scripture as sacred doctrine puts him in need of conceptual and expository portions of Scripture in order to anchor his spiritualization of the narrative portions of the text. In fact, his very understanding of the act of

---

[90] Ibid., 602.
[91] Ibid., 603. Cf. *ST* I-II.106.1-2.
[92] Ibid., 603. Cf. *ST* I-II.107.4 c.
[93] Ibid., 604-605.

interpretation requires the text at hand to be one that can be drawn into a scientific model, and this is only possible with texts that expound meaning and do not merely reiterate events. The many examples from Thomas' exegetical practice and his exegetical presuppositions have confirmed that Thomas relies on expository works (such as much of the Johannine corpus, the Pauline corpus, the Catholic Epistles, etc.) so preponderantly as to leave no doubt that they are indispensable to his exegetical enterprise and are where he is most able to apply his principles of interpretation naturally and without adaptation.

Moving from these insights to the question of whether or not Thomas can succeed at biblical interpretation, the criticisms of Torrance, Black and Pesch give us even deeper insights into Thomas' actual situation as an exegete. In dialogue with Torrance we have once again confirmed that Thomas depends on the non-narrative to make his exegesis possible (a dependence which Torrance mistakenly characterizes as overly philosophical). Black (and also Yaffe) help to show that Thomas' exegesis is as constructive as it is interpretive, and that this type of theological exegesis is one at which he excels. Finally, with Pesch we see that in this activity specifically as Thomas engages in it in relation to the Pauline corpus, he shows tremendous insight and not only spares the text from violence, but also allows Paul to guide him so thoroughly that the result is as truly Pauline as it is Thomistic. These insights demand to be foundational to any approach to Thomas' biblical exegesis if such an approach is to be fruitful. Thus, a warrant is given to the formulation of a new approach, one which does not ignore the mass of scholarship in this field, but utilizes its manifold insights.

One thing remains before such an approach can be proposed. Throughout these two chapters we have referred to Thomas as being most at home with portions of Scripture that are expository, argumentative, speculative and conceptual. At times we have employed the broadest possible term to identify this all-important trait of Thomas as an exegete: we have referred to his predilection for the use of (and his facility at interpreting) "non-narrative" portions of Scripture. As the analysis progressed, many of the elements of such non-narrative texts and Thomas' use of them have become more clear. But a more direct consideration of what is meant by "non-narrative" must be undertaken before its crucial role both in Thomas' exegesis and as an object of it can be fully appreciated.

E) *Non-Narrative Scripture*

It has long been recognized that in dealing with the Bible, one is dealing with a collection of diverse texts and literary genres that must be recognized as such before they can be properly understood. Thomas himself was aware of this fact.[94] But I have been able to locate only one scholar who has studied how awareness of literary genre effects Thomas' practice as an exegete: Wilhelmus Valkenberg. This he does particularly in considering Thomas' Pauline exegesis; he notes that since "the Pauline Epistles are argumentative texts instead of narrative texts, the style of Aquinas' explanation in his commentaries on these Epistles is different from the style in his commentaries on the Gospels."[95] In light of this he recognizes that Thomas finds in Paul a use of Scripture similar to his own, considering him "as a theologian who uses the same procedures in theological argumentation as the theologian in the thirteenth century."[96] Although Valkenberg's statistical conclusion in this section is not decisive for the present study, it nevertheless demonstrates that in Thomas' exegesis "a distinction ensues between an exposition of the Gospels in the mode of 'narrative theology' and an exposition of the Epistles in the mode of 'argumentative theology.'"[97]

But Valkenberg's distinction between narrative and argumentative texts, though precise enough for his own purposes, does not do full justice to the differences of genre in Scripture as they apply to the issue of Thomas' exegesis. In the first place, argumentative texts are not the only kind of texts that are distinguishable from narrative. Second, Valkenberg's distinction does not reflect Thomas' own categories, which are of paramount importance in the present study because they give us an invaluable glimpse into how Thomas perceives the various books of the Bible. To this end, let us consider Thomas' own delineation as it is given in the *Postilla super Psalmos*:

> The modes or forms to be found in Sacred Scripture are manifold.
> There is narrative, as Sirach 22 says, "Has not God made his saints
> narrate all of his miracles?" This is found in the historical books.

---

[94] *Super Psalmos*, Proemium.

[95] VALKENBERG, "'Did not our Heart Burn?' Place and Function of Holy Scripture in the Theology of St. Thomas," 252.

[96] Ibid., 252. Here we have a characterization very much like Pesch's, but by no means as dismissive as his.

[97] Ibid., 253. Valkenberg notes here as well "that the argumentative style" of the Pauline text under analysis "entails a commentary in the same fashion; more elements of *quaestiones* and less spiritual explanations..." [Ibid., 252-253].

There is admonishing, and exhorting, and the giving of precepts, such as Titus 2: "Say these things. Exhort and argue with all authority"; and also II Timothy 2: "Remind people of all these things, bearing witness before God." This mode is found in the Law, the Prophets, and the Books of Solomon. There is disputation, and this is in Job and the Apostle, as Job 13 says: "I desire to argue with God." There is deprecation but also praise; and this is found in this book [Psalms]; because whatever is said in the other books of other modes is said here through the mode of praise and prayer, as Psalm 9 says below: "I will confess to you, Lord," etc., and "I will narrate," etc.[98]

A careful analysis of this passage is necessary if its full implications are to be appreciated. The first thing that should be noticed is that Thomas is not interested in giving absolute distinctions. Rather, he categorizes the biblical texts according to a general characterization of their contents (for instance, he either doesn't recognize or at least doesn't comment that some of the biblical books, even some he mentions, have a mixture of modes). Also, the list he gives is obviously not meant to be an exhaustive one, as it leaves out all of the NT corpus except for the writings that Thomas associates with Paul. But the gaps he leaves can (in most cases) be easily filled according to the general description of content that he gives for each mode. For instance, under "historical books" the Gospels and Acts can surely be placed along with the books of the OT that traditionally bear the name "historical." Also, the

---

[98] "*Modus seu forma in Sacra Scriptura multiplex invenitur. Narrativus, Eccli. 22. Nonne Deus fecit sanctos suos enarrare omnia mirabilia sua? Et hoc in historialibus libris invenitur. Admonitorius, et exhortatorius, et praeceptivus, ad Titum 2. Haec loquere, et exhortare, et argue cum omni imperio: Secundum Tim. 2. Haec common, testificans coram Deo etc. Hic modus invenitur in Lege, Prophetis, et Libris Salomonis. Disputativus; et hoc in Iob, et in Apostolo: Iob 13. Disputare cum Deo cupio. Deprecativus, vel laudativus; et hoc invenitur in isto libro; quia quicquid in aliis libris praedictis modis dicitur, hic ponitur per modum laudis, et orationis: infra (Ps 9) Confitebor tibi, Domine, etc. narrabo etc.*" [*Super Psalmos*, Prol.]. The Latin text and English translation are from the website "Aquinas' Commentary on the Psalms: In Latin with an English Translation," trans. by Hugh McDonald. This division of Scripture is not the only one provided by Thomas; his inaugural lecture ("*De Commendatione et Partitione Sacrae Scripturae*") is much more comprehensive and detailed than this later one. But this short excerpt from the postilla on the Psalter is the only one in which Thomas divides the works of Scripture according to their genre; in the case of the inaugural lecture Thomas categorizes the books of the Bible according to what these books do, with the most general categories being "mandating" (*praecipiendo*) and " helping" (*adiuvando*).

non-Pauline Epistles clearly fit into the "disputative" category along with the Pauline corpus.

In regard to the distinction presently being considered, all of those categories which fall outside of the narrative category are of primary interest. But it is necessary, on the basis of all that has been discovered about Thomas' exegetical practice so far, to consider first the narrative category itself, and then the rest. What all of the narrative texts of Scripture have in common is that they confront the reader with people, places, things and events in a primary way - that is, either the communication of the basic existence and description of these people, places, etc. is of primary importance (in the case of what can be called "mere narration"), or the text mediates a message by proceeding with this communication in a certain way. We have already observed that Thomas is limited in his ability to deal with narration. In the case of the most developed form of biblical narration (the transmission of meaning through narration), Thomas is not adept at perceiving this as anything more than "confirmative testimony" and "objective information,"[99] and so deals with it as mere narration. And in the case of mere narration, Thomas must doctrinalize the text by recourse to spiritual senses or by applying (in fact, imposing) a complex of non-narrative intertextual scriptural citations with which he glosses the text. In doing this, Thomas trumps the text with those portions of Scripture that are non-narrative, and the uniqueness of the text as well as much that it is intended to mediate is lost in the interpretive process. So it is not surprising that Thomas' exegesis of narrative texts (with the exception of the *lectura* on John, which contains much non-narrative material in the discourses of Jesus) has never been lauded. In trying to pierce through to the meaning of the text, Thomas very often ends up further away from it.

But what about the non-narrative portions of Scripture? The most significant aspect of these for understanding Thomas' exegetical practice and also for approaching his exegetical corpus productively is their defining characteristic: they all relate to the question of the meaning of things and to the significance of people, places, things and events in a way not mediated by a story. Each of these modes does this in a different way, and not all of them do this to the same degree. But each lays meaning bare, even if only to the corner of the eye or from a particular angle, so that a text of any non-narrative type can be used as the basis for other maneuvers regarding meaning - for manifesting interrelations and connections, the further explication of meaning, and the implications of it for other questions of meaning. Interestingly, these

---

[99] VALKENBERG, 196-197.

aspects are all part and parcel of the Thomistic interpretive building process
we analyzed above. That is, they correspond to the very process of exegesis
Thomas employs: discerning the divisions of the text (interrelations and
connections), expounding the meaning of the individual parts (further
explication), and applying what is found in the text to other issues in the mode
of the *quaestio*.[100]

The distinction between narrative and non-narrative texts is so
obvious that it may be objected that it is unnecessary to delineate it.
However, it is stated here not to introduce it, but to apply it to Thomas'
exegetical practice. The key element at present is not the novelty of this
distinction, but the emphasis that it is too often overlooked when Thomas'
relationship to the Bible is under analysis. At times it is recognized in some
fashion or other, such as in the case of Valkenberg. But he stands alone as the
only one who ever explores it. Most often the question of whether there is
any difference in Thomas' treatment of the narrative as opposed to the non-
narrative is not even raised. As observed in Chapter I, the exegetical presuppositions are just laid out, explained, and illustrated. But with this distinction we encounter an aspect of Thomas' exegesis which is not detectable
in this manner. It requires sustained contact with his exegetical practice itself,
and not merely a familiarity with it. With this in mind, we can continue our
analysis.

Each non-narrative type is open to interpretive activity (such as
Thomas envisaged it) in different ways and to differing degrees. Of course,
without further investigation into Thomas' exegetical practice it would be
impossible to isolate all of the different ways Thomas uses these various non-
narrative modes. At present, however, it is both possible and necessary to
give a basic outline of how Thomas deals with the non-narrative modes, using
his own categories as he expounds them in the Proemium to the Psalms
postilla.

Doubtless, the non-narrative mode *par excellence* for Thomas is the
"disputative" mode, such as Job, Paul, the non-Pauline letter-writers, and the
Johannine writer(s) (in many parts). This has already been amply demonstrated above. These authors write in a fashion not far removed from Aristotelian argumentation. Therefore Thomas accesses them with greater success
than he does any other biblical texts, and also uses them in citations more

---

[100] See CHENU, *Toward Understanding*, 250-253, for the best explanation of Thomas'
basic exegetical method.

often than any other. He is hermeneutically well-prepared to tackle their content in a way similar to the way that their content is presented. Valkenberg's analysis of the qualities of *In 1 Cor.,* 15 is a fitting example of Thomas' exegesis of texts of this type: more elements of *quaestiones* and less spiritual interpretations are found within it than in the Gospel commentaries.[101]

In the case of "admonishment," "exhortation" and "legislation," we encounter a non-narrative mode that is very easily accessible from the point of view of its meaning, and so does not often pose Thomas with insurmountable difficulties. Without going into detail, it is well-known that Thomas' view of morality was such that his overwhelming emphasis was on the reasonable foundations for the commands of God. As this is not unique to Thomas and is a perspective he shares with much of the preceptive literature of the Bible (especially the prophetic and sapiential, but also the legislative), when he approaches texts of this nature he usually engages in fruitful interpretation and theological construction, especially when the reasons for these commands are given or their connection to points of meaning are manifest. Thomas' exegesis of the last three chapters of Ephesians demonstrates this fruitfulness well, as shall be seen.

In the last case (the Psalms) we encounter a unique mode which entails a unique difficulty. The adjectives "deprecative" and "laudative" are definitely apropos for this mode and are soundly descriptive of psalmody. But in Thomas' eyes the Psalms, taken together, are a restatement of the contents of all the other modes, "because whatever is said in the other books of other modes is said here through the mode of praise and prayer."[102] He can assert this only because of another assertion regarding the Psalms - that they are christological in their literal sense. In his own words:

> Regarding the mode of exposition, it should be known that in expounding upon the Psalms, *as in other prophecies* [emphasis mine], we should avoid an error that was condemned in the Fifth Synod. Theodore of Mopsuestia said that in Sacred Scripture and the prophecies nothing is explicitly said about Christ, but about certain other things... This mode is condemned in that Council... St. Jerome therefore expounding on Ezekiel passed on to us a rule

---

[101] VALKENBERG, 252-253.
[102] *Super Psalmos,* Prol.

CHAPTER II. CONTEMPORARY CRITICISM OF THOMAS' EXEGESIS:
A CALL FOR A NEW APPROACH?

87

that we will observe in the Psalms, namely, that events are to be
expounded as prefiguring something about Christ or the Church.[103]

In other words, Aquinas believes the biblical author (i.e., David) to be
speaking consciously in prophecy about Christ and the Church in the Psalms.
Because of this, "this book has the general material of theology as a whole"
and "it contains the whole of Scripture"[104] in the form specific to the Psalms,
which is prayer.

The difficulty this pre-understanding poses is obvious - it handicaps
Thomas in his interpretation of the Psalms, to the extent that he mis-
understands the mind of the human author from the outset. In short, the
writer(s) of the Psalms did not intend to write about Christ, or to repeat in
advance the words of Christ. So from the perspective of direct interpretation,
the *Postilla super Psalmos* is burdened by the same weaknesses as Thomas'
exegesis of narrative texts. This is also the case with much that is contained
in the commentaries on Isaiah, Jeremiah and Lamentations. This is not to say
that Thomas is thoroughly incapable of sound exegesis in these cases (nor, for
that matter, is he incapable of it in the *lectura* on Matthew). But if we recall
that Thomas is not just exegeting bits and pieces but also constructing a
theological model in any given commentary, then we must conclude that in
these cases the exegetical project is in many ways doomed, even if some of its
constituent parts may be well-crafted.

However, Thomas does not only engage in direct interpretation of the
Psalms. In fact, he cites the Psalter in his exegesis of other works so often
that it is without a doubt his predominant OT source and may even be his
predominant biblical source. In the *In Ephesios*, for instance, he cites it 97
times, more than any other source with the exception of Romans (which is
cited the same number of times). For now, it should be noted that in this latter
use of the Psalms they contribute greatly to Thomas exegetical project, and
provide it with a spiritual emphasis which it might otherwise lack. As Torrell

---

[103] "*Circa modum exponendi sciendum est, quod tam in Psalterio quam in aliis Prophetiis
exponendis evitare debemus unum errorem damnatum in quinta Synodo. Theodorus enim
Mopsuestenus dixit, quod in Sacra Scriptura, et prophetiis nihil expresse dicitur de Christo, sed
de quibusdam aliis rebus... Hic autem modus damnatus est in illo Concilio... Beatus ergo
Hieronymus super Ezech. tradidit nobis unam regulam, quam servabimus in Psalmis; scilicet
quod sic sunt exponendae de rebus gestis, ut figurantibus aliquid de Christo, vel Ecclesia*"
[Ibid., Prol.].

[104] "*...hic liber generalem habet totius Theologiae... continet totam Scripturam*" [Ibid.,
Proemium.].

and Bouthillier note: "If we are seeking a reason for the great predominance of the Psalms over all the other books [in Thomas' exegesis], we might in the first place hear an echo of Thomas' prayer. He did not just work with a concordance; the material that came spontaneously to his heart and mind is that on which he had meditated longest."[105]

With this working definition of non-narrative texts and a basic grasp on how the different non-narrative modes function both in Thomas' exegesis as well as subject to it, we are now able to advance to the formulation of a way of approaching the individual works that make up Thomas' exegetical corpus.

---

[105] TORRELL and BOUTHILLIER, "Quand saint Thomas," 9.

CHAPTER III

A SYSTEMATIC APPROACH
TO
THOMAS' BIBLICAL COMMENTARIES

A) *A Brief Review of the Literature*

Several scholars have made attempts to place Thomas' biblical commentaries under closer scrutiny than do the cursory examinations that have predominantly characterized scholarship in the domain of Thomas' relationship to the Bible. It is necessary to take a broad perspective on their work, as it represents a most promising sub-field of inquiry, one that is relatively recent and is still in its formative stages. What are the general characteristics of these inquiries? What do they offer as potential components of a new approach? We will attempt an answer to the second question when the approach is proposed; however the first one must be considered before this can be undertaken.

The various attempts at understanding Thomas' exegetical corpus can be broadly characterized by certain aspects that they share in common. The first category would include all attempts that are oriented thematically/topically in a primary way, without a specific focus on any one biblical commentary. The works of O'Connor, Lawrence Boadt,[1] Valkenberg and Romanus Cessario[2] would fit this category. The next category would include all of the works that are primarily thematic/topical, but that limit their scope to specific works (or parts thereof) within the exegetical corpus.[3] This is by far the largest group, and would contain works by Mary Daly,[4] Swierzawski,[5]

---

[1] Lawrence BOADT, "St. Thomas Aquinas and the Biblical Wisdom Tradition," *The Thomist* 49 (1985) : 575-611.

[2] Romanus CESSARIO, *The Godly Image: Christ and Salvation in Catholic Thought from Anselm to Aquinas*, Studies in Historical Theology 6 (Petersham, MA: St. Bede's, 1990), 27-51.

[3] My own M.A. thesis fits into this category.

[4] Mary S. DALY, "The Notion of Justification in the Commentary of St. Thomas Aquinas on the Epistle to the Romans" (Ph. D. diss., Marquette University, 1971).

Pesch, Ti-Ti Chen, Michel Corbin,[6] Cuéllar, Bertrand De Margerie,[7] Black and Denis Billy.[8] The final category would be works which do not limit themselves to particular themes, but focus rather on the commentaries as individual works with their own organic unity. Works that fit into this category would be all of the various introductions to translations (such as Lamb's, Weisheipl's and Philippe's), and also a monograph coauthored by Torrell and Bouthillier.[9]

This is by no means an exhaustive list, nor is it a qualitative one - works of varying degrees of precision and interpretive success are listed in common categories indiscriminately. But it is helpful in that it aids us in considering the approach to be proposed in relation to works that have gone before it.

One significant work that is not listed above is Yaffe's, whose interpretive essay is not easily categorized. It resembles the third category in that it gives priority to the fact that Thomas' commentary on Job is a biblical commentary, recognizing that this OT book dictates the order and character of Thomas' work.[10] But it also labors to discern Thomas' native themes and the possibilities for contemporary retrieval,[11] treating the work as a theological model. Here Yaffe combines the best of both the second and the third categories - his approach is thematic, but the themes are Thomas', and he

---

[5] Waclaw SWIERZAWSKI, "God and the Mystery of his Wisdom in the Pauline Commentaries of St. Thomas Aquinas," *Divus Thomas* 74 (1971) : 466-500; "Faith and Worship in the Pauline Commentaries of St. Thomas Aquinas," *Divus Thomas* 75 (1972) : 389-412; "Christ and the Church : *Una Mystica Persona* in the Pauline Commentaries of St. Thomas Aquinas," in *S. Tommaso Teologo,* ed. A. Piolanti, 239-250 (Rome: Libreria Editrice Vaticana, 1995).

[6] M. CORBIN, "Le Pain de Vie. La Lecture de Jn 6 par S. Thomas d'Aquin," *Recherches de Science Religieuse* 65 (1977) : 107-138.

[7] Bertrand DE MARGERIE, "Mort sacrificielle du Christ et peine de mort chez Thomas d'Aquin, commentateur de Saint Paul," *Revue Thomiste* 83 (1983) : 394-417.

[8] Denis J. BILLY, "Grace and Natural Law in the *Super epistola ad Romanos lectura*: A Study in Thomas' Commentary on Romans 2:14-16," *Studia Moralia* 26 (1988) : 15-37.

[9] TORRELL and BOUTHILLIER, "Quand saint Thomas méditait sur le prophète Isaïe." To further specify this categorization it is possble to conceive of a sliding scale in each category, with works being placed along it in terms of their secondary similarity to other categories. In this case, the works of Cuéllar and Swierzawki would be placed nearer the first category (as they focus on all of the Pauline commentaries rather than on any particular one), and the work of Black would be placed nearer the third category (as it gives considerable attention to Thomas as exegete of the Fourth Gospel).

[10] YAFFE, 12.

[11] Ibid., 6-8.

never forgets that Thomas is in dialogue with a text. In this sense he stands alone in a fourth category, and it is one that has at the very least the benefit of eclecticism. But while his exposition of the *Expositio super Iob* is truly peerless, he does not endeavor to formulate a comprehensive approach for the benefit of those who would attempt to consider other Thomistic biblical commentaries in the same fashion.

It is to this end that the present approach is being proposed, with the recognition that all of the other authors listed above can and do contribute essential components to it as well. We will call this the "Genre-Identification Approach," designating it by referring to what immediately distinguishes it from the bulk of scholarship in this field; namely, the importance we attribute to the recognition of the genre of the biblical text under analysis. The word "approach" in the title is of importance as well, as this is not meant to be an infallible or even inalterable way to analyze Thomas' exegetical works, but rather a helpful guide that incorporates the insights and techniques of the best inquiries which have preceded it.

It is best to consider this approach in its totality first; hence, it is presented in outline form below. However, each part requires explanation, and so a detailed analysis of each element will also be given, with examples from various works in Thomas' exegetical corpus, as well as insights from those contemporary scholars who best incorporate the kind of analysis each step requires into their own enterprises. Finally, its fullest and most organic illustration will be its actual application to the *Lectura super epistolam ad Ephesios* in Part II of the present study.

B) *The Genre-Identification Approach*

The Genre-Identification Approach can be briefly outlined as follows:
I. Pre-Analysis
    a) Textual Pre-Analysis
        1) Provenance
        2) Integrity
        3) The biblical text itself
            3a) The type of text
            3b) Its theme(s) and characteristics according to
            current exegesis
    b) Thomas' Exegetical Framework
        1) The theme of the text according to Thomas
        2) Major divisions of the text according to Thomas

3) Relationship(s) to other texts according to Thomas
4) Characteristics of author and authorship according to
Thomas

   c) *Auctoritates*

1) Biblical citations - preliminary inquiry into the place and
function of Scripture
2) Extra-biblical *auctoritates* - preliminary inquiry into the
place and function of extra-biblical *auctoritates*

II. Thomas' Analysis of the Parts of the Text

   a) The minor divisions of the text according to Thomas
   b) Examination of Thomas' word and phrase analyses

1) Examination of significant terms and phrases
2) Examination of significant (or insignificant) terms and
phrases in the text as understood by Thomas

   c) Interpretive conclusions

1) The 'literal sense'

1a) Thomas' conclusion(s) regarding the 'literal
sense'
1b) Its relationship to the text itself in the light of
current exegesis
1c) Its relationship to similar ideas and themes in
Thomas' other works

2) Spiritual senses

2a) Illuminative or non-illuminative usage in relation
to Thomas' understanding of the 'literal sense'?

3) *Quaestiones* arising from the text

3a) Exegetical or pedagogical?

   d) Examination of the use of *auctoritates* in interpretation

1) Biblical citations
2) Non-biblical citations

III. Overall Evaluation - Thomas' Work and its Potential Contribution

   a) Similarities to and differences from Thomas' other works
   b) The *lectura / expositio / postilla* as a theological model of its pre-
designated theme
   c) Miscellaneous data

A few preliminary characteristics of this approach should be noted in advance. First, the approach itself is neither absolute nor monolithic; parts of it can be omitted in circumstances where they are not applicable. For instance, **II.c.2** will not always be applicable because Thomas does not always posit spiritual senses; in the same way, **II.d.2** will not always be necessary because Thomas does not always cite extra-biblical authorities in his exegesis. Also, the importance of each step will vary from passage to passage depending on how important the passage is in Thomas' interpretation. If it is of minor importance, a more cursory exposition is admissible; if it is of major importance, then a more extended treatment will be required. We will discuss ways that the varying degrees of importance can be discerned in the detailed treatment below.

Another significant feature of this approach is that it demands of the analyst an attention to recurring features and techniques in Thomas' exegetical practice. In this way the approach is open to the insights of others who have studied Thomas' exegesis, and also can contribute to the formation of a general patrimony regarding the exegetical corpus, one that gains its insights first and foremost from that exegesis itself. In this way a collective "clinical experience" of the Thomistic biblical corpus can be gained, one that will make the use of this approach into a self-refining activity.

I. Pre-Analysis
I.a) Textual Pre-Analysis
I.a.1) Provenance
I.a.2) Integrity

The first part of this approach, the pre-analysis, contains elements that are conventional to any study of ancient and/or medieval documents (**I.a.1, I.a.2**) as well as those that are more specific to analysis of the Thomistic exegetical corpus. We will limit our consideration to the latter elements (**I.a.3a-b**), as the exigencies of the former are well-known and are neither original nor specific to the present study.

I.a.3) The biblical text itself
I.a.3a) The type of text

It has already been demonstrated to a clear if limited degree that Thomas' exegesis is dictated in many ways by the text on which he is commenting. Therefore it is necessary to have a firm grasp of the characteristics of the biblical text itself if one is to discern how this text gives an underlying framework to Thomas' efforts. Such a grasp is necessarily comprised of two aspects. In **I.a.3a** the goal is to ascertain the most basic defining characteristic of the text insofar as Thomas' exegetical practice is concerned; namely, whether the text is narrative, non-narrative, or a mixture of both. Once this is determined, it is necessary to further categorize the text if it contains non-narrative elements in order to identify what Thomistic category (or combination of categories) of non-narrative the text fits into. The categorization that Thomas gives in the *Postilla super Psalmos* is decisive in this regard, but is also open to further specification based on Thomas' actual practice.

I.a.3b) The themes and characteristics of the text according to modern exegesis

In **I.a.3b** some consideration of the most important characteristics of the biblical text is undertaken. Some things to be investigated are major themes, specific concerns, major literary features and relationships to other biblical texts. As a rule of thumb, what is to be attempted here is not detailed exegesis but a general background to Thomas' own interpretation which will help demonstrate to what degree he is successful in his attempts to understand the text.

I.b) Thomas' Exegetical Framework
I.b.1) The theme of the text according to Thomas

I.b involves understanding in the most comprehensive possible terms how Thomas understood the biblical text he has under comment. In **I.b.1** an examination of the overall theme Thomas discerns in the text is undertaken. Such a consideration is key; it gives the most important indication of what kind of theological model Thomas' commentary will be. For instance, Hebrews is considered by Thomas to be principally about the existence of grace in the Head of the Church, who is Christ.[12] This alerts the reader to the fact that Thomas sees Hebrews as being primarily christological, and also to the possibility that a distinct christological model may emerge from his encounter with the text. At the very least, one can certainly say that it is crucial for ascertaining Thomas' understanding of Hebrews and of how this particular biblical work functions as a whole.

---

[12] *Super epist.*, Prol.,11

I.b.2) Major divisions of the text according to Thomas

In this step, the way that Thomas divides the text is investigated. This is an activity that needs to be clarified, as it involves a deviation from a certain trend among scholars.

It has long been a commonplace in considerations of Thomas' exegesis that the text of the commentary be introduced by recourse to a textual outline in which Thomas' divisions of the text are given in brief.[13] This practice logically fits with Thomas' actual practice, which is to divide and subdivide the text (*divisio textus*). Lamb is a good example of this; he gives an excellent three-page outline of the *In Ephesios* in the introduction to his translation of the same.[14]

However, one must add an observation. Just as the "sophisticated divisions" of Thomas' actual presentation can strike one as "dry intellectualism which seems to have forgotten the vivid originality of the Holy Scriptures,"[15] even more so do these divisions, when they are distilled from the text, seem totally foreign to the work under comment. In the case of Lamb's translation they stand at the entrance to the *lectura* forbiddingly, and are so numerous and exact that they are quickly forgotten at the turn of the page. Yaffe has developed an approach more amenable to exposition. In his essay he presents the major divisions of the text at the beginning of his treatment. As he continues, he gives the minor divisions of these sections only when he sees a necessity in doing so. For instance, he gives the minor divisions of Job 1-2 in detail because the history it gives "is premised as a foundation for the whole debate" according to Thomas.[16]   Yet when he begins to consider Thomas' commentary on this debate, he only focuses on the minor distinctions when doing so is necessary for following Thomas' presentation.[17]

---

[13] Cf. J.-M. VOSTÉ, "S. Thomas epistularum," 270-272, and BLACK, 683 for two examples.

[14] LAMB, 32-34.

[15] PESCH, 586. Cf. Brevard S. CHILDS, *Biblical Theology of the Old and New Testaments: Theological Reflection on the Christian Bible* (Minneapolis: Fortress, 1992), 41, who holds a similar position: "His [Thomas'] use of conventional scholastic categories and the endless subdivision of phrases will remain a major barrier to most modern readers." We must disagree with him, however, when he concludes that "a direct appropriation" of Thomas' biblical commentaries is not where Thomas' contribution to biblical theology is to be located.

[16] YAFFE, 16.

[17] See Ibid., 45-51, for an example of Yaffe's method.

This may seem to be only a matter of taste, but it is far more. If we are to take seriously the charge leveled by Pesch (and countless others throughout the centuries) of "dry intellectualism" on Thomas' part, then we must admit that a weakness of Thomas' approach to the Bible lies in that it is "top-heavy." Thomas' divisions tend to draw attention away from the biblical text as often as they draw attention to it because they are so minute and hair-splitting. When the interpreter of Thomas puts forward this aspect first, he is offering Thomas' weakness, from the modern perspective, as a guide to modern readers. Another justification for leaving this comprehensive treatment of the textual divisions out is given by Corbin, who distinguishes the *divisio textus* from the *expositio textus*, although noting their interrelation.[18]

So what is the subject of this step? Rather than draw out a lengthy diagram, it is here that the major divisions alone are analyzed with an eye for what they indicate of Thomas' interpretive slant. For Thomas, these major divisions are almost always related to his opinion regarding the biblical author's literary intention, and so are key to his understanding of the biblical text under comment. In particular, their connection to the theme Thomas detects for the entire work should be considered.

I.b.3) Relationships to other texts according to Thomas

In this step the relationship of the text Thomas is exegeting to other texts is considered. This is another helpful indicator of the direction Thomas' interpretation will take. For instance, in his Johannine commentary Thomas refers to the Gospel of John in relation to the other gospels in an attempt to distinguish what its defining characteristics are: it makes known the divinity of Christ (whereas the others concentrate on the mysteries of his humanity), it was written later than the other gospels, and it is polemical in nature.[19] These are obviously decisive indicators regarding what Thomas considers to be the subject matter of the Gospel as contrasted with the other gospels. This contrast is decisive, for it shows that Thomas understands that he is dealing with a text quite different from these others.

I.b.4) Characteristics of author and authorship according to Thomas

What is true of the last step is also true of this one - Thomas' understanding of the biblical author may offer some clues regarding his understanding of the author's work. The long exposition of the nature of John

---

[18] CORBIN, "Le Pain de la Vie," 108.

[19] *In Io.*, Prol., 10.

the Evangelist's contemplation which we considered above[20] shows that Thomas considers himself to be confronted by a biblical text of particular theological profundity, a crucial key to understanding how he interprets the text itself.

A final note for this part (**I.b**) of the Genre-Identification Approach: the analyst should never underestimate the scriptural *accessus* which Thomas uses in his prologues to introduce his commentaries. The particular *accessus* may describe the author (as in the case of *In Ioannem*), or characterize the subject-matter of the text (as in the case of *In Philippenses*), or both (as in the *lectura* on Ephesians). In any case it represents the one biblical verse that Thomas would use to characterize what it is essential to know about the biblical work under analysis as a starting point for that analysis. Because of this it often offers indispensable information about where Thomas will be going with his interpretation; in the case of the *Lectura super Iohannem*, Black has already demonstrated for us that the indication of Isaiah's vision of God is how Thomas would characterize John's contemplation (and therefore, his Gospel).[21] Likewise, when Thomas goes to lengths to discuss Paul's strengthening of the pillars of the Ephesian church, he demonstrates to us that he sees Paul as a pastor involved in pastoral work in writing this Letter.[22]

I.c) Auctoritates

I.c involves taking preliminary stock of the resources which Thomas chose to aid him in his task of exegesis. As a work of pre-analysis this is not grounds for any final conclusions. However, it is an excellent basis for developing hypotheses regarding the text. To borrow terms from Valkenberg, it is at this level that the "place" of scriptural citations and non-scriptural authorities are identified; only in the next part of the inquiry (**II**) can definite conclusions regarding the "function" of these be drawn.

I.c.1) Scriptural citations

One lacuna in the existing literature regards the consideration of the biblical sources which Thomas uses in commenting on biblical texts. Little has been done in this area - only over the past fifteen years have there been any investigations into this telling aspect of Thomas' exegetical practice.

---

[20] See pp. 62-63.

[21] See BLACK, 686-688, for an example. We have already considered his treatment of Thomas' use of an *accessus* in some detail above.

[22] *In Eph.*, Prol., 1.

Boadt's article is the first example of a monograph that inquires into how often Thomas uses a genre of biblical literature (i.e., wisdom literature), and this he does only briefly.[23] (We have already noted Torrell and Bouthillier's astute observation of Thomas' use of Psalms citations.[24])

However, it is Valkenberg who deserves credit for being the first to clear a real path towards understanding the significance of Thomas' use of biblical citations. In this step, we will adopt (with some modifications[25]) his heuristic device for tracing the place of Scripture in any given work by Thomas. It can be broken down into two basic tasks (to which we will add a third): 1) a tally is made of the total number of citations in the entire work (or part thereof);[26] 2) the number of citations per 1,000 words is quantified in order to create a basic standard of comparison between the work under analysis and Thomas' other works (since this is for the sake of comparison between entire works, it will not be performed in the present case).[27] Valkenberg also offers a consideration of which works are most frequently cited by Thomas,[28] but it is here that his approach needs to be augmented in order to maximize the benefit of his method for understanding Thomas' biblical commentaries. Rather than identifying only the twenty sources (biblical and non-biblical) most frequently used as Valkenberg does, the third task would be: 3) to list all the biblical sources that Thomas cites and the number of times they are cited. This will not only identify what Thomas' major sources are, but will also demonstrate with what frequency Thomas cites certain genres of biblical literature, allowing clusters of citations to be

---

[23] BOADT, 576.

[24] TORRELL and BOUTHILLIER, "Quand saint Thomas méditait sur le prophète Isaïe," 9.

[25] Valkenberg's approach is extremely detailed and involves a certain knowledge of and experience with the rules of statistical analysis. The basic elements of his approach are detailed here, recognizing that most Thomistic scholars (including the author) have limited backgrounds in this advanced field of mathematics.

[26] To accomplish this, Valkenberg relies mainly on Roberto BUSA, ed., *Index Thomisticus S. Thomae Aquinatis Operum Omnium Indices et Concordantiae*, 50 vols. (Stuttgart: 1979-1980). Since the completion of Valkenberg's thesis, Busa has published a CD-ROM database which offers electronic search capacities [*Thomae Aquinatis Opera Omnia cum hypertextibus in CD-ROM* (Milan: Licosa/Editel, 1992)]. We will use this latter tool in our investigation.

[27] VALKENBERG, 20-25. This step of Valkenberg's heuristic device does not allow for the possibility of differences in the frequency of citation in the various parts of the same work. However, as part of the approach being proposed it is augmented by step **II.d.1,** where such phenomena come under consideration. Here Valkenberg's device helps to differentiate the work under analysis from other Thomistic writings that incorporate biblical citations.

[28] Ibid., 44-46.

more easily identified. Also, in the case of less frequently cited texts, this will alert the reader to be aware of the reasons why these sources are cited infrequently and also to the possibility that these play a particular role in the commentary.

One difficulty in this step which cannot be avoided by recourse to either electronic search devices or to Thomistic concordances is the enumeration of Thomas' use of citations from the text being commented on in reference to itself (usually signalled by the use of the words *"infra"* and *"supra"*). The difficulty arises from the fact that in Thomas' technique of dividing the text, he also cites upcoming (and at times, preceding) passages using these same terms (i.e. *infra* and *supra*). These latter are not really citations, but in a concordance or electronic search they will seem to be so. A manual count is necessary to isolate those instances where Thomas is actually commenting on the text. These "false citations" (i.e. his divisions) invariably are placed at the beginning of Thomas' treatment of a passage, and so are easy to locate.

In Part II of this study, we will apply this part of our approach specifically to the Ephesians commentary.

I.c.2) Extra-Biblical Auctoritates

In this final part of **I.c**, preliminary stock is taken of what extra-biblical *auctoritates* Thomas uses in commenting on the text, as well as his frequency of recourse to these authorities. Interestingly, there is a much longer precedent in Thomistic scholarship regarding his use of extra-biblical authorities than there is regarding his use of Scripture citations. Spicq was the first to enumerate Thomas' use of patristic authorities in a specific commentary (*In Ioannem*);[29] others have followed his lead.[30]

Valkenberg offers an exhaustive and very useful list of the various types of authorities Thomas relies on, one which we will also adopt: a) Holy Scripture (which we have considered in a separate category); b) the Fathers of the Church (a complicated group: *symbola*; Councils; Latin Fathers; Greek Fathers; Pseudo-Dionysius; Boethius and John Damascene; early popes; Apostolic Fathers; general references to Fathers; general references to the Church; negative authorities such as *Haeretici*, *Graeci*, Nestorius, etc.; litur-

---

[29] SPICQ, *D.T.C.*, col. 722-723.

[30] REVUELTA, 575-576; Leo J. ELDERS, "Thomas Aquinas and the Fathers of the Church," in *The Reception of the Church Fathers in the West*, ed. Irena Backus, vol. I, (Leiden; N.Y.: E.J. Brill, 1997), 347-348.

gical sources; and early medieval saints); c) Philosophers (including all sources of classical antiquity); and d) Interlocutors (another complicated group: predecessors and contemporaries; well-known sayings; Scriptural glosses, including the *Glossa Ordinaria* and Peter Lombard's *Magna Glossatura*; the non-glossular works of Peter Lombard; other *Magistri*; and Thomas' own works). These are listed in descending order in terms of their authority for Thomas. After Scripture, the Fathers are the most important sources, having authority bestowed on (or withheld from) them through their reception (or rejection) in the Church. The Philosophers exerted great influence on the *artes* of Thomas' age, and so have a real (yet relativized) authority for him. The final group is significant because Thomas saw it as necessary to take all opinions into account in searching for truth.[31]

In this part of the pre-analysis, a parallel enumeration to the preceding part is undertaken: 1) a tally is made of the total number of direct and indirect citations in the entire work (or part thereof);[32]   2) the number of direct and indirect citations per 1,000 words is quantified; 3) a list of these is made showing how many times each of these non-scriptural authorities are used. After this, some preliminary observations of the same hypothetical nature as those in I.c.1 can be made.

As in the case of **I.c.1**, we will refrain from illustrating this step until we approach the Ephesians commentary in Part II. In terms of our approach considered generally, it is at this point that emphasis shifts to Thomas' consideration of the biblical text under comment; with the pre-analysis accomplished, we are well-prepared for such a venture.

II. Thomas' Analysis of the Parts of the Text

Part II of the Genre-Identification Approach is designed to be flexible for the analyst in a number of ways. First, it is designed to be applied and reapplied to major and minor sections of the text, but it does not specify which sections (chapters, lectures, etc.).   It can also be modified and rearranged as needed. Finally, the extent to which it or its component steps are utilized is not dictated. All of this implies that the user must make judgments about the various parts of the text that he/she is commenting on in order to determine what steps should be applied to the text and to what degree in each individual case. There are no specific rules for determining this. For instance,

---

[31] Ibid., 25-31. Cf. ELDERS, "Fathers," 349-342, for a more developed treatment of Thomas' understanding of the authority of the Fathers.

[32] Unlike enumerating Thomas' use of Scripture citations, this is much more easily and precisely accomplished through manual counting.

length of exposition on the part of Thomas may be decisive in many cases regarding his emphases, but not always. However, there are two general rules which should always be followed; one which relates to Thomas, the other which relates to contemporary scholarship.

The first involves always remembering Thomas' main theme in light of the established fact that he is building a theological model as much as interpreting a text. In fact, for Thomas the former *is* the latter. Therefore, care should be taken to judge all major and minor sections in their significance for the main theme, be it a direct or indirect significance.[33] Thomas will labor to do this for the reader, but it is also the analyst's job to ask whether or not he is always successful. Sometimes Thomas' intention to connect the various parts to the main theme will trip him up and cause him to stretch the meaning of unrelated passages in order to connect them to it. In other cases, attention to minute details may cause Thomas to overlook a passage's connection to the main theme. In this case, it is also the analyst's job to ask how this and other exegetical maneuvers affect, for better or for worse, Thomas' understanding of the text as a whole and in its parts.

The second point to remember is that, in this approach, the analyst is laboring to make Thomas accessible to modern biblical and theological scholarship. Hence it is important to develop a readable exposition, one which always keeps in sight the relation of the analysis to the modern mind-set. Care should be taken not to develop a "commentary on the commentary" - this only exacerbates the problem in much the same way as the diagram method criticized above. In this new approach some commentary may have to be sacrificed, but only that which stands as an obstacle to capturing the heart of Thomas' interpretation. To draw an analogy - the tour-guide may know (and should know) every minor detail of the art of the Louvre, but attempting to heave it all at once on even the unsuspecting art expert will probably bring him/her to confusion. In the modern exposition of Thomas' painstaking style, sometimes less is more.

---

[33] Although it is not counter-productive to trace secondary themes in Thomas' commentaries, one must recognize that to do so it is necessary to capture them in the framework which Thomas gives them and sees the biblical text as giving them. Daly gives us an example in her doctoral dissertation on justification in the commentary on Romans; she is careful to establish it in relation to the grace of Christ considered in itself, the main theme of Romans according to Thomas [DALY, 12-14]. An even better example is that of Corbin, who considers the commentary on John 6 in relation to "the Chalcedonian formula of the two natures" of Christ [CORBIN, 107].

II.a) The minor divisions of the text according to Thomas

We have already noted that Yaffe has developed an efficient method for following both the major and minor divisions of Thomas' *Expositio super Iob* in proportion to their respective significance for Thomas' interpretation. Using his analogy to architecture, Yaffe takes great pains to make sure that he gives all of the details of the foundations of the commentary,[34] and then gives broader accounts of what Thomas builds on that foundation, offering greater detail at the more significant points,[35] and briefly summarizing other less decisive aspects.[36] In this he discerns what is significant to Thomas' main theme (Thomas believes the Book of Job to be about "showing through plausible argumentation that human affairs are ruled by divine providence"[37]), and gives greatest weight to what Thomas himself emphasizes.

A similar approach should be adopted at this stage, and the text under analysis should be treated accordingly. At all times Thomas' divisions of the text should be given pride-of-place, and not merely the chapter divisions which were imposed on the text before it was received by Thomas.[38] These are often significant for Thomas as well, but not always - lecture and non-structural thematic divisions are also of import, especially as they approximate to the main theme. Again, the analyst must judge to what degree the contents of each division are treated.

II.b) Examination of Thomas' word and phrase analyses

One helpful aspect of Thomas' approach to the biblical text for the analyst is his effort to leave no word or phrase unconsidered. At times, even prepositions and conjunctions come under intensive analysis.[39] This is helpful for the reader in that it is at this "micro-level" that length and detail are very decisive. Almost invariably, the longer Thomas spends with a word or phrase, the more important it is for understanding the overall commentary.

---

[34] YAFFE, 18-22.

[35] Ibid., 31-37 on *In Iob* 7.

[36] Ibid., 31-33 on *In Iob* 6.

[37] *In Iob*, Prol.

[38] Raphael LOEWE, "The Medieval History of the Latin Vulgate," in *The Cambridge History of the Bible*, Volume 2, *The West from the Fathers to the Reformation*, ed. by G.W.H. Lampe (Cambridge: Cambridge University Press, 1969) : 147. As Loewe notes, the Paris Vulgate which Thomas had at his disposal had chapter divisions

[39] *In Io.*, 1.1.44-45.

II.b.1) Examination of significant terms and phrases

This step involves identifying words and phrases which Thomas sees as significant in the biblical text, and also analyzing Thomas' treatment of these linguistic units. In this area there have been some excellent contributions for understanding Thomas' exegesis; we will consider two examples.

O'Connor's monograph gives an exhaustive analysis of one word, *"mysterium,"* in Aquinas' exegesis. On the basis of Thomas' use of the term in various places in his interpretation of biblical texts, he concludes that "the basic meaning of 'mystery' for Thomas is 'something hidden'" (*in aliquo occulto*), and nothing more, allowing Thomas to deal with mysteries in various stages of being revealed (or remaining hidden). Thomas allows "all the 'mystery texts' to decide what sense the word has," showing (according to O'Connor) that his definition is actually superior to the one given so often in our day, namely: "a truth which was once hidden but is now revealed."[40] As he puts it elsewhere,

> If Aquinas saw a book entitled *The Theology of the Mystery*, he would ask, 'What mystery?' He would accept the observation of J.B. Lightfoot on the word 'mystery' that "on the nature of the truth itself the word says nothing. It may be transcendental, incomprehensible, mystical, mysterious, in the modern sense of the term; but this idea is quite accidental, and must be gathered from the special circumstances of the case, for it cannot be inferred from the word itself.[41]

In this instance, O'Connor builds a convincing case that in regard to this important Pauline term, Thomas is more restrained than some modern interpreters, and so is in a better position to interpret Pauline "mystery texts."

Swierzawski gives a good example of phrase analysis when he considers Thomas' understanding of the NT concept of "glory." He locates what he considers to be the *"locus classicus"* of Thomas' theory of glory: *In Heb.* 1.2, where Thomas comments on the phrase "the splendor of his glory" in reference to the Son. Here Thomas reviews a definition by Ambrose, but actually opts for his own, defining it in reference to God *"antonomastice"*; that is, specifying glory to refer to God in its most proper sense: "only the

---

[40] O'CONNOR, "The Concept of Mystery in Aquinas' Exegesis," 207-208.

[41] Ibid., 273. Cf. J.B. LIGHTFOOT, *Colossians and Ephesians* (London: Macmillan, 1912), 166.

knowledge that God has of himself is perfectly called 'glory'."[42]   He
continues to demonstrate the relationship of glory to light in Thomas'
exegesis, continuing this close examination to its conclusion - the glory of
God is communicated to us through "the *Verbum Patris*', which is the concept of God's intellect.... the brilliance of his wisdom"; this is why Paul calls
the Son "*splendor gloriae*."[43]

Both authors offer excellent paradigms for analyzing words and
phrases in Thomas' commentaries. However, in both cases a trans-textual
approach is taken, with each author drawing from many sources both exegetical and non-exegetical. This does not allow the possibility that Thomas
was capable of giving specific emphases to a term in one commentary that he
would not give to it in another place. To address this difficulty, the analyst
should always attempt to demonstrate the meaning of a term first by its
immediate context, than by other uses in the same work, and only as a last
resort through recourse to other works, giving pride-of-place to works of the
same period or general topic (i.e., other Pauline commentaries in the above
two cases).

*II.b.2) Examination of significant (or insignificant) terms and phrases in the
text as understood by Thomas*

II.b.2 is really a function of the preceding step because it involves the
same kind of analysis with a different angle - namely, attending to the
coherence or divergence of uses of specific words and phrases between the
biblical author and Thomas as interpreter. To give a purely hypothetical example: if Thomas were to remain unaware of the significance of the term
"Word" while commenting on the Johannine Prologue, it would obviously
effect his exegesis of the text. And if he were to overemphasize any particular
word or phrase, this would also be a clear indicator of a particular emphasis
arising from Thomas and not the text itself. Attending to such possibilities
helps the analyst to focus on the strengths and weaknesses of Thomas'
construction, and also to identify precisely where the text leaves off and
Thomas begins.

II.c) Interpretive conclusions

The combination of analyses in **II.a** (regarding Thomas' minor
divisions of the text) and **II.b** (regarding Thomas' analysis of words and

---

[42] "*...sola cognitio Dei de seipso perfecte dicitur gloria*" [*In Heb.*, 1.2.26].

[43] SWIERZAWSKI, "God and the Mystery of his Wisdom," 483-484.

phrases) cover the two most basic elements in Thomas' practice of interpretation. Once the section has been considered in how it breaks down according to these two steps, the analyst is ready to expound on the section itself, considering it in relation to the major theme(s), the biblical text itself, Thomas' other works and its implications for contemporary theology (once the entire work is accounted for, larger conclusions of this sort can be drawn regarding the whole work in Part III of our approach). The interpretive conclusions break down along the lines of the three most basic interpretive maneuvers that Thomas engages in with the biblical text: detecting the literal sense, positing spiritual sense(s), and producing *quaestiones* that arise from the text. These latter two are not considered in the same depth as the first, because in Thomas' understanding they arise from the literal sense of the text and so can be evaluated as complementary to it.

II.c.1) The 'literal sense'

The definition of the literal sense which is given by Thomas is well-known: it is "that mode according to which things [in Scripture] are signified by words."[44] Here I refer the reader unfamiliar with this aspect of Thomas' exegetical presuppositions to the consideration of Thomas' understanding of the literal sense offered by Kennedy, who demonstrates how absolutely crucial this doctrine is to Thomas' understanding of Scripture.[45] It will suffice to note that two norms give form to Thomas' quest for the literal sense. The first is his rule that one ought not hold anything false as being the literal sense of the text, since Scripture is divine revelation. The second is that "the circumstances of the letter must be preserved," demonstrating a concern for "context and contextual coherence."[46]

II.c.1a) Thomas' conclusion(s) regarding the 'literal sense'

The first point to be examined is the proposed literal meaning of the section itself. This is not a mere restatement of the commentary or even a brief reformulation of it, but should involve an attempt to form a deeper understanding of Thomas' exposition than merely its surface intent. Here one must recognize not only its accuracy or inaccuracy, but also the style and

---

[44] *Quodl.*, VII.14.

[45] KENNEDY, "Thomas Aquinas and the Literal Sense of Sacred Scripture," 98-144. Cf. *Quodl.*, VII.14-15; *In Gal.*, 4.7; *ST* I.1.10 for the major sources of Thomas' doctrine of the literal sense.

[46] John F. BOYLE, 96-97. Cf. *De pot.*, 4.1 ad 5.

fuller implications of it. The last three parts of **II.c** exist only to help the interpreter reach the fullest possible understanding of what is uncovered in this first step.

A significant aspect of **II.c.1a** involves analyzing the relation of the literal sense of any given section to the main theme which Thomas attributes to the whole of the biblical work under analysis. At times, no connection is made between the former and the latter, and in turn signals to the analyst that the section itself is not of primary importance to Thomas in the case of the particular work under analysis. But when the section under consideration is clearly connected to that theme which Thomas himself asserts to be central, then it is a clear indication to the analyst that he/she have reached a crucial place in Thomas' commentary. Such a recognition will facilitate the analyst in correctly identifying how much attention to give to a section – if it is connected to the main theme, then it must be given the fullest possible consideration

II.c.1b) The relationship of the 'literal sense' to the text itself in the light of current exegesis

This step focuses on the accuracy of Thomas' exegesis from the standpoint of modern exegesis (see step **I.a.3**). It involves asking whether or not Thomas has a basic grasp of the meaning of the text under analysis, or if his understanding is either partially or totally inaccurate. At times Thomas is thrown off by the Vulgate text which gives faulty renderings of specific verses. At other times false etymologies, anachronistic interpretations, and other obstacles intrude and obscure his vision of the text to some (usually partial) degree. We considered an example of this in the preceding chapter as part of our analysis of Black's insights.[47] However, one should be cautious not to demand of Thomas an accuracy of modern proportions; rather, the fact that Thomas is involved in theological construction and not mere interpretation is a key aspect that should not be neglected. In this way we can speak of a primary accuracy (which is to be evaluated in this step) and a secondary accuracy, in which Thomas' construction remains at least basically connected to the foundation of the text. These two "accuracies" are certainly connected, but are not identical.

---

[47] BLACK, 695.

*II.c.1c   The relationship of the 'literal sense' to similar ideas and themes in
Thomas' other works*

For the fullest possible consideration of Thomas' exegesis, it is often
necessary to go beyond the confines of his commentary in order to fill out
areas that are vague and need clarification (see **II.b.2**). This is especially true
of attempts to trace how Thomas' ideas on the subject of the section have
developed or remained static throughout his career. However, there are two
excesses which must be avoided in this activity. First, one must be wary of
excess in the use of other texts for the purpose of interpreting the text; if there
is no license already present in the text for deepening its significance by
recourse to other works, one should not be inserted. Second, one must beware
the tendency to use the synthetic works (i.e. the *Summae*) as primary
interpretive guides- these are not necessarily the best works for this activity,
especially in the case of the Pauline commentaries. In all cases, the commentary itself must be given pride-of-place; it is the work under analysis, and
no other.

*II.c.1d   The relationship of the 'literal sense' to Thomas' understanding of the
overall theme*

At every opportunity, the relationship of the literal sense of the
passage to the main theme should be examined. At some points this relationship is not yet evident because Thomas has not yet worked this
relationship in, and will do so in an upcoming section. At other times there is
no discernible relationship - Thomas does not see the main theme to be the
only theme. However, he will take the opportunity to connect minor themes
to the major one as often as possible. This demonstrates the necessity of
treating the biblical commentaries as distinct works and not just as doctrinal
mines - unless the main theme is being investigated, it is often lost when
interpreters pick-and-choose from various places without reference to the
order which Thomas discerns in the text.

*II.c.2) Spiritual Senses: Illuminative or non-illuminative usage in relation to
Thomas' understanding of the literal sense?*

"The second role that the literal sense plays in Thomas' thought is as
the foundation for the spiritual or mystical sense."[48]   Although not auth-

---

[48] John F. BOYLE, 97.

oritative,[49] these senses are nonetheless part of Thomas' exegesis, much as this can confound the modern scholar, and so must be taken account of. However, this account is secondary to the account that is taken of the literal sense, and can actually serve it; the question here is not of accuracy (how could one judge this?) but rather of illumination. Does the spiritual sense shed light on the literal sense of the passage under consideration (or of other passages)? It may be a helpful tool in filling out the analyst's understanding of the literal sense Thomas gives, and so should not be neglected.

II.c.3) Quaestiones *arising from the text: exegetical or pedagogical?*

Chenu's masterful account tells the analyst everything he/she needs to know regarding the detection of *quaestiones*, the bulk of which (the origin, development and defining characteristics of the latter) must be omitted.[50] However, he does deserve direct quotation in regard to this:

> In the XIIIth century, the differentiation of these genres [*quaestio* and biblical *lectio*] had reached the stage of completion, with the disputed questions unquestionably having become school exercises different from the commentary on the text. The latter, however, as a result of the pressure its rational analysis brings to bear, involves anew the emergence of short *quaestiones* that, to be sure, are linked to the text, yet enter nonetheless into theological elaborating. *Hic oritur quaestio* [The question arises here]; *Hic est duplex quaestio* [There is here a twofold question]; *Potest aliquis quaerere* [One may ask]; *Hic oritur dubitatio* [A doubt arises here]. Even where a formula is not employed, exegesis develops along the lines of doctrinal research, argumentation, arguing from suitabilities, and, lengthily at times, refuting errors.[51]

When these textual modules are encountered, the analyst must answer a question similar to the one regarding the spiritual senses: Does the *quaestio* arise directly or only occasionally from the text? Can it be neatly separated from the rest of the commentary, or does it illumine the literal sense of the passage it is connected to? Determining this will not be difficult, and will

---

[49] *ST* I.1.8

[50] CHENU, *Towards Understanding*, 85-88.

[51] Ibid., 253. His conclusion is worth quoting: "The *magister in sacra pagina* begets the *magister in theologia*, exegesis, scholasticism" [253].

very often be fruitful, as it is in the *quaestio* that Thomas most clearly fuses the horizon of his day with the horizon of the text.[52]

II.d) Examination of the use of auctoritates in interpretation

The implications of Thomas' exposition of the literal sense cannot be fully discerned until his sources, opponents and dialogue partners have been investigated. We have considered the broad characteristics of Thomas' use of biblical and non-biblical authorities in some detail, both in this chapter and also in the preceding one. In this step the roles that both play in any given section are examined.

II.d.1) Biblical citations

In the case of biblical citations, some questions should be asked in every section under analysis: does Thomas demonstrate any patterns of citation (i.e., groups of texts similar in message and/or genre, or all coming from a specific biblical work)? Does he cite Scripture to reinforce his interpretation, or to challenge it for the purposes of clarification? And finally, what does the data regarding biblical citations tell us about the passage being investigated? These questions (along with others) can be more readily answered on the basis of the chart of biblical citations composed in **I.c.1**, which serves as a helpful indicator of Thomas' tendencies in citation in the work under analysis. The analyst should also keep in mind the uses of Scripture displayed by Thomas in earlier sections in order to detect major patterns as well as minor ones.

II.d.2) Non-biblical citations

In the case of extra-biblical authorities in specific sections, certain questions arise: Does Thomas use the authority in question positively, negatively, or as one of a number of different possible interpretations? How important is the citation to the interpretation he is making? Does it lead Thomas to misunderstand the text, or does it situate him for developing an authentic understanding? What *kind* of authorities does he use the most in any particular section, and why? For instance, Swierzawski notes that in commenting on Hebrews Thomas quotes Ambrose, but not as an absolute source; in fact Thomas seems to define glory in mildly stated opposition to

---

[52] BLACK, 697.

Ambrose's definition.[53] Obviously this affects his interpretation of the literal sense in a different way than if he had proposed Ambrose's definition unquestioningly.

Once again, it should be obvious that everything involved in the first two parts of the Genre-Identification Approach revolves around the literal sense with the aim of developing the fullest possible understanding of it. In the last step we come to the place where the analyst examines the ramifications of his/her findings for the present-day.

III. Overall Evaluation - Thomas' Work and its Potential Contribution

III.a) Similarities to and differences from Thomas' other works

Of crucial importance to evaluating one of Thomas' commentaries as a specific theological model is to consider ways that it is different from and particularly exceeds the limits of other works, especially the synthetic works but others as well. How does the approach differ from Thomas' other works? How is it similar? One important criteria to evaluate is the appearance of new elements that are not addressed elsewhere. Seeing these differences in the light of the biblical text provides the analyst with an excellent perspective with which to demonstrate the unique value of the work under analysis. Here we take Thomas' own claim seriously; if biblical study is reserved for those most proficient in theology,[54] then surely in his biblical commentaries we find works of great value which merely await the proper treatment for their genius to be revealed.

III.b) The lectura/expositio/postilla as a theological model of its pre-designated theme

This is perhaps the most crucial step of **Part III**, as it is the most comprehensive, drawing the whole analysis into a final summary that uses the value of hindsight to the advantage of underscoring the most crucial elements of the theological model created by Thomas in his exegesis of the biblical text. We have relied significantly on Yaffe's consideration of the *Expositio super Iob*, and now turn to him again. At the level of overall evaluation for the sake of making Thomas' thought and theological model accessible to the modern reader, he once again demonstrates his profound grasp of Thomas' thought, and is therefore an excellent example for the analyst to imitate. He challenges the present-day reader to approach the *expositio* as a protreptic

---

[53] SWIERZAWSKI, "God and the Mystery of His Wisdom," 483. Cf. *In Hebr.*, 1.2.

[54] *ST*, Prol.

work - it is an exhortation to philosophy and not necessarily a cut-and-dried theodicy that solves all problems and is not open to new insights. In fact, Yaffe notes that the work poses a challenge to modern philological scholarship in this regard, which tends to focus on the *minutiae* of Job rather than on how it engages its readers.[55]

Yet this is not his final word on what the *expositio* offers the modern reader. Thomas' work provides a fitting lesson for the Christian reader who, albeit at a much later time than Job, may tend to measure his/her own religious merit in terms of his/her intellectual competence in academic debates.[56] Thomas interprets Job's stunned repentance (39:34-35) as a turning away from superficiality to a deeper estimation of God;[57] and he concludes, "no man can contend with God in wisdom and in power."[58] As Yaffe concludes regarding the *expositio*:

> The reader is offered the edifying insight that Christian wisdom is more than an academically satisfying argument. It is also humility, prudence and charity. By stooping to lift his coreligionists who falter along the way of truth, by enlarging the vision of those whose purview is limited to the academic cloister, and by inspiring others with his own divinely inspired genius, Thomas becomes an example of one who is, in the spiritual if not the literal sense, feet to the lame, eyes to the blind, and a patron to those of us who would be much poorer in spirit without him[59]

This brings the reader back to the main theme; in expounding on what divinity entails (incomprehensibility), Thomas demonstrates not only that divine providence governs natural things, but also how we should perceive this governance and so respond to it. In this way Thomas' protreptic approach takes the message of Job a step further, adding a direct exhortation to respond in humility to the sufferings of Job and one's own sufferings as well.

As in all good things, the only criticism of Yaffe's efforts to give the modern reader access to the *expositio* and also to show its applicability today is that it is too brief. This is the case because of Yaffe's purpose - he is trying

---

[55] YAFFE, 7-8.
[56] Ibid., 65.
[57] Ibid., 63.
[58] *In Iob*, 40.
[59] YAFFE, 65.

to introduce the work and not perform a full-scale analysis of it. Yet even in its brevity he manages to capture the heart of Thomas' interpretation and also to connect the modern reader to it. Thomas is not forced into the service of modern exegesis, but modern exegesis is kept in mind as providing at least a wide boundary to delimit the allowable space which Thomas can legitimately wander through in his own interpretation. This is basically what the analyst using this approach should labor to do as well.

III.c) Miscellaneous data

In this final step, findings of the most potential value to the general and comparative analysis of Thomas' biblical commentaries are examined. General patterns in Thomas' exegetical practice are stated for the purpose of serving other analysts in a collective/collaborative approach to Thomas' exegetical corpus. These are not to be considered as unquestionable governing principles but as limited observations, careful steps in a direction that will further deepen our knowledge of Thomas' exegetical practice in a way that only direct study can.

Now that the model of approach has been laid out in detail, such an analysis can be fruitfully undertaken. This initial part of the present study has situated us well for approaching the *Lectura super Epistolam ad Ephesios* and the ecclesiological themes it contains. We are capable of seeing it both as a rich source of theological themes and a work of biblical commentary, employing a method that marries these oft-separated aspects by basing its inquiry on the fact that for Thomas the former and the latter are truly identical. If its application is successful, a deeper appreciation of these two distinct aspects will emerge together. In fact, the success of this approach will completely depend on maintaining this unity between exegesis and theology which is an extremely valuable exegetical trademark of St. Thomas Aquinas.

PART II

"BUILT INTO A HOLY TEMPLE":
THE CHURCH IN
THE *LECTURA SUPER EPISTOLAM AD EPHESIOS*

CHAPTER IV.

A PRE-ANALYSIS OF THE
LECTURA SUPER EPISTOLAM AD EPHESIOS

A) *Textual Pre-Analysis of the Lectura super epistolam ad Ephesios*[1]

When we approach Thomas' *lectura* on Ephesians, we encounter a text which has a provenance that becomes less and less defined the more closely the analyst examines it; considered as a part of a larger group of commentaries on the Pauline corpus, we have a good idea of the general time span within which it was composed; considered as an individual work, it is shrouded in mystery.

Mandonnet's explanation of the genesis of the Pauline commentaries is an excellent place to begin a treatment of the subject, as his basic position has been held by many scholars for many years. He maintains that Thomas gave lectures on the Pauline corpus twice, once at Orvieto (1259-1265), and once at Naples (1271-1273). The first course was taken down by a secretary, and the second course (an abortive venture including only Romans and 1 Cor 1-10) was written by Thomas himself, probably using the notes from the first course as the basis for this *expositio*.[2] Mandonnet's position is held, with very few modifications, by Bouillard,[3] Glorieux,[4] Lamb,[5] and many others.

---

[1] This section corresponds to **I.a** of our approach.

[2] P. MANDONNET, "Chronologie des écrits scripturaire de s. Thomas d'Aquin," *Revue Thomiste* 33 (1928) : 222-225. Mandonnet bases his theory on a combination of factors: the witness of the catalogues, all of which distinguish between the two parts of the *Super epist.* (Rom 1:1 - 1 Cor 10; 1Cor 11 - Heb 13:25) [227-228]; and an internal critique in which he analyzes the evolution of Thomas' doctrine of the sin of drunkenness. He is led by these to assert that not only is the *reportatio* of Reginald older than the part which Thomas wrote himself, but that the two are separated by many years [229-235].

[3] Henri BOUILLARD, *Conversion et grâce chez saint Thomas d'Aquin* (Paris: Aubier, 1944), 225-241.

[4] P. GLORIEUX, "Essai sur les commentaires scripturaires de saint Thomas et leur chronologie," 254-258.

[5] LAMB, 22-23.

As our focus is on the first and largest section of commentary, it is necessary to consider Torrell's critique of Mandonnet's thesis. In noting that the *Expositio super Iob* was composed in Orvieto (1261-1265),[6] and also in noting that scholarly consensus has abandoned Mandonnet's idea that Thomas taught simultaneously on two biblical books at once (one from the OT and one from the NT), he concludes that it was virtually impossible for Thomas to have commented on Job and Paul simultaneously. He would therefore assign the first course on St. Paul to Thomas' sojourn in Rome (1265-1268), although he recognizes that this is far from certain.[7] We concur with Torrell, if only by default; none of the other possibilities proposed fit the normal pattern of Thomas' pedagogical activity. This probably places the *lectura* on Ephesians in the middle of Thomas' Roman sojourn, circa 1266-1267; but as Torrell notes himself, "until future labors on the critical edition are completed, it is impossible to verify the validity of these views more fully."[8]

It is important to ask what this time period involved for Thomas, as this will help put the work into its proper context as part of Thomas' overall activity. We will rely on Torrell's chronology[9] here as well; in his schema, the original non-extant course on Romans would have been the fifth biblical commentary Thomas executed, and the first on a NT text (granted that Thomas lectured on the Pauline corpus in their present order, for which we have clear evidence[10]). The *lectura* on Ephesians would have been his fifth in the overall course and the ninth of all of his biblical commentaries.

---

[6] TORRELL, *Saint Thomas,* 120.

[7] Ibid., 250-255. P. SYNAVE, "Les Commentaires scripturaires de saint Thomas d'Aquin," 464, gives the same date as a possibility, but offers no reason for it. See M.D. JORDAN, "Thomas Aquinas," in *Dictionary of Biblical Interpretation: K-Z,* ed. John H. Hayes (Nashville: Abingdon Press, 1999), 574; FROEHLICH, 87, for two recent proponents of Torrell's dating.

[8] Ibid., 252.

[9] Ibid., 327-329.

[10] For instance, in the *In Ephesios,* Thomas discusses the "ranks of angels" (*ordines Angelorum*); he gives both the classification of Gregory the Great and the classification of Dionysius, noting their difference. Since Dionysius' approach is in accord with the text, he chooses to follow it, "reserving Gregory's classification until we lecture on the Letter to the Colossians" (*reservata ordinatione Gregorii, usquequo legamus epistolam ad Colossenses*) [*In Eph.* 1.7.61]. Since Ephesians precedes Colossians, it is a good possibility that Thomas follows the canonical order still in use today. This possibility is augmented by the fact that the Paris Vulgate followed the canonical order of Stephen Langton [LOEWE, 147], which has Ephesians before Colossians, and the evidence of Thomas' own ordering of the epistles in his Prologue, which does the same [*Super epist.,* Prol. 11].

This course on St. Paul would have taken place in a setting that was rare in Thomas' life up until that time and after - one almost entirely devoid of an established learning center. Torrell concurs with Boyle's thesis that this was an experimental *studium*, a *studium personale*, so that Thomas could initiate a program of study of his own design.[11] Torrell's explanation is worth quoting in full:

> Parallel to his commentaries on Scripture, he had the task of forming the friars in moral theology and in the pastoral work of confession, which went along with the mission of preaching that had been entrusted to his order. For this, he had at his disposal the manuals published by the first generations of Dominicans; but that predominance of practical theology in the formation of friars, as we have said, gave them only a partial and narrow view of theology; this resulted in a marked imbalance, to the detriment of dogmatic theology, which could not help but leave Thomas dissatisfied. We must therefore read what he was about to do in Rome as an attempt to put the formation of the friars on a broader basis.[12]

"What he was about to do" was to begin the composition of the *Summa Theologiae*; he would complete the *Prima Pars* before he would leave Rome for his second regency in Paris.

Yet this was not the only work which was contemporaneous with the *Super Epistolas Pauli Apostoli*. During his Roman sojourn he would also complete the *Catena Aurea*, compose the *Sententia libri De Anima* (the first of his commentaries on Aristotle), the *De regno ad regem Cypri*,[13] and the *De Potentia*; he would also begin the *Compendium Theologiae*, a work he would never finish.[14] All of this Thomas labored to complete in this three-year period, yet the only evidence of any original teaching activity during this time is his commentary on the Pauline Epistles.

---

[11] TORRELL, *Saint Thomas*, 143-144. Cf. L. E. BOYLE, *The Setting of the Summa Theologiae of Saint Thomas*, Etienne Gilson Series 5 (Toronto: 1982), 15ff.

[12] Ibid., 144.

[13] It seems to this scholar that great benefit might come from comparing the *De Regno* to the commentary on Philemon; both pertain to the duties of temporal authorities, and so may contain similarities and/or differences which will help confirm/disprove Torrell's thesis regarding the first course on Paul.

[14] TORRELL, 160-178.

In terms of learned company, Thomas commented on the Pauline corpus with no companionship but that of his students; Torrell does not see "any assistant or any lector alongside Thomas."[15] This is significant, for it certainly dictates that any significant dialogue concerning the Pauline corpus (including Ephesians) with other *magistri* could not have taken place during his course; Thomas was left alone to comment on the text. Thus what we have in the *reportationes* on Paul (excepting, of course, Romans and 1 Cor 1-10) is work which Thomas performed in relative isolation.

And what of the text itself? The integrity of the *lectura* on Ephesians must be considered on two levels. First, the integrity of the text as we now have it must be considered - are the Latin editions available to us reliable? After this, another question arises, one which is even more fundamental. This commentary, unlike the commentary on Job or on Romans, was not composed by Thomas directly, but consists of the notes of a secretary/student.[16] Can such a text be considered a reliable source for Thomas' thought?

As to the first question, the *lectura* on Ephesians offers a unique situation. Although the Leonine Commission has yet to produce an authoritative critical Latin edition, there are a number of published Latin editions which are more or less reliable. The most recent is the Marietti edition (1953), which is a revision by Raphael Cai of the *Editio Piana* of 1570. As this is the most recent (the second most recent being the Parma edition of 1862), it has the benefit of dealing with the text in the light of the many older editions as well as the MSS. We take the Marietti edition as the basic source for the Latin text, keeping in mind that this is by no means an infallible one;[17] almost fifty years have passed since its publication, and it is the work of a single scholar, lacking the objectivity and wealth of expertise that a group approach brings to such an endeavor (which is the great strength of the Leonine Commission).

So in Cai's work we do have a basically reliable edition, but not one that stands alone. This would pose a difficult obstacle to the present study were it not for the work of Matthew Lamb, who in 1966 published the first and only English translation of the *In Ephesios*. He combines a reading of the Parma (itself a simple reprint of the Piana), the Marietti and, to a lesser degree, other even earlier editions. In cases of variation between the editions, Lamb either chooses between them by reference to context or notes that such

---

[15] Ibid., 144.

[16] WEISHEIPL, *Friar Thomas*, 248.

[17] Ibid., 247, refers to all of the editions of the Pauline commentaries as "badly corrupted".

a choice is not possible. Through this process he detects and removes additions to the text, all of which were made by Remigius Nannini in his 1562 edition. In short, what Lamb offers us in his translation is an English version in many ways more critically astute than the Latin editions currently available. With this in mind, our approach will be a combined reading of the Marietti edition in the light of Lamb's translation; his helpful notes will signal to us when careful inquiry into the integrity of the former is required.

With this said, it must also be noted that Lamb's translation itself can be problematic at times – as he notes, it is not "word-for-word,"[18] and so there are occasions where his translation of words and even phrases lacks precision and loses the original sense of the text. While the aim of the present study is not to hone Lamb's translation, it will be necessary to make some corrections of it, which will be identified as such through the use of brackets within the citations from his work and corresponding remarks in the notes. In this way at least, those inaccuracies which most affect the present study will be addressed.[19]

To this combination will be added a third source; the CD-ROM version of the complete works of Aquinas compiled and edited by Roberto Busa. Although not created for cover-to-cover reading, Busa's work is helpful for its excellent search capacities, which allows the enumeration of words, phrases and citations in any combination of Thomas' works (individually or in groups).[20] The only difficulty with this otherwise wonderful tool is that it does not contain a critical edition itself (since none exists), but an electronic version of the Marietti edition. Because of this its use will need to be supplemented in those cases where the search involves dubious passages detected by Lamb, whose opinion will serve as the final word in areas of doubt in this regard.

This threefold combination of texts will serve to give us the best reading possible to date, with deference to the Leonine Commission which at this time has only produced a critical edition of the Romans *expositio* from the collection of Pauline commentaries (which is not very helpful, as it is not from the same composition as the rest, as has already been noted).

---

[18] LAMB, 35.

[19] LAMB also uses brackets to mitigate "the laconic abruptness of Reginald's transcription… in order to form a complete sentence or clarify a hazy reference" [Ibid., 35]. These will be distinguishable from my own corrections in that the former will remain unremarked.

[20] We have already utilized Busa's electronic index in Chapter III to enumerate the number of biblical citations contained in the lectures on John 6.

What about the basic nature of the text? Does the fact that this work is a *reportatio* and not Thomas' own direct composition decrease its reliability as a source for Thomas' thought? One point cannot be contested; it does not have the same high level of reliability as a work for which Thomas provides us with an autograph manuscript. But were this the criterion for reliability, many if not most of Thomas' works would have to be set aside; in order to cope with his prodigious output, an entire team of secretaries was at his disposal from the first Parisian regency through the end of his life, during which time he produced as much as 12.48 pages on average per day during certain periods. Some of these works can be traced to particular secretaries (as in the case of the *lectura* on Matthew, which is clearly the work of Léger of Besancon).[21] One such secretary was continually at Thomas' side, and it is to him that we owe the *lectura* on Ephesians, the rest of the Pauline commentaries (excepting Romans and perhaps 1 Cor 1-10), as well as the largest part of the dictated works of Thomas Aquinas. This individual was Thomas' fellow Dominican and *socius*, Reginald of Piperno. Of this fact there is no doubt; all of the catalogues attribute it to his hand.[22]

So it is fair to say that the *lectura* on Ephesians, being itself a *reportatio* of Reginald, is as reliable as the many other works for which this secretary was responsible. This may be why no one has ever questioned its basic integrity. It exhibits all of the exegetical characteristics which mark Thomas' work, combined with the abrupt style of a work which is a collection of notes;[23] this latter characteristic, involving the omission of obvious words (such as "*quaestio*") and short, awkward abbreviations of scriptural citations poses no real challenge to the analyst.

B) *The Epistle to the Ephesians and Thomas' Exegetical Framework*

Of first priority is the matter of Thomas' text of Ephesians, a Latin translation which formed part of the Paris Vulgate edition of the Bible that Thomas had at his disposal. In the words of Raphael Loewe, this text was "a heavily interpolated and corrupt representation of the Vulgate" of Alcuin, which suffered from its frequent pairing with the *Glossa ordinaria* and its subsequent harmonization with it.[24] It was not a uniform text, coming under the editorial control (or lack thereof) of the various *scriptoria* which produced

---

[21] TORRELL, *St. Thomas*, 241.

[22] WEISHEIPL, *Friar Thomas*, 248.

[23] LAMB, 31.

[24] LOEWE, 146-147.

its many versions. Only in the areas of canonical order and chapter divisions (the latter probably inherited from Stephen Langton) did these many editions of the Paris text possess any uniformity[25]; and as we shall see, Thomas not only includes these chapter divisions but also gives them theological significance.

Thomas also had at his disposal the *Correctoria* which had been produced by members of his order for the sake of supplementing this badly corrupted text, but these often were corrupt themselves.[26] In summary, the text which Thomas commented on is by no means a wholly reliable one. Care must be taken in any analysis, including our own, to consider how such corruptions have the potential to derail Thomas' exegesis because of their misguiding influence. Perhaps we can take consolation from Markus Barth, who points out that the problems of the text have not been solved even through modern critical analysis. In his words: "In sum, the genuine text of Ephesians is as little available as is the authentic meaning of its words, sentences and paragraphs."[27]

Regarding the modern, critical resources available to us in our analysis, the Epistle under comment in Thomas' *lectura* is the subject of a very rich and outstanding modern exegetical tradition. A number of monographical treatments of the various aspects of Ephesians are listed in the bibliography. These will be referred to occasionally as their relevance to the various aspects of the Epistle permits; they are only circumstantial resources, and so demand no particular treatment here. However, three works do need to be considered directly, as they will serve as important guides to the whole of Ephesians, leading us through the text along with Thomas, and offering a vantage point from which we will be able to evaluate Thomas' exegesis.

The first of these is the commentary by Markus Barth,[28] whose work has not been rivaled by any commentator since its publication for its extensive treatment of the Epistle. Barth wonderfully summarizes all of the work that has gone on before him and offers the best of it to his reader. He also offers insights and judgments which have deservedly lent a whole new direction to inquiry into this text. Although Ephesians has not lacked great commentators

---

[25] Ibid., 147.

[26] Ibid., 22.

[27] Markus BARTH, *Ephesians*, vol. I-II, Anchor Bible Series 34-34A (Garden City, NY: Doubleday, 1974) : 53.

[28] Ibid.

in our century (Schlier, Abbot, Robinson, et al.), the great advantage of Barth is his masterful handling of these and other authors whose opinions can often be diverse and contradictory; though original, his work is also a compendium of many other points of view. In this way it is a good index of scholarly consensus (or lack thereof) regarding Ephesians.

But perhaps the greatest service Barth renders to the present task is his all-too-rare attempt to dialogue not only with the critical, but also with the pre-critical exegetical history of this Epistle. His bibliographical section entitled "I. Commentaries and Special Studies"[29] is a comprehensive list of the major extant patristic, medieval and Reformation commentaries on Ephesians, including authors as diverse as Theophylact, Pelagius, John Calvin and most significantly, Thomas Aquinas, who is cited here more often than any other patristic and medieval commentator (in fact more than any other pre-Enlightenment commentator besides Calvin). Barth offers Thomas' opinions on various aspects of the Epistle and considers how Thomas' point of view compares to his own as well as to those of other ancient and modern sources. To those skeptical of this approach he offers these words, which also serve to justify his own doctrinal maneuvers and reflections: "Since Ephesians is a theological document it must be explained in theological terms - or else the exposition would not be literal."[30] Rather than disallow or ignore the ramifications of the Epistle for dogma and for the life of the modern reader, Barth recognizes that theologizing on the basis of the text is a necessary step in exegesis, and so affords a place for the voices of those who see exegesis as a primarily theological enterprise, most notably Thomas Aquinas.

Although Barth is certainly our primary source for understanding Ephesians in the present study, it would be unwise to read the text with only his assistance. Two other works will be used to supplement Barth's guidance. The first, A.T. Lincoln's "masterful" and "very thorough"[31] contribution to the Word Biblical Commentary Series,[32] has the benefit of being both recent and extremely well-documented, but also comparatively brief (unlike Barth's two volume commentary). In this case it is helpful because of the effort Lincoln makes to maintain a focus on what is most significant in each verse/passage/chapter, allowing for referencing that is both quick and thorough.

---

[29] Ibid., 831-823.

[30] Ibid., 60.

[31] William W. KLEIN, *The Book of Ephesians : An Annotated Bibliography*, Vol. 8, Books of the Bible Series (NY, London : Garland, 1998), 32.

[32] A.T. LINCOLN, *Ephesians*, Word Bible Commentary (Dallas : Word, 1990).

The second (by E. Best) has the benefit of being the most recent critical commentary on Ephesians, and so can offer to us the latest products of research.[33] The combined reading of these two works along with Barth's and the support of excellent monographs will give a clear and reliable standard for judging the basic exegetical precision/imprecision which Thomas displays in his interpretation of Ephesians.

A primary and indispensable service which modern exegesis of Ephesians can offer to the present study is to demonstrate the genre of the Epistle and its defining characteristics as a text (corresponding to **I.a.3a** and **I.a.3b** of the approach proposed in Chapter III). Although Barth focuses on specific questions of style and linguistics which are much too advanced for applicability to how Thomas would have read the text,[34] Lincoln focuses on the more general questions of textual character which are easily detected by any intelligent reader. Along with Barth[35] and the overwhelming majority of commentators (including Best[36]), he distinguishes two parts to the Epistle; chaps. 1-3 and chaps. 4-6, "with the 'Amen' at the end of chap. 3 and the change to direct exhortation at the beginning of chap. 4 as clear division markers."[37] This is significant for understanding the style of Ephesians as it would have been read by Thomas, because each part is characterized by a different style; although both parts are overwhelmingly non-narrative, each falls into a definite place in the categories of genre which we encountered in the Prologue to the *Postilla super Psalmos*. The first part is characterized by the preeminence of a non-narrative genre which Thomas calls "disputative;" that is, theological/doctrinal exposition makes up the large part of these first chapters.[38] The second part is concerned with paraenesis; ethical considerations and exhortations predominate.[39] As has been noted, these are literary waters which Thomas is skilled in navigating; we can assert that at the very

---

[33] Ernest BEST, *Ephesians*, The International Critical Commentary, ed. J.A Emerton, C.E.B. Cranfield and G.N. Stanton (Edinburgh: T&T Clark, 1998). Like Barth, Best also dialogues with ancient commentators, including Thomas.

[34] BARTH, 4-6.

[35] Ibid., 53.

[36] BEST, 353-355.

[37] LINCOLN, xxxvi.

[38] Ibid., xxxvi, though he would warn us that there is more to this part than merely doctrine.

[39] Ibid., xxxvii.

least this Epistle fits Thomas' preconceived notion of biblical revelation
already considered.

In terms of the Letter's basic purposes, Lincoln offers a very succinct
enumeration of five (although he gives no indication that this list is an
exhaustive one): to give its readers "inner strength, further knowledge of their
salvation, greater appreciation of their identity as believers and as members of
the Church, increased concern for the Church's unity, and more consistent
living in such areas as speech, sexuality and household relationships."[40] This
enumeration of themes is very similar to Thomas'; although he gives only one
theme directly, "the origination of ecclesial unity,"[41] he hints at other
characteristics of the text in his prologue to the *lectura*.

In order to fully comprehend Thomas' designation of this main theme
and his entire exegetical framework (corresponding to **I.b.1-I.b.4** of our
approach), it is helpful to recall the general prologue to the *Super epistolas*;
this is where Thomas gives us his overall schema for the Pauline corpus:

> The Apostle wrote fourteen Epistles: nine of them instruct
> the Church of the Gentiles; four the prelates and princes of the
> Church, as well as kings; the last is addressed to the Hebrews, the
> sons of Israel... The teaching bears entirely on Christ's grace,
> which we can consider under a triple modality.
>
> In the first place, according to its existence in the Head
> himself, Christ, and it is thus that we find it in the Epistle to the
> Hebrews; then, as it is in the principal members of the mystical
> body, and it is thus that we find it in the Epistles addressed to the
> prelates; thirdly according as it is in the mystical body itself, which
> is the Church, and it is thus that we find it in the Epistles addressed
> to the Gentiles.
>
> There is another distinction, for Christ's grace is
> susceptible of a triple consideration. First, in itself, as in the Epistle
> to the Romans. Second, in the sacraments of grace, as in the two
> Epistles to the Corinthians - of which the first treats of the

---

[40] Ibid., lxxxi.

[41] Church unity is posited as an important theme by both of our commentators (BARTH, 55-
56; LINCOLN, xciv) as well as many others: cf. H. CHADWICK, "Die Absicht des
Epheserbriefes," *Zeitschrift für die neutestamentliche Wissenschaft und die Kunde der älteren
Kirche* 51 (1960) : 145-154; P. POKORNY, *Der Epheserbrief und die Gnosis* (Berlin:
Evangelische Verlagsanstalt, 1965), 17-21; E. KÄSEMANN, "Ephesians and Acts" in *Studies in
Luke-Acts*, ed. L.E Keck and J.E. Martyn (London: S.P.C.K., 1968), 291; L.E. KECK and V.P.
FURNISH, *The Pauline Letters* (Atlanta: John Knox, 1975), 127; A.G. PATZIA, *Colossians,
Philemon, Ephesians* (New York: Harper & Row, 1984), 113-118.

sacraments themselves and the second of the dignity of their ministers - and in the Epistle to the Galatians, in which are found excluded superfluous sacraments against those who wish to add the ancient sacraments to new ones. [Third], Christ's grace is considered according to the work of unity that it realizes within the Church.

The Apostle therefore treats first of the origination of ecclesial unity in the Epistle to the Ephesians; then its confirmation and progress in the Epistle to the Philippians; then its defense; against errors in the Epistle to the Colossians; against the present persecutions in I Thessalonians; against future persecutions and, above all, persecutions in the time of the Antichrist in II Thessalonians.

As to Church prelates, it instructs equally the spiritual as well as the temporal. For the spiritual, he speaks of the origination, of the construction, and of the government of ecclesial unity in I Timothy; of firmness against persecutors in II Timothy; of the defense against heretics in the Epistle to Titus. As to temporal lords, he instructs them in the Epistle to Philemon.[42]

---

[42] "*Scripsit enim quatuordecim epistolas quarum novem instruunt Ecclesiam Gentium; quatuor praelatos et principes Ecclesiae, id est reges; una populum Isräel, scilicet quae est ad Hebraeos. Est enim haec doctrina tota de gratia Christi, quae quidem potest tripliciter considerari. Uno modo secundum quod est in ipso capite, scilicet Christo, et sic commendatur in epistola ad Hebraeos. Alio modo secundum quod est in membris principalibus corporis mystici, et sic commendatur in epistolis quae sunt ad praelatos. Tertio modo secundum quod in ipso corpore mystico, quod est Ecclesia, et sic commendatur in epistolis quae mittuntur ad Gentiles, quarum haec est distinctio: nam ipsa gratia Christi tripliciter potest considerari. Uno modo secundum se, et sic commendatur in epistola ad Romanos; - alio modo secundum quod est in sacramentis gratiae et sic commendatur in duabus epistolis ad Corinthios, in quarum prima agitur de ipsis sacramentis, in secunda de dignitate ministrorum, et in epistola ad Galatas in qua excluduntur superflua sacramenta contra illos qui volebant vetera sacramenta novis adiungere; - tertio consideratur gratia Christi secundum effectum unitatis quem in Ecclesia fecit. Agit ergo Apostolus, primo quidem, de institutione ecclesiasticae unitatis in epistola ad Ephesios; secundo, de eius confirmatione et profectu in epistola ad Philippenses; tertio de eius defensione, contra errores quidem, in epistola ad Colossenses, contra persecutiones vero praesentes, in I Thessalonicenses, contra futuras vero et praecipue tempore Antichristi, in secunda. Praelatos vero ecclesiarum instruit et sprituales et temporales. Spirituales quidem de institutione, instructione et gubernatione ecclesiasticae unitatis in prima ad Timotheum, de firmitate contra persecutores in secunda, tertio de defensione contra haereticos in epistola ad Titum. Dominos vero temporales instruit in epistola ad Philomonem*" [*Super Epist.*, Prol., 11]. The English translation above is taken from TORRELL, *St. Thomas*, 255-256, who translates *tertio* as "finally". I have changed it to "third."

In the opinion of Cuéllar, this part of the general prologue is replete with ecclesiological implications. He focuses on the first categorization that Thomas offers, where the fourteen Epistles are categorized according to the existence of grace in Christ the Head, in the prelates and finally in the larger Church. As he notes, this first image of the Pauline corpus is one in which the Church as mystical body predominates, with each member being given a specific place within it.[43] In his opinion, "the proposed schema of St. Thomas is clear. All the letters of St. Paul have an ecclesiological orientation with a base christology."[44] He notes that among these fourteen texts Thomas sees the preeminently ecclesiological Epistle to be Ephesians, although all the Epistles which follow it also carry its theme, which is "Church unity as the effect of grace."[45]

While we basically agree with this characterization, is there more that can be detected about this theme of Ephesians? Our first clue (one which Cuéllar also recognizes) is that Thomas does not locate Church unity as a static subject or a mere object to be described by Paul, but rather refers to the *institution* (or origination) of ecclesial unity as the theme of Ephesians.[46] Although this designation of an activity rather than a static reality characterizes his description of the themes of many other Epistles in the Pauline corpus, not all of them are characterized this way - Hebrews, Romans, 1-2 Corinthians and Galatians have formal nouns for their subjects rather than activities. Why the "origination of ecclesial unity" rather than ecclesial unity itself? The prologue to the *lectura* on Ephesians gives us no indication; in fact it does not even restate the major theme that Thomas detects in the Epistle. But we do have an indication in the body of the commentary itself; at the beginning of Chapter 4, Thomas notes that a shift is occurring in the Letter (one also detected by modern exegetes, as we have seen above): "The Apostle recalled above the divine blessings through which the Church's unity has originated and been preserved (Ch. 1-3). Now he admonishes the Ephesians

---

[43] CUÉLLAR, 21-23.

[44] Ibid., 23.

[45] Ibid., 31.

[46] Significant for understanding this point is Thomas' mention of "divine blessings" through which unity originates and is preserved. As he states in his general prologue to the *Super epistolas*, the teaching of the Pauline corpus is on the grace of Christ; this is borne out by another passage in the general prologue, where Thomas characterizes Ephesians, Philippians, Colossians, I-II Thessalonians, I-II Timothy, Titus and Philemon as the "place" where Christ's grace is considered according to the work of unity that it realizes within the Church.

to remain within this ecclesial unity."[47]   This comment demands closer inspection, as it is the one of the only ones within the *lectura* that attempts to characterize the entire Epistle.

In order to catch the full implications of this division, it is necessary to recycle a common criticism of Thomas' exegesis, one which we confronted in the work of Pesch in Part I. The anachronistic systematizing of the Pauline corpus that Pesch so easily dismisses can actually help us to understand how Thomas deals with the various Epistles, if we but remember the *ordo disciplinae* approach that characterizes Thomas' theological method.   As Chenu describes Thomas' work (and that of his contemporaries): "In the process of becoming a science - even if only in a relative sense - theology strove to organize its object and objects, and hence to build them up from broad architechtonic principles [such as the concept of grace] borrowed from the rational structures of mind working under the light of faith."[48]   This explains the movement from broad concepts to more specific ones; Thomas demonstrates his allegiance to this method perhaps unconsciously when he omits Hebrews from the last categorization in the general prologue; as it is about Christ, who must serve as a controlling principle because of his centrality to theology, it should not come last, and so is bracketed.[49]   The rest of the Pauline corpus has enough fluidity to avoid being likewise omitted or rearranged, although the *ordo disciplinae* method forces Thomas to reduce each work to a single theme (with the possible exception of 1 Timothy).

Therefore the *de institutione ecclesiasticae unitatis* theme Thomas detects in Ephesians sets it at the head of a group of related and/or more specific topics in the Epistles that follow it (minus Hebrews). As it is the only one that is described as treating the origination of ecclesial unity *qua* the origination of ecclesial unity, it is a bridge Epistle for Thomas. It is related to the core concept ("grace in itself" via Romans) in its primary part (chaps. 1-3), and it also prepares for the diverse Epistles to come in its second part (chaps. 4-6). Therefore in Thomas' schema the "Amen" in 3:21b (not to mention the praise and thanksgiving directly preceding it in 3:20-21a) is not only a division marker for the first part of Ephesians, but for the entire first part of the Pauline corpus. Likewise, 4:1 ff (especially 4:3 a direct statement

---

[47] "*Supra commemoravit Apostolus divina beneficia per quae unitas ecclesiae constituitur et conservatur, hic monet eos Apostolus ad permanendum in ecclesiae unitate*" [*In Eph.*, 4.1.187].

[48] CHENU, *Towards Understanding*, 299.

[49] Notice that in the first distinction Hebrews is dealt with first.

of the general admonishment that Thomas sees all of Eph 4-6 to be) is the launching point of all the latter Epistles.

This is borne out in the change from static to dynamic concepts noted above; we have grace, sacraments of grace and the ancient sacraments on the one hand, then a series of active concepts following. On closer inspection, these are all paraenetic concepts: confirming, progressing, defending, constructing, governing, standing firm, ruling ethically. The two-part division of Ephesians (and Ephesians itself) is practically a microcosm of Thomas' vision of the Pauline corpus; the general switch from theology to ethics is not only the pattern of Ephesians in Thomas' view, but also of this entire group of texts. This is not an absolute distinction; Thomas would not isolate out the paraenetic elements of the earlier epistles, but seems to subordinate them for the sake of discerning an order of presentation within the *corpus paulinum*.

It would be unwarranted to consider the meaning of Thomas' main theme at this point, as to do so would be to preempt the actual analysis of the *lectura* - the *institutione ecclesiasticae unitatis* is precisely what must be left undeveloped so as to allow Thomas to develop it. However, it is possible to assert an important fact about this theme. Noting that it stands at the hinge of the Pauline corpus reinforces the observation of Cuéllar that Thomas' conception of the entire Pauline corpus is overwhelmingly ecclesiological. The analysis of grace leads to the subject of the formation of the Church, which carries with it a host of other topics, all of which revolve around the themes of grace and its effect, ecclesial unity. The one Epistle (Ephesians) which most comprehensively includes all of the major topics of the corpus (because it is both theological *and* paraenetic as Thomas reads it) has as its theme not grace but grace's ecclesial product, unity. So although we should expect to find many ecclesiological subtopics, we must be primarily attentive to those places in the *In Ephesios* where Thomas makes transitions from his former topic to his new one if we are to detect his larger pattern at work within the commentary.

Thomas' conception of St. Paul as he describes him in both the general prologue and in the prologue to the *lectura* on Ephesians fills out our basic understanding of Thomas' designation of the Epistle.[50] This picture is

---

[50] It should be noted that Thomas, in accord with the entire pre-critical tradition, considers Paul to be the author of the all of the works which comprise the Pauline corpus, including Ephesians. With him, we will refer to the author of Ephesians as Paul. This is not an implicit judgment in favor of Pauline authorship (a point regarding which we are not qualified to make an assertion), but rather a matter of deference to Thomas' viewpoint, the influence of which on his exegesis will be one of the objects of our analysis.

bounded by two points; the two Scriptural *accessus* Thomas uses to describe Paul in his respective prologues, Acts 9:15 and Ps 74:4. In the first case, using a verse which refers to Paul directly ("...this man is a chosen vessel of mine to carry my name before Gentiles, kings and Israelites"), Thomas focuses on the word "vessel" (*vas*). He designates four reasons for which persons are compared to vessels in Scripture: their "constitution, fullness, value and fruitfulness (*constitutionem, repletionem, usum et fructum*). Paul's nature is best symbolized by a vessel of gold adorned with precious stones (Sir 50:10), the gold representing wisdom and charity, the stones representing all the virtues. His writings attest to Paul's high quality as a vessel, because in them "he demonstrated the most excellent divine mysteries" (*docuit enim excellentissimae divinitatis mysteria*).[51] He was a vessel full of the name of Christ, which he held in both knowledge and love;[52] he was also a useful vessel, for he carried the divine name which was distant from humanity because of sin.[53] He fulfilled the office of carrying God's name with excellence,[54] and so was a fruitful vessel clean of sin and error, best typified by his own words in 2 Tim 2:21.

This summary of Thomas' vision of St. Paul demonstrates that it was a multi-faceted one, offering many aspects from which he could choose in order to introduce Paul's authorship of the Epistle to the Ephesians: wisdom, excellence in teaching, virtue, etc. But rather than focus on these in themselves, Thomas chooses to focus on Paul in his particular relationship to the Ephesian church. The Scriptural *accessus* of the Ephesians *lectura*, "I have strengthened its pillars" (Ps 74:4) characterizes what Paul does in connection to the Ephesians, and describes the Epistle as much as it does the Apostle. He uses another Psalm quotation ("By the word of the Lord the heavens were established" - Ps 32:6) to accentuate his point - the word of the Lord "written through Paul" (*per Paulum scripto*) establishes the Ephesians, who are signified by "the heavens" (*caeli*). Here we see that Thomas also locates other aspects or themes in this text; this singular description of Paul's authorship tells us that he sees the Epistle to be a positive endeavor (not a polemical one), a confirmation more than a correction; to use Lincoln's words, he sees Paul building up his readers in "inner strength, further

---

[51] *Super Epist.*, Prol., 1.

[52] Ibid., 2.

[53] Ibid., 4.

[54] Ibid., 8.

knowledge of their salvation, greater appreciation of their identity as believers and as members of the Church."[55]   We can also see Thomas' high regard for the Letter itself reflected by his characterization of Paul; we need only read the other biblical citations he uses to detect his enthusiasm about what he reads in Ephesians: "And thou, being once converted, confirm thy brethren" – Lk 22:32; "Thy words have confirmed them that were staggering" – Job 4:4; "I have found David my servant: with my holy oil I have anointed him. For my hand shall help him: and my arm strengthen him" – Ps 89:21-22; "But thou hast upheld me by reason of my innocence: and hast established me in thy sight forever." – Ps 40:13; "But God is faithful, who will strengthen and keep you from evil" – 2 Thess 3:3; and especially "Command thy strength, O God: confirm, O God, what thou hast wrought in us." – Ps 67:9. These are all quoted in the first article of the prologue; is there any doubt that what we are hearing is a note of anticipation in the voice of a *magister* about to comment on a favorite text?

C) *Thomas' Use of Auctoritates in the In Ephesios*[56]

The electronic search capacities of the CD-ROM edition of Thomas' works developed by Busa made the otherwise arduous task of taking count of Thomas' biblical citations relatively easy. Using the form-search capacity for each biblical text allowed for a specific enumeration of the total citations from them individually, which then allowed the total number of biblical citations to be enumerated through simple addition. The only manual search necessary was for the evaluation of the intra-referencing of Ephesians itself, which cannot be electronically accounted for because of Thomas' habit of dividing the text using brief references to upcoming or preceding passages.

The results are surprising. In the *Lectura super epistolam ad Ephesios*, Thomas cites biblical sources 1,030 times, with 628 citations from the NT and 402 from the OT. The frequency of biblical citation on average is high not only by modern standards but also by Thomas', at least when we consider his systematic works: 21.3 citations per 1,000 words (the *lectura* contains 48,331 words altogether) as compared to 2.2 for the *Scriptum super Libros Sententiarum* or 5.2 for the *Summa Theologia*.[57]   This represents a larger trend; Thomas does quote Scripture much more often in his biblical commentaries than in his other works; in fact 20+ quotations per 1,000 words

---

[55] LINCOLN, lxxxi.

[56] This section corresponds to **I.c** of our approach.

[57] VALKENBERG, 29.

are not uncommon in the former. The tables below list each biblical text cited and the frequency of citation from each work: the first table lists the NT citations and the OT citations separately, the second lists all citations together:

Table I : NT and OT Citations
(separately and according to frequency)

I. NT Citations	**II. OT Citations**	
1) Romans - 97	1) Psalms - 97	26) 4 Kings - 1
2) 1 Corinthians - 83	2) Isaiah - 53	27) 1 Chronicles - 1
3) John - 61	3) Sirach - 44	28) 2 Chronicles - 1
4) Matthew - 43	4) Proverbs - 30	29) Judith - 1
5) Ephesians - 40	5) Job - 26	30) Esther - 1
6) Colossians - 37	6) Wisdom - 24	31) Joel - 1
7) Luke - 36	7) Jeremiah - 19	32) Micah -1
8) Galatians - 32	8) Deuteronomy - 12	33) Habakkuk - 1
9) Acts - 26	9) Ecclesiastes - 12	34) 3 Esdras - 1
10) Hebrews - 25	10) Genesis - 11	
11) 1 Peter - 25	11) Ezechiel - 9	
12) 2 Corinthians - 23	12) Hosea - 9	
13) Philippians - 21	13) Song of Songs - 8	
14) James - 16	14) Zechariah - 7	
15) Revelation - 12	15) Exodus - 5	
16) 1 Timothy - 10	16) Leviticus - 5	
17) 1 John - 9	17) Daniel - 3	
18) 2 Peter - 6	18) Malachi - 3	
19) Mark - 5	19) Numbers - 2	
20) 1 Thessalonians - 5	20) Judges - 2	
21) 2 Thessalonians - 5	21) 1 Kings - 2	
22) 2 Timothy - 5	22) Tobit - 2	
23) Titus - 5	23) Lamentations - 2	
24) Philemon - 2	24) Amos - 2	
25) Jude - 2	25) 3 Kings - 1	

Table II. All Biblical Citations
(according to frequency)

1) Psalms - 97	2) Revelation - 12	47) Amos - 2
2) Romans - 97	25) Genesis - 11	48) Philemon - 2
3) 1 Corinthians - 83	26) 1 Timothy - 10	49) Jude - 2
4) John - 61	27) Ezechiel - 9	50) 3 Kings - 1
5) Isaiah - 53	28) Hosea - 9	51) 4 Kings - 1
6) Sirach - 44	29) 1 John - 9	52) 1 Chronicles - 1
7) Matthew - 43	30) Song of Songs - 8	53) 2 Chronicles - 1
8) Ephesians - 40	31) Zechariah - 7	54) Judith - 1
9) Colossians - 37	32) 2 Peter - 6	55) Esther - 1
10) Luke - 36	33) Exodus - 5	56) Joel - 1
11) Galatians - 32	34) Leviticus - 5	57) Micah - 1
12) Proverbs - 30	35) Mark - 5	58) Habakkuk - 1
13) Job - 26	36) 1 Thessalonians - 5	59) 3 Esdras - 1
14) Acts - 26	37) 2 Thessalonians - 5	
15) Hebrews - 25	38) 2 Timothy - 5	
16) 1 Peter - 25	39) Titus - 5	
17) Wisdom - 24	40) Daniel - 3	
18) 2 Corinthians - 23	41) Malachi - 3	
19) Philippians - 21	42) Numbers - 2	
20) Jeremiah - 19	43) Judges - 2	
21) James - 16	44) 1 Kings - 2	
22) Deuteronomy - 12	45) Tobit - 2	
23) Ecclesiastes - 12	46) Lamentations - 2	

The tables above offer an excellent foundation to make some observations as well as to develop some basic hypotheses. Regarding the NT, the overwhelming majority of citations come from the Pauline corpus (including Hebrews); 387 of the total (62 %). When one adds to that number the other non-narrative NT texts (James, 1 Peter, 2 Peter, 1 John, Jude), excluding the Gospels (even John), Acts and Revelation, the number jumps to 436 (69 %), which is more than all of the OT citations combined. Here Thomas displays his basic pattern, which is to rely on texts which mediate their messages conceptually and directly in order to develop an understanding of the text under comment. As could be expected due to their narrative character, the gospels are not nearly as prominent, making up only 14% of the total citations.

Of these NT texts, two stand out: Romans and 1 Corinthians, which comprise 29 % of all NT citations. Perhaps the significance of this can be deduced from their standing in the Pauline corpus as Thomas schematizes it. First, Romans is the theme Epistle; it discusses grace in itself, whereas the rest consider grace in relation to some more specific topic. This unfolding of the Pauline corpus would naturally lead Thomas to link the other Epistles to Romans, to illuminate them with what had been expounded there and to draw them into a scientific union with it. 1 Corinthians shares many of the characteristics of Romans as Thomas reads it; it has a static topic (grace in the sacraments), which is a key sign in this format that it is a point of departure, an essential part of an intellectual root system for the Epistles which follow it (this would also explain why Galatians and 2 Corinthians rank highly in the list of NT citations). Given the aforementioned two-part structure which Thomas assigns to Ephesians, one would expect that these four, as well as other highly theological non-narrative sources, would predominate in the properly theological and expository part of the Epistle (chaps. 1-3), although would not necessarily be limited to it. It is not as clear what place the gospels might play; this is an area of Thomas' exegetical practice that can be enlightened by a more direct consideration of the *lectura*.

In the OT citations, we see the predominance of the Psalms in Thomas' citations (ranking first with Romans); Isaiah also emerges as a favored text, as do the wisdom books (13%). The prophetic literature makes up 8% of the citations in the former text; similarly, they make up 11% of the citations here.

Thomas' use of the OT to exegete the NT is an almost entirely unexamined subject; as such we have no basis to draw out detailed hypotheses on the basis of prior research. It will certainly be an important task in the upcoming analysis to observe Thomas' reliance on the Psalms in citation, as their frequent use is obviously a trademark exegetical maneuver; however, it is as likely as not that Thomas' specific use of Psalms citations is not significantly different from his use of any other OT source. At this point all that can be hypothetically asserted is that Thomas will probably rely on those works which he sees as containing "admonishing, and exhorting, and the giving of precepts" (namely, "the Law, the Prophets, and the Books of Solomon"[58]) in the second part of the *lectura* on Ephesians 4-6, which is the predominantly paraenetic section of the Epistle. Yet this is gathered from

---

[58] *Super Psalmos*, Proemium.

what Thomas says in the *lectura* itself, not from any particular pattern in OT citation.

To this general profile of the biblical sources that Thomas uses in his exegetical project must be joined his use of extra-biblical *auctoritates*. Thomas is much more restrained in this form of citation; he cites extra-biblical sources 47 times in the Ephesians commentary, a total of a little less than one citation (.97) per 1,000 words. The following table demonstrates a number of aspects of his use of these resources, including the sources themselves, the frequency of citation, and works cited:

Table III: Extra-Biblical *Auctoritates*[59]

Peter Lombard – 13
Collectanea in epistolis S. Pauli - 13

Augustine of Hippo: 13
De Trinitate - 2
De Civitate Dei - 2
Ennarationes in Psalmos – 2
De Gratia Christi et Peccato Originali – 1
De Gratia Christi et Peccato Originali - 1
De Catechizandis Rudibus – 1
Super Genesim ad Litteram - 1
Soliloquiorum - 1
De Natura Boni – 1
De Diversis Quaestionibus - 1

Gregory the Great - 5
Homilia 30 in Evangelia – 2
Homilia 34 in Evangelia – 1
Spurious citations - 2

Pseudo-Dionysius – 4
De Coelestia Hierarchia – 2
De Divinis Nominibus – 1
Ecclesiastica Hierarchia - 1

Aristotle – 3
Politics – 2
Nichomachean Ethics – 1

Origen – 2
General Allusions – 2

Prayer of Manasseh – 1

Athanasius of Alexandria – 1
De Morte Arii – 1

Ambrose – 1
Spurious citation – 1

Jerome – 1
Epistula 22 – 1

John Damascene – 1
De Fide Orthodoxa - 1

Ovid – 1
De Arte Amatoria

---

[59] In enumerating Thomas' extra-biblical sources, Lamb's edition was particularly helpful. There he recognizes every extra-biblical source in his notes as they occur in the *lectura*.

Thomas' use of extra-biblical sources in the *lectura* on Ephesians displays some distinctive characteristics which should be noted from the outset. First of all, the frequency of citation is much lower here than in the systematic works; in the *Scriptum super Libros Sententiarum*, Thomas cites extra-biblical sources 7.5 times per 1,000 words, and in the *Summa Theologiae*, he does so 10.7 times per 1,000 words.[60] Here we see a reverse pattern from the biblical citations, which increase dramatically in Thomas' exegetical works as compared to his systematic works. (Another important characteristic has already been mentioned in Chap. II: the relative paucity of references to philosophical sources when the *lectura* is compared to Thomas' systematic corpus.)

Besides a clear preference for Augustine, only one distinct pattern emerges - Thomas' reliance on the *Collectanea in epistolis s. Pauli* (or "*Glossa*") of Peter Lombard.[61] On the basis of initial observation, this practice is difficult to explain - as a near contemporary (or "Interlocutor"), Peter Lombard does not carry the same weight as the Fathers in Thomas' general schema,[62] but he outstrips them in importance in the most significant area of extra-biblical citation - his is the only work of commentary on Ephesians which is even cited by Thomas (at least explicitly). All other citations are diverse and obviously occasional; even the references to Augustine are to many different works, with no more than two citations per work Therefore, why it is that Thomas takes the Lombard as his preeminent dialogue partner needs to be explored.

Marcia Colish's excellent study of the life, thought and works of Peter Lombard provides some indications for determining the reasons for Thomas' exclusive reliance on the *Collectanea*. As she notes, Lombard's exegesis of Psalms and the Pauline Epistles (dubbed the *Magna Glossatura*) had swiftly superseded the earlier *Glossa ordinaria* and a number of other glosses as "the scholastic commentary of choice" by the time of Thomas' course on St.

---

[60] It should be noted that Thomas' use of *auctoritates* in the *Summa Theologiae* is dictated to a certain extent by the genre; every article had to include *auctoritates* in its objections and in its *sed contra*, while no such standard existed for exegesis. However it is still noteworthy, if only because it demonstrates that Thomas had a certain freedom to cite extra-biblical sources as often (or as seldom) as he pleased in the *In Ephesios*, and that with this freedom he opted for a degree of independence from the tradition that could just as easily have been a strong *dependence* upon it.

[61] *PL* 191-192.

[62] VALKENBERG, 28-29.

Paul.[63]   While the other glosses available broke the text up into minute and unconnected divisions, Peter gives the reader the whole text in clear subdivisions with running commentary.[64]   He offers historical/contextual *accessus* which actually play an important part in his reading of the text.[65] And unlike Peter Abelard (whose commentary on the Pauline corpus was widely popular up until it was superseded by the *Collectanea*), his *quaestiones* are always rooted in the context of the text under comment. In the words of Colish, the *Collectanea* demonstrate Peter Lombard's desire "to present Paul to his readers as a working theologian, and not just a source of raw theological materials."[66] On the basis of this, it seems clear that Thomas chose the *Collectanea* simply due to the fact that it was the best glossular source available during his time.

This observation calls for close attention not only to Thomas' direct citations of the Lombardian gloss, but also to the possibility that Thomas' framework for the Ephesians commentary (and possibly for the whole Pauline corpus) may be dictated by it. A number of questions emerge: Does Thomas use the same basic approach to Ephesians as Lombard? Is his theme for the text the same or similar to the *Collectanea*? What about his major divisions? Are the other extra-biblical references derived in large part from this older work? Answering these questions will allow an answer to an even more crucial question: Does Thomas' commentary maintain its own identity, or does it turn out to be a rehashing of the Lombardian gloss?

A first indication that Thomas' use of the *Collectanea* is not a complete or even partial abdication of his exegetical project is that his use of this work is rather erratic; the frequency of his citation of it varies widely from work to work. For instance, Thomas refers to it thirty-five times in his commentary on Galatians but only thirteen times in the Ephesians commentary, although the two works are nearly the same length. Also, the commentary on 1 Thessalonians contains only three references while the shorter commentary on 2 Thessalonians contains seven. Yet this is not conclusive evidence of Thomas' autonomy as a commentator, and other statistics seem to point in the other direction; if one compares the amount of references in the commentary on Romans (45) to the mere nineteen references in the Johannine

---

[63] Marcia L. COLISH, *Peter Lombard*, vol. I (Leiden, New York, Köln : E.J. Brill, 1994), 156-157.

[64] Ibid., 193.

[65] Thomas refers to the Lombard's *accessus* for Ephesians approvingly in the prologue to the *lectura* (*In Eph.*, Prol., 2).

[66] COLISH, 194-195.

commentary (to its own glossular source, the *Glossa Ordinaria*), it certainly seems as if the former is much more dependent on a glossular source than the latter.

A comparison of the two texts (i.e., the *Collectanea* on Ephesians and the *lectura* on Ephesians) is much more decisive for proving that Thomas' commentary is really his and not Lombard's. First of all, we see characteristics of Thomas' approach that are not found in the *Collectanea*. Peter gives no overall theme to the Epistle, whereas Thomas does; he also gives no introductory scriptural *accessus* for any of the Pauline Epistles, whereas Thomas always gives one. In fact, Peter rarely gives scriptural quotations at all in comparison to Thomas' copious usage. Their sources are often different as well; Peter is constantly citing Ambrose while Thomas only cites him once; both rely on Augustine but usually on different works; Gregory the Great and Pseudo-Dionysius do not show up at all in the Lombardian Gloss but are cited relatively often by Thomas. This collective evidence certainly favors the conclusion that the later commentary is clearly distinct from its predecessor.

The difference can also be demonstrated by the absence in the older commentary of a key element in the *lectura*; the division of Ephesians into two parts. For Thomas it is of major importance, as we have seen. But he does not borrow it from the Lombard, who makes no mention of the shift that occurs at the beginning of Ephesians 4. This outlines another difference between the two works; while Colish's observation that Peter gives clear subdivisions of the text is true, it is also true that he does not give reasons for his subdivisions. For Thomas, on the other hand, this is a key exegetical maneuver.

The difference between the two is clearest in the manner Thomas uses the Lombardian Gloss. Of the thirteen references to it, four are examples of Thomas either offering it as an alternative interpretation (as in 2.5.116) or an erroneous one (as in 3.3.161), and one example is not even a reference to the section on Ephesians but on Romans (1.3.23). In the other eight references Thomas concurs with the Lombard, but in these cases his opinion is clearly delineated and also specifically tied to a given word or phrase. Never does he rely on the *Collectanea* for his interpretation of a whole section, and it seems that his reliance on it decreases as his commentary continues: he cites it six times in commenting on Chap. 1, but only once on Chap. 2, three times on Chap. 3, once on Chap. 4, once on Chap. 5 and on Chap. 6, not at all.

In summary, then, all of the evidence demonstrates that Thomas' commentary on Ephesians is an original work in the fullest sense, one which obviously utilizes the approach of Peter Lombard but also advances it in those very areas which Colish praises in the *Collectanea*. Thomas' reliance on it decreases as his own perspective develops in a chapter-by-chapter reading of the Epistle; in this and all uses of extra-biblical sources we see a *magister* clearly mastering his materials, forging ahead with his own vision of the Epistle that forms a foundation for the theological model that is the *lectura*.

CHAPTER V

THE BUILDING OF A HOLY TEMPLE:
IN EPHESIOS 1-3

As we begin our consideration of the Ephesians *lectura*, it is necessary to return to the Genre-Identification Approach which was proposed in Chapter III, which we have been following since the beginning of Chapter IV through an application of **Part I** of the approach (i.e. the pre-analysis) to the commentary. The next two chapters involve the application of the various steps involved in **Part II** of the approach, in an effort to follow Thomas' analysis of the various parts of the text of Ephesians.

As we have already noted,[1] this part of the Genre-Identification Approach involves a certain selectivity on the part of the analyst, as the many steps involved will not always be applicable or even necessary. Because of this the order, extent of application, and even inclusion of each individual step are not easily demonstrable. Therefore we will refrain from identifying each step as it is applied, using the outline and remarks contained in Chapter III as a checklist to be followed as the components of **Part II** are applied to each individual section. We will also keep in mind the two general rules composed as governing principles to this kind of application: a) the necessity of judging all major and minor sections in their significance for the main theme, be it a direct or indirect significance; and b) the necessity of a readable exposition that labors to make Thomas' work accessible to modern biblical and theological scholarship. In this way all of the components that have been identified as necessary to achieve a successful analysis of Thomas' exegesis will be utilized, but only when they are helpful in achieving this end.

A) *Chapter One: Christ, the Temple Blueprint.*

If the past 70 years of intellectual ferment regarding Thomas' ecclesiology could speak with one voice regarding the most essential aspect of his vision of the Church, it could perhaps be summed up in one short

---

[1] Pp. 99-100.

sentence: "The Church is dynamic." This is certainly one of the many great insights of Yves Congar, who uncovers in Thomas an ecclesiology which depicts the Church not as a static reality but rather a movement, the dynamism of "the life of humanity moving Godwards," "the economy of the return of personal beings to God, *reditus creaturae rationalis in Deum*"[2]; this he describes as "the first and deepest notion that can be had of the Church."[3] His enthusiasm is echoed by many others, including Avery Dulles, who also points to this dynamic movement towards God as the most essential definition which Thomas offers of the Church.[4] Ti-Ti Chen, in her analysis of the Ephesians *lectura*, presents no less than six sections which focus, in one way or another, on the ecclesial *dinamismo*.[5]

We would affirm the insight of these and other scholars. Yet the dynamism they detect, although compelling in how Thomas describes it, is encountered in much of his work (for instance, in the *Summa Theologiae*) as an entirely interior dynamism - something that goes on inside a sphere of graced existence that can be described in general and is offered as a working principle. In the most exciting terms which he is capable of (using words like *reditus* and *via*), Thomas describes for us in manifold ways the scope of this ecclesial dynamism and how it touches human life.[6] But outside of the Ephesians commentary, we never hear of how this dynamism touches specific lives. It remains abstract, without concrete specificity.

This is where we can detect the first unique emphasis that is provided to Thomas' ecclesiology by the text of Ephesians. In the *lectura* he is forced by the text under comment, the work in which his work is rooted, to step into new territory, to consider the theoretical in relation to the actual, the abstract

---

[2] Yves CONGAR, "The Idea of the Church in St. Thomas Aquinas," in *The Mystery of the Church*, translated by A.V. Littledale (Baltimore: Helicon Press, 1960), 103.

[3] Ibid., 103.

[4] Avery DULLES, "The Church according to Thomas Aquinas," in *A Church to Believe In* (NY: Crossroad, 1982), 150.

[5] TI-TI CHEN, "La unidad de la Iglesia según el Comentario de Santo Tomás a la Epístola a los Efesios," 131-132; 135-136; 140-141; 157; 172-173; 183-184.

[6] This multidimensional understanding of the Church is at the heart of Congar's famous and widely-held thesis that Thomas would not have crafted a formal systematic treatise on the Church (commonly referred to as *De ecclesia*) even if to do so was a prevalent practice in his day (which it was not), because "the Church pervaded his theology in all its parts" [CONGAR, "The Idea of the Church," 117.]. We will not address this issue in the present study, other than to point out that our reading of the *lectura* on Ephesians in particular and Thomas' ecclesiology in general supports Congar's point of view. For an interesting analysis of this question, see SABRA, 19-33.

in relation to the concrete and even historical. Ironically, he does so in commenting on an Epistle whose connectedness to specific issues and problems has actually been downplayed by modern biblical scholarship.[7] Yet he does it nonetheless, prompted by references which he takes to be quite specific as well as essential. Three concrete poles bound Thomas' exposition, and all three figure strongly in Thomas' general notion of the Church as it is developed in the *lectura*. These are: a) the spiritually thriving Ephesian church; b) Paul and, in the background, the other Apostles; and c) the general population of Jews and Gentiles who have converted to Christianity (some of whom are members of Paul's audience). As we begin our consideration, we would do well to be attentive to these three important aspects.

Thomas begins Lecture 1 by considering the first of these three, the Ephesian church. Although he spends a little time on its geographical location, he is much more interested in its relationship to Paul. Although they had been previously converted, (Thomas bases this assertion on Acts 19:1), Paul came to them as part of his missionary work and fortified them in their faith. In writing his letter to them, he aims to continue this fortification. Thus "they were entitled to encouragement rather than reprimand; and Paul's Letter has the tone of reassurance and not rebuke."[8] We have heard this before, in the prologue - Thomas' repetition notes how important he thinks this fact to be. This is also clear in how he describes Paul's *modus agendi*; every aspect of the Letter is presented for encouragement. Thomas demonstrates this by dividing the text into four parts according to how Paul encourages the Ephesians:

> First, the greeting, in which he shows his affection for them. Secondly, the narrative, in which he strengthens them in good habits (1:3-3:21). Thirdly, the exhortation, in which he urges them to greater perfection (4:1-6:9). Fourthly, the conclusion of the Letter, in which he fortifies them for spiritual combat (6:10-24).[9]

---

[7] BARTH, 58-59; LINCOLN, lxxiv; BEST, 64-65.

[8] "...*consolatione digni erant. Ideo Paulus eis non increpatoriam, sed consolatoriam scribit epistolam*" [*In Eph.*, 1.1.3].

[9] "*Primo ergo ponit salutationem, in qua suum affectum ad eos demonstrat; secundo narrationem, in qua eos in bonis habitis confirmat, ibi **Benedictus Deus**, etc., usque ad iv cap.; tertio, exhortationem, in qua eos ad ulteriora bona provocat, a cap. IV usque ad locum illum cap. VI **De caetero, fratres, confortamini in Domino**, etc.; quarto epistolae conclusionem, in qua eos ad certamen spirituale confortat a loco isto **De caetero**, usque in finem* [Ibid., 1.1.3]. It is interesting to note that Thomas seems to negate a basic principle of the present study here:

Shortly after, this division is further specified regarding the first three chapters. According to Thomas, Paul strengthens the Ephesians in good (*in bono confirmat*) in three ways, each of which corresponds to a chapter. Chap. 1 strengthens them by describing Christ and the gifts he has given them; Chap. 2 by focusing on their conversion; and Chap. 3 by drawing their attention to Paul, who strengthens them by his apostolic activity.[10]

In Lecture 1 Thomas is focused on the gifts of Christ in general,[11] a signal that he believes Paul to be expounding the subject-matter of the chapter in the broadest possible way. What Thomas offers to us by way of explanation is a long meditation on the blessings of God's election and of predestination, one which finds its culmination in the words "grace" and "glory," terms which Thomas pairs together to compare and contrast the Church militant and the Church triumphant.[12] This eschatological interpretation is initiated by v. 5, which refers to the Father's "adoption of children through Jesus Christ unto himself." Thomas takes "unto himself" to refer to conformity in likeness; he cites 1 Jn 3:1-2 in explanation of this point.[13] Specifically, this is a likeness to the Son of God and one that involves two aspects - an imperfect likeness of grace, which concerns only the partial reformation of the soul, and a likeness of glory which will be perfect "both as regards the body... and in regard to the soul."[14] Although Thomas notes that this verse could possibly refer to "the imperfect assimilation to the Son of God possessed in this life through grace" (*imperfectam assimilationem Filii Dei, quae habetur in hac vita per gratiam*), he holds it to be "better" (*melius*)

---

he calls the section which we have called expository "*narrationem*," when it has already been argued that this is precisely what it is not. Here we must remember that Thomas' concept of narration is not as deeply and inextricably connected with the concept of story as it is in contemporary theological usage. Deferrari translates Aquinas' *narratio* not only as "story" but also as "a relating;" and *narrare* not only as "to recount" and "to report" but also simply as "to set forth" [Roy J. DEFERRARI, *A Latin-English Dictionary of St. Thomas Aquinas* (Boston: St. Paul Editions, 1960), 678]. Here it does not exclude what we have classified as "non-narrative," and should be a reminder that to be "non-narrative" is not to be "anti-narrative." We would concur with Ryken, who notes that the various types of writing found in Scripture are often found to be intertwined; "one of them usually dominates a given passage, but not to the exclusion of others" [RYKEN, 14]. Interestingly, he uses a passage from the part of Ephesians Thomas refers to as "narrative" to demonstrate this - i.e., Eph 2:4-8.

[10] Ibid., 1.1.5.

[11] Ibid., 1.1.5.

[12] TI-TI CHEN, 58 n.156. As she notes, "grace-glory" is only one terminological pair that Thomas employs in making this distinction.

[13] *In Eph.*, 1.1.9.

[14] "...*quantum ad corpus... et secundum animam*..." [Ibid., 1.1.10].

to interpret it as referring to "the perfect assimilation to the Son of God which will exist in the fatherland" (*perfectam Filii Dei assimilationem, quae erit in patria*).[15]

Indeed, Thomas extends this "better" interpretation to the whole passage, as can be seen from still another *divisio textus* which is offered at the beginning of the lecture. According to Thomas, Paul enumerates six blessings offered to the human race in the first seven verses of Ephesians 1. The first three are preeminently eschatological: "First, that of praising [God] in the certainty of future beatitude (1:3). Secondly, that of being chosen in the foreordained separation from those headed toward destruction (1:4). Thirdly, that of predestination in the foreordained community of the good, namely, of the adopted sons (1:5)."[16]

This can be seen throughout his actual interpretation. "Every spiritual blessing" (*omni benedictione spirituali*) in v. 3 is interpreted eschatologically, with reference to the resurrection of the body; Thomas justifies his addition of the body here by noting that, in the future, "the body will be spiritual."[17] One has to wonder why he is stretching this point - why the repeated emphasis on eschatology when many other interpretations are possible which do not involve the future so directly?[18] Perhaps we already have the answer in what Congar, Dulles and others have demonstrated regarding Thomas' ecclesiology. If the Church is "the economy of the return of personal beings to God," is it surprising that Thomas would see in Ephesians, Paul's tract on "the origination of ecclesial unity," an emphasis on the end-point of this return?

There can be no doubt that this is what Thomas is about; it comes forth most clearly in his interpretation of v. 6a, "unto the praise of the glory of his grace": "Nor does he say 'of the glory' but adds 'of his grace,' as though it were a glorious grace. And grace is just this; *the greatness of grace is revealed in that it consists in the greatness of glory* [emphasis mine]."[19] In

---

[15] Ibid., 1.1.10.

[16] "*Primum benedictionis, in certitudine futurae beatitudinis, ibi* **Benedictus**, *etc. Secundum electionis, in praeordinata separatione a massa perditionis, ibi* **Sicut elegit nos in ipso**, *etc. Tertium praedestinationis, in praeordinata associatione cum bonis, scilicet cum filiis adoptionis, ibi* **Quae praedestinavit nos,** *etc.*" [*In Eph.,* 1.1.5].

[17] "*Tunc enim erit corpus spirituale*" [Ibid., 1.1.7].

[18] Cf. BARTH, 77-82; LINCOLN, 19-25; BEST, 113-129.

[19] "*Nec solum dicit* **gloriae**, *sed addit* **gratiae**, *quasi gloriosae gratiae, quae est gratia, in qua ostenditur magnitudo gratiae, quae consistit etiam in magnitudine gloriae...* " [*In Eph.,* 1.1.13].

other words, Paul is depicting for the Ephesians the glory of God's plan for them, precisely by showing them that it is a plan of glory. The faithful church he addresses is destined for the fullness of blessings; because of their fidelity in grace, glory is their destiny. Knowing what we do about Thomas' most basic definition of the Church, it should be clear that, without even mentioning the word *ecclesia*, Thomas portrays the Epistle as beginning right at the heart of the matter regarding the Church. Is it possible that it is from these opening verses of Paul's "ecclesiological Epistle" that Thomas acquires his basic insight regarding the Church?

In short, Thomas portrays Paul as fortifying the members of the Ephesian church with the glorious "bottom-line" for the Church that appears in these verses. This is also significant from another angle - the relationship between the Church and the preaching of the Word. In this case (and throughout the entire *lectura*) Thomas sees the fundamental pastoral activity (both apostolic and otherwise) to be one of proclamation and teaching; he will fill out this particular aspect of his ecclesiology further along in the *lectura*. What is important to note from the outset is that this is a deviation from Thomas' usual practice in expounding the mission of the institutional Church, which is to emphasize the sacraments above all else.[20] In the Ephesians *lectura*, however, he takes his emphasis from the Epistle itself, which is on the ministry of the word both in preaching the Faith (Ephesians 1-3) and in moral instruction (Ephesians 4-6). The fact that Thomas never offers a systematic treatment of the ministry of the word in any of his works[21] underscores the importance of attending to it here.

Lecture 2 continues along the theme of God's six blessings for the Ephesian church, here focusing on the blessing "of being pleasing [to God] through the gift of grace."[22] This is a meditation on the redemptive work of Christ,[23] the bestowal of "sanctifying grace, which makes us pleasing and acceptable to God."[24] Thomas makes no significant assertions here which are of importance to his main theme; he does however continue to emphasize the eschatological tone he attributes to the beginning of the Epistle by making the interpretive comment that Paul's references to predestination are specifically

---

[20] SABRA, 143-146.

[21] Ibid., 146.

[22] "...*gratificationis in collatione gratiae*" [*In Eph.*, 1.2.14].

[23] CUÉLLAR, 31, is correct in identifying redemption as a primary theme of this lecture, although it must be noted that this is not what Thomas designates to be the main theme of the verses under comment.

[24] "...*gratia gratum faciens, quae nos facit Deo gratos et acceptos...*" [*In Eph.*, 1.2.15].

to "eternal predestination" (*aeterna praedestinatione*) and not merely to "present justification" (*praesentis iustitiae*).[25]

But in Lecture 3 (vv 8-10) Thomas turns to a topic which figures significantly in the ecclesiology he is building on the basis of the text - that of apostolicity. Although most modern commentators would disagree with his decision to do so,[26] Thomas takes the "us" in v.8 ff. to refer to the Apostles; and therefore devotes his entire lecture to investigating "those favors especially granted to the Apostles."[27] The sanctifying grace considered in Lecture 2 "has superabounded" (*superabundavit*) in them, who have it more fully than anyone else.[28] Before we scoff at what seems to be a hierarchialization of God's favor and help, it behooves us to investigate exactly where Thomas' emphasis lies. In particular, what are the implications of this heralding of the graces of apostleship?

What must be considered first are the graces themselves. Thomas expounds on three apostolic graces that he detects in these verses. First, God enriched them with "all wisdom" (*omni sapientia*); he also gave them "prudence" (*prudentia*), so that they would be able to guide others.[29] Finally, he blessed them with an "excellent wisdom" (*excellentiam sapientiae*); and this so that they might fulfill their special purpose - that through them, God "might make known to us the mystery of his will" (v. 9).[30]

But the interesting thing to note is that Thomas' emphasis is not on this last point, which is what sets the Apostles apart from all other Christian leaders (in his actual exposition of v. 9, Thomas focuses on the mystery itself and not on those who dispense it). Rather, his emphasis is on the first two gifts, which are available to all who are placed in leadership in the Church. That is, rather than emphasizing the apostolic mission to the whole of humanity, Thomas emphasizes the pastoral role of the Apostles for the Church of their day. They are given all wisdom and prudence because they "are set over the Church to be her pastors."[31]   When giving the reason for this, Thomas does not emphasize the *excellentiam sapientiae* it fell to them to deliver, but rather the essential duties of all who administer pastoral care:

---

[25] Ibid., 1.2.19.

[26] BARTH, 84-85; LINCOLN, 29-30; BEST, 132-133.

[27] "...*beneficia specialiter Apostolis collata*" [*In Eph.*, 1.3.21].

[28] Ibid., 1.3.22.

[29] Ibid. 1.3.24.

[30] Ibid., 1.3.25.

[31] "...*praepositi sunt ecclesiae sicut pastores*" [Ibid., 1.3.24].

"Two qualities should characterize pastors: a profound knowledge of divine truth and an assiduous fulfillment of religious actions."[32] Lecture 4 (which offers little more than a *quaestio* on the ethics of casting lots to decide religious affairs) continues this emphasis on pastoral activity; after the coming of the Holy Spirit, casting lots for spiritual elections is no longer licit (Thomas maintains), since to use them would be to fail to realize "that the Holy Spirit will provide his Church with *good pastors* [emphasis mine]."[33]

Several scholars have remarked on Thomas' special treatment of the Apostles, noting that Thomas places them second only to the Virgin Mary in the supereminence of grace.[34] However, none of these remark on the particularly strong emphasis Thomas places on the basic pastoral function of the Apostles in his vision of the Church. Sabra comes closest in his analysis of the institutional aspect of the Church in Thomas' theology (though without reference to the Apostles); he is worth quoting at length on this point:

> Beginning with the episcopacy - itself the backbone of the institutional church - one finds that Thomas conceives its very essence in terms of its operation or function, 'through which it intends the good of one's fellowmen' [*ST* II-II.185.1]. Its function is its principle and final *raison d'être*, and that function is always directed towards serving others... [this] is perhaps best captured in a seemingly unimportant comment he makes in connection with the last few verses of the *Epistle to the Colossians*. The Apostle here instructs the community, i.e. the Colossian church, to convey something to Archippus. Why, asks Thomas, is the Apostle addressing himself to the Church directly and not to the prelate (Archippus)? 'Why did he not write to the prelate?' His answer is striking in its clarity and ecclesiological depth: 'Because a prelate is (there) for the church and not conversely' [*In Col.*, 4.1.193].[35]

Sabra concludes by noting correctly that Thomas practically reverses the saying *ubi episcopus, ibi ecclesia* into *ubi ecclesia, ibi episcopus* in his

---

[32] "*Duo autem spectant ad pastores, scilicet ut sint sublimes in cognitione divinorum, et industrii in actione religionis*" [Ibid., 1.3.24].

[33] "*...quod Spiritus Sanctus providet ecclesiae suae de bonis pastoribus*" [Ibid., 1.4.33].

[34] See especially Nicholas HALLIGAN, "The Teaching of St. Thomas Aquinas in regard to the Apostles," *American Ecclesiastical Review* 144 (1961) : 32-47; see also O'CONNOR, "The Concept of Mystery in Aquinas' Exegesis Part I," 188-189; TI-TI CHEN, 150; CUÉLLAR, 258.

[35] SABRA, 116-117.

theology.[36]   We agree entirely with Sabra, but would add one point which he does not mention - this element of Thomas' theology could not be anywhere clearer than in his comments in the lecture we are presently considering. The presence of such an emphasis in a passage which Thomas believes to be referring directly to the Apostles only serves to demonstrate how deeply this particular emphasis on pastoral activity runs in Thomas' vision of the Church. It also serves to qualify the superiorizing tendency which Thomas adopts from the tradition that gives the Apostles an almost superhuman status.[37]   What he emphasizes for us in the Ephesians commentary is Paul working as a tireless servant for the community he addresses, and the Apostles in general as models for (not the exception to) fruitful, basic pastoral activity.

A final aspect of Lecture 3 deserves mention, and that is Thomas' commentary on the phrase "reestablish all things' (*instaurare omnia*) which concludes v. 10 (and the lecture as well). Thomas relies on Amos 9:11 to help establish the meaning of this expansive phrase, which is worth quoting here: "In that day I will raise up the tabernacle of David, that is fallen; and I will close up the breaches of the wall thereof, and repair what was fallen."[38] This building image is a crucial clue to where Thomas' interpretation of Ephesians is heading. He equates three things here: the reestablishment of all things, the redemption of mankind (which he sees as the cause and/or occasion of universal reestablishment), and the image of the temple under construction. As indicated by the title of the present study, this final image will become a crucial image for the ecclesiology of the *lectura*, one which takes up its central position in the final lecture on Ephesians 2.

Thomas' exegesis of Ephesians 1 turns more decidedly towards the Church in Lecture 5; it is here that he gives his first direct designation of the Church, referring to it as the "the flock of the Lord" (*grex Domini*) This is significant for three reasons: a) it is an ecclesial designation not found in the text of Ephesians, a biblical concept which Thomas "imports" into his

---

[36] Ibid., 117.

[37] The notion of the "apostolicity" of the Church in Thomas' ecclesiology exhibits the exalted status which Thomas gives to the Apostles in their relation to the Church; see CONGAR, "L'apostolicité de l'Eglise chez S. Thomas d'Aquin," *Revue des sciences philosophiques et théologiques* 44 (1960) : 209-224, for the best treatment of this aspect of his ecclesiology.

[38] "*Suscitabo tabernaculum David quod cecedit, et reaedificabo aperturas murorum eius, et ea quae corruerant, instaurabo*" [*In Eph.*, 1.3.29].

interpretation of the Epistle;[39] b) this first direct mention of the Church occurs in the context of a passage (vv 13-14) that concerns the Holy Spirit; and c) this ecclesiological designation (i.e., "flock") is an uncommon one for Thomas;[40] and offers another angle from which he considers the Church that needs to be addressed. We will consider (b) and (c) first, in order to return to the more central subject of (a).

It has long been recognized that Thomas' ecclesiology is a predominantly pneumatological one. Mahoney, in his article "'The Church of the Holy Spirit' in Aquinas," identifies Thomas' conception of the Spirit's action in the world as a crucial source from which his ecclesiology flows:

> All springs from his magisterial statement that the law of the Gospel of Christ is principally the interior grace of the Holy Spirit present and operative in the heart of the believer. Everything else, whether it be the written law of Scripture and record of Jesus' own teaching, the institutional Church, its sacraments or its authority, is of secondary... importance.[41]

Thus, the "deep internal action of the Spirit of Christ" is the "*raison d'être* of the Church itself."[42] Thomas identifies this internal action of the Spirit as charity,[43] the love of God poured into the hearts of believers and uniting them. A closely related aspect of Thomas' vision of the Church is the

---

[39] It is unclear what biblical source Thomas has in mind when he uses this term. It (i.e. "*grex Domini*") is not unique to him; it occurs in the Vulgate text at least once (in Jer 13:17) and also occurs often in the patristic commentaries on this OT passage. However, Thomas never mentions Jer 13:17 in this lecture. A similar reference to the Church as flock can be found in Acts 20:28, which details Paul's address to the presbyters of Ephesus: "Keep watch over yourselves, and over the whole flock the Holy Spirit has given you to guard. Shepherd the church of God, which he has acquired at the price of his own blood." Thomas makes reference to this NT verse in 1.5.44, but only to the last phrase, "which he has purchased with his own blood" (as translated by LAMB). It therefore seems unlikely that Thomas is relying on either verse in any significant way in this case. A much more likely possibility is that the source is Jn 10:16, which will figure significantly into his interpretation of Ephesians 2 as well as other places in the Epistle.

[40] It is not mentioned by SABRA, whose account of Thomas' titles for the Church is perhaps the most comprehensive treatment in existence; see Idem, 34-71. Nor is it noticed by TI-TI CHEN, who undertakes an analysis of the images of the Church specifically contained in the Ephesians *lectura*; see Idem, 114-186.

[41] J. MAHONEY, "The Church and the Holy Spirit in Aquinas," *Heythrop Journal* 15 (1974) : 19-20.

[42] Ibid., 19.

[43] Ibid., 20.

compact but profound assertion that the Holy Spirit unifies the Church by dwelling in all of its members while remaining numerically one.[44] In fact, Vauthier notes that for Thomas, it is precisely through the gift of charity that the Holy Spirit unifies the Church.[45] With this in mind, it should not be surprising to observe this same idea in his consideration of ecclesial unity in Ephesians, which we do in Lecture 3.

The "trigger-phrase" which sets Thomas onto this particular discussion of the Church as "flock of the Lord" is in v. 13, where the Vulgate text asserts that the readers "were signed with the Holy Spirit of promise" (*signati estis spiritu promissionis sancto*).[46] This is the first mention of the Spirit in the Epistle, and on cue Thomas takes his interpretation into an ecclesiological direction. He notes that three things are predicated of the Spirit in the two verses under examination: "he is a sign, the Spirit of promise, and the pledge of inheritance."[47] The first aspect is taken by Thomas to be concerned primarily with charity - "He is a sign inasmuch as through him charity is infused into our hearts, thereby distinguishing us from those who are not the children of God."[48] This signing has set the Ephesians apart from the "flock of Satan" (*grege diaboli*).[49]

In explaining this, Thomas launches into an important comparison between the Jews of the Old Testament and the "*populum christianum.*" According to him, God cared for his people in the old dispensation in a way that was primarily bodily - he fed them "on the earthly pastures of material teachings and temporal goods."[50] Thomas uses Is 1:19 as an example of this

---

[44] E. VAUTHIER, "Le Saint-Esprit principe d'unité de l'Église d'après Saint Thomas d'Aquin," *Mélanges de science religieuse* 5 (1948) : 175-196. Vauthier analyzes several passages in Thomas' works which carry this idea, among them *In III Sent.* 13.2.1, 13.2.2; *De Ver.* 29.4; *In I Cor.* 12.3.734; *In Col.* 1.5.46; *In Io.* 6.7.972; *ST* II-II.1.9 ad 5, II-II.83.2 ad 3, III.8.1 ad 3; *In Symb.* 12.

[45] Ibid., 60-61.

[46] The original Greek text reads "sealed." However, the Vulgate is not incorrect; BEST, 150, notes that this passage definitely connotes a visible sign with the term "seal", and refers to the activity of the Holy Spirit in the baptized.

[47] "...*quod est signum, et quod est spiritus promissionis, et quod est pignus haereditatis* [*In Eph.* 1.5.40]."

[48] "*Signum quidem est inquantum per eum infunditur charitas in cordibus nostris, qua distinguimur ab his qui non sunt filii Dei* [Ibid., 1.5.41]."

[49] Ibid., 1.5.41.

[50] "...*in pascuis corporalibus pascebatur, scilicet in doctrina corporali et in bonis temporalibus*" [Ibid., 1.5.41].

shepherding by God of his people - they are promised security in the land for their obedience. In accord with this, he asserts, they were differentiated by a bodily sign, circumcision.[51]

But in the case of the New Testament, God's flock "is fed on spiritual doctrine and spiritual favors, hence the Lord differentiated it from others by a spiritual sign. This is the Holy Spirit... *But since the Holy Spirit is love, he is given to someone when that person is made a lover of God and neighbor* [emphasis mine]."[52] Thomas' emphasis on the Church's distinguishing characteristic should not be overlooked. It is charity; the Holy Spirit who cannot be seen is manifested by love in action.[53] This is the flip-side of Thomas' normal emphasis when he discusses charity, which is more decidedly focused on ecclesial unity itself. Instead of this, Thomas dwells on the manifestation of the Church to the world by noting its differentiation from the world as being one of love. It is a group branded by activity, the activity of loving God and neighbor. The simultaneity between the Holy Spirit being given to a person and that person being made a lover of God and of neighbor should not go unnoticed either - Thomas offers the two here as one and the same without qualification or even addition.

Charity remains central when Thomas moves to consider the meaning of the phrase "*pignus haereditatis nostrae*" in v. 14. Here he makes a keen and telling interpretive decision based on the Lombardian Gloss, which notes that "a variant reading" (*alia littera*) for this verse has "earnest" (*arra*) instead of "pledge" (*pignus*).[54] Thomas opts for this variant reading for reasons which are clearly founded in the notion of charity as the brand of the *gregis Domini*:

---

[51] Ibid., 1.5.41.

[52] "*...iste pascitur in pascuis doctrinae spiritualis et spiritualibus bonis, ideo eum signo spirituali ab aliis Dominus distinxit. Hoc autem est Spiritus Sanctus... Quia autem Spiritus Sanctus amor est, ergo tunc Spiritus Sanctus datur alicui, quando efficitur amator Dei et proximi*" [Ibid., 1.5.41].

[53] *Pace* TI-TI CHEN, 208-209, who would connect the "spiritual sign" here too directly with the sacramental character given in Baptism. But this is to miss the point; Thomas' use of the *grex* image places the emphasis on the sign as one that is visible to others in a permanent way. In other words, Thomas' usage places the accent on visibility, not sacramentality.

[54] Ibid., 1.5.43; cf. BARTH, 96; LINCOLN, 40-41; BEST, 151-153, who all note that the original Greek is in fact "earnest" (*arrabon*). Here as in many cases, Thomas demonstrates his perception regarding the literal sense even in the face of obstacles (in this case, a faulty Vulgate translation).

...perhaps this is a better rendering. For a pledge differs from the object in place of which it is given, and it must be returned once he who has received the pledge obtains the object due him. An earnest, however, does not differ from the object in place of which it is given, nor is it returned since it is a partial payment of the price itself, which is not to be withdrawn but completed. God communicates charity to us as a pledge, through the Holy Spirit who is the spirit of truth and love. Hence, this is nothing else than an individual and imperfect participation in the divine charity and love; *it must not be withdrawn but brought to perfection* [emphasis mine]. More fittingly, therefore, it is referred to as an earnest rather than as a pledge.[55]

The fact that Thomas is willing to part ways with the Paris Vulgate here underlines his emphasis that the differentiating characteristic of the Church is the love manifested by its members. It is this that will be brought to perfection *in patria*; only regarding the gifts that will not last (namely, faith and hope) "on account of their imperfection" (*propter sui imperfectionem*) can the Spirit be called a pledge: "Hence, the Spirit is called an earnest in reference to what will remain, and a pledge with respect to what will be done away with."[56]

With all of this in mind, how should Thomas' use of this image, *grex Domini*, be understood? The difficulty of this question is accentuated by how seldom Thomas uses the term outside of this lecture, as well as how he uses it in those few instances when he does. It appears only twice more in the Ephesians *lectura*, and in both cases it is used only to help define the ministries of Church leaders.[57] This is the case also with the one other place in Thomas' work where the word "*grex*" figures prominently - *ST* II-II.184-185, two *quaestiones* which deal in large part with the duties of prelates and

---

[55] "...*et forte melius, quia pignus est aliud a re pro qua datur, et redditur postquam ille, qui pignus recipit, rem sibi debitam recipit. Arra autem non est aliud a re pro qua datur, nec redditur; quia datur de ipso pretio, quod non est auferendum, sed complendum, Deus autem dedit nobis charitatem tamquam pignus, per Spiritum Sanctum, qui est spiritus veritatis et dilectionis. Et ideo huiusmodi non est aliud, quam quaedam particularis et imperfecta participatio divinae charitatis et dilectionis, quae quidem non est auferenda, sed perficienda, ideo magis proprie dicitur arra quam pignus*" [Ibid., 1.5.43].

[56] "*Sic ergo Spiritus Sanctus dicitur arra per respectum ad ea quae manent, pignus vero per respectum ad ea quae evacuabuntur*" [Ibid., 1.5.43].

[57] Ibid., 4.4.211.

with the episcopal state.[58]   Therefore, in terms of direct development of this image of the Church, the lecture under analysis stands alone.

Yet we can be aided by a title of the Church which makes a brief appearance in relation to this image in the lecture, the term "Christian people" (*populum Christianum*).[59] As Congar has noted, Thomas uses this latter term to connote the notion of law in its relation to the Church.[60] Yet it also refers to the Church's "sacramental context," whose unity "is expressed and assured by *certain signs* [translation/emphasis mine]."[61] In this respect Congar references *ST* III.70.2 ad 2 where Thomas discusses circumcision as the necessary *sign* by which the OT people was gathered together. Here we find a point of connection between the two ecclesiological titles "people" and "flock," and so can conclude that the latter carries many of the same connotations as the former.

Yet while the Church as a people is a starting-point for understanding this image, the latter carries an emphasis which the former does not. What is emphasized beyond the fact that this people is gathered together by love is the concept of love as the locus of differentiation and, therefore, of manifestation. Thomas' basic awareness of agrarian society suffices to remind him that among owners of free-ranging animals the ability to distinguish between them regarding ownership is essential. The brand is what is sought out when the flocks are separated, and is the silent presence of the owner. In this way, what Thomas emphasizes with this image is the witness of the Church to the world, in which charity appears as the bottom-line and also the fundamental characteristic of membership.

A final aspect of Thomas' development and use of the notion of the Church as "flock" can be found in the words "the redemption of acquisition" (*redemptionem acquisitionis*) in v. 14. In commenting on this phrase, Thomas ties it to the notion of an outward sign, giving the following explanation: "He adds the purpose for which we are signed as **unto the redemption**. For when a man buys new animals and adds them to his flock, he puts a mark on them

---

[58] It occurs 14 times in these two questions, which is more than half of all occurrences of the term in this part of the *Summa*.

[59] *In Eph.*, 1.5.41.

[60] CONGAR, "'Ecclesia' et 'populus (fideles)' dans l'ecclésiologie de S. Thomas," in vol. I, *St. Thomas Aquinas, 1274-1974, Commemorative Studies,* ed. A. Maurer, et al. (Toronto: Pontifical Institute of Medieval Studies, 1974), 166.

[61] Ibid., 162

to the effect that he has purchased them."[62] For a second time in this lecture
he references John 10, but this time he uses a verse (16) which alludes to more
than just the Good Shepherd imagery: "Other sheep I have that are not of this
fold; them also I must bring. And they shall hear my voice; and there shall be
one fold and one shepherd." It is obvious that this is a continuation of the
comparison/contrast between Jews and Christians developed earlier in the
lecture, but with an emphasis on the former as constituting the latter; "acquisition" refers here to the Gentiles who are "added" to a flock that is already
made up of Jewish converts. This is a foreshadowing of a theme that Thomas
will detect and address in his comments on chapter two of the Epistle.

Lecture 6 represents a prayerful, pastoral pause for Thomas in what
he has interpreted so far as a doctrinally packed chapter. His interpretation
will not lose (in fact, never loses) its theoretical emphasis, but it will not
contain any more directly ecclesiological exposition until Lecture 8.
However, this is a pause that is by no means void of important implications
for Thomas' vision of the Church, as is demonstrated by the unusually
personal, almost informal cast which Thomas gives to the passage: "After
enumerating the blessings conferred on the Ephesians, the Apostle now
reveals how his affection for them has grown."[63] The Apostle demonstrates
this affection by focusing on the "good reports" (*bonorum*) which he has
received about them (v. 15), then by giving thanks for the ways God has
blessed them (v. 16a), and finally by asking for "future blessings" (*futuris
beneficiis*) in vv16b-19a,[64] which becomes another opportunity for Thomas to
engage in eschatological exposition.

The significance of Thomas' focus on the relationship between Paul
and the Ephesians is revealed by what the lecture does not contain. In particular, Thomas refrains from in-depth exploration of some favorite themes
which present themselves in the verses under analysis. For instance, the first
verse contains references to both faith and love, giving Thomas the chance to

---

[62] *"Ad quid autem signati sumus, subdit, dicens* **in redemptionem**. *Nam si aliquis de novo
aliqua animalia acquireret et adderet gregi suo, imponeret eis signa acquisitionis illius"* [Ibid.,
1.5.44].

[63] *"Postquam enumeravit Apostolus beneficia Ephesiis collata per Christum, hic ostendit
quomodo affectus suus crevit ad eos"* [Ibid., 1.6.45].

[64] Ibid., 1.6.45.

pursue two concepts which are extremely important to his ecclesiology.[65] Yet Thomas passes this opportunity by, devoting only one paragraph to this aspect of the verse (which briefly calls to mind the previous lecture with a reference to love as "a spiritual sign that one is a disciple of Christ"[66]). What he does instead is to concentrate on his assertion regarding Paul's affection for the Ephesians in expressing his personal care and concern for them.

Thus, Paul's "attitude of thanksgiving" (*affectus gratias agendi*) for the Ephesians is continually with him;[67] he prays for special gifts for them;[68] his use of the phrase "the riches of the glory" (*divitiae gloriae*) is interpreted by Thomas to refer to the spiritual riches of the Ephesian church in its final inheritance.[69] We have already noted that the superhuman aspect of the Apostles that is so prevalent in Thomas' theology is balanced in the Ephesians *lectura* by a rare glimpse of an apostolic figure involved in basic pastoral activity. The picture Thomas paints of Paul both here and elsewhere in the *lectura* is one which could be painted of any good pastor - strengthening and affirming his flock, as well as fervently praying for their greatest possible good.

It is this picture of Paul and the other Apostles as pastors which helps to frame and mitigate some of the errors that Thomas makes in his interpretation of particular verses that seem to him to be related to the Apostles exclusively, such as vv 8-10 (which we have already considered) and also v. 19. The contemporary reader of Ephesians can easily agree with Best when he points out that Aquinas is incorrect when he asserts that "we who believe" in v. 19 refers only to Paul and the other Apostles, excluding its recipients both past and present.[70] Indeed, Thomas presents us with an almost absurd hermeneutic (from a contemporary perspective, at least) when he interprets verses that seem to be singularly potent in this way; consider his interpretation of v. 19, for example: "He [Paul] seems to say: Although he bestows the riches of his glory abundantly on all the saints, he grants them in

---

[65] For example, see O. DOMINGUEZ, "La fé, fundamento del Cuerpo Místico en la doctrina del Angélico," *Ciencia Tomista* 76 (1949) : 550-586, for his consideration of the importance of faith in Thomas ecclesiology.

[66] "*...spirituale signum, quod homo sit discipulus Christi*" [*In Eph.*, 1.6.46].

[67] Ibid., 1.6.47.

[68] Ibid., 1.6.50.

[69] Ibid., 1.6.54.

[70] BEST, 168.

an exceedingly great measure to the Apostles."[71]   The bridge between such statements and a more egalitarian reading of the Epistle is offered in the very human portrait of Paul which we see most clearly in this lecture.   He is (deliberately or not) pulled from his pedestal and placed in relation to a specific church whose members he knows and loves personally.   This allows Thomas to present the Apostles as models of Church leadership rather than unattainable ideals.   This can be clearly seen at the end of this lecture, where he applies his interpretation to his audience, who are not even bishops but lowly friars: "Those among you, therefore, through whom others are taught and called to the faith - such as the doctors - will be rewarded in a preeminent way."[72]   The teaching activity of the friars is placed here in the same category with the teaching activity of the apostles, and not merely as its continuation.

In summary, the Apostles continue to hold their exalted status, but it is one in which all Christian teachers and pastors can participate, because it is entirely *pro nobis*; their supereminent place, their extraordinary supernatural gifts, even their exalted place in heaven, is tied to their loving care of the members of the Church.   This way of understanding apostolic authority and power brings to mind the patristic ideal for the pastoral activity of bishops, summed up in advice reputedly given to Ambrose while he was still a layman: "Act not as a judge but as a bishop."[73]

Thomas considers the next lecture (i.e. Lecture 7) to be a continuation of Paul's enumeration of future blessings for the Ephesian church which he has considered in the preceding verses (17-19b), one which consists of an exploration of these benefits through a discussion of their "form and exemplar" *(formam et exemplar)*, Christ.[74]   This is not the first time Thomas' interpretation of Ephesians 1 has taken a christological turn; for instance, a large part of Lecture 2 was devoted to the part Christ plays in the giving of grace.[75]   Yet this is the first lecture in which Thomas interprets a passage as

---

[71] "*Quasi dicat: Licet omnibus sanctis abundanter divitias gloriae tribuat, supereminentius tamen tribuet Apostolis*" [*In Eph.*, 1.6.55].

[72] "*Ideo illi inter vos per quos alii instructi sunt et vocati ad fidem, sicut doctores, praeeminentius praemiabuntur...*" [Ibid., 1.6.55].

[73] "*Age non ut iudex sed ut episcopus.*"   This was spoken by Anicius Probus, prefect of Italy, upon Ambrose's departure from Rome for Milan after having been appointed as a consular prefect by Valentinian I.   See J. PLASSMAN and J. VANN, ed., *Lives of Saints: With Excerpts from Their Writings* (New York: J.J. Crawley, 1954) : 63-64.

[74] *In Eph.*, 1.7.56.

[75] Ibid., 1.2.17.

being primarily about Christ (a trend which will continue in Lecture 8), and
although in reality he devotes more time to angels than to anything or anyone
else, he does so in a long *quaestio* which is easily separable from his exposition. Yet the properly interpretive part is overwhelmingly christological,
and is significant for Thomas' major theme in two ways: a) because it is in
this lecture that he first refers to Christ as "head" (*caput*), a title which is as
ecclesiological as it is christological, alluding as it does to the Church as body
(*corpus*); and b) in his division of the text, Ephesians 1 has Christ for its
principal subject, making it clear that Thomas believes himself to have
reached the heart of this chapter in these final two lectures.

The phrase in which this mention of Christ as head occurs, "exalting
that head" (*exaltans caput illud*) could easily serve as the summary of both
lectures, especially if we include the words that directly follow it: "in this way
he will mightily act in us" (*ita virtuose operabitur in nobis*).[76] Christ exalted
as "form" and "exemplar" (terms which naturally point to something distinct
yet related to themselves) will be continuously connected with the exaltation
of the Church in Thomas' interpretation of the final verses of Ephesians 1;
and it is the title "head" which he will use to manifest the connotations of
Christ' role as exemplar and form. In Lecture 7 this is done in anticipation of
the first reference to Christ as head in the Epistle itself (v. 22). In the final
lecture, Thomas will devote his interpretive energy entirely to this theme of
head and body.[77]

The significance of Lecture 7 is found in the fact that it serves as a
necessary prelude to the message of Lecture 8. One important aspect can be
located in Thomas' assertion that in this passage (vv 19b-21), Paul is
"speaking of Christ inasmuch as he is man" (*loquendo de Christo inquantum
est homo*).[78] For Thomas, this is Paul's emphasis; it is as man that Christ is
raised from the dead and set at the Father's right hand (vv 20b-21), and it is
also as man that he receives from the Father "an elevation to the greatest of
power" (*sublimatio ad potentiam maximam*),[79] a subject considered in Lecture
8. The long meditation on the various ranks of angels, though obviously an
exercise in pedagogically tangential thinking (especially from a modern

---

[76] Ibid., 1.7.57.

[77] Thomas' perspective here is not dissimilar to LINCOLN, 47, who notes that this section of
Ephesians 1 involves a thanksgiving which "shades into... confessional material in praise of
God's power in Christ's resurrection and exaltation *and the use of this material to highlight the
role of the Church in God's purposes* [emphasis mine]..."

[78] *In Eph.*, 1.7.58.

[79] Ibid., 1.7.58.

exegetical perspective), is summarized by Thomas in an almost dismissive way in favor of his main theme:

> Christ is above all these ranks that have been discussed. The Apostle only makes a special mention of four of them. The reason is that the names of these four ranks are given them for their dignity, and since he is dealing with the dignity of Christ, he names them especially to show that Christ surpasses all created dignity.[80]

He surpasses "all created dignity" specifically as man and particularly as head. Thomas' final remarks are even more expansive, and are clearly preparing for the lecture to come: Christ "has been exalted above every spiritual creature" (*Christum exaltatum esse communiter supra omnem creaturam spiritualem*); "as man" (*secundum quod homo*) he is exalted "over everything capable of being named" (*super omne nominabile*).[81] This total exaltation is so far-reaching that it only halts at the *substantia divinitatis*.[82]

Yet Thomas is only preparing for what is clearly the pinnacle of his exposition, and in this way closely follows Paul.[83] Lecture 7 has focused on Christ's exaltation itself. Yet in Lecture 8, the focus (according to Thomas) changes to "the immense power of his exaltation," concerning which Paul does two things: "First, he discusses the power of Christ with respect to the whole of creation. Secondly, then his power in relation to the Church (22b-23)."[84] The flip-side of exaltation is power for both Thomas and Paul; the former is truly on the mark exegetically when he notes that "The phrase **under his feet**... is a figurative and [similar] way of saying that every creature

---

[80] "*His ergo expositis, Christus super omnes est. De his vero quatuor Apostolus specialem mentionem facit. Cuius ratio est, quia horum quatuor ordinum nomina a dignitate imponuntur; et quia agit de dignitate Christi, ideo hic specialiter eos nominat, ut ostendat Christum omnem dignitatem creatam excedere*" [Ibid., 1.7.63].

[81] Ibid., 1.7.64.

[82] Ibid., 1.7.64.

[83] See BARTH, 157, who notes: "The interconnection between the cosmic and ecclesiastic dimensions of the Messiah's kingship appears to be the very point Paul wants to make in singing the praise of the resurrected Christ. The Church cannot claim for herself a Lord other than the one who is also Lord over the world."

[84] "*...primo agit de Christi potestate respectu totius creaturae; secundo de eius potestate respectu ecclesiae*" [*In Eph.*, 1.8.65].

is totally subject to the power of Christ."[85]   This leads Thomas to discuss a
favorite tangent (i.e. the error of Origen with regard to universal salvation),
but he does not tarry there long.   Rather, he turns quickly to v. 22b, where
Paul "deals with Christ's power with respect to the Church" (*agit de potestate
Christi respectu ecclesiae*).[86]   It is interesting that Thomas does not place any
emphasis on the Church's subjugation to Christ in his treatment, which he
only mentions briefly as one aspect of the Church's relation to Christ.[87]   It is
this broader term, "relation" (*habitudo*), that is repeated several times, hinting
at the possibility that Thomas aims to consider more about the Church than
what the passage would normally warrant.   This possibility is strengthened to
a probability when we recall that Thomas is lecturing, and has reached the
first mention of the Church in Ephesians.

And this is precisely what we see - Thomas takes the opportunity
given by the text to offer his students the broadest possible treatment of the
Church under the aspect of mystical body and particularly in its relation to
Christ considered as head.   In the latter case, Thomas defines what it means
for Christ to be head:

> Concerning the first, he says God the Father **hath made him head
> over all the Church**, both of the Church militant, composed of men
> living in the present, and of the Church triumphant, made up of the
> men and angels in the fatherland.   On account of certain general
> reasons, Christ is even head of the angels - "who is head of all
> principality and power" (Col 2:10) - whereas Christ is spiritually the
> head of mankind for special reasons.   For the head has a threefold
> relationship with the other members.   First, it has a preeminent
> position; secondly, its powers are diffused since all the senses in the
> members are derived from it; thirdly, it is of the same nature.[88]

---

[85] "...*quod hoc quod dicit* **sub pedibus**... *ut sit locutio figurativa et similitudinaria, ut
scilicet per hoc detur intelligi, quod omnis creatura totaliter est subiecta potestati Christi*"
[Ibid., 1.8.66]. LAMB, 80, translates "*similitudinaria*" as "symbolic." "Similar" is actually
closer to the original meaning of the term.

[86] Ibid., 1.8.68.

[87] Ibid., 1.8.70. The term used is "*subiecta*," the same term used to describe the relation of
every creature to Christ in 1.8.66.

[88] "*Quantum ad primum dicit* **et ipsum dedit**, *Deus Pater*, **caput super omnem ecclesiam**,
*scilicet tam militantem, quae est hominum in prasenti viventium, quam triumphantem, quae est
ex hominibus et angelis in patria.*

*Christus enim secundum quasdam communes rationes caput est etiam angelorum, Col. c.
II, 10: Qui est caput omnis principatus et potestatis; sed secundum speciales rationes est
Christus caput hominum spiritualiter.*

The main thing that should be noticed here is the almost complete similarity of this paragraph to the many other instances where Thomas treats the headship of Christ,[89] an idea he develops most fully in *ST* III.8.[90]   In other words, we are not in new territory in terms of Thomas' basic idea of the Church. However, what is new (or at least unique) is the emphasis that results from the interplay of Epistle and exposition, as we shall see.

Thomas takes a notable amount of time qualifying one aspect of Christ's headship, that he is "head of the angels." This should not confuse us into attributing too much importance to this aspect of Thomas' teaching; although it does seem to come up almost every time Christ's headship does, this does not necessarily imply that it is central and in fact very often (both in this context and elsewhere) seems almost tacked on.[91]   In this instance it makes much more sense as the completion of the considerations in Lecture 7 of Christ's exaltation over the angels. The fact that Thomas emphasizes that Christ is not the head of the angels in regard to "a conformity of nature" (*naturae conformitatem*) makes this clear; in this regard "he is head of men only" (*est caput hominum tantum*).[92]

And it is on this last characteristic that Thomas places his greatest emphasis in this section; he mentions it three times in only four paragraphs. In context, it becomes clear that Thomas singles out this aspect in order to achieve two goals: a) to establish a relationship of identity between head and body, Christ and Church; and b) to prepare for his exposition of the enigmatic (now as then) identification of the Church as "the fullness of him who is filled all in all" (*plenitudo eius, qui omnia in omnibus adimpletur*).[93] These two

---

Nam caput triplicem habitudinem habet ad membra. Primo quidem quo ad praeeminentiam in situ; secundo, quo ad diffusionem virtutum, quia ab eo omnes sensus derivantur in membra; item, quo ad conformitatem in natura" [Ibid., 1.8.70].

[89] For example, see *ST* III.8; *De Ver.*, 29.4-5; *In I Cor.*, 11.1.587; *In Col.*, 1.5.46; *Comp. Theol.*, 1.214.

[90] SABRA, 85.

[91] *Pace* TI-TI CHEN, 162-166, who takes the title much further than it merits.

[92] *In Eph.*, 1.8.69.

[93] The debate over this verse and the meaning of "pleroma" makes up a large part of the research on Ephesians 1 undertaken during the last 50 years. For various opinions on its meaning see C.F.D. MOULE, "'Fullness' and 'Fill' in the New Testament," *Scottish Journal of Theology* 4 (1951) : 79-86; P. BENOIT, "Corps, tête et plérôme dans les Épîtres de la captivité," *Revue biblique*   63 (1956) : 5-44; A.R. MCGLASHAN, "Ephesians 1:23," *Expository Times* 76 (1964-1965) : 132-133; H.A. MERKLINGER, "Pleroma and Christianity," *Concordia Theological Monthly* 36 (1965) : 739-743; R. YATES, "A Re-examination of Ephesians 1:23," *Expository Times* 83 (1972) : 146-151; G. HOWARD, "The

goals are actually part of one larger goal - the transfer of Christ's exaltation to
the Church in an explication of the term "fullness," which Thomas uses to add
a whole new category to the head/body metaphor which he uses so often.

It behooves us, dealing as we are with an ambiguous but crucial
passage, to consider the insights of others who have noticed Thomas'
exposition of Eph 1:23. Swierzawski emphasizes that Thomas' use of Paul's
"definition" of the Church is such that "we cannot speak about [the Church
as] some absolute complement, but only about a subjective contribution" if we
are to continue to assert (with Thomas) that the merits of Christ as head of the
Church are infinite.[94] Yet this merely qualifies Thomas' exposition, and fails
to shed a greater light on it. Sabra takes much the same approach, making the
correct argument that Thomas does not take this verse as an "ecclesiological
hypostatization."[95] Cuéllar goes further towards an adequate consideration
by noting especially that for Thomas the Church is "fullness" precisely
because it represents "the redemption *in actu secundo*, manifesting - 'body' in
the hebraic sense - Christ."[96]

With these comments in mind, how does Thomas understand this
passage? Although it is entirely possible for him to take Eph 1:23 in such a
way that his emphasis on Christ's power is continued (the final phrase "who is
filled all in all" is ambiguous enough for this, and in fact Thomas does place
an emphasis on Christ's activity in the Church when he deals with this final
phrase), this is not his intention, as is clear when we consider the main portion
of the passage:

> He explains **which is his body** by adding **the fulness** [sic]
> **of him**. To one asking why there are so many members in a natural
> body - hands, feet, mouth, and the like - it could be replied that they
> are to serve the soul's variety of activities. [The soul] itself is the
> cause and principal of these, and what they are, the soul is virtually.
> For the body is made for the soul, and not the other way around.
> From this perspective, the natural body is a certain fullness of the

---

Head/Body Metaphors of Ephesians," *New Testament Studies* 20 (1974) : 351-354; I. DE LA
POTTERIE, "Le Christ, Plérôme de l'Église (Ep 1,22-23)," *Biblica* 58 (1977) : 500-524; S.
SAWATSKY, "Pleroma in Ephesians 1:23," *Taiwan Journal of Theology* 11 (1989) : 107-115.
For the opinions of our commentators, see BARTH, 200-210; LINCOLN, 73-78; BEST, 183-
189.

[94] SWIERZAWSKI, "Christ and the Church," 249.
[95] SABRA, 190-191.
[96] CUÉLLAR, 114-115.

soul; unless the members exist with an integral body, the soul cannot fully exercise its activities.

This is similar in the relation of Christ and the Church. Since the Church was instituted on account of Christ, the Church is called the fullness of Christ. *Everything which is [truly] in Christ is, as it were, filled out in some way in the members of the Church* [emphasis mine]. For all spiritual understanding, gifts, and whatever can be present in the Church - all of which Christ possesses superabundantly - flow from him into the members of the Church, and they are perfected in them.[97]

The key word here is *"impleantur,"* "filled out." All that has been predicated about Christ in this chapter is filled out by the members of the Church taken together and as individuals (Thomas' use of the term "members" here emphasizes the Church as a complete body while not neglecting the fact that this body can be considered in its parts). This rather abrupt shift to the soul/body (vs. head/body) analogy is crucial as well as unusual, as Thomas nearly always identifies the Holy Spirit as the soul of the Church.[98] Yet here Christ is presented as the *anima ecclesiae*, even if only to clarify the image of the Church as Christ's fullness.[99] Perhaps this demonstrates that Thomas is on unfamiliar ground, but also that he requires a new analogy for a new theological purpose - namely, to show that all which Christ has is given to and manifested by the Church. Anyone who is familiar with Thomas' anthropology knows that the close identification between body

---

[97] *"Exponit autem quod dixit,* **quae est corpus ipsius,** *subdens* **et plenitudo eius,** *etc. Quaerenti enim cur in corpore naturali sint tot membra, scilicet manus, pedes, os et huiusmodi, respondetur hoc esse ideo ut deserviant diversis operibus animae, quorum ipsa potest esse causa, principium, et quae sunt virtute in ipsa. Nam corpus est factum propter animam, et non e converso. Unde secundum hoc corpus naturale est quaedam plenitudo animae. Nisi enim essent membra cum corpore completa, non posset anima suas operationes plene exercere. Similiter itaque est hoc de Christo et de ecclesia. Et quia ecclesia est instituta propter Christum, dicitur quod ecclesia est plenitudo eius, scilicet Christi, id est, ut omnia, quae virtute sunt in Christo, quasi quodam modo in membris ipsius ecclesiae impleantur, dum scilicet omnes sensus spirituales, et dona, et quidquid potest esse in ecclesia, quae omnia superabundanter sunt in Christo, ab ipso deriventur in membra ecclesiae et perficiantur in eis"* [*In Eph.,* 1.8.71]. LAMB, 82, translates *"virtute"* as "virtually." A better, more contemporary translation of the term is "truly," as has been substituted above.

[98] SABRA, 103. For examples of the more general usage, see *In III Sent.,* 13.2.2; *In Symb.,* 9; *ST* II-II.183.2 ad 3; *In Col.,* 1.5.46.

[99] Thomas never uses this exact term, but in the analogy the term *"anima"* has no other possible referent.

and soul in his Aristotelian mindset makes the two so inseparable for him that he can (and does) offer a famous formula to the Christian understanding of the human person: "The soul is the form of the body."[100]   This radical inseparability is carried here into the relation of Christ to the Church; as he says above: "From this perspective, the natural body is a certain fullness of the soul; unless the members exist with an integral body, the soul cannot exercise fully its activities."   Christ, therefore, requires the Church in order to exert his influence in the world; it was instituted "on his account."

This is not a theory of the Church as an *incarnatio continuata* - Thomas makes this clear by his qualification of the analogy, noting that it is "*similar* [emphasis mine] in the relation of Christ and the Church," not identical.   But only to note this is to miss the point.   For the way Thomas deals with this passage definitively demonstrates that he sees this last verse of the chapter to be its pinnacle.   We have noted already that in Thomas' per-spective Ephesians 1 is about the gifts which Christ has given to the Eph-esians,[101] and in this last verse the greatest gift is revealed - that in giving gifts Christ has given himself in a unity so radical that the Church becomes his manifestation, and not just any manifestation, but the one proper to him.   The blessings are so complete that as the Church Paul's audience can be Christ's very fullness.   Here the seemingly disparate themes of the lectures on Ephesians 1 come together in a final crescendo: like Christ the members of the Church are destined for glory, pleasing to God, filled with grace; hence they share his exaltation by making him present.   Yet this is not an exaltation in power primarily so much as an exaltation in charity, and here is where the image of the *grex Domini* must be recalled - Christ rules all things in love, and it is his flock that, sealed with his love, radiates this charity to the world.

B) *Chapter Two: The Building of the Temple*

The first chapter of the Ephesians *lectura* succeeded in painting a picture of a Church that is profoundly evangelistic, its boldest strokes (i.e., the image of the clearly branded flock and even more so, the Church as *plenitudo*) revealing an overwhelming emphasis on signification and presence.   How-ever, it still remained very much in the general idiom of Thomas' eccle-siological vision, which is abstract and general.[102]   Although he has made

---

[100] *ST* I.76.1.

[101] *In Eph.*, 1.1.5.

[102] Thomas recognizes this fact himself at the beginning of Chapter 2 of the *lectura*; as he notes: "Above [i.e. Chapter 1], the Apostle enumerated the blessings bestowed on the human

overtures toward a more concrete and specific interpretation of the Epistle, he will enter into this most fully only in the lectures on Chapter 2, which also expound the hinge metaphor of the Epistle - the Church (and most particularly the Ephesian church) as temple.

The first paragraph of Lecture 1 demonstrates this emphasis on the historical - it is a reformulation of the primary theme of Ephesians 2 which Thomas gives at the beginning of his exposition.[103] As he points out: "Here the Apostle sets them [i.e. the blessings of God on the human race in general] in relief by comparing them to their own former condition."[104] In other words, Thomas portrays Paul as describing the former condition of the members of the Ephesian congregation in order to bring them to understand and appreciate their post-conversion status most fully, and he devotes this entire lecture to probing the significance of this former state.

It is a grim picture which is painted by Paul,[105] one which Thomas succeeds in darkening even further in his exposition. The Ephesians were spiritually dead, and kept up "their pace in going from bad to worse" (*de malo in peius procedentes et ambulantes*),[106] "attracted by the things of the world" (*alliciebantur a rebus mundi*)[107] and serving devils along the way.[108] Their

---

race *in general* [emphasis mine] through Christ" (*Supra enumeravit Apostolus beneficia humano generi per Christum communiter exhibita...*) [Ibid., 2.1.72].

[103] Ibid., 1.1.5.

[104] "*...hic Apostolus commemorat eadem per comparationem ad eorum statum praeteritum*" [Ibid., 2.1.72]. LAMB, 84, adds "mankind" in brackets in his translation, so that the passage reads "...[mankind's] own former condition." But this begs the question of whether or not this is what Thomas means by using "*eorum*" here. This is unlikely, as Thomas has already specified (as noted above) what the theme of Ephesians 2 is: to strengthen the Ephesians "*by reason of themselves* [emphasis mine] who have been transformed from a former evil condition to their present good one" (*ratione sumpta ex parte ipsorum, qui de praeterito statu malo, ad bonum praesens translati sunt...*) [Ibid., 1.1.5]. While it is true that their own former condition is identical to Thomas' conception of fallen mankind, the stress should be on the former, not the latter.

[105] Thomas clearly considers Paul's emphasis to be on the horror of their condition, even to the point of hyperbole; Lecture 2 begins with a summary of these verses that is quite revealing of Thomas' conception: "After exaggerating their state of festering sin, the Apostle..." (*Postquam exaggeravit Apostolus statum culpae inficientis...*) [Ibid., 2.2.84]. This corresponds to Thomas statement in his exegesis proper of Eph 2:1: "**Wherein in time past you walked** is added to exaggerate the great number of sins" (***In quibus aliquando ambulastis***, *quod ideo dicit, ut multitudinem peccatorum exaggeret*) [Ibid., 2.1.74]. Thomas does not object to this exaggeration; in fact, he participates in it.

[106] Ibid., 2.1.74.

[107] Ibid., 2.1.75.

futile way of life is on display among the "children of distrust" (*filios diffidentiae* – Eph 2:2) - that is, those "who reject the fruit of Christ's passion" (*qui a se repellunt fructum passionis Christi*) as well as those who "have no faith in eternal realities nor hope in salvation through Christ" (*de aeternis non habent fidem, nec spem salutis per Christum*).[109] That this past state is one of paganism is clear from the aforementioned reference to the service of devils, specified as worship (in his exposition) by a reference to Wis 14:27 and the worship of idols.[110] Thomas accentuates his dark interpretation with a final twist which the passage does not even merit: "Perhaps **of distrust** means those whom we should distrust because they sin out of malice, the prince of this world doing whatever he pleases in them."[111]

It is at this point that Thomas makes a sudden shift of interpretation, at the beginning of v. 3. As mentioned above, it is clear that vv 1-2 are taken to be in reference to paganism, particularly the lifestyles of the Gentile converts who are the Ephesian recipients of the Epistle. Yet now the subject changes to one much more personal to Paul, revealing another stratum of the early Church's population which has previously not been alluded to by Thomas in this passage. This change is occasioned by the appearance of the first-person plural, which calls to Thomas' mind Paul's ethnic and religious background: "Now the Apostle recalls the sinful state of the Jews..."[112]; that is, of himself and of those Jewish Christians who now compose some part of the Ephesian church's membership. They are distinguished from the sordid past of their Gentile counterparts only in regard to idolatry, "hence, the Apostle only mentions their sin as arising from worldly causes."[113]

---

[108] Ibid., 2.1.76.

[109] Ibid., 2.1.78.

[110] Ibid., 2.1.76.

[111] "*Vel **diffidentiae**, id est de quibus eis est diffidendum, id est qui ex malitia peccant, in quibus princeps huius mundi etiam operatur ad nutum*" [Ibid., 2.1.78].

[112] "*...commemorat Apostolus statum culpae quantum ad Iudaeos...*" [Ibid., 2.1.80]. BARTH, 216, gives the same basic interpretation, while BEST, 207-208, maintains that the "all" in v 3 excludes the possibility of a specific reference to Jews. It is interesting that the former maintains Pauline authorship, while the latter does not - for Thomas, the assertion of Pauline authorship is crucial.

[113] "*...ideo Apostolus non facit mentionem de culpa eorum, nisi quantum ad causam quae est ex parte mundi.*" [Ibid., 2.1.80]. Thomas' rather negative assessment of the state of the Jewish people is reminiscent of the fifth lecture of Chapter , which is mild by comparison. Later, he will take an entirely different stance, calling them "the society of the saints" (*societatem sanctorum*) in 2.4.106, implying as well that the Jews possessed "the fundamental truth of Christ" (*Christi dignitatem*) by way of promise. Such an ambivalent picture of the

This interpretation of v. 3 is very significant for Thomas' interpretation of the whole chapter. Although some modern commentators would
disagree with Thomas' decision to give priority to this aspect of the
chapter,[114] it nevertheless remains that one of the concrete poles which
bounds Thomas' exposition of Ephesians is his concern for the relationship
between Jewish and Gentile Christians (one which is reflected by the Epistle).
This important theme of Ephesians 2 becomes for Thomas its major theme, as
can be seen in his readiness to delve into it even in this early passage which is
several verses removed from the place where it becomes explicit in the text
(i.e. vv 11ff.).[115] This shows that Thomas is concerned to trace a progression
in the chapter, a progression which is very much one of building, in this case
the building of a congregation. This begins (much like the first creation
account in Genesis) out of chaos and darkness, an outward division between
one darkness (paganism) and another (Judaism), but a division thinly
camouflaging an inward unity in sin. In regard to this last point, it is not
accidental that Thomas moves from a discussion of the Gentile *statum culpae*
to the Jewish *statum culpae* to a general account of sin in itself. He
emphasizes oneness among Jews and Gentiles in the evil state of fallen nature
even though the first-person plural in "we were by nature children of wrath" is
not far removed from the first "we" of the passage which led him to focus on
the Jews in the first place: "Original sin is hinted at in **and we were by
nature children of wrath**. This sin of the first parent was not only passed on

---

Jewish people is typical of Thomas, who often passes back and forth between negative and
positive evaluations of the latter. For the most in-depth treatment of this ambivalence, see J.
Y.B. HOOD, *Aquinas and the Jews*, The Middle Ages Series (Philadelphia: Univ. of
Philadelphia Press, 1995) : 38-76.

[114] See esp. BEST, 286, who takes issue with Thomas' interpretation in his comments on
2:21: "Nowhere else does AE [author of Ephesians], unlike Paul, have individual
communities... in mind, least of all individual believers, but always the whole church... AE is
not then thinking here of the growth of each separate congregation which receives his Letter,
still less of Jews and Gentiles being built together (Jerome, Aquinas), but of the one church of
God." Once again we see the influence of the question of Pauline authorship; it is natural for a
pro-Pauline exegete such as Thomas to see Ephesians in the light of the rest of the Pauline
corpus, while a different point-of-view causes Best to adopt a more general, universal view of
its meaning.

[115] See S. HANSON, *The Unity of the Church in the New Testament, Colossians and
Ephesians*, Acta seminarii neotestamentici upsaliensis (Uppsala: Almquist, 1946), 141-148,
for the best modern treatment of this theme.

to the Gentile but to the Jew also."[116] Rather than digress on a favorite topic, Thomas emphasizes a universal state of hopelessness in which all the members of the Ephesian church were formerly united. It is from here that he will follow Paul's spiral of hope as the latter describes the transformation of this unity of sin into a unity of holiness.

Lecture 2 begins this ascent; Thomas correctly considers the principal theme of the verses he considers here (i.e., vv 4-7) to be "the divine blessing of justification" (*beneficium gratiae divini iustificantis*). Yet just as important in his exposition itself is the reality of God's mercy in his work of justification - nearly one-third of the lecture is devoted to explaining the phrase "who is rich in mercy" (*qui dives est in misericordia*).[117] Thomas begins by defining mercy; it is the source of any love which "causes goodness in the beloved" (*causat bonitatem in dilecto*). Therefore, since God is presented here as the agent of justification, Thomas asserts that Paul presents mercy in this passage as "the root of divine love" (*radix amoris divini*).[118] A long explanation follows which consists in a contrast between the finite mercy of man and the infinite and the unfailing mercy of God. In providing this, Thomas is reinforcing his earlier interpretation in Lecture 1, placing stress now as then on human weakness. Yet now this stress is informed with a new goal, that of demonstrating God's power and willingness to save. This level, focused as it is on the individual believer and God's solicitude for him/her, is clearly the "first phase" of the building process - God, as it were, refining the materials which will go into construction.

This is all that Lecture 2 offers by way of Thomas' principal theme. But this encouraging message of Paul is, as we shall see, building up to something profoundly ecclesiological, as Thomas is aware. A final point that should be observed in this regard is the renewal of the eschatological perspective of Chapter 1 with an important new emphasis in Thomas' comments on v. 6, "And [God] raised us up together and hath made us sit together in heavenly places in Christ Jesus" (*Et conresuscitavit, et consedere fecit in caelestibus in Christo Iesu*): "In these [words] the Apostle uses the

---

[116] "*Peccatum vero originis insinuat dicens et eramus natura filii irae. Quod quidem peccatum ex primo parente non solum in Gentiles, sed etiam in Iudaeos transfunditur*" [*In Eph.*, 2.1.83]. LINCOLN, 99, would agree with Thomas that the phrase "by nature children of wrath" is a reference to the innate sinfulness of human nature, as does D.L. TURNER, "Ephesians 2:3c and peccatum originale," *Grace Theological Journal* 1/2 (1980) : 195-219. BARTH, 231-232, and BEST, 211-212, on the other hand, do not consider this a plausible interpretation.

[117] Ibid., 2.2.86.

[118] Ibid., 2.2.86.

past tense in place of the future, proclaiming as already accomplished what has yet to be done on account of the certitude of hope."[119] This interpretation serves two purposes for Thomas. First, from an exegetical perspective, it allows him to accentuate the full force of Paul's many eschatological statements; the Ephesian believers, a community filled with hope, can receive all of Paul's references to future beatitude as fulfilled in the present because of their firmness of hope. Second, from a theological perspective, it underlines the glory of the Church's destiny by reference to its consummation in heaven - "in the next life" (*in alia vita*), signified by the words "in the ages to come" (*in saeculis supervenientibus*), he will manifest "the abundant riches of his grace" (*abundantes divitias gratiae suae*) by "the numerous saints who will participate in eternity" (*multitudinem sanctorum participantium aeternitatem*).[120]

Thomas ties the verses under examination in Lecture 3 closely to those of Lecture 2; in the latter Paul mentions briefly (in v. 5) that Christ's grace has saved us; "now he intends to prove that" (*nunc autem illud probare intendit*).[121] Thus Thomas is still mainly treating the "first phase" of construction - the salvation of the individual believer. In terms of his manner of proceeding, the pilot concept is faith, which appears in what for Thomas is the key verse (i.e., v. 8) of the passage: "For by grace you are saved through faith; and that not of yourselves, for it is the gift of God" (*Gratia enim estis salvati per fidem, et hoc non ex vobis, Dei enim donum est*). But here Thomas changes his emphasis from believer to Church - in his estimation, "faith... is the foundation of the whole *spiritual edifice* [emphasis mine]" (*fidem... est fundamentum totius spiritualis aedificii*)[122] - in this first direct reference to the building metaphor, Thomas shifts into the fully ecclesiological mode within which he will stay for the remainder of the chapter.

Why is faith so foundational? It is clear that Thomas gives it such priority because in his understanding (and certainly in the sense of the passage[123]) it comes entirely from God. In his interpretation Paul eliminates

---

[119] "*Utitur autem in his Apostolus praeterito pro futuro, enuntians tamquam iam factum quod futurum est, pro certitudine spei*" [Ibid., 2.2.88].

[120] Ibid., 2.2.90.

[121] Ibid., 2.3.92.

[122] Ibid., 2.3.94.

[123] See BARTH, 224-225; LINCOLN, 111-112; BEST, 225-227. Thomas' conception of this verse (indeed, of the entire passage) is profoundly Pauline, a correct perception of the emphasis of the author.

two "errors" here. First, he dismisses the opinion that "faith itself originates within ourselves and that to believe is determined by our own wishes" (*fides esset a nobis et quod credere in nostro arbitrio constitutum est*) by asserting "and that not of yourselves" (*et hoc non ex vobis*). In the next case, with the words "not of works" (*non ex operibus*) he rejects the error that "anyone can believe that faith is given by God to us on the merit of our preceding actions" (*Posset enim aliquis credere quod fides daretur nobis a Deo merito operum praecedentium*).[124]

All of this is summarized for Thomas in the words "For we are his workmanship, created in Christ Jesus in good works" (*Ipsius enim factura sumus, creati in Christo Iesu in operibus bonis*):

> There are two essential characteristics of grace, they have already been spoken of. The first of these is that what exists through grace is not present in man through himself or by himself, but from the gift of God. In reference to this he states **For we are his workmanship**, whatever good we possess is not from ourselves but from the action of God...
> The second essential characteristic of grace is that it is not from previous works; this is expressed when he adds **created**.[125]

The point, that man is unable to save himself, is further emphasized by Thomas in his comments on v. 10b, which he takes as a reference to predestination.

Does this overwhelming stress on God's work in founding the spiritual edifice (as opposed to man's inability to do so) result in a vision of the Church which involves no human effort in its existence? So far, these two lectures have given the impression that there is no human element in the fashioning of the Church - God seems to be the only one at work in its construction. Yet Thomas himself is aware of this stress and the need to balance it, as is demonstrated by his interpretation of the final words of the passage ("that we should walk in them [i.e., good works]"). The key word here is "walk," initiating a qualification on Thomas' part which nicely

---

[124] *In Eph.*, 2.3.96

[125] "*Duo autem ad rationem gratiae pertinent, quae etiam iam dicta sunt, quorum primum est ut id quod est per gratiam, non insit homini per seipsum. vel a seipso, sed ex dono Dei. Et quantum ad hoc dicit **ipsius enim factura sumus**, quia scilicet quidquid boni nos habemus, non est ex nobis ipsis, sed ex Deo faciente. Secundo, pertinet ad rationem gratiae, ut non sit ex operibus praecedentibus, et hoc exprimitur in hoc quod subdit **creati**" [Ibid., 2.3.98].

balances his primary focus, which is the construction of the Church as the work of God:

> Lest anyone imagine that good works are prepared for us by God in such a way that we do not cooperate in their realization through our free will, he annexes **that we should walk in them**. As though he said: Thus has he prepared them for us, that we might perform them for ourselves through our free will. "For we are God's coadjutors" (1 Cor 3:9). For this reason the Apostle said himself: "But, by the grace of God, I am what I am. And his grace in me hath not been void; but I have laboured more abundantly than all they. Yet not I, but the grace of God with me" (1 Cor 15:10). He expressly said **we should walk** to designate a progress in good works, in line with that saying: "Walk whilst you have the light, that the darkness overtake you not" (Jn 12:35). "Walk then as children of the light" (Eph 5:8).[126]

Besides being an excellent specimen of Thomas' exegetical acumen, this passage offers a glimpse of another aspect of ecclesial unity in Ephesians, one which will be evident in Thomas' exposition of Ephesians 4-6 (as hinted at by the citation of Eph 5:8). At this point it suffices to maintain a balance between human and divine freedom, reminding the reader that another side of the Church exists than the one currently being emphasized.

As Paul returns to his first theme (i.e., the former state of his audience) in vv 11-13, Thomas will devote his fourth lecture on Ephesians 2 to the same. In his interpretation, this passage is one of exhortation, Paul calling the Ephesians to recall their past state so that they would remember "that everything comes to us by God's grace" (*quod omnia sint nobis data ex Dei gratia*).[127] Paul's reference to their former state is taken by Thomas to be a direct allusion to their activity in that state - worshipping idols, involvement in carnal living - but also the fact that they were despised and rightly held in

---

[126] "*Sed ne aliquis intelligeret bona opera sic esse nobis praeparata a Deo, ut nihil ad illa per liberum arbitrium cooperaremur, ideo subdit **ut in illis ambulemus**, quasi dicat: Sic nobis ea praeparavit, ut ea nos ipsi nobis per liberum arbitrium impleremus. 'Dei enim adiutores sumus,' ut dicitur I Cor. III,9. Propter quod dicebat de seipso Apostolus I Cor. c. xv, 10: 'Gratia eius in me vacua non fuit, sed abundantius omnibus laboravi, non ego autem, sed gratia Dei mecum.' Signanter autem dicit **ambulemus**, ut designet boni operis profectum, secundum illud Io. xii, 35: 'Ambulate, dum lucem habetis. ' Infra, v, 8: 'Ut filii lucis ambulate'*" [Ibid., 2.3.100].

[127] Ibid., 2.4.102.

contempt by the Jews.[128] The last point is particularly significant from the
standpoint of the lectures to come, where (as we have noted) the relationship
between Jews and Gentiles will take center-stage.

This priority again becomes clear in Thomas' interpretation of v. 12.
Here Paul is portrayed as recounting the good things (*bona*) of which the
Ephesians had formerly been deprived: "First, from a share in the sacraments.
Secondly, from a knowledge of God..."[129] Yet Thomas does not mean the
seven sacraments in this case;[130] in particular, he lists three *sacramenta* which
have reference not to Christianity but to Judaism. First, "that you were at that
time without Christ" (*qui eratis illo in tempore sine Christo*) is taken to refer
not to a Christian knowledge of Christ, but rather to "the promise of a Christ,
as was made to the Jews [emphasis mine]" (*promissione Christi, quae facta
est Iudaeis*). The second sacrament from which they were deprived was "the
society of the saints" (*societatem sanctorum*) - yet not from the Christian
community, but rather from "Israel's way of life" (*conversatione Israêl*),
"since the Jews were not permitted to mix with the Gentiles" (*quia scilicet
Iudaeis cum Gentibus non erat licitum conversari*). As part of this they were
also deprived of "the testaments" (*testamentorum*), "since the Old Testament
was offered to the Jews and the New was promised" (*quia Iudaeis Vetus
Testamentum erat exhibitum, et Novum erat promissum*). Finally, they were
without "the hope of future goods" (*spem futurorum bonorum*).[131] Besides
the fact that this is a startling departure by Thomas from his usual emphasis,
i.e., Christianity (a departure which is vindicated by modern exegesis[132]), his

---

[128] Ibid., 2.4.104. For a similar interpretation, see BARTH, 255.

[129] "...*primo participatione sacramentorum; secundo Dei cognitione...*" [Ibid., 2.4.105].

[130] *Pace* SWIERZAWSKI, "Faith and Worship in the Pauline Commentaries of St. Thomas
Aquinas," 391. For an in-depth treatment of this more comprehensive notion of sacrament in
Thomas' thought, see Peter B. GARLAND, *The Definition of Sacrament according to Saint
Thomas* (Ottawa: Univ. of Ottawa Press, 1959), 21-62.

[131] *In Eph.,* 2.4.106.

[132] See BARTH, 255-260; LINCOLN, 136-138; BEST, 240-244. The deftness of interpretation which Thomas demonstrates here is best captured by LINCOLN, 136, who makes this
remark in regard to the phrase "apart from Christ" in v 12: "It would be a striking thought for
Gentile Christians to have to entertain that having been apart from Christ can be set in parallel
to having been separated from Israel. Yet the writer can make this point because he conceives
of Christ as the Messiah belonging to Israel." In much the same way, it is just as striking that
Thomas, dealing with a reference to Christ, does not make the easiest interpretation, which
would certainly have been to refer to paganism in reference to itself (i.e., "They were without
Christ because they were pagans.") rather than to Judaism (i.e., "They were without Christ
because they were not Jews"). The astuteness of his attention to the context causes Thomas to
make the correct interpretation.

direction is quite revealing. From the overwhelming emphasis on God's activity he has moved to a focus on the relationship of one group of people (the Gentiles) to another (the Jews). If there is any doubt that such a change is indicative of his central concern, one need only observe his interpretation of the final verse (13) of the passage - "But now in Christ Jesus, you, who some time were afar off, are made nigh by the blood of Christ" (*Nunc autem in Christo Iesu, vos qui aliquando eratis longe, facti estis prope in sanguine Christi*). Though the two-fold mention of Christ offers Thomas the possibility of returning to a primarily theocentric interpretation, only two paragraphs are offered in explanation of this verse, whereas v. 12 receives twelve paragraphs of exposition. In fact, Thomas' interpretation of v. 13 itself is focused not only on the issue of the unity of the Gentiles with Christ but also with "the saints"; that is, the Jews:

> **You**, I say, **who some time were afar off**, severed from God, not by space but by what you deserved since "salvation is far from sinners" (Ps 118:155), as well as association with the saints and a share in the covenants, as has already been said. Now you **are made nigh** to God and to his saints and covenants.[133]

This emphasis can only be attributed to Thomas' concern for the main theme of Ephesians: the origination of unity. The illustration of division prepares for a consideration of how these two peoples are united, a reconciliation from which Thomas will draw manifold conclusions regarding the nature of the Church. This horizontal element is absolutely crucial for Thomas, and he will have much to say about it in the next lecture.

---

remark in regard to the phrase "apart from Christ" in v 12: "It would be a striking thought for Gentile Christians to have to entertain that having been apart from Christ can be set in parallel to having been separated from Israel. Yet the writer can make this point because he conceives of Christ as the Messiah belonging to Israel." In much the same way, it is just as striking that Thomas, dealing with a reference to Christ, does not make the easiest interpretation, which would certainly have been to refer to paganism in reference to itself (i.e., "They were without Christ because they were pagans.") rather than to Judaism (i.e., "They were without Christ because they were not Jews"). The astuteness of his attention to the context causes Thomas to make the correct interpretation.

[133] "*Vos, inquam, qui aliquando eratis longe, id est elongati a Deo, non loco, sed merito, Ps. CXVIII, 155: 'Longe a peccatoribus salus,' et a conversatione sanctorum et participatione testamentorum, ut dictum est, iam facti est prope, Deo scilicet et sanctis eius, et testamentis*" [*In Eph.*, 2.4.109].

examining. He asserts that Paul performs this more precise treatment of the
blessings of the Ephesians by tracing two movements. The first of these is the
convergence of the Ephesians with the Jewish people; the second, their being
drawn close to God.[135] In regard to the first, "Christ is the cause of this
drawing together" (*causa autem appropinquationis est Christus*); hence Paul
says "he is our peace" (*ipse est pax nostra*). Christ is considered by Thomas
in terms of this peace he has caused through an enumeration of the various
ways he manifested peace to the world in the course of the Incarnation:

> In the same way, whatever peace we possess is caused by Christ
> and, as a result, whatever convergence [men have with one
> another]. For when a man is at peace with another he can surely
> walk towards or approach him. Hence, **he is our peace**. Angels
> announced peace at his birth: "Glory to God in the highest; and on
> earth peace to men of good will" (Lk 2:14). Indeed, while Christ
> lived in the body the world enjoyed the greatest peace, the like of
> which it had never before possessed. "In his days justice shall
> spring up, and abundance of peace" (Ps 71:7). He himself
> proclaimed peace when he arose from the dead: "He saith to them:
> Peace be to you" (Lk. 24:36).[136]

Yet it is not the cause of peace (Christ) so much as it is peace itself
which occupies Thomas. With the words "[he] hath made both one" (*qui fecit
utraque unum*), Thomas turns to this main object of his attention: "It follows
that he **has made both one**, joining into unity both the Jews who worshipped
the true God and the Gentiles who were alienated from God's cult."[137] Here
he uses a double citation (Jn 1:16; Ez 37:22) to show that this union is in
God's plan; his maneuver underscores how important this fact is to Thomas,
signaling that we have reached a crucial juncture in his exposition. But here
Thomas diverges from his usual practice when considering Church unity.

---

[135] Ibid., 2.5.110.

[136] "*Quia ergo quidquid pacis est in nobis causatur a Christo, et per consequens quidquid
appropinquationis, quia homo quando pacificatus est cum alio, secure potest ambulare seu
appropinquare ad ipsum, ideo dicit quod est pax nostra. Nam in eius nativitate angeli
annuntiaverunt pacem. Lc. II,14: 'Gloria in altissimis Deo, et in terra pax,' etc. Ipso etiam
Christo in corpore existente, mundus maximam pacem habuit, qualem ante non habuerat. Ps.
LXXI, v.7: 'Orietur in diebus iustitia,' etc. Ipse etiam resurgens pacem annuntiavit. Lc. ult.:
'Dixit eis: 'Pax vobis'*" [Ibid., 2.5.111].

[137] "*Sequitur **qui fecit utraque unum**, quia scilicet Christus utrumque populum, videlicet
Iudaeorum colentium Deum verum et gentilium, ab huiusmodi Dei cultura alienatorum,
coniunxit in unum*" [Ibid., 2.5.111].

Rather than focus on his more common themes (i.e., the Holy Spirit as the principle of unity,[138] and the unity of the Church as a unity of faith and love,[139] among others), Thomas gives his attention to the human, historical event of unity. The section is worth quoting in full:

> The manner of convergence is revealed when he states **and breaking down the middle barrier of partition**. The method, then, consists in removing what is divisive. To understand the text we should imagine a large field with many men gathered on it. But a high barrier was thrown across the middle of it, segregating the people so that they did not appear as one people but two. Whoever would remove the barrier would unite the crowds of men into one multitude, one people would be formed.
>
> What is said here should be understood this way. For the world is likened to a field, "and the field is the world" (Mt 13:38); this field of the world is crowded with men, "Increase and multiply and fill the earth" (Gn 1:28). A barrier, however, runs down the field, some are on one side and the rest on the other. The Old Law can be termed such a barrier, its carnal observances kept the Jews confined: "Before the faith came, we were kept under the Law shut up, unto that faith which was to be revealed" (Gal 3:23). Christ was symbolized through the Old Law: "Behold, he standeth behind our wall" (Cant 2:9). Christ, however, has put an end to this barrier and, since no division remained, the Jews and the Gentiles became one people. This is what he says: I affirm that he **hath made both one** by the method of **breaking down the middle barrier**.[140]

---

[138] See above, n. 42; see also SABRA, 100-104.

[139] In the Ephesians commentary, see 1.5.36-44; 4.1.195. In Thomas' other works, see *In III Sent.*, 13.2.1 ad 2; *In Symb.*, 9.973-975; *In II Cor.*, 13.3.539; *In Io.*, 6.7.972-973; *ST* II-II.183.2 ad 1.

[140] "*Modus autem appropinquationis ostenditur cum subdit et medium parietem, etc. Hic autem modus est per remotionem eius quod dividebat. Debemus autem ad intellectum litterae imaginari unum magnum campum, et multos homines ibi congregatos, in quo quidem per medium protendatur et elevetur unus paries dividens eos, ita quod non videatur populus unus, sed duo. Quicumque ergo removeret parietem, coniungeret illorum hominum congregationem in turbam unam, et efficeretur populus unus. Sic intelligendum est quod hic dicitur. Mundus enim iste sicut ager. Matth. XIII, 38: 'Ager est mundus'; hic autem ager, scilicet mundus, plenus est hominibus, Gn I, 28: 'Crescite, et multiplicamini, et replete terram. In isto autem agro est paries, quia quidam sunt ex una parte, quidam ex alia; hic autem paries potest dici lex vetus, secundum carnales observantias, in qua Iudaei conclusi custodiebantur, ut dicitur Gal. c. III, 23: 'Sub lege custodiebamur conclusi in eam fidem, quae revelanda erat.' Cant. II, v.9: 'Ipse stat post parietem nostrum'; quia videlicet Christus per veterem legem figurabatur.*

Three elements make this section remarkable. In the first place, Thomas is on entirely new ground, dealing with the topic of unity from an angle that he takes nowhere else. The closest he comes to it elsewhere would be in his section on the Old Law in the *Summa Theologiae* (II-II.98-105), but even there the emphasis is decidedly different - Thomas is considering the Law with reference to morality in general, and not to ecclesiology. But in the present case what stands out is the dilemma which the Law poses to the unity of the human race. Thomas adopts the Pauline ambivalence to the Law in its totality when he discusses, in one and the same section, the Law as both a symbol of Christ and as a jailer, one which did not keep the Gentiles confined in sin so much as the Jews confined from fellowship with the Gentiles. It is the elected people, not the worshippers of devils, who are penned in, and after the removal of the Law, no barrier remains: "the Jews and the Gentiles became one people." This interpretation, so striking because of its radical emphasis on peace and unity even to the expense of the divinely revealed Law, becomes even more striking when we consider that the Lombardian Gloss offers Thomas a more mutual cause of division which he rejects: "This [i.e., his own interpretation] appears to be the Apostle's intention, yet in the Gloss the barrier is duplicated. On the side of the Jews the law is set up as the obstacle, while on the Gentile's side it is idolatry."[141]

The second element of note is the shift Thomas makes from the discussion of the special blessings of a particular Christian people to a more universal outlook; he is no longer discussing the situation of the Ephesians so much as he is the very formation of the primitive Church. This reveals how central Thomas sees this reconciliation to be for the message of the Epistle to the Christian reader. His labors to demonstrate the special situation of the Ephesian congregation as a part of a larger, more universal blessing to the whole Church (i.e., the making of peace between separated peoples) show the enormous ramifications this event has for Thomas' theology. In fact, he will go so far as to develop this as a new factor of his soteriology in the coming paragraphs when he discusses how Christ brings this peace about.

Finally, the word-picture Thomas offers to his audience provides a glimpse of a fractured human community longing for unity. This division/

---

*Christus autem hunc parietem removit, et ita cum nullum remaneret interstitium, factus est populus unus Iudaeorum et Gentium. Et hoc est quod dicit: Dico quod fecit **utraque unum**, hoc modo scilicet **solvens medium parietem**" [In Eph., 2.5.112].*

[141] "*Et licet ista videatur esse intentio Apostoli, tamen in Glossa paries duplicatur: quia ex parte Iudaeorum ponitur lex quasi obstaculum, ex parte Gentium est idololatria*" [Ibid., 2.5.116].

unity paradigm is different from the more basic sin/salvation paradigm which characterizes much of Thomas' work, including and especially the very structure of the *Summa Theologiae* (which treats sin in the *prima secundae pars* and then moves to discuss salvation in the *tertia pars*), although the former paradigm will be shown to be related to the latter paradigm in the coming paragraphs. In the final analysis it is not sin but its temporary remedy that divides the one human family into two peoples, and both peoples are portrayed as awaiting an original unity that has eluded them and which will be reestablished in Christ's act of reconciliation (which still has yet to be specified).

The axis of Thomas' interpretation is the word "*maceriae*," or barrier. He distinguishes between what this word signifies and the word "*murus*," or wall,[142] a distinction which is not supported by the text itself[143] but which is nonetheless key to Thomas' exposition. According to Thomas, the reason the division is described as a barrier of partition is because it was not meant to be permanent: "A barrier of partition is one in which the stones are not mortared together with cement; it is not built to last permanently but only for a specified time."[144] It was a temporary barrier "because it was not mortared together with charity" (*quia non conglutinabatur charitate*), the "cement" which unites people together and to Christ.[145] A "law of fear" (*lex timoris*), it was persuasive by way of "punishments and threats" (*poenas et comminationes*), unlike "the New Testament which is the law of love" (*Novum Testamentum... quod est lex amoris*).[146]

Yet this *paries* was in itself not entirely divisive:

> The Old Law contained both moral and ceremonial precepts. The moral commandments were not destroyed by Christ but fulfilled in the counsels he added and in his explanations of what the Scribes

---

[142] Ibid., 2.5.113. See LAMB, 282 n. 55.

[143] According to our commentators, the Greek word *phragmos* does not carry the connotations of a temporary partition which Thomas assigns to it; for their own interpretations, see BARTH, 263; LINCOLN, 141-143; BEST, 252-259. All would agree with Thomas, however, that the barrier refers to the Law, an interpretation clearly supported by the text.

[144] "*Tunc enim est est paries maceriae, quando lapides in eo non conglutinantur cemento, nec ad hoc erigitur, ut duret in perpetuum, sed usque ad tempus praefinitum*" [*In Eph.*, 2.5.113].

[145] Thomas is hard to follow here, as he offers a metaphor which refers to the unity of the barrier itself, and not of the peoples on either side of it.

[146] Ibid., 2.5.113.

and Pharisees had wrongly interpreted... He abolished the
ceremonial precepts with regard to what they were in themselves,
but he fulfilled them with regard to what they prefigured, applying
what was symbolized to the symbol.[147]

This ceremonial law is also called "the carnal law" (*legis carnalis*) by
Thomas; it is the aspect of the law where the division is located: "To break
down this barrier of partition is to destroy the hostility between the Jews and
the Gentiles. The former wanted to observe the law and the latter had little
inclination to do so, from which anger and jealousy sprung up between
them."[148]   And just as it is the carnal law which divides, so Christ abolishes
this animosity "in his flesh" (*in carne sua*).[149]   That is, the sacrifice of his
flesh (which Thomas sees alluded to in the reference to flesh in v. 14[150]), puts
away any need for further ceremonial sacrifices - he quotes Heb 10:14 as
support for this conclusion. The barrier of religious custom, so often in
human history a cause for division, is torn down by Christ who fulfills the end
of religious custom by achieving what it attempted.

The reference in v. 15 to "the law of the commandments" (*lex
mandatorum*) is taken by Thomas as a confirmation of his interpretation of

---

[147] "*Moralia quidem praecepta Christus non solvit, sed adimplevit, superaddendo consilia,
et exponendo ea quae Scribae et Pharisaei male intelligabant... Caeremonialia vero praecepta
solvit quidem quantum ad eorum substantiam, sed adimplevit quantum ad illud quod
figurabant, adhibens figuratum figurae*" [Ibid., 2.5.114]. Thomas' example of Christ's
correction of the Scribes and Pharisees is Mt 5:43-44, an interesting choice in the present
context, especially considering that the "cement" which should hold the Law together is love in
his understanding. But once again, this is an unusual way of making his point; would not the
addition of love then make the barrier between the peoples a permanent one if it is identified as
the cement which is absent from the barrier?

[148] "*Et solvere hoc, scilicet parietem maceriae, est solvere inimicitias quae erant inter
Iudaeos et Gentiles: quia isti volebant legem servare, illo vero minime, ex quo oriebatur inter
eos ira et invidia*" [Ibid., 2.5.114]. LAMB, 283 n. 58, notes that the text is ambiguous at this
point. In his words, "According to literal usage, '*isti*' and '*illi*' would make the passage read:
'between the Jews and Gentiles, the latter wanting to observe the law and the former least
(wanting it).' If Thomas was asserting that the Gentiles were eager to observe the law, then
either the Jews were not eager to observe it themselves or they were not eager to let the
Gentiles do so. Old Testament history, however, offers so few instances of this phenomenon -
not to mention Paul's struggles with the judaizing Christians in the New - that I have taken
'*isti*' to refer to the Jews and '*illi*' to the Gentiles." We concur with this observation, as it
seems to make better sense in the present context.

[149] Ibid., 2.5.114.

[150] BEST, 255, agrees with Thomas that the reference to "flesh" in v 14 includes the idea of
death.

this passage; it is called this because of the multiplicity of injunctions contained within it, or possibly (here the Pauline influence surfaces again) because it is a law "of works" (*factorum*). Here Thomas has recourse to his well-known contrast between the Old and New Laws: "...the Old Law was termed of works because it ordained only what must be done, but did not confer the grace through which men would have been assisted in fulfilling the law. The New Law, on the other hand, regulates what must be done by giving commands, and it aids in fulfilling them by bestowing grace."[151] Christ makes the Old Law void "as the imperfect is made void by the perfect and the shadow by the truth" (*sicut imperfectum evacuatur per perfectum, et umbra per veritatem*).[152] Yet this is the last Thomas says about this - he moves quickly back to the main theme once again:

> He reveals the purpose of the convergence when he states **that he might make the two in himself into one new man.** The end is that the aforementioned two peoples would be formed into one people. [Whatever is to be united] must come together in some unity, and since the law divided they could not be united in that law. But Christ took the place of the law, and faith in him, as the truth of those symbols, made them one in himself.[153]

This reference to the new man is taken not as a reference to the Church as distinct from Christ, but rather to Christ himself, an interpretation clearly dictated by the upcoming reference to "one body" (*uno corpore*) in v. 16. His newness, stemming from the new manner of his conception, the novelty of his grace and his new commands, is transferred to the Church by way of its union with him.

---

[151] "...*lex vetus dictur lex factorum, quia praecipiebat tantum quid facere deberent, sed non conferebat gratiam, per quam ad legem implendam iuvarentur. Lex vero nova dirigit in agendis, praecipiendo, et iuvat ad implendum, gratiam conferendo*" [*In Eph.*, 2.5.115]. For an excellent account of this contrast between the two laws, see Brian DAVIES, *The Thought of Thomas Aquinas*, 257-262.

[152] Ibid., 2.5.115.

[153] "*Finem vero appropinquationis ostendit, dicens **ut duos condat in se**, etc. Qui quidem finis est ut dicti duo populi efficiantur unus populus. Quae autem uniuntur, oportet uniri in aliquo uno, et quia lex dividebat, non poterant in lege uniri; Christus autem in lege succedens, et fides eius (sicut veritas figurae) eos in semetipso condidit*" [Ibid., 2.5.116]. LAMB, 107, translates "*quae autem uniuntur*" as "whatever unites"; I have changed it to read "whatever is to be united."

Now that Thomas has explored the ways in which the two peoples are made into one, he moves to discuss how both draw near to God. Thomas focuses first on love of neighbor as a means to this movement toward the divine:

> It should be realized that love of neighbor is the way to peace with God; for as is mentioned in 1 Jn 4:20: 'He that loveth not his brother whom he seeth, how can he love God whom he seeth not?' Let no one pretend he has peace with Christ, Augustine asserts, if he quarrels with another Christian. Hence, he first mentions the peace among themselves Christ brought to men and then the peace of men with God. For this reason he says that **he might reconcile both** the united peoples **in one body** of the Church, namely, in Christ... Then he reconciles us **to God** through faith and charity.[154]

Once again we encounter the unexpected; Thomas not only posits that peace with God depends on peace with neighbor, but goes so far as to say that the action of God in uniting the two peoples is prior to (and necessary for) unity with God. There is no doubt that the text of Ephesians leads Thomas to a whole new conception of reconciliation in this case - because the text posits a unity in one body prior to a unity with God, Thomas does the same.

Now Thomas brings in the sin/salvation paradigm; just as by fulfilling the Old Testament symbols Christ "killed" (*interfecit*) the division between Jews and Gentiles, so did he kill in himself the hostility between God and humanity through death on the Cross. But this is an afterthought; it is interesting that this latter reconciliation does not carry the same ecclesiological weight as does the first. The blessing of reconciliation with God, though certainly not unimportant to Thomas, is mentioned because it results in the flowering of peace between peoples, which is "the manifestation of reconciliation" (*manifestationem... reconciliationis*). As Thomas notes:

---

[154] "*Sciendum est quod dilectio proximi est via ad pacem Dei; quia ut dicitur I Io. IV, 20: 'Qui enim non diligit Fratrem suum quem videt. Deum quem non videt quomodo potest diligere?' Et Augustinus dicit quod nullus putet habere pacem cum Christo, si discors fuerit cum Christiano. Primo ergo ponet pacem hominum invicem factam per Christum, et exinde pacem hominum et Deum. Propter quod dicit **ut reconciliet ambos**, iam unitos, **in uno corpore** ecclesiae, scilicet in Christo... Reconciliet, inquam, **Deo** per fidem et charitatem*" [Ibid., 2.5.118]. Thomas is paraphrasing Augustine; to locate the idea in Augustine's writings, see his comments on Psalm 124 in *Ennarrationes in Psalmos* (*CCSL* 40, pp. 1843-1844).

The reconciliation of God to man through Christ has been made
known because Christ himself not only reconciled us to God and
destroyed the hostilities, but also coming in the flesh **he preached**
and proclaimed **peace**. Or, **coming** after the resurrection when he
stood in the midst of the disciples and said: "Peace be to you" (Lk
24:36). "He hath sent me to preach to the meek, to heal the contrite
of heart" (Is 61:1). "How beautiful upon the mountains are the feet
of him that bringeth good tidings and that preacheth peace, of him
that sheweth forth good, that preacheth salvation" (Is 52:7).[155]

Here we have come back full circle to Christ, the destroyer of division
and the giver of peace. Thomas has completed a full-scale consideration of
the event of reconciliation, but not without reference to its cause. Although
his emphasis is the former, Thomas is quick to remind his audience that this
ecclesiology is founded on an even more essential christology. In fact, he has
forged what could be called an ecclesiological soteriology in response to the
text, in which Christ saves humanity by uniting it.[156]

A final historical contingency is addressed in the exposition of v. 17;
that is, the manner of the transmission of peace from Christ to the Ephesian
congregation and, for that matter, all peoples. Thomas brings the Apostles
back into his exposition at this point: **"He preached,** I say, not to one people
only but **to you** Gentiles **that were afar off**; although not in his own person,
nonetheless he proclaimed the peace to you through his Apostles... Christ in

---

[155] "*Est ergo manifesta Dei reconciliatio ad hominem per Christum, quia ipse Christus non
solum reconciliavit nos Deo, et interfecit inimicitias, sed etiam **veniens**, scilicet in carne,
evangelizavit, id est annuntiavit, **pacem**. Vel veniens per resurrectionem, quando stetit in
medio discipulorum, et dixit eis 'Pas vobis,' Lc. ult., Is LXI, 1: 'Ad annuntiandum mansuetis
misit me, etc.' Et Is LII, 7: 'Quam pulchri pedes supra montes annuntiantis et praedicantis
pacem, annuntiantis bonum, praedicantis salutem, etc.'"* [Ibid., 2.5.120].

[156] Admittedly, this interpretation (especially the parts concerning the division caused by
religious custom and the abolishment of the ceremonial law through the sacrifice of Christ) is
as eisegetical as it is magnificent, although it is not without some support in the text (see
BARTH, 290-291; LINCOLN, 141-142; BEST, 260). Here we must once again recall a point made
in Chapter II, that to dismiss Thomas' exegesis because of his development of the literal sense
is to treat the very thing that is unique to Thomas' encounter with the text of Ephesians as an
unwanted accretion. Another more constructive possibility is to treat this development of the
literal sense for what it is - a unique theological model which, although not entirely contained
in the text, is inextricably tied to it and inspired by it.

his own person announced the **peace to them that were nigh**."[157] Again the importance of the Apostles is stressed, but not without the point that their importance is entirely *pro nobis*.

In the last verse (18), the text finally offers Thomas the opportunity to expound on a favorite theme, one which we have already discussed: the pneumatological dimension of the Church. Yet his time with it is brief; he offers only one sentence regarding it: "He indicates the cause and form of peace by saying **For by him we have access both**, that is, the two peoples, **in one Spirit**, meaning we are joined by the union of the Holy Spirit."[158] Knowing how important this theme is to Thomas' ecclesiology, as well as the fact that he has not treated it to any significant length in the *lectura* thus far, should demonstrate without a doubt that we are correct in asserting that Thomas' real emphasis in this case is on the human aspect of unity, on the mechanics of human reconciliation rather than on those of the Spirit's action in bringing about reconciliation. Although Thomas gives no indication (here or elsewhere) that he would have separated these two elements, or even conceived of them as separable, we can see that the text has won the day - his anthropocentric and Christocentric interpretation, focused as it is on the event of unity, allows little room for other considerations. And when one adds the fact that Thomas goes so far as to identify the theme of this lecture as the theme of the entire Epistle when he asserts that Ephesians is about "the origination of ecclesial unity,"[159] it is safe to conclude that Thomas is truly forging a very new conception of the Church, one not unrelated to his "base ecclesiology" but also one that stands on its own, undergirded by the text of Ephesians.

This final point recalls a principle asserted in Part I of the present study; namely, that the ecclesiological model provided by Thomas in the Ephesians *lectura* can only be sufficiently understood when the work is treated as a work of exegesis, as a work tied inextricably to a text as Thomas understands it. This is confirmed by the lack of attention which the historical, human event of reconciliation receives in the work of other scholars. Ti-Ti Chen, whose work is closest to that of the present study, treats Lecture 5

---

[157] "*Evangelizavit, inquam, non uni populo tantum, sed **vobis** gentibus **qui longe fuistis**, quibus etsi non in persona propria, tamen per Apostolos suos annuntiavit pacem... Et **pacem his qui prope**, supple* [sic] *annuntiavit Christus in persona propria*" [*In Eph.*, 2.5.120].

[158] "*Causam autem pacis et formam ostendit dicens **quoniam per ipsum habemus accessum ambo**, id est, duo populi, in uno spiritu, id est, uniti unione Spiritus Sancti*" [Ibid., 2.5.121].

[159] *Super epist.*, Prol., 11.

briefly as one which demonstrates that the Christian people are "radically distinct" from the Jewish people, "because it [i.e., the former] has the Holy Spirit as its distinctive sign."[160] Elsewhere, she refers to the lecture again as one which portrays the Israelite people and the Christian people as "two phases of the Church universal," citing Thomas' comments on Eph 2:14 for support.[161] Yet as we have seen, these are not Thomas' emphases, and she does not even mention the origination of unity as an historical event, but rather as the work of the Holy Spirit in a general sense. Cuéllar does treat this historical event, albeit briefly, but only as a small part of Thomas' notion of the Old Testament as one of two phases in the history of the Church, a figure foreshadowing a future reality.[162] For his part, Sabra takes no notice of this aspect at all, even in his section on the relationship of Christ to the Church,[163] which is one part of his treatment of the Church's "constitutive principles."[164] What is lacking in their respective approaches is an attention to the organic unity of the commentary, which when recognized reveals a new side to Thomas' ecclesiological vision.

This lecture also sheds a new light on the images of the Church which Thomas develops in the first chapter; that of the Church as the flock of the Lord and as his fullness. As we noted earlier,[165] Thomas' emphasis is on ecclesial unity as the feature element of the witness of the Church to the world through the "brand" of charity and as the plenitudinous manifestation of Christ. In retrospect, the work of God in uniting two estranged peoples into one people against-all-odds only accentuates the identity of the Church as *grex Domini* and *plenitudo Christi*. Those who lived in alienation and enmity are now one flock, which lives in the world as a sign of contradiction. In particular, the first image is quickly emerging as an essential metaphor for Thomas' ecclesiological model, as is demonstrated by Thomas' repeated citation of Jn 10:16, first in his initial explanation of the Church as flock,[166] then in this lecture,[167] in Chapter 3[168] and for a final time in Chapter 4.[169]

---

[160] TI-TI CHEN, 116.
[161] Ibid., 126.
[162] CUÉLLAR, 177-181.
[163] SABRA, 77-94.
[164] Ibid., 72.
[165] Pp. 149; 160-161.
[166] *In Eph.*, 1.5.44.
[167] Ibid., 2.5.111.
[168] Ibid., 3.1.142.

    In Lecture 6, Thomas' exposition of the historical origination of
ecclesial unity in Lecture 5 is explored in its theological ramifications. The
first verse which Thomas examines there is 2:19, one which signals (through
the use of the phrase "Now, therefore") a transition by Paul from the
description of the event of unity to some significant conclusions regarding
it.[170] Thomas is definitely aware of this shift, and in accord with it enters into
what is surely the most systematic lecture of his entire exposition. Though the
purpose he assigns to the passage is the demonstration of the Gentiles' equal
access to the blessings of Christ,[171] Thomas perceives that this is achieved by
Paul through a description of the one people now formed by the reconciliation
of the two. This unified people, of course, is the Church, and Thomas uses
two illustrations (which are provided by the text) to describe it. The first, in v.
19, is a comparison of two images, city and household; the second is the
exploration of one image, that of the Church as temple.
    Thomas' exposition of the first image is based on v. 19b, "but you are
fellow citizens with the saints and the [family] of God" (*sed estis cives
sanctorum et domestici Dei*). His analysis is initiated by the contrast with
"strangers and foreigners" in v. 19a, and is worth quoting at length:

> To understand this text it must be realized that the
> community of the faithful are sometimes referred to as a house in
> the Scriptures: "that you may know how you ought to behave
> yourself in the house of God, which is the church of the living God"
> (1 Tim 3:15). At other times it is called a city: "Jerusalem, which is
> built as a city..." (Ps 121:3). A city possesses a political community
> whereas a household has a domestic one, these differ in two
> respects. For those who belong to the domestic community share
> with one another private activities; but those belonging to the civil
> community have in common with one another public activities.
> Secondly, the head of the family governs the domestic community;
> while those in the civic community are ruled by a king. Hence:
> what the king is in the realm, this the father is in the home.
>   The community of the faithful contains within it something
> of the city and something of the home. If the ruler of the com-
> munity is thought of, he is a father: "Our Father, who art in heaven"
> (Mt 6:9); "you shall call me Father and shall not cease to walk after
> me" (Jer 3:19). In this perspective, the community is a home. But

---

[169] Ibid., 4.4.217.
[170] BARTH, 268; LINCOLN, 150; BEST, 276.
[171] *In Eph.*, 2.6.122.

if you consider the subjects themselves, it is a city since they have in common with one another the particular acts of faith, hope and charity. In this way, if the faithful are considered in themselves, the community is a civil one; if however, the ruler is thought of, it is a domestic community.[172]

Here we encounter a section of the *lectura* that has been well explained by others,[173] and we have recourse particularly to Sabra's insights in order best to understand it. Noting that this passage is only one of three in which Thomas elaborates on the idea of the Church as a city, he identifies its origin as an appropriation of a political model, "i.e., from an analogy with a state or public society."[174] As he summarizes it: "When Thomas likens the Church to a city in this text, there immediately comes to his mind a conception of men who live by faith, hope and love. Just as the members of a city share in public acts, so do members of the Church... the Church as city is primarily a theological communion." Therefore it is a "horizontal designation" of the Church, whereas the other image involved in the passage, i.e. the Church as household, is a "vertical" one.[175] As Sabra notes, this is an analogy which is unique to the *lectura*.[176]

Thomas completes his exploration of the verse by commenting on what it means for the Ephesians to be fellow citizens with the saints:

---

[172] "*Ad intellectum autem litterae sciendum est, quod collegium fidelium quandoque in scripturis vocatur domus, secundum illud I Tim. III,15: 'Ut scias quomodo in domo Dei oporteat te conversari, quae est Dei ecclesia.' Quandoque autem vocatur civitas, secundum illud Ps. CXXI, 3: 'Ierusalem quae aedificatur ut civitas.'*

Civitas enim habet collegium politicum: domus autem oeconomicum, inter quae quidem duplex differentia invenitur. Nam qui sunt de collegio domus communicant sibi in actibus privatis; qui vero sunt de collegio civitatis, communicant sibi in actibus publicis. Item, qui sunt in collegio domus, reguntur ab uno qui vocatur paterfamilias; sed qui sunt in collegio civitatis reguntur a rege. Ita enim est paterfamilias in domo, sicut rex in regno.

Sic igitur collegium fidelium aliquid habet de civitate, et aliquid de domo. Sed si consideretur rector collegii, pater est Matth. VI, v.9: 'Pater noster, qui es in caelis,' etc. Hier. c. III, 19: Patrem vocabis me, et post me ingredi non cessabis'; et sic collegium est domus. Si vero ipsos subditos consideres, sic civitas est, quia communicabant sibi in actibus praecipuis, scilicet fidei, spei et charitatis. Et hoc modo si fideles considerentur in se, est collegium civitatis; si vero rector collegii attendatur, est collegium domus." [Ibid., 2.6.124].

[173] See SABRA, 36-43; TI-TI CHEN, 127-136; SWIERZAWSKI, "Christ and the Church," 241; CONGAR, "'Ecclesia' et 'populus (fideles)' dans l'ecclésiologie de S. Thomas," 164.

[174] SABRA, 36-37.

[175] Ibid., 37.

[176] Ibid., 40.

As if he had said: Since the community of the faithful is termed a
city in relation to its subjects, and a home relative to its ruler, the
assembly to which you [the Ephesians] are called is the city of the
saints and the house of God. "Glorious things are said of you, O
city of God" (Ps. 86:3). Hence Augustine remarks: "Two loves have
formed two cities. For the love of God, even to the contempt of
self," namely, of the man loving, "builds the heavenly city of
Jerusalem. But the love of self, even to the contempt of God, builds
the city of Babylon." Everyone, then, either is a citizen with the
saints if he loves God to the contempt of self ["All of her domestics
are doubly clothed," Prov 31:21]; or if he loves himself to the
contempt of God, he is a citizen of Babylon.[177]

Thomas' wholesale borrowing of Augustine's famous image of the
two cities is significant here, because in the various references to the Church
as city in Thomas' works, he only adopts it on this occasion. In this regard,
Sabra's insights are again helpful; he notes that while Augustine's use of the
image of Church as city is normally a reference to its "celestial state" (as in
this case), Thomas' ideas about the Church as city are usually in reference to
the Church in its present condition.[178] As such, the tendency of Thomas to
interpret the message of Ephesians in a predominantly eschatological way is
certainly reflected by his use of Augustine's concept in this instance; the
reference to building is not to be ignored either, especially when one
considers the next illustration of the Church, which Thomas seems to be
preparing for.

While he does give a significant portion of his lecture over to this first
illustration (seven paragraphs in all), Thomas seems to be interested in it more
for pedagogical reasons (i.e. for using the occasion of the appearance of the
city and household images as an opportunity to instruct his students regarding

---

[177] "... quasi dicat: Quia collegium fidelium dicitur civitas in comparatione ad subditos, et
domus in comparatione ad rectorem, collegium, ad quod vocati estis, est civitas sanctorum et
domus Dei. Ps. LXXXVI, v.3: 'Gloriosa dicta sunt de te, civitas Dei.' Unde Augustinus: 'Duas
civitates faciunt duo amores. Nam amor Dei usque ad contemptum sui,' scilicet hominis
amantis, 'facit civitatem Ierusalem caelestem, amor vero sui usque ad contemptum Dei, facit
civitatem Babylonis.' Quilibet ergo vel est civis sanctorum, si diligit Deum usque ad
contemptum sui, Prov. ult.: 'Omnes domestici eius vestiti sunt duplicibus'; si vero diligit se
usque ad contemptum Dei, est civis Babylonis." [Ibid., 2.6.125]. LAMB omits the quote from
Proverbs from his translation, which is included in the original text, although its meaning is
obscure. I have added it above in brackets. For the original quote from AUGUSTINE, see De
Civitate Dei, XIV.8 (CCSL 48, pg. 451).
[178] SABRA, 39.

them) than for reasons of interpretation. Though the situation which he proposes to address is the new status of the Gentiles, he spends most of his time explaining the images themselves rather than what they signify in regard to this primary theme. When we come to the second and final illustration of the lecture (on vv 20-22), Thomas gives much more attention to this aspect; it is clear that the notion of temple construction in v. 21 draws him back to the theme of the origination of unity. This will also allow him to develop a compact but comprehensive model of the Church (i.e. as spiritual edifice) on the basis of the text.

Thomas begins by considering how Paul uses the imagery of a building as a literary device for describing the Church:

> It is customary in the scriptures that the figure, called metonymy, is used where the container is substituted for what it contains, as a house sometimes refers to those who are in the house. The Apostle employs this figure of speech concerning those who are in the house of God, the faithful; as though they were one house, he compares them to a building.[179]

This raises the question of what it is that the faithful are contained in. The way Thomas explains it here possibly alludes to a place of worship, especially if we consider the direct reference to "a holy temple" in v. 21.[180] Yet in this passage, with its discussion of foundations and frame, the term *domus Dei* is almost certainly a reference to the Catholic Faith. Thomas' repeated references to doctrine in this lecture reinforces this understanding, and so it is clear that what is dwelt in by the faithful is what Thomas would call the Gospel - that which has been handed on by the Apostles and the Prophets in perpetuity to the Church as summarized by the Apostle's Creed.

This is clear when we consider what provides the foundation for the temple; Thomas' exposition places its emphasis not so much on the Apostles and Prophets as on their teaching and its essential orientation to Christ:

---

[179] "*Consuetum est in scripturis quod in figura, quae metonymia dicitur, continens ponatur pro contento, sicut quandoque domus pro his qui sunt in domo: secundum hunc ergo modum loquitur Apostolus de his qui sunt in domo Dei, scilicet de fidelibus, sicut de una domo, et comparat eos aedificio*" [*In Eph.*, 2.6.126].

[180] See SWIERZAWSKI, "Faith and Worship in the Pauline Commentaries of St. Thomas Aquinas," 389-412, for the centrality of worship in Thomas' interpretation of the Pauline corpus.

In this regard he states that they [the Ephesians] are not strangers
but fellow citizens who belong already to the spiritual edifice which
is **built upon the foundation of the Apostles and Prophets**, that
is, upon the teaching of the Apostles and Prophets. Or, **upon the
foundation of the Apostles and Prophets** means upon Christ who
is the foundation of the Apostles and the Prophets. As though he
said: You are built upon the same foundation on which the Apostles
and Prophets, who were Jewish, were built.[181]

The passing reference to the Jewishness of the Apostles and Prophets
is Thomas' attempt to keep the idea of the unity of the two peoples in the
foreground, reinforcing its primacy as the main theme. He continues to qualify the foundational status of these individuals in relation to the primary
foundation of the edifice, who is Christ: "...they proclaimed Christ alone,
and not themselves. To accept their doctrine is to accept Christ crucified."[182] This reference to the sacrifice of Christ once more recalls the
vision of Christ as the surpasser of religious custom to the effect of unity; he
is the foundation for both because he is common ground, as Thomas will
himself emphasize in explaining the symbolism of the cornerstone:

He is called cornerstone on account of the convergence of both
[Jews and Gentiles]. As two walls are joined at the corner, so in
Christ the Jewish and Pagan peoples are united: "The stone which
the builders rejected; the same is become head of the corner" (Ps
117:22): "This is the stone which was rejected by you, the builders,
which has become the head of the corner. Neither is there salvation
in any other" (Acts 4:11-12). And Christ applies this text to himself
in Mt 21:42: "Have you never read in the Scriptures: The stone

---

[181] "*Et quantum ad hoc dicit eos non esse hospites, sed cives, qui iam pertinent ad
aedificium spirituale, utpote* **superaedificati supra fundamentum Apostolorum et
Prophetarum**, *id est, qui sunt Apostoli et Prophetae, id est, super doctrinam eorum. Vel aliter:*
Supra fundamentum Apostolorum et Prophetarum, *id est, supra Christum qui est
fundamentum Apostoloum et Prophetarum; quasi dicat: In eodem fundamento superaedificati
estis in quo Apostoli et Prophetae sunt aedificati, qui ex Iudaeis fuerunt*" [Ibid., 2.6.127]. See
CONGAR, "L'apostolicité de l'Eglise chez S. Thomas d'Aquin," *Revue des sciences
philosophiques et théologiques* 44 (1960) : 212-213, for an excellent explanation of how the
teaching of the Apostles serves as a foundation for the Church.

[182] "*cum Christum tantum, non seipsos, praedicaverint; unde accipere eorum doctrinam est
accipere Christum crucifixum*" [Ibid., 2.6.127].

which the builders rejected, the same is become head of the corner?[183]

The barrier which once divided them has been smashed, to become the very place where the two peoples (to refer as Thomas does to the original image in Lecture 5) are now cemented together with charity,[184] joining on Christ who unites them. The triple enumeration of citations regarding Christ as the rejected stone adds an element of irony; the very one who was cast aside for not fitting the barrier is the one who does away with it and becomes the source of unity. It should be noted that here Thomas shifts to metonymy himself; the Jews and Gentiles are identified as walls of the temple, rather than dwelling within it. Thomas will use this literary device for the rest of the lecture.

This edifice is spiritual, a fact which Thomas now emphasizes by offering one of the most unusually beautiful images of the Church to be found in his writings:

> The foundation of a spiritual edifice contrasts with that of a material building. For a material building rests on a foundation in the earth, the more important the foundation is, the deeper it must be. A spiritual structure, on the other hand, has its foundation in heaven; as a result, the more principal the foundation, the higher it necessarily is. Thus we could imagine a city, as it were, coming down from heaven with its foundation in heaven and the building itself appearing to come downwards towards us below...[185]

---

[183] *"Angularis autem dicitur propter utriusque coninunctionem; nam ut in angulo duo parietes uniuntur, sic in Christo populus Iudaeorum et Gentium uniti sunt. Ps [cxvii, 22]: 'Lapidem quem reprobaverunt aedificantes, hic factus est in caput anguli.' Act. IV, 11s.: Hic est lapis qui reprobatus est a vobis aedificantibus, qui factus est in caput anguli, et non est in aliquo alio salus.' Et hoc idem de se introducit Matth. XXI, 42: 'Numquid legistis in scripturis: Lapidem quem reprobaverunt aedificantes, hic factus est in caput anguli, etc."* [Ibid., 2.6.129]. Thomas' interpretation of *"angulari lapide"* in v. 20 is affirmed by the latest scholarship. As Michael CAHILL notes, it is reasonable to translate the term *"akrog_niaion"* as "cornerstone" in Eph 2:20, as it is concerned with "the initial phase of building" [Idem, "Not a Cornerstone! Translating Ps 118, 22 in the Jewish and Christian Scriptures," *Revue Biblique* 106 (1999) : 351]. However, CAHILL would call into question Thomas' use of Ps 118:22, Acts 4:11-22 and Mt 21:42 as supportive of his interpretation of Eph 2:20, as these refer not to a cornerstone but rather to a capstone [245-357].

[184] Ibid., 2.6.113.

[185] *"Sed non est idem de fundamento in aedificio spirituali et in aedificio materiali. Materiale namque aedificium fundamentum habet in terra, et ideo oportet ut principalius*

When one considers how much stress Thomas places, both in this *lectura* and elsewhere, on the eschatological dimension of the Church and its status as a pilgrim Church,[186] this image is all the more surprising, as it portrays the Church as being pointed away from heaven and toward earth, manifesting the former to the latter. This recalls once again the *grex Domini* and *plenitudo Christi* imagery, in which the orientation of the Church is outwards rather than upwards, a missionary Church witnessing its character to the world.

Thomas completes his picture of the temple with his interpretation of Ephesians 2:21-22. He considers these to be a chronicle of the construction of the temple, which involves four necessary phases: the foundation, the construction on the foundation, the increase of the construction and its final completion.[187] He devotes only one sentence to the first, as he has already considered it in detail; however, the final three steps are given much more attention.

In describing the second step, Thomas asserts that he is engaging in an allegorical interpretation, one which he will continue to identify as such throughout his treatment of the stages of building. In his understanding, the Church is the building being constructed, although it is unclear why he suddenly identifies this as an allegorical sense of the passage when this has been his literal interpretation throughout. Perhaps he does so to distinguish this more primary interpretation from a new moral sense which he attributes to it: the temple as not only Church but also as the sanctified soul (*animam sanctam*):

> Understood allegorically, this signifies the Church herself which is built up when men are converted to the faith. Taken morally it signifies a sanctified soul, and then this building is erected when good works are built upon Christ. "A wise woman builds her house" (Prov 14:1); "let every man take heed how he builds thereupon" (1 Cor 3:10). With Christ as the foundation, every spiritual edifice - whether of Jews or of Gentiles - is constructed by

---

fundamentum sit magis infimum. Spirituale vero aedificium fundamentum habet in caelo, et ideo oportet quod fundamentum quanto est principalius, tanto sit sublimius: ut sic imaginemur civitatem quamdam descendentem de caelo, cuius fundamentum in caelo existens, et aedificium demissum ad nos videatur inferius..." [Ibid., 2.6.130].

[186] CUÉLLAR, 263-280, amply demonstrates how much attention Thomas devotes to the future destiny of the Church in his Pauline commentaries.

[187] *In Eph.*, 2.6.131.

God's power... Yet the building is constructed instrumentally either by the man who builds up himself, or by prelates.[188]

To extricate the purely ecclesiological interpretation here would perhaps be to miss a crucial point - that the moral sense is actually a function of the allegorical sense. God, who works in each person, prepares them as individual materials in order to incorporate them into the edifice. The mention of prelates in the final sentence extends the building process into Thomas' day and beyond - this work is not solely the work of the Apostles, but of all who labor in every age. Also crucial is the repeated mention of the two peoples, an indicator that Thomas has not left off this more historical interpretation, which he will bring in once again in his interpretation of v. 22.

The third step is really an extension of the second: "He touches on the third when he states **grows up into a holy temple**; this happens when the number of those saved increases... It also grows when a man makes progress in good works, and he grows in grace to the degree that he becomes a holy temple."[189] It is here that Thomas locates the chief element of temple identity - holiness: "A temple is the dwelling place of God and must be holy... Since we should be inhabited by God, that he might live in us, we ought to prepare ourselves in order to be holy."[190] This holiness consists in charity, the "cement" which fuses the individual building stones into one structure. Thus the perfection and completion of the temple occurs when charity indwells each member with intensity. This is what the passage means when it says that the temple is **in the Lord**; and "temple" here refers to both the individual soul as well as the Church.[191]

---

[188] "*Et quidem si intelligatur allegorice, designat ipsam ecclesiam, quae tunc construitur quando homines ad fidem convertuntur. Si autem moraliter intelligatur, significat animam sanctam, et tunc eiusmodi aedificatio construitur, quando bona opera superaedificantur super Christum. Prov. XIV, 1: 'Sapiens mulier aedificat domum suam.' I Cor III, 10: 'Unusquisque videat quomodo superaedificet.' In hoc ergo fundamento, scilicet Christo, omnis aedificatio spiritualis construitur, Iudaeorum vel Gentilium, a Deo per auctoritatem... Sed instrumentaliter construitur aedificium vel ab homine qui seipsum aedificat, vel a praelatis*" [Ibid., 2.6.131].

[189] "*Tertium tangit cum dicit **crescit in templum**, etc.; quod quidem fit quando multiplicantur qui salvi fiunt... Crescit etiam quando homo crescit in bonis operibus, et in gratia crescit quantum ad hoc, quod fit templum sanctum*" [Ibid., 2.6.131].

[190] "*Templum enim a Deo inhabitatur, et ideo oportet quod sit sanctum... Et quia nos debemus inhabitari a Deo, ut Deus in nobis habitet, ad hoc nos parare debemus, ut sancti simus*" [Ibid., 2.6.131].

[191] Ibid., 2.6.131.

Thomas uses v. 22 as a final opportunity to raise his main topic once again: the union of the two peoples:

> Finally, (v. 22), he indicates how the Gentiles have become participants of the building. **In which** building not only are the Jews incorporated, but also you Ephesians **are built together**, that is, you are incorporated like the others. "Unto whom coming, as to a living stone, rejected indeed by men, but chosen and made honorable by God, you also as living stones are built up, a spiritual house" (1 Pet 2:4-5). Therefore he adds **into a habitation of God** that God may dwell in you through faith. "That Christ may dwell by faith in your hearts" (Eph 3:17). Yet this cannot happen without charity since "he that abides in charity abides in God, and God in him" (1 Jn 4:16). And charity is bestowed on us through the Holy Spirit: "the charity of God is poured forth in our hearts by the Holy Ghost who is given to us" (Rom 5:5). Thus he adds **in the Spirit**.[192]

The reference to the Holy Spirit and the Spirit's gift of charity draws a connection between the universal, historical picture of the Church/temple and its growth and the more fundamental theme of the union of the two peoples into one through the work of Christ. Charity is the key which shows the increase of the Church in all nations and cultures to be a function of the initial reconciliation of the Jews and Gentiles. Thus the construction of the temple is continuous with the whole history of the Church, reaching back to Christ's act of peace and also forward in perpetuity.

As we conclude our consideration of the second chapter of the *lectura*, it is certain that with it we have reached the heart of Thomas' understanding of the Epistle's message. Nowhere else does the theme of the origination of ecclesial unity take such a central position; nowhere else does it receive such concentrated attention and systematic exposition. Therefore it

---

[192] "*Consequenter cum dicit* **in quo et vos**, *etc., ostendit quomodo Gentiles facti sunt participes huius aedificii, dicens* **in quo**, *scilicet aedificio, non solum superaedificantur Iudaei, sed etiam vos Ephesii* **coaedificamini**, *id est ad similitudinem aliorum aedificamini. I Petr. II, 4 s.: 'Ad quem accedentes lapidem vivum, ab hominibus quidem reprobatum, a Deo autem electum et honorificatum, et ipsi tamquam lapides vivi superaedificamini domus spiritualis.' Et ideo subdit* **in habitaculum Dei**, *ut scilicet Deus in vobis inhabitet per fidem. Infra III, 17: 'Habitare Christum per fidem in cordibus vestris.' Hoc autem non potest fieri sine charitate, quia qui manet in charitate, in Deo manet, etc. I Io. IV, 16: Charitas autem datur nobis per Spiritum Sanctum. Rom. V, 5: 'Charitas Dei diffusa est in cordibus nostris per Spiritum Sanctum qui datus est nobis.' Ideo subdit* **in Spiritu Sancto**" [Ibid., 2.6.132].

must serve as the central reference point for the rest of our analysis, as the various topics which Thomas will explore in the upcoming lectures shall have their importance revealed by their connection to this one. Although it is tempting to stop at this point in order to explore the ramifications of this incredibly rich section of the Ephesians commentary, to do so would preempt a full consideration of Thomas' vision of the Church in his interpretation of the Epistle, as four chapters remain to be considered. As we consider those, the relation of each to Thomas' central theme can be fully appreciated.

C) *Chapter Three: The Mystery Revealed*

"The Apostle has previously recounted the many blessings of God granted to the human race and the Apostles themselves, here he turns to God's special blessings bestowed on himself."[193] As Thomas begins his consideration of Ephesians 3, he repeats what he believes to be its theme - the special situation of the Apostle who is writing about his ministry to the Ephesian congregation as well as to the larger Church.[194] We have already considered the preeminently pastoral emphasis which Thomas gives to the role of the Apostles in the *lectura*, one which he develops in more detail in the context of this chapter. However, this treatment of Paul's ministry and special blessings as an exemplary specimen of apostleship need not be considered in any more detail in the present study - others have already treated it thoroughly,[195] and Thomas general treatment of it is as digressive as is its function in the text of the Epistle.[196] It should also be noted that this emphasis is not unique to the *lectura* but rather to many of Thomas' Pauline commentaries, and also does not figure prominently in his consideration of the main theme.

However, certain sections of Thomas' interpretation of Ephesians 3 do stand out for the present study because of some significant places wherein Thomas is offered the opportunity to develop further his theology of ecclesial unity as well as his vision of the Church. In particular, his exposition of 3:6,

---

[193] *"Supra commemoravit Apostolus multa Dei beneficia humano generi et ipsis Apostolis collata, hic commemorat specialia Dei beneficia sibi tradita"* [Ibid., 3.1.133].

[194] Thomas' understanding of this chapter is upheld by modern exegetes; see BARTH, 327; LINCOLN, 167; BEST, 292-293.

[195] See CONGAR, "L'apostolicité de l'Eglise," 193-198; Nicholas HALLIGAN, "The Teaching of St. Thomas Aquinas in regard to the Apostles," 32-47; TI-TI CHEN, 193-198; CUÉLLAR, 251-261.

[196] BEST, 293.

3:10, and 3:18-21 must be explored in order to comprehend fully the theological model which Thomas has produced thus far.

In the case of 3:6, we find him weaving his exposition around the synonymous terms "*sacramentum*" and "*mysterio Christi*,"[197] which first appear in the Vulgate text with vv 3-4. Paul's special blessing in this case is to have a full knowledge of this mystery,[198] a knowledge which was given to the "Old Testament fathers" (*patribus Veteris Testamenti*) but only in "certain generalities, whereas [it was disclosed] to the Apostles clearly and completely" (*in quadam generalitate, Apostolis vero clare et perfecte*).[199] This is a sacrament (or mystery) of faith according to Thomas, which Paul discloses to the Ephesian believers; namely, that "the Gentiles should be fellow heirs" (*Gentes esse cohaeredes*) in Christ. In a passage packed with biblical citations (which we shall omit), Thomas explains what this means:

> ... it should be recognized that the Jews enjoyed three prerogatives with respect to the Gentiles. They had the promised inheritance... Another was their special election; they were set apart from the Gentiles... Finally, they had the promise of a Christ...
>
> These three the Gentiles did not enjoy... By faith, however, they have received them. First, they share in the inheritance; concerning this he says **fellow heirs** with the Jews in the heavenly inheritance. Second, [they are admitted] to the chosen community of believers; thus he states **of the same body**, that is, in one body... Third, [they are admitted] to a participation in the promised grace; he says they are **co-partners of his promise**, the promises made to Abraham.[200]

---

[197] For the immense importance of these terms to Thomas, see Donal J. O'CONNOR, "The Concept of Mystery in Aquinas' Exegesis, Pt. I-II," 183-210, 261-282; SWIERZAWSKI, "God and the Mystery of his Wisdom in the Pauline Commentaries of St. Thomas Aquinas," 466-500. For an exploration of the meaning of the term in Ephesians, see esp. C. CARAGOUNIS, *The Ephesian Mysterion: Meaning and Content* (Lund: CWK Gleerup, 1977), 96-112.

[198] *In Eph.*, 3.1.138.

[199] Ibid., 3.1.142.

[200] "*Circa quod sciendum est quod Iudaei triplicem prerogativam habebant respectu Gentilium, scilicet promissionis haereditatis. .. Item per specialem a gentibus aliis distinctionem et electionem... Item per Christi promissionem. Haec autem tria Gentes non habebant... Sed ad haec tria recepti sunt per fidem. Primo quidem, quantum ad participationem haereditatis, et, quantum ad hoc, dicit **cohaeredes**, scilicet ipsis Iudaeis in haereditate caelesti... Secundo ad speciale collegium fidelium, et quantum ad hoc, dicit et concorporales, id est unum corpus... Tertio, ad participationem, gratiae repromissae, et, quantum ad hoc, dicit **et comparticipes**, scilicet promissionum quae factae sunt Abrahae*" [Ibid., 3.1.142].

Here Thomas cites Jn 10:16 once again in regard to the Gentiles, counterbalancing a citation of Ps 19:3 in reference to the Jews: "We are his people and the sheep of his pasture" (*Nos autem populus eius et oves pascuae eius*). He also cites Eph 2:12, and with all three citations shows his recognition of the connection of the verse under comment (3:6) to Ephesians 2. In fact, his comments here fill out his interpretation of the latter, which was more focused on the event of unity than on the blessings it carries: namely, a heavenly inheritance, admission to the *speciale collegium fidelium*, and participation in grace. All of these are the blessings of Christ, who (in Pauline fashion) is contrasted with Moses:

> The Gentiles have acquired all this, not through Moses, but **in Christ**: "For the Law was given by Moses; grace and truth came by Jesus Christ" (Jn 1:17), "by whom he has given us most great and precious promises" (2 Pet 1:4). Moreover, these did not come through fulfilling the law, whose burden "neither our fathers nor we have been able to bear" (Acts 15:10), but **by the gospel** through which all men are saved.[201]

The next significant interpretation by Thomas for his main theme is in regard to 3:10: "That the manifold wisdom of God may be made known to the principalities and powers in heavenly places through the church" (*Ut innotescat principatibus, et potestatibus, in caelestibus, per ecclesiam, multiformis sapientia Dei*). The manifestation of God through the Church is a theme we have encountered three separate times already in the *lectura*, and in each case this emphasis was provided by Thomas rather than by the Epistle. In this case it is the text which provides the impetus, one which Thomas is eager to follow. He begins by identifying the recipients of the revelation of God's manifold wisdom: "the holy angels by whom the saints are directed and protected" (*sanctis Angelis, per quos diriguntur, et defenduntur sancti*).[202] Yet this presents "great difficulty" (*magnam difficultatem*); Thomas takes issue with the interpretation of Peter Lombard (without rejecting it outright), who holds that the angels are given this wisdom "by the Apostles preaching in

---

[201] "*Et haec omnia consecutae sunt Gentes non per Moysem, sed in Christo. - Io. I, 17: 'Lex per Moysem data est, gratia et veritas per Iesum Christum facta est.' II Petr. I, 4: 'Per quem maxima et pretiosa nobis promissa donavit,' etc. - Item, nec per impletionem legis, quia hoc est iugum quod 'neque patres nostri, neque nos portare potuimus,' ut dicitur Act. XV, 10, sed per evangelium, per quod omnes salvantur*" [Ibid., 3.1.142].

[202] Ibid., 3.3.159.

the Church" (*per Apostolos in ecclesia praedicantes*).²⁰³   This does not
address the question of how the Angels, who "immediately intuit the divine
nature" (*immediate naturam divinam vident*), could need to be taught outside
of that intuition. Here Thomas resorts to epistemological subtleties in order to
save the original sense of the text:

> Therefore, it must be asserted that the angels are instructed
> **through the church**, that is, through the apostolic preaching, as the
> Gloss maintains, in such a way that they are not taught by the
> Apostles, but in them...
>   Further, there exist certain intelligible patterns [operative
> in] the mysteries of grace which transcend the whole of creation.
> These intelligible patterns are not impressed on the angelic minds
> but are hidden in God alone. Thus the angels do not grasp them in
> themselves, nor even in God, but only as they unfold in the events
> [which the mysteries] effect. Now, the intelligible patterns relative
> to God's manifold wisdom belong to this category. They are hidden
> in God and gradually unfold in external effects. Clearly, therefore,
> the angels will understand them neither in themselves, nor in the
> Word, nor by the Apostles or any other wayfarer. Rather, they
> know [the mysteries of grace] hidden in the Divine Mind as they
> unfold in the Apostles themselves.²⁰⁴

Yet this interpretation is only one of two possibilities which Thomas
offers; he sees another, in which the conjunction "*ut*" is taken not causally but
consecutively. In this case, the text would indicate that it is directly after the
creation of the Principalities and Powers that the mystery of God's work is
revealed to them, through the revelation of the Church's heavenly archetype
and exemplar: "The sacrament was concealed in God in such a manner that he

---

²⁰³ Ibid., 3.3.160. For the original context of the quote by Peter LOMBARD, see *PL* 192 col.
189, B.

²⁰⁴ "*Dicendum est ergo, quod innotuit Angelis per ecclesiam, id est per Apostolos
praedicantes, ut dicit glossa, non quod Angeli hoc didicerint ab eis, sed in eis... Ulterius
notandum est, quod sunt quaedam rationes mysteriorum gratiae totam creaturam excedentes, et
huiusmodi rationes non sunt inditae mentibus Angelorum, sed in solo Deo sunt occultae. Et
ideo Angeli non cognoscunt eas in seipsis, nec etiam in Deo, sed cognoscunt eas secundum
quod in effectibus explicantur. Cum igitur rationes pertinentes ad multiformem sapientiam Dei,
sint huiusmodi, scilicet in solo Deo absconditae, et postmodum in istis forinsecis effectibus
explicatae, manifestum est, quod Angeli eas, nec in seipsis, nec in ipso Verbo, nec etiam ab
Apostolis, nec a viatoribus aliis congnoverunt; sed in ipsis Apostolis explicatas, prius in mente
divina latentes, cognoverunt*" [Ibid., 3.3.160].

later revealed it... This was not through the earthly Church but through the heavenly one - the true Church who is our mother and to whom we tend; on her is our militant Church patterned."[205]

What of this confusing array of possibilities? For its importance to Thomas' central concern, which is certainly not angelic epistemology, we must look at what both of the offered possibilities have in common. In each case, what Thomas labors to demonstrate is that in some real sense the angels are taught through the Church, and particularly through that mystery which is the reconciliation of the two peoples into one Church, the incorporation of the Gentiles as co-heirs. Be it taken simply (as in the case of the Lombardian Gloss), or as a supernatural spectatorship in which the angels watch the event of unity unfold through intuition of the Divine Mind, or whether they contemplate by special privilege the ecclesial *exemplata* from the very beginning of their creation, the place which Thomas gives to the event in the plan of God is so central that it transcends the scope of human history and is placed in the heavens, itself the substance of angelic contemplation. Here we have a manifesting function *par excellence* - not only does the Church manifest heaven to humanity but to heavenly beings as well.[206]

As he completes his consideration of Ephesians 3, Thomas offers a final reflection which offers a key to understanding not only the event of the origination of ecclesial unity, but also its very substance. He devotes his final two lectures to the prayer of Paul for the Ephesians, which is primarily a prayer for an increase in charity.[207] Here Thomas is afforded an opportunity by the text to give a fitting end to his sustained inquiry into unity with a focus on this key virtue. When he encounters the famous reference to the dimensions of love in v. 18, Thomas enters into a meditation on the charity of Christ:

---

[205] *"...istud sacramentum ita fuit absconditum in Deo, quod inde innotuit... et hoc non per ecclesiam terrenam, sed caelestem, quia ibi est vera ecclesia, quae est mater nostra et ad quam tendimus et a qua nostra ecclesia militans est exemplata*" [Ibid., 3.3.161].

[206] It has been suggested that Thomas' interpretation of Eph 3:10 demolishes the possibility that Thomas' ecclesiology in the *lectura* carries a decidedly historical emphasis, because it makes the event of unity (i.e. the "mystery" and/or "manifold wisdom") something which is a property of the heavenly Church, almost in the Platonic sense of the latter serving as the form of the earthly unity of the Church, which is secondary and inferior to it. But this interpretation is only one of two possibilities offered by Thomas, the first of which (i.e. that the Angels know the mystery through an intuition into the Divine Mind only as it unfolds in the Apostles) preserves the importance of the historical element.

[207] Best, 335.

For whatever occurred in the mystery of human redemption and
Christ's incarnation was the work of love. He was born out of
charity: "For his exceeding charity wherewith he loved us even
when we were dead in sins, has quickened us together in Christ"
(Eph 2:4-5). That he died also sprang from charity: "Greater love
than this no man has, that a man lay down his life for his friends"
(Jn 15:13). And "Christ also has loved us and has delivered himself
for us, an oblation and sacrifice to God" (Eph 5:2). On this account
St. Gregory exclaimed: "O the incalculable love of your charity! To
redeem slaves you delivered up your Son."[208]

But this passage can also be read in regard to "the perfection of our
charity" (*perfectionem charitatis nostrae*):

As though he stated: Be strong, rooted and founded in charity, that
you may comprehend - and not merely know - **with all the saints**;
since this gift of charity is common to all, no one can be holy
without charity, as the third chapter of Ephesians indicates. **May
you, I say, comprehend what is the breadth** of charity, extending,
as it does, even to one's enemies... For charity is broad in its
diffusion... Its **length** is seen in its durability, never stopping, it
begins in this life and is perfected in glory... Its **height** is perceived
in its motivation which is heavenly; God is not loved to obtain
temporal advantages - which love would be sickly - but he is loved
for his own sake alone... **Depth** signifies the source of charity
itself. For our love of God does not spring from ourselves, but from
the Holy Spirit, as Romans (5) mentions: "The charity of God is
poured forth in our hearts, by the Holy Spirit who is given to us."[209]

---

[208] "*Ubi sciendum est quod quidquid est in mysterio redemptionis humanae et incarnationis
Christi, totum est opus charitatis. Nam quod incarnatum est, ex charitate processit. Supra II,
4: 'Propter nimiam charitatem suam qua dilexit nos,' etc. Quia vero mortuus fuit, ex charitate
processit. Io. XV, 13: 'Maiorem hac dilectionem nemo habet,' etc.; infra V, 2: 'Christus dilexit
nos, et tradidit semetipsum pro nobis oblationem et hostiam Deo.' Propter hoc dicit
Gregorius: 'O inaestimabilis dilectio charitatis! ut servum redimeres, filium tradidisti'*" [*In
Eph.*, 3.5.178]. Thomas mistakenly attributes this quote from the Easter Vigil Exultet to
Gregory; see LAMB, 280 n. 48.

[209] "*...quasi dicat: Corroboramini in charitate radicati et fundati, et hoc **ut possitis
comprehendere**, non solum cognoscere, **cum omnibus sanctis**, quia hoc donum, scilicet
charitatis, commune est omnibus, cum nullus possit esse sanctus sine charitate, ut dicitur
Ephes. c. III. **Possitis**, inquam, comprehendere **quae sit latitudo**, scilicet charitatis, quae se
extendit usque ad inimicos... Lata est enim charitas ad suam diffusionem... **Longitudo** autem
eius attenditur quantum ad sui perseverantiam, quia numquam deficit, sed hic incipit et
perficitur in gloria... **Sublimitas** autem eius attenditur quantum ad intentionem caelestium, ut*

The lesson to be learned from this final reference to the charity of Christ is rendered by Thomas as one which teaches the necessity of a resort to charity in all things. Each aspect has a connection to the subject of unity - it is common to all, it extends to enemies (recalling the "enmities" in Eph 2:14), it never ceases, it has God for its object, it comes from the Holy Spirit (who is the source of unity). All that Thomas has said about the initial event of unity is shown to be true of charity in general. As such, it is the most important characteristic of Church and Church membership, a sentiment with which he completes his exegesis of Ephesians 3 - Thomas shifts into thanksgiving along with the Epistle as he makes his final comments:

> The subject matter of the thanksgiving is the twofold blessing God has bestowed upon us. The first is the institution of the Church, and the second the Incarnation of his Son. Hence he says **to him**, God the Father, **be glory**, in **the Church** for all he has done in the Church he established, **and in Christ**, that is, through Christ; or for Christ whom he gave to us. **To him**, I repeat, **be glory** that his glory might shine forth, not only now, **but unto all generations of the age of ages**, meaning in the age which embraces all things. "Now to the King of ages, immortal, invisible, the only God, be honor and glory forever and ever. Amen." (1 Tim 1:17).[210]

This final passage reveals the enthusiasm of Thomas for what he has uncovered in the Epistle. Indeed, "all he [God] has done in the Church" has been revealed to be a drama of reconciliation, and has inverted Thomas' usual emphasis from a pilgrim Church moving away from earth to one which

---

scilicet Deus non diligatur propter temporalia, quia huiusmodi charitas esset infirma, sed ut diligatur propter se tantum... **Profundum** *vero attenditur quantum ad originem ipsius charitatis. Nam hoc quod Deum diligimus, non est ex nobis, sed a Spiritu Sancto, quia, ut dicitur Rom. V, 5: 'Charitas Dei diffusa est in cordibus nostris per Spiritum Sanctum,' etc."* [Ibid., 3.5.179]. LAMB, 291, n.102, notes that some manuscripts identify the phrase "*ut dicitur Ephes. c. III*" as "a superfluous addition to the text," an assertion which neither he nor we contest.

[210] "*Materia autem gratiarum actionis dicitur esse duplex beneficium quod nobis contulit Deus. Primum est ecclesiae institutio; secundum est Filii incarnatio. Dicit ergo* **Ipsi**, *scilicet Deo Patri,* **gloria**, *sit, supple* [sic], **in ecclesia**, *id est pro his quae fecit in ecclesia, quam instituit: quo ad primum;* **in Christo**, *id est per Christum, vel pro Christum, quem nobis dedit. Ipsi, inquam, sit gloria, ut gloriosus appareat, non solum in praesenti sed* **in omnes generationes saeculi saeculorum**, *id est saeculi omnia continentis. I Tim. I, 17: 'Regi autem saeculorum immortali, invisibili, soli Deo honor et gloria in saecula saeculorum.'* **Amen**" [*In Eph.*, 3.5.186].

faces earth, shining forth as the most unlikely example of human reconciliation in history. Its very existence is remarkable and God-given, as it points to the rarest of events - peace between those once separated by alien customs, beliefs, and mores. A sign of contradiction by virtue of its harmony, the only cause of the Church can be God, in Christ, whose perfect charity has brought it about.

The properly theological section of the *lectura* is now complete. However, Thomas has more to say. The divine gift of unity is now a matter of human responsibility, one which belongs to each individual member of the Church. It is to this aspect of unity that Thomas, following Paul, will devote the rest of his commentary.

CHAPTER VI

TEMPLE MAINTENANCE:
IN EPHESIOS 4-6

Markus Barth has beautifully summarized the last three chapters of Ephesians in the following manner:

> [It] encourages the readers to let their light shine. All that was and is done and revealed to them has but one purpose: *to be shown* [emphasis mine], to be made known by word and deed, by labor and suffering, to their fellow men on earth, and also to heavenly powers that may seek to obstruct them. The gospel is not for private possession and enjoyment; it is for all. No situation in life, whatever one's position in marriage, one's age, or one's social or economic bracket, is an excuse or obstacle preventing the fulfillment of the mission entrusted to the Church. All earthly situations, including suffering, are opportunities to be seized for attesting to God's love. It is God himself who provides the equipment to stand one's ground and to proceed on his course.[1]

Thomas' understanding of this latter section of the Epistle is much the same as Barth's. We have already seen his strong emphasis on the Church as witness in the first three chapters; the final three offer him the chance to comment on how ecclesial unity can be witnessed; namely, through its maintenance and increase at each level of its manifestation. The "ethics section"[2] of the Epistle allows him to develop a praxis of witness, one which is ecclesiologically oriented.

However, this latter section of the *lectura* is by no means solely a treatise on individual or even communal responsibility. It includes passages

---

[1] BARTH, 56.

[2] R. WILD, "'Be Imitators of God': Discipleship in the Letter to the Ephesians," in *Discipleship in the New Testament*, ed. F.F. Segovia (Philadelphia: Fortress Press, 1985), 133.

which carry various doctrinal emphases, particularly regarding the Church. Thomas will respond in kind by continuing to explore the issue of the nature of the Church and Church unity as the opportunity arises. Hence, the present study will undertake an exploration of both aspects. In the first place, Thomas' interpretation of the ethical imperatives of ecclesial unity will be considered, especially from the perspective of how each ethical category ties into the larger issue of the Church's oneness. Along with this, Thomas' reflections on the more expository and ecclesiologically descriptive passages will be given special notice.

A) *Chapter Four: The Pattern of Unity*

We have already considered Thomas' primary division of Ephesians in the pre-analysis of the *lectura*; however, we do well to remember it here: "The Apostle recalled above the divine blessings through which the Church's unity has originated and been preserved (Ch 1-3). Now he admonishes the Ephesians to remain within this ecclesial unity."[3] These final chapters are taken as an admonishment, therefore, and it is interesting that in his opening comments Thomas begins by separating ecclesial unity from the behavior of the Ephesians, as something not so much to be maintained (though he does use this term in several places), as to be dwelt in.[4] This accords well with the picture of the Church he has given thus far - it is one body, a holy temple, etc., and its members, though part of it, are only part insofar as they remain holy and unified. Its reality includes them but is also distinct from them. The picture of the temple in Chapter 2, Lecture 5 was separated by Thomas into two senses - it is both the Church and the soul - for this very reason; only if the latter is maintained can it be part of the former.

Lecture 1 of the present chapter consists of Thomas' exposition of Paul's encouragement of the Ephesians for the purpose of unity (vv 1-4). The Apostle's love, his imprisonment, and the fact of their call are offered by the Apostle to give them incentives to behave uprightly, and it is the third reason that is particularly important to Thomas; it will be reiterated by him several times throughout the rest of the *lectura*:

---

[3] "*Supra commemoravit Apostolus divina beneficia, per quae unitas ecclesiae constituitur et conservatur, hic monet eos Apostolus ad permanendum in ecclesiae unitate*" [*In Eph.*, 4.1.187].

[4] *Pace* BEST, 365, who attributes to Thomas an interpretation that makes unity "something created by the community and therefore able to be lost by it."

He also stimulates them by a consideration of the divine blessings:
that you walk worthy of the vocation in which you are called.
You should be attentive to the dignity to which you are summoned,
you ought to behave in a way conformable to it. If someone had
been chosen to a rank of nobility in a kingdom, it would be an
indignity for him to perform peasant work.[5]

In other words: be what you are.[6] The greatness of the Church' unity
calls for admiration and conformity on the part of its members.

To live in this unity requires four virtues, which are listed in v. 2:
humility, mildness, patience and charity. But it is the unlisted vices which are
opposite to these that most interest Thomas and which he treats in detail. This
treatment becomes a sustained criticism of negative human qualities which
disrupt harmony among fellows. Each virtue, through its opposite vice, is
treated more for how it disposes one for unity with neighbor than for unity
with God, indicating that Thomas is still allowing the idea, that drawing close
to God means to live in peace with one's neighbor, to be his hermeneutical
principle. We quote the passage at length, omitting only the numerous biblical citations for which the biblical wisdom literature and James provide the
rich moral wells from which Thomas draws support for his interpretation:

> The first vice which he rejects is pride. When one arrogant
> person decides to rule others, while the other proud individuals do
> not want to submit, dissension arises in the society and peace
> disappears... To eliminate this he says **with all** interior and exterior
> **humility**...
> Anger is the second vice. For an angry person is inclined
> to inflict injury, whether verbal or physical, from which
> disturbances occur... To discard it he says **with all mildness**; this
> softens arguments and preserves peace...
> The third is impatience. Occasionally, someone who
> himself is humble and meek, refraining from causing trouble,
> nevertheless will not endure patiently the real or attempted wrongs
> done to himself. Therefore, he adds **with patience** in adversities...
> An inordinate zeal is the fourth vice. Inordinately zealous
> about everything, men will pass judgment on whatever they see.

---

[5] "*Ex consideratione vero divinorum beneficiorum inducit eos, dicens **ut digne ambuletis
vocatione qua vocati estis**, id est attendentes dignitatem ad quam vocati estis, ambuletis
secundum quod ei convenit. Si enim quis vocatus esset ad nobile regnum, indignum esset quod
faceret opera rusticana*" [*In Eph.*, 4.1.190].

[6] LINCOLN, 224-225, attributes the same theme to this section of Ephesians 4.

Not waiting for the proper time and place, a turmoil arises in society... Hence he says **supporting one another in charity**; mutually bearing with the defects of others out of charity. When someone falls he should not be immediately corrected - unless it is the time and the place for it. With mercy these should be waited for since "charity bears all things" (1 Cor 13:7).[7]

The two references to "society" leave little doubt that Thomas is aiming his interpretation of this verse directly at the friars who are the primary recipients of the lecture.[8] Yet this only underscores the importance of the original event of unity for Thomas' vision of the Church in the *lectura*; this event is translated into its ramifications for the situation of the ecclesial life Thomas is most familiar with - that of the Dominicans. Its relevance is timeless, touching even the life situation of those who stand many centuries removed.

This call to avoid the elements of dissension is for the sake of producing a "bond of peace" (*vinculo pacis*) in the Church:

For charity is a union of souls. Now the fusion of material objects cannot last unless it is held by some bond. Similarly, the union of souls through love will not endure unless it is bound. Peace proves to be a true bond; that peace which is, according to Augustine, the

---

[7] "*Primum autem vitium quod excludit est superbia. Dum enim unus superbiens vult alii praeesse et alius similiter superbus non vult subesse, causatur dissensio in societate et tollitur pax... Ad quod excludendum dicit* **cum omni humilitate**, *scilicet interiori et exteriori... Secundum est ira. Iracundi enim sunt propinqui ad iniuram inferendam verbis vel factis, ex quo turbationes oriuntur... Ad hoc excludendum dicit* **et in mansuetudine**, *quae mitigat rixas, et pacem conservat... Tertium est impatientia. Quandoque enim aliquis humilis est et mansuetus in se, abstinens a molestiis inferendis, non tamen patienter sustinet molestias sibi illatas, vel attentatas. Ideo subdit* **cum patientia**, *scilicet adversorum... Quartum inordinatus zelus. Cum enim inordinate omnia zelantes, quae vident iudicant, nec tempus, nec locum servantes, concitatur turbatio in societate... Et ideo dicit* **supportantes invocem in charitate**, *scilicet mutuo sustinentes defectus aliorum, et hoc ex charitate. Quia quando deficit aliquis, non debet statim corrigi, nisi adsit locus et tempus, sed misericorditer expectari, quia charitas omnia sustinet, I Cor XIII, 7*" [*In Eph.*, 4.1.191].

[8] See CONGAR, "'In dulcedine societatis quaerere veritatem.' Notes sur le travail en équipe chez S. Albert et chez les Prêcheurs au XIIIe siècle," in *Albertus Magnus, Doctor Universalis, 1280/1980*, ed. G. Meyer, A. Zimmerman and P-B. Lüttringhaus (Mayence: Matthias Grünewald Verlag, 1980), 52-53, for his discussion of Thomas' use of the term "*societas*" in reference to his order.

balanced harmony between the measure, form, and order of a thing. This is achieved when each possesses what is proper to himself.[9]

Thomas follows this thought by explaining, in conjunction with v. 4, what it is that is proper to each, using the reference to "one body and one spirit" (*unum corpus et unus spiritus*) in v. 4 as an analogy for the two levels of unity in the Church. As Thomas explains it: "Now in man there is a twofold unity. The first is the ordered structure of the organs among themselves, the second is the union of the body and soul constituting what neither are separately."[10]   Thus, "one body" refers to the ordering of the faithful among themselves, and "one spirit" to "a spiritual consensus through the unity of your faith and charity" (*spiritualem consensum per unitatem fidei et charitatis*). Here Thomas makes a distinction between the social and possibly hierarchical aspect of the church and its invisible essential character, yet not a separation – the two (body and soul) constitute a "third" (*tertium*). Thus the two aspects themselves (the ordered visible structure manifesting the interior aspect as its expression, the former receiving the latter as its form) are impossible to consider fully without seeing them as one.

When we proceed to Lecture 2, Thomas' exposition takes a speculative turn. The verses he considers (vv 5-6) are treated as a glimpse of "the pattern of unity" (*formam dictae unitatis*).[11] In explaining the passage, he resorts to the image of the Church as city (an image he imports into the passage) to explain how each of the unities posited by the text are integral exemplars of the unity that is to be striven for by the Church's members. Sabra, whose analysis of the city image was our primary source for understanding Thomas' exposition of Eph 2:19, has some important insights into this passage as well, most significantly that Thomas does not succumb to juridicalism by reducing the "forms" of unity to fit only the aspect of the visible, hierarchical Church.[12] However, what must be given more attention is that the passage (and for that matter, much of Thomas' exegesis of

---

[9] "*Charitas enim est coniunctio animorum. Nulla autem rerum materialium coniunctio stare potest, nisi ligetur aliquo vinculo. Eodem modo nec coniunctio animorum per charitatem stare potest, nisi ligetur; huiusmodi autem verum ligamen est pax, quae est, secundum Augustinum, tranquillitas modi, speciei et ordinis, quando scilicet unusquisque habet quod suum est*" [*In Eph.*, 4.1.194]. For the original quote from AUGUSTINE, see *De Natura Boni*, III (*CSEL* 25, pg. 860).

[10] "*Nunc autem, quia in homine est duplex unitas, una scilicet membrorum ad invicem simul ordinatorum, alia corporis et animae tertium constituentium*" [Ibid., 4.1.195].

[11] Ibid., 4.2.197

[12] SABRA, 37-38.

Ephesians 4) is united closely to his main theme as it appears in the "heart" of the Epistle, which for Thomas is Ephesians 2 and its treatment of the reconciliation of the Jews and Gentiles. Therefore, the fact that Thomas proposes the city image as a necessary product of the event of reconciliation at the very beginning of the Church's historical existence must be of central concern.

With this in mind, let us consider how Thomas uses the *civitas* image. He begins by introducing it:

> Since the Church of God is likened to a city, it is one and distinct, although this unity is not uncomposed but composed of different parts... The solidarity of any city demands the presence of four common elements: one governor, one law, the same symbols, and a common goal. The Apostle affirms that these are present in the Church also.[13]

When the earlier treatment of the reconciliation of the Jews and the Gentiles is recalled, it becomes apparent that in the case of each of these four, Thomas is patterning Church unity after that event, as each element which makes a city one has already been demonstrated as an element of the alienation of the two peoples.

In the case of governance, Jews and Gentiles were without "one Lord" (*unus Dominus*): "...she [the Church] has one leader, Christ. [Obeying] **one Lord**, not many, conflicts do not arise from trying to comply with divergent demands."[14] It is not Christ's lordship *per se* that interests Thomas here, so much as the opportunity it provides for concord. One recalls the situation described in regard to Eph 2:1-3, and the service of devils which was attributed to the Gentiles there. The abandonment of idolatry serves harmony in the same way it serves the purity of faith.

The same is true of the Church's law:

> Secondly, her law is one. For the law of the Church is the law of faith... **Faith** is sometimes applied to the reality believed in, as with

---

[13] "*Ubi sciendum est, quod cum Ecclesia Dei sit sicut civitas, est aliquod unum et distinctum, cum non sit unum sicut simplex, sed sicut compositum ex diversis partibus... In qualiibet autem civitate, ad hoc ut sit una, quatuor debent esse communia, scilicet unus gubernator, una lex, eadem insignia, et idem finis: haec autem quatuor dicit Apostolus esse in ecclesia*" [*In Eph.*, 4.2.197].

[14] "*...habet ducem unum, scilicet Christum; et quantum ad hoc dicit* **unus Dominus**, *non plures, pro quorum diversis voluntatibus oporteat vos discordare*" [Ibid., 4.2.198].

"This is the Catholic faith...," meaning this is what must be believed. At other times, faith refers to the habit of faith by which a man believes what he must in his very heart. **Faith** in both these senses can be called one.[15]

Thomas' inclusion of the second notion of faith (i.e. the habit of faith) draws the connection between faith and unity, alluding to a unanimity among those who share faith's content: "**One faith** designates the unity of the habit of faith by which all believe. I mean that it is specifically one - not numerically one - since the same faith is present in each one's heart; just as when many persons want the same thing, they are said to be of one will."[16] Since it is human unity which preoccupies Thomas, he dwells not on the perfect oneness of revealed truth but rather on the oneness of the heart which it makes possible. This also eluded the Jews and Gentiles, who did not believe as one.

The clearest case, however, is that of the Church's *insignia*, or "symbols": "Thirdly, the Church shares the same symbols. They are Christ's sacraments, of which baptism is the first and the entrance to the rest. Hence he says **one baptism**."[17] As it was the ceremonial precepts of the old, superseded law which was the main issue of contention between the Jews and Gentiles according to Thomas, so now in Christ the aspects of ritual are held in common by both. The reference to baptism is taken to be to the whole Christian sacramental system, and although he does explore the nature of the sacrament of baptism briefly, this is a pedagogical tangent. The main point is that in Christ religious custom now has a unitive function rather than a divisive one.

All of this leads to the heart of the matter - the Church's one goal, which is God.[18] Thus the functioning of the city towards its goal is itself a unity, as its citizens strive in common for a single goal.

---

[15] "*Secundo quia lex eius est una. Lex enim ecclesiae est lex fidei... Sed fides quandoque sumitur pro ipsa re credita, secundum illud: 'Haec est fides catholica,' etc., id est, ista debent credi. Quandoque vero sumitur pro habitu fidei, quo creditur in corde. Et de utroque hoc potest dici*" [Ibid., 4.2.199].

[16] "*...**una est fides**, id est unus habitus fidei quo creditur; una, inquam, non numero, sed specie, quia idem debet esse in corde omnium; et hoc modo idem volentium dicitur una voluntas*" [Ibid., 4.2.199].

[17] "*Tertio eadem sunt insignia ecclesiae, scilicet sacramenta Christi, inter quae primum baptisma, quod est ianua omnium aliorum. Et ideo dicit **unum baptisma***" [Ibid., 4.2.200].

[18] Ibid., 4.2.201.

As a final consideration, we can now return to a point already considered, that Thomas' city imagery, in the words of Sabra, is concerned primarily with the Church as "a theological communion."[19] Accepting that the image is molded by such a conception sheds light on why (as Ti-Ti Chen observes) Thomas pursues the city image on three separate occasions when it is only mentioned fleetingly in the text.[20] For although the temple image is the hinge metaphor of the Epistle, the one which is most naturally connected to the idea of human harmony is that of a peaceful society of individuals, the *civitas Dei*.[21]   So far, Thomas has interpreted the beginning of Ephesians 4 as a manifesto of unity, proclaiming the common duty of all of the Church's members. With the verses (7-13) of Lectures 3 and 4, Thomas now faces a change in the text,[22] positing that Paul "manifests this same [unity] from the viewpoint of what is personal and specific to each of the faithful members of the Church" (*ostendit quantum ad hoc quod singulis fidelibus membris ecclesiae est proprium et speciale*).[23] This presents a more difficult angle than the consideration of what is common, which is a perspective that naturally lends itself to a vision of harmony. Thomas now must deal with the acknowledgement by Paul of the various roles and ministries in the Church, with the matter of how these too, even in their distinctiveness and diversity, make for its unity.

It is v 7 which first offers Thomas the theme of diversity. In his words: "each of us has the diverse graces especially granted to him - **to every one of us is given grace**" (*sed tamen diversas gratias diversis particulariter*

---

[19] SABRA, 37.

[20] TI-TI CHEN, 127-128.

[21] It has been suggested that Thomas does not have the original event of unity in mind in this section on Eph 4:5-6, and that the issue of the Jews and Gentiles is no longer present, ruling out the interpretation I have given it. This assertion is supported by the fact that Thomas does not mention either in the lecture. However, other aspects rule out the possibility that there is no connection between this section and Thomas' interpretation of Ephesians 2. In the first place, Thomas' use of the city metaphor both here and there establishes at least one link between them, especially since 4:5-6 does not even mention the word *"civitas."* Also, in the present section Thomas asserts that Paul is showing his readers "unity's pattern"; certainly in a chapter that falls into that part of the Epistle which Thomas maintains is an exhortation "to remain within" the original unity of the Church, an exhibition of a pattern of unity would have reference to that original unity. In fact, he poses his interpretation in very similar terms: "Hence he [Paul] says: You ought to have one body and spirit since you belong to *the one unified Church* [emphasis mine]" (*Dicit ergo: Dico quod debetis habere unum corpus et unum spiritum, quia estis in unitate ecclesiae, quae est una*) [*In Eph.*, 4.2.198].

[22] BEST, 241.

[23] *In Eph.*, 4.3.204.

collatas habemus, quia **unicuique nostrum data est gratia**).[24] For the sake of precision, Thomas gives his own reformulation of the meaning of the verse, affirming that this diversity is not accidental:

> As though he said: None of us lack [*sic*] a share in divine grace and communion, "of his fullness we have all received, and grace for grace" (Jn 1:16). This grace, however, is certainly not bestowed on everyone uniformly and equally but according to the measure of Christ. Christ is the donor who metes out grace to each, who have "different gifts according to the grace that is given us" (Rom 12:6). The variation does not spring from fate or chance, nor from a difference of merit, but from the giving of Christ; that is, according as Christ allots it to us.[25]

The rest of the lecture is spent discussing Christ as the giver of grace; "that he might fill all things" (*ut adimplerit omnia*) in v. 10 is taken to refer to the bestowal "on every race of men the fullness of spiritual gifts" (*omne genus hominum spiritualibus donis repleret*).[26]

It is with Lecture 4 that Thomas begins to discuss more specifically what these gifts are (v. 11) and their benefit for the Church (vv 12-13). The former is a discussion of the charisms associated with each ministry listed in v. 11, and is a passage which has been well-explored by Ti-Ti Chen.[27] As she notes, Thomas' treatment of it is not very different from *ST* II-II.183.2, where Eph 4:11 figures prominently.[28] While it is an important ecclesiological topic, Thomas treats it distinctly from his main theme, and so we will refrain from exploring it here.

But the second half of the passage returns Thomas to the main issue, precisely by its mention of the "body of Christ" (*corporis Christi*) in v. 12 and "the unity of faith" (*unitatem fidei*) in v. 13. Earlier, we observed Thomas

---

[24] Ibid., 4.3.205.

[25] "*...quasi dicat: Nullus nostrum est qui non sit particeps divinae gratiae et communionis. Io. I, 16: 'De plenitudine eius omnes accepimus gratiam pro gratia. Sed certe ista gratia non est data omnibus uniformiter seu aequaliter, sed* **secundum mensuram donationis Christi***, id est secundum quod Christus est dator, et eam singulis mensuravit. Rom. XII, 16: 'Habentes donationes secundum gratiam quae data est nobis differentes.' Haec differentia non est ex fato, nec a casu, nec ex merito, sed ex donatione Christi, id est secundum quod Christus nobis commensuravit*" [Ibid., 4.3.205].

[26] Ibid., 4.3.209.

[27] Ti-Ti CHEN, 151-153.

[28] Ibid., 151.

move from the eschatologically-oriented perspective of his first lectures to a more historical interpretation. However, the glorious destiny of the Church has never been far from his mind, and it takes center-stage again here. The key word in Thomas' analysis is *"congregatio,"* or "a gathering together":

> He goes on [v. 13] to discuss the ultimate fruit [of the Church's preaching] which can be understood in two ways. One sees it as touching on the absolutely ultimate effect: the resurrection of the saints. In this perspective two facts are asserted. First is the spiritual and corporeal [gathering together] of all who have risen. The physical [gathering together] will consist in this, that all the saints will be drawn together toward Christ... Concerning this he says **until we all meet**, as if to say: the above ministry, the perfecting of the saints, and the edifying of the Church will continue until we all meet Christ in the resurrection... We shall meet one another also...[29]

Here the eschaton is analyzed according to the pattern set in the earthly formation of the Church; it will be a reunion, both between Christ and his body as well as between the various relations among its human members. This will come about through the work of Christ, whose human body is the exemplar of the Church's future perfection due to its "mature and robust age" (*perductum ad plenam aetatem virilem*) of thirty-three, which will be the age of all the saints in heaven.[30] In this way the "perfect man" (*virum perfectum*), a metaphor which Thomas notes "is used here rather in contradistinction to boy than as opposite of woman" (*vir magis sumitur secundum quod dividitur contra puerum, quam secundum quod dividitur contra*

---

[29] *"Deinde cum dicit* **donec occuramus**, *etc., assignat fructum ultimum, et potest intelligi dupliciter. Uno modo de fructu simpliciter ultimo, qui erit in resurrectione sanctorum. Et, secundum hoc, duo declarantur. Primo quidem congregatio resurgentium et corporalis et spiritualis. Corporalis quidem erit congregatio in hoc, quod omnes sancti congregabuntur ad Christum... Et quantum ad hoc dicit* **donec occurramus omnes**, *etc., quasi dicat: Usque ad hoc extenditur praedictum ministerium et consummatio sanctorum et aedificatio ecclesiae, donec in resurrectione occurramus Christo... Et etiam occurramus nobis invicem"* [*In Eph.*, 4.4.215]. LAMB, 165-166, translates *"congregatio"* as "convergence"; an unusual choice, since the phrase "a gathering together" is closer to the original meaning. I have changed the translation above accordingly.

[30] *In Eph.*, 4.4.216. Thomas does not explain why Christ's body specifically serves as the exemplar of the Church's future perfection; according to his explanation, the body of any healthy thirty-three year old would fulfill the requirements necessary for this important function.

foeminam), refers to the ultimate maturity in unity which the Church is growing towards.[31] The diversity and distinctiveness of the members will be a real part of this unity when the Church reaches its heavenly destiny.

Yet Thomas also offers another interpretation of this verse which allows him to tie this passage more securely to the Epistle's main theme: "In another way [this] can be understood as referring to the ultimate fruit [of the Church's ministry] *in the present life* [emphasis mine]. This will happen when all the faithful come to her in **the unity of faith** and **knowledge** of the truth."[32]   Here Thomas cites what has become an important scriptural motif for his main theme: Jn 10:16. This is a direct assertion of a foundational principle for Thomas' interpretation of the Epistle, that the unity of the two peoples is to be the pattern for the ongoing life of the Church. Still other sheep who belong to Christ have yet to be added to his fold. The overcoming of alienating factors between Christians and those whom they evangelize is the path to bringing about the Church's ultimate fruition in its ministry to the world. To look for a specific referent (i.e., Jewish contemporaries, Muslims, etc.) would be to miss the point. It is a general program rather than a specific mission; the Church must always be about the process of reconciliation, of uniting persons so as to unite them to Christ.

This meditation on the Church as the body of Christ, a union of diverse members whose very diversity makes for maturity, is continued in Lecture 5. Here it is Christ's headship which is initially considered, but not in itself; the main part of Thomas' exposition is given over to the unified structure of the Church and the interrelationship of its members as being infused into it through Christ as its head. This is clear from the three aspects of the body image which are identified by Thomas as central to the passage:

> Three points concerning an organic body are to be kept in mind: its organs are interrelated, they are bound together by tendons, each member serves the rest. "If the foot should say: because I am not the hand, I am not of the body; is it therefore not of the body? And if the ear should say: because I am not the eye, I am not of the body; is it therefore not of the body? If the whole body were the eye, where would be the hearing? If the whole were hearing, where would be the smelling? (1 Cor 12:15-17). [Spiritually understood], therefore, the one body [of the Church] is composed of many

---

[31] Thomas will use the distinction between man and boy for the same purpose in 4.5.219.

[32] "*Alio modo potest intelligi de fructu ultimo praesentis vitae, in qua quidem sibi occurrent omnes fideles ad unam fidem et agnitionem veritatis*" [*In Eph.*, 4.4.217].

members in these three ways: through its structured whole or unity, through its connective bindings, and through its reciprocal actions and assistance. Just as all these actions of interrelating organs, the connecting of tendons, and movements take their initiative from the body's head, so the spiritual counterparts of these flow from Christ, our head, into his body, the Church.[33]

Sabra has noted that unity is a theme which is always present whenever Thomas considers the body metaphor for the Church,[34] and this is as true here as it is in Thomas' other writings. Just as the diversity of the Church's members has been considered, Thomas moves inexorably to the way in which the mutual harmony among members, itself a grace given by the Church's head, functions to make it one. The stress in the above passage is on the intra-dynamic aspect of unity: the actions of organs, connecting of tendons, movements. It is not surprising that this dynamic unity will be revealed to be one of service, where each individual unit exists to serve the rest.[35]   In fact, one word runs through the whole analysis of v. 16, and is predicated both of Christ and the Church's members - *subministrationis*, the act of aiding by giving.[36]

In the first case (the interrelation of organs), what Thomas observes in the Church is "a structured unity through faith" (*compactio per fidem*), given to it by Christ. Thomas uses biblical citations to remark on this passage - in each of the three cited the emphasis is on the work of Christ as he serves Church unity by gathering its members together:·

> Whence he says **from** Christ who is our head, as was already mentioned, **the whole body being compacted** is joined together in a unity. "He will gather together the dispersed of Israel" (Ps 146:2).

---

[33] "*Ubi sciendum est, quod corpus naturale tria habet, scilicet compactionem membrorum ad invicem, ligationem per nervos et mutuam subministrationem. I Cor XII, 16 s.: 'Si dixerit pes: quoniam non sum manus, non sum de corpore; non ideo non est de corpore? Et se dixerit auris; quoniam non sum oculus, non sum de corpore, etc. Si totum corpus est odoratus, ubi auditus?' Spiritualiter ergo, sicut unum corpus efficitur ex multis his tribus modis, scilicet per compactionem seu adunationem, per ligationem et per mutuam operationem et subventionem: ita et omnia, quae sunt a capite corporali, scilicet compactio, nervorum ligatio, ad opus motio, fluunt a capite nostro Christo in corpore ecclesiae*" [Ibid., 4.5.225]. LAMB, 171, leaves "*spiritualiter*" untranslated. I have added its English equivalent above.

[34] SABRA, 64.

[35] LINCOLN, 262, gives the same interpretation: "Through the proper functioning of the parts, the whole body is to be active in promoting its own growth."

[36] DEFERRARI, "*subministro*," in *A Latin-English Dictionary of St. Thomas Aquinas.*

"He will gather together to himself all nations, and heap together to him all people" (Hab 2:5). Christ is "the head, from which the whole body, by joints and bands, being supplied with nourishment and compacted, grows into the increase of God" (Col 2;19).[37]

Along with this structured unity is given "a connecting and binding force" (*connexio et colligatio*), which "emanates from Christ, the head, into his body, the Church" (*fluit a Christo capite in corpus ecclesiae suae*): "On this account he says **fitly joined together, by what every joint supplies**, that is, through the faith and charity which unite and knit the members of the mystical body to one another for mutual support."[38] For this, the prayers of the Philippians for Paul serve as the example *par excellence*: "Thus the Apostle himself, confident of this mutual being-of-service which reigns among the members of the Church due to the divine unifying action, had said: 'I know that this shall happen to me unto salvation, through your prayer and the assistance of the Spirit of Jesus Christ' (Phil 1:19)."[39] Thus the service of the members for one another is spiritual, though Thomas does not restrict this service to prayer. In fact, with the third element Thomas emphasizes action:

> Third, from Christ the head there is infused into his members the power to act in order that they may grow spiritually. For this reason he states **according to the operation in the measure of every part, makes the increase of the body**. As if he said: Not only is the structured unity of the members of the Church through faith, and their connection or being joined together through the mutual service of charity, from Christ the head. Indeed, from him comes the actual operation or movements of the members needed for action, and this according to the measure and competency of each member... Therefore, the body not only grows through the faith which

---

[37] "*...scilicet Christo, qui est caput nostrum, ut modo dictum est, **totum corpus compactum est**, id est, coadunatum. Ps. CXLVI, 2: 'Dispersiones Israël congregabit.' Abac. II, 5: 'Congregabit ad se omnes gentes, et coacervabit ad se omnes populos.' De hoc dicitur Col. II, 19: 'Caput ex quo totum corpus per nexus et coniunctiones subministratum et constructum crescit in augmentum Dei*" [*In Eph.*, 4.5.226].

[38] "*Et propter hoc dicit **et connexum per omnem iuncturam subministrationis**, id est per fidem et charitatem, quae connectunt et coniungunt membra corporis mystici ad mutuam subministrationem*" [Ibid., 4.5.227]. The reference to faith and charity would seem to imply the action of the Holy Spirit; see SABRA, 100-105.

[39] "*Unde ipse Apostolus, confidens de ista mutua subministratione quae est inter membra ecclesiae per divinam coniunctionem, dicebat Phil I, 19: 'Scio enim, quia hoc proveniet in salutem per vestram orationem et subministrationem spiritus Iesu Christi'*" [Ibid., 4.5.227].

compacts it into a structured whole and through charity's mutual
assistance, but also through the actual [binding force which flows
out from each member according to the degree of grace given him,
and also through the actual] impulse to act which God effects in
us..."[40]

To whom is this impulse to act directed? In the context one would
think that it is the other members of the body, but the distinction between the
mutual assistance of charity and the actual impulse to act may suggest
something closer to general goodwill that extends even to those outside the
Church. This would be in keeping with Thomas' emphasis on the Church's
missionary character which we have already considered.

Thomas completes his interpretation of the chapter with a reference to
charity, a predictable move even were it not offered to him by the text itself:

> But why does God make each member grow? To build up the body.
> "In whom all the building, being framed together, grows up into a
> holy temple in the Lord. In whom you also are built together into a
> habitation of God in the Spirit" (Eph 2:21-22). So 1 Corinthians 3
> (9) affirms that "you are God's building." All this occurs **in** the
> **charity** of which it is said that "charity edifies" (1 Cor 8:1). Or **in**
> **charity** refers to the purely gratuitous love with which God
> accomplishes all this. "Yea, I have loved thee with an everlasting
> love: therefore have I drawn thee, taking pity on thee. And I will
> build thee again, and thou shalt be built" (Jer 31:3-4). This is what
> he states in **unto the edifying of itself in charity**.[41]

---

[40] "*Tertio, a capite Christo in membris, ut augmententur spiritualiter, influitur virtus
actualiter operandi. Unde dicit **secundum mensuram uniuscuisque membri, augmentum
corporis facit**; quasi dicat: Non solum a capite nostro Christo est membrorum ecclesiae
compactio per fidem, nec sola connexio, vel colligatio per mutuam subministrationem
charitatis, sed certe ab ipso est actualis membrorum operatio sive ad opus motio, secundum
mensuram et competentiam cuiuslibet membri... quia non solum per fidem corpus mysticum
compaginatur, nec solum per charitatis subministrationem connectentem augetur corpus, sed
per actualem [compositionem ab unoquoque membro egredientem, secundum mensuram
gratiae sibi datae, et actualem] motionem ad operationem, quam Deus facit in nobis*" [Ibid.,
4.5.228]. The bracketed portions are an interpolation by Remigius Nannini in his edition of
1562. See LAMB, 296, n.121.

[41] "*Sed ad quid augmentat Deus unumquodque membrum? ut corpus aedificet. Supra II,
21: 'In quo omnis aedificatio constructa crescit in templum sanctum in Domino, in quo et vos
coaedificamini, etc.' Unde II Cor III, 9: 'Dei aedificatio estis.' Et haec omnia fiunt **in**
charitate, quia, ut dicitur I Cor c. VIII, 1: 'Charitas aedificat.' Vel **in charitate** facit Deus
haec omnia, id est ex mera dilectione. Ier. XXI, 3: 'In charitate perpetua dilexi te, ideo attraxi*

With the reference to the temple image in Ephesians 2 we are left no doubt that the body image of Ephesians 4 complements this earlier image with which the main theme of the Epistle is illustrated; the temple built out of the two peoples on the foundation of Christ, mortared together by charity. This dynamic process of construction begins with this event but is not limited to it, an emphasis which Thomas repeats here as is seen by the open-ended orientation of this passage; the "building up" of the Church and the "growth" of the members are treated as dynamic and ongoing rather than static and complete.

At this point we come to another major *divisio textus*; as Thomas begins Lecture 6, he signals a change by Paul to a more purely paraenetic approach: "The Apostle previously admonished the Ephesians to persevere in ecclesial unity by describing to them its quality and pattern. In the part that follows he teaches them the way to remain within the Church's unity."[42] This new section consists of two parts. In the first, Eph 4:17-6:9, precepts are offered both for all in common (4:17 - 5:21), but also for "particular classes" (*ad singulos gradus*) within the Church (5:22 - 6:9). In the second part (6:10 - 6:24), Paul "shows them where they can find the strength to fulfill these commands" (*ostendit potestatem hanc ad implenda praecepta*).[43] This division of the text corresponds to that of modern exegesis,[44] which sees the imperatives given as having in common their relation to "the need to maintain the unity of the community."[45] In kind, the task for interpreting Thomas' commentary in regard to Paul's paraenesis requires attention to how well Thomas achieves the union between these disparate topics and the main theme, as well as any important developments which may come along with this endeavor. We will attend especially to those places where Thomas is clearly engaged in deepening the vision of the Church's unity, those in which he continues to elaborate his theological model.

Thomas' attention to the necessity of a structured exposition guides him in this endeavor. The structure of his major synthesis, the *Summa Theologiae*, is well known for its movement from the general to the specific.

---

*te miserans. Rursusque: Aedificabo, et aedificaberis.' Hoc est ergo quod dicit **in aedificationem sui in charitate**"* [Ibid., 4.5.229].

[42] "*Supra monuit Apostolus Ephesios ut manerent in ecclesiastica unitate, describendo modum eius et formam, in hac parte docet eos viam per quam possint manere in ecclesiastica unitate*" [Ibid., 4.6.230].

[43] Ibid., 4.6.230.

[44] BEST, for instance, divides this final part precisely as Thomas does.

[45] LINCOLN, 442.

Hence, it is not surprising that in the first verses of Paul's moral instruction Thomas asserts that he is expressing "certain general precepts to which all the others can be reduced" (*quaedam praecepta generalia ad quae reducuntur omnia alia*)[46]; this occurs in his exegesis of 4:17-24 and offers him a basic theme which he will use to unify his exegesis of Ephesians 4.

This passage is the subject of Lectures 6-7, which cover 4:17-19 and 4:20-24 respectively. The first lecture, dealing as it does with the admonition "to walk not as also the Gentiles" (*iam non ambuletis sicut et Gentes*), offers little for analysis which has not already been noted in his exegesis of the contrasts offered in the early verses of Ephesians 2. This is a reminder to the Ephesians of the life they have abandoned, and it is only with Lecture 7 that the question of how this old way must be left behind is raised:

> How should they live? He adds **to put off, according to the former way of life, the old man**. The passage has two variant readings. One is the infinitive, **to put off**; then it would be construed with what preceded to read: The truth about which you were instructed in Jesus was to put off the old man. The more common reading has an imperative, **put off**; in this case the signification is: Since the life and teachings of the Gentiles are contrary to those of Jesus, in which you have been taught, the only alternative is that you discard the old man.[47]

This is achieved through renewal "in the spirit of your mind" (*spiritu mentis vestrae*), a process involving one of two possibilities (according to how the passage is taken) - through the cause of the mind's renewal, which is the Holy Spirit, or more directly through the renewal of the rational powers. In either case, what is called for is a total rehabilitation of the darkened human spirit. Thomas here acknowledges with the text that the price of unity is individual reformation. The old division of the peoples corresponds to the "oldness" of sin; Thomas' indictment of this oldness is accompanied by a Pauline reference to the non-necessity of circumcision, one of the ceremonial precepts of the Law:

---

[46] *In Eph.*, 4.6.230.

[47] "*Sed quomodo? Subdit **deponite vos**, etc. Quae quidem littera potest legi dupliciter. Uno modo, ut dicatur deponere, et tunc construitur cum praecedentibus sic: Ita est veritas in qua edocti estis in Iesu, deponere vos, etc. Si autem dicatur deponite, quae littera communis habetur, dicemus quod quia contaria est et vita et doctrina Gentilium, vitae et doctrinae Iesu, in qua edocti estis, restat ut deponatis, etc.*" [Ibid., 4.7.240].

And put on the new man discloses in whom this renewal takes place. Adam introduced sin into all men, and thus became for everything the primary source of oldness. Likewise, the primary source of newness and renovation is Christ. In Adam all die and in Christ all will be brought back to life. "For in Christ Jesus neither circumcision avails any thing, nor uncircumcision; but a new creature" (Gal 6:15). Therefore, "put ye on the Lord Jesus Christ" (Rom 13:14).[48]

The contrast between new and old will henceforth be the unifying thread of Thomas' exegesis of many of the ethical imperatives which are given in the text.

However, he is not always concerned with the connection of these imperatives to his main topic. Thomas often strays from the sense of the text to take the opportunity to expound it according to his vision of morality, interpreting the text according to the various divisions of the human person, such as in the beginning of Lecture 8, where Thomas interprets 4:25-28 as forbidding sin according to how it effects human "rational powers" (*rationalem*), "irascible emotions" (*irascibilem*), and "concupiscible emotions" (*concupiscibilem*).[49] In particular, such sections bear the mark of *ST* I.75-102, which Thomas composed during the period in his career in which he lectured on Ephesians. In these cases he is content to leave unconsidered the connection to the issue of unity, although not in every case - it is still present, and arises in certain places within his consideration.

One such place is v. 25, which he considers in Lecture 8; here veracity of speech is the subject:

> Then he urges them on to *newness* [emphasis mine] of life, saying with Zacharias (8:16) **speak the truth, every man with his neighbor**. And why? Because **we are members of one another**. For members are to love and mutually assist one another in truth.

---

[48] "*In quo autem haec renovatio consistat, quantum ad secundum, subdit cum dicit **et induite novum hominem**, etc.*

Hic advertendum est quod sicut uniuscuiusque rei primum vetustatis principium fuit Adam, per quem peccatum in omnes intravit, ita principium primum novitatis et renovationis Christus est; quia sicut in Adam omnes moriuntur, ita et in Christo omnes vivificabuntur. Unde Gal. ult.: 'In Christo Iesu neque circumcisio, neque praeputium aliquid valet, sed nova creatura.' Induimini ergo Dominum nostrum Iesum Christum, Rom. c. XIII, 14" [Ibid., 4.7.245].

[49] Ibid., 4.8.247.

'We being many, are one body in Christ; and every one members of one another' (Rom 12:5).[50]

In this case the mention of membership draws Thomas briefly back to the issue of unity, but he leaves it just as quickly - no significant additions are made. As he moves on to consider the question of anger in accord with v. 26 he is drawn to other concerns, such as when anger is appropriate and to whom it can be appropriately directed. In short, in this and many other cases Thomas is content to explore the subject and leave its connection to the main theme unspoken.

In fact, it is not until his consideration of v. 28 in Lecture 9 that Thomas goes back to the main issue once more. Here the topic is the disharmony caused by evil speech; Thomas sees the passage as calling for a way of speaking that builds an atmosphere of peace:

> Man should possess a threefold inner relationship; namely, to himself, that all his powers are subject to reason; to God, so that his reason submits to him; and to his fellow man when he loves him as himself. Hence a word is evil when it shows that a man is not properly related within himself. This is the false word by which he means one thing and says another; futile and vain talk also belong to this category. Again, there are wicked words which indicate that a man is not properly related to God, such as perjury, blasphemy, and the like. Finally, there is also evil talk which is against one's neighbor, such as injurious, deceitful, and fraudulent words Therefore does he say **Let no evil speech proceed from your mouth**. "No" is equivalent to "none"...[51]

---

[50] "*Et postea inducit ad novitatem, dicens Zac. c. VIII, 16:* '**Loquimini veritatem unusquisque cum proximo suo**.
Et quare? **Quoniam sumus invicem membra**. *Membra enim se invicem diligunt et se iuvant mutuo in veritate. Rom. XII, 5:* '*Unum corpus sumus in Christo, singuli autem alter alterius membra*'" [Ibid., 4.8.248].

[51] "*Tripliciter autem homo ordinatur interius, scilicet ad se, ut scilicet omnia sint ratione subiecta; ad Deum, ut ratio sit ei subdita; ad proximum, quando diligit eum ut seipsum. Est ergo quandoque sermo malus, quando indicat hominem inordinatum in se, et hic est sermo falsus eius, qui aliud loquitur et aliud intendit: et similiter sermo inutilis et vanus. Item, est sermo malus qui indicat hominem inordinatum contra Deum: sicut periuria, blasphemiae, et huiusmodi. Item, etiam est sermo malus, quando est contra proximum suum: sicut inuriae, doli, et fallaciae. Et ideo dicit* **omnis sermo malus ex ore vestro non procedat**. '*Omnis non*' *vero aequipollet huic signo,* '*nullus*'..." [Ibid., 4.9.259].

Thus Paul compels the Ephesians to say only what is good:

> With **that which is good** he encourages them on toward newness because a good word, spoken at the right time and place, is blessed... He adds **to the edification of faith** in order, that is, for faith to be strengthened in the hearts of the weak: "Let all things be done for edification" (1 Cor 14:26).[52]

Here Thomas is back on course, discussing the issue of speech as an essential element of newness and "edification," a word which subtly ties the passage to the building theme that characterized the first half of the Ephesians *lectura*. The final addition to this discussion involves bitterness and its illicit expression; in this case Thomas considers v. 31 and its admonition to avoid every manifestation of bitterness, as well as its accompanying remedy, which is kindness:

> Next, when he says **be kind to one another** he determines what pertains to the new man which is contrary to the above mentioned passions. Opposed to bitterness is kindness; so he says **be kind to one another** since "the spirit of wisdom is benevolent" (Wis 1:6). Mercy is contrary to anger, thus he mentions **merciful**: "Be therefore merciful, as your Father is also merciful" (Lk 6:36). Opposed to indignation is a pardoning attitude; whence he says **forgiving one another just as God has forgiven you in Christ**.[53]

Once again newness is the subject - the "profile" of the new man is one of mercy and long-suffering.

But the reference to the unifying virtues of kindness and mercy is very brief, much less detailed than the accompanying treatment of anger and its concomitants. With this we begin to see a pattern. As far back as his commentary on 4:2 we noticed that Thomas spends more time on the vices being condemned than on the virtues being prescribed; in that case, Thomas

---

[52] "*Sequitur* **sed si qui bonus est**, *etc. Inducit ad novitatem, quia sermo bonus benedicendus est pro loco et tempore... Et ad quid? Subdit* **ad aedificationem fidei***, id est ut corroboretur fides in cordibus infirmorum. I Cor XIV, 26: 'Omnia ad aedificationem fiant'*" Ibid., 4.9.260-261].

[53] "*Deinde cum dicit* **estote autem**, *etc., ponit pertinentia ad novitatem contrariam passionibus praemissis: contra amaritudinem, benignitatem. Unde dicit* **estote autem invicem benigni***. Quia benignus est siritus sapientiae, etc. - Contra iram, misericordiam; unde dicit misericordes. Lc. VI, 36: 'Estote ergo misericordes, sicut et Pater vester misericors est.' - Contra indignationem, condonationem; unde dicit* **donantes invicem***, etc.*" [Ibid., 4.10.265].

even imported the opposing vices in order to treat them, since they were not mentioned in the text. He continues this way of commenting on the text in every case; he explores the vices and their effects and gives only a passing treatment of the correct behavior being proposed.

This trend is accompanied by another characteristic that was not present earlier, a certain rhetorical questioning of the text, which can be seen throughout his exegesis starting with 4:17. Stringing these together helps give the flavor of this new approach: "How should they be [in accordance with how they learned Christ]?" "How should they live?" "And why [should they speak the truth]?" "And what [is a good word] for?" In each case Thomas cites the text, then interrogates it, and finally defends it. The purpose is clear - to give his own stress to the text, to underscore Paul's exhortations with his own. Here we must recall that Thomas is teaching other friars. His decision to add a certain pedagogical enthusiasm to his lecture, as well as to thoroughly identify and excoriate the negative, may well stem from the fact that along with his teaching on the Pauline corpus, Thomas also had the responsibility of teaching moral theology and preparing the friars for "the pastoral work of confession" and preaching.[54] Therefore, it seems likely that Thomas is monopolizing on the opportunity the biblical text is offering him to draw a connection between the Scripture course and the other courses, for which the manuals at his disposal were unsatisfactory.[55] The connection thus established between the Bible and morality/pastoral work would definitely have been of great value to Thomas; in fact, it is exactly what he labors to achieve with the writing of the *Summa Theologiae*.[56]

This recalls another factor into the construction of this theological model of Church unity, i.e. that it is an exercise in pedagogy and pastoral formation.[57] Also, while he would certainly not limit his exhortations to friars, there should be no doubt that this type of community life is in his mind as he comments on all of the paraenetic sections of Ephesians.

---

[54] TORRELL, *Saint Thomas*, 144.

[55] Ibid., 144.

[56] Ibid., 120.

[57] See L.E. BOYLE, "Notes on the Education of the *Fratres communes* in the Dominican Order in the Thirteenth Century," in *Xenia medii aevi historiam illustrantia oblata Th. Käppeli O.P.*, ed. R. Creytens and P. Künzle, 249-267, vol. 1, Storia e Letteratura, Raccolta di Studie Testi 141 (Rome: 1978), for a consideration of the formation of the friars during the time of Thomas.

B) *Chapter Five: Christ, the Bridegroom and the Church, His Bride*

In his exegesis of Ephesians 5, Thomas offers ten lectures which are of the same basic character as the last five lectures of Ephesians 4 (at least until Lecture 7). Yet his emphasis is much less "communocentric" - nowhere does Thomas wander further from a direct consideration of his main theme. Even his repeated references to the "newness," to which the members of the Church are called, are absent.[58] The new unifying concept (at least from Lecture 4 forward) is the contrast between light and darkness first offered by the text in 5:8. It is only with the verses under consideration in Lecture 7 (vv 18-21) that Thomas will begin to adopt a perspective that pertains directly to the life of the Church as Church, and even there we encounter what is perhaps Thomas' first significant failure to adopt a communal perspective - the exhortation of v. 19, which calls for "speaking to yourselves in psalms and hymns, etc." (*loquentes vobismet ipsis in psalmis, hymnis*, etc.), is taken in large part as a call to personal prayer rather than as a way of greeting and speaking with other Christians.[59] This is a fitting end to a series of lectures where Thomas has dwelt on moral imperatives from a clearly individualistic perspective.[60]

Yet in the end, Thomas will turn his attention to the issue of the Church again, and in fact does so in his treatment of the very same passage for which we have criticized him above - vv 18-21. Thomas sees this passage as an elaboration of what it means to be filled with the Holy Spirit (as *per* the exhortation of v. 18). As such, the call for "singing and making melody" (*cantantes et psallantes*) in v. 19 triggers the following observations:

---

[58] Only once more will this theme be taken up again, and only in passing, as Thomas completes his treatment of the paraenetic section of the Epistle: "The Apostle has previously written down many general and particular instructions aimed at destroying the old man of sin and encouraging the newness of grace" (*Supra posuit Apostolus multa praecepta generalia, et specialia ad destruendam vetustatem peccati, et inducendam novitatem gratiae...*) [*In Eph.*, 6.3.351].

[59] Ibid., 5.7.312.

[60] Perhaps this is too harsh a judgment of Thomas' pattern of exegesis. LINCOLN, 299 has noted the fact that the "general applicability" of the moral imperatives given by Paul unhinges them from the "setting" of the Letter's recipients. That is, Paul is no longer commenting directly on the issue which Thomas has chosen as the main theme; therefore, it is not reprehensible that Thomas ceases to do so as well. Also, we must remember again that he is not only exegeting the text, but teaching it - Ephesians is his classroom text, and so he should not be indicted for his tendency to treat each subject which arises in it with at least a basic degree of individual importance.

> This refutes the error of those heretics who claim that it is useless to sing vocal canticles to the Lord; that only spiritual ones matter. In the praises of the Church there is an essential element to consider, what the apostle refers to as **in your hearts**. Yet there is another element [the external expression in song] which has a twofold purpose. One is that it is for us, to stimulate our minds to an interior devotion. If someone is moved rather to frivolity or vain glory by it, this is contrary to the Church's intention. Its second purpose is for others, since by it the illiterate become more devout.[61]

The comment is sparse, but at least demonstrates how easily Thomas makes his way back to the subject of the Church. At the same time, it also demonstrates how far Thomas has moved from his main subject; the joyful noise of singing, an easy tie-in to the harmony of once estranged peoples, is not taken by Thomas as a chance to point towards unity within the Church. Only the *divisio textus* at the beginning of Chapter 4 remains to remind us that this is his theme, and Thomas ends the *lectura* without another explicit reference to it.

However, he is not finished discussing the Church; the subject will arise once more in the context of 5:22-33. As we have already noted above, 5:22 begins the section of Ephesians which Thomas characterizes as pertaining to specific classes within the Church. In this passage the subject is the relationship of husband and wife. However, this is not the main focus of Thomas' exposition, but rather the corresponding relationship between Christ and the Church,[62] as he himself notes at the end of Lecture 10 with reference to the citation by Paul of Gn 2:24:

> ...there are certain passages in the Old Testament which can be said only of Christ. For instance, Psalm 21 (17): "they have dug my hands and feet; they have numbered all my bones"; or Isaiah 7 (14): "Behold, a virgin shall conceive, and bear a son; and his name shall

---

[61] *"Ex hoc error haereticorum confunditur dicentium quod vanum est cantare Domino cantica vocalia sed spiritualia tantum. Nam in laudibus ecclesiae est aliquid per se considerandum, et hoc est quod Apostolus dicit* **in cordibus**. *Aliquid vero propter duo, scilicet propter nos, ut mens nostra incitetur ad devotionem interiorem; sed si ex hoc aliquis commoveatur ad dissolutionem, vel in gloriam inanem, hoc est contra intentionem ecclesiae. Item, propter alios, quia per hoc rudes efficiuntur devotiores"* [Ibid., 5.7.31].

[62] Others have also taken note of this passage, albeit wth differing emphases. See D.J. O'CONNOR, "The Concept of Mystery in Aquinas' Exegesis, Part II," 276-282; SWIERZAWSKI, "Christ and the Church," 245-247.

be called Emmanuel." Other passages, however, can be explained as referring to Christ and others; to Christ principally, and to others as they were types of Christ. The above example (Gn 2:24) is of this category.

Thus it must first be interpreted in reference to Christ, and afterwards concerning others. Hence he says **Nevertheless, let every one of you in particular love his wife**, as though he asserted: the above example is principally related of Christ, but not only about him since it must be interpreted and fulfilled in other persons as types of Christ.[63]

Therefore Gn 2:24 is, in Thomas' opinion, primarily about Christ and only secondarily about matrimony, and just as he places the emphasis on the christological aspect in this case, so does he place his emphasis on the christological sense of the whole of the passage in which it is contained - the relationship of husband and wife is used by Thomas principally to illustrate the way in which Christ is head of the Church.

The parameters of this relationship of Christ to the Church are set out here in a manner very similar to his treatment of the head/body analogy in other places.[64] The emphasis is on the Church's subjection to Christ; this can be seen in his comments on v. 24:

> As though he said: it is not proper for an organ to rebel against its head in any situation; but as Christ is head of the Church in his own way, so a husband is the head of his wife; therefore the wife must be obedient to her husband **as the Church is subject in Christ.** "Shall not my soul be subject to God?" (Ps 61:2), **so also let the wives be subject to their husbands.**[65]

---

[63] "...*sunt in sacra scriptura Veteris Testamenti, quae tantum dicuntur de Christo, sicut illud Ps. XXI, 17: 'Foderunt manus meas, etc.'; et illud Is. VII, 14: 'Ecce virgo concipiet, etc.' Quaedam vero de Christo et aliis exponi possunt, sed de Christo principaliter, de aliis vero in figura Christi, sicut praedictum exemplum. Et ideo primo exponendum est de Christo et postea de aliis. Et ideo dicit* **verumtamen et vos singuli, unusquisque uxorem suam diligat,** *quasi dicat: De Christo dicitur principaliter et si non singulariter, quia exponendum et implendum est in aliis in figura Christi*" [Ibid., 5.10.335].

[64] See *In III Sent.*, 13.2; 18.1.6; *De Ver.*, 29.4; *Comp. Theo.*, 1.214; *ST* III.8; III.19; *In I Cor.*, 11.1.587; *In Col.*, 1.4.47-52.

[65] "*Quasi dicat: Non est conveniens, quod membrum repugnet ipsi capiti in aliquo; nunc autem, sicut Christus caput est ecclesiae, suo modo, ita vir est caput mulieris: non debet ergo mulier inobediens esse viro,* **sed sicut ecclesia subiecta est Christo**" [*In Eph.*, 5.8.318].

This is a headship not of domination but of love: "This is not for his own utility, but for that of the Church, **since he is savior of the body**."[66] Here we see the soteriological dimension of headship underlined, and this will be the principal element which Thomas will continue to emphasize throughout his exposition of this passage, in accordance with the emphasis of the text itself. One part of this consideration is how this salvation is tranferred from head to body; namely, through baptism:

> As a result of this sanctification he cleanses it from the stain of sin. Hence he adds **cleansing it by the laver of water**. This washing has a power from the passion of Christ. "All we who are baptized in Christ Jesus are baptized into his death; for we are buried together with him by baptism into death" (Rom 6:3-4). "And I will pour upon you clean water and you shall be cleansed from all your filthiness" (Ez 36:25). "There shall be a fountain open to the house of David and to the inhabitants of Jerusalem; for the washing of the sinner and of the unclean woman" (Zach 13:1). This occurs **in the word of life** which, coming upon the water, gives it the power to cleanse: "Going, therefore, teach all the nations; baptizing them in the name of the Father and of the Son and of the Holy Spirit" (Mt 28:19).[67]

Sabra notes that for Thomas, the instrumentality of the sacraments in conferring grace is a function of the instrumentality of Christ's humanity in effecting salvation.[68] Therefore, it is not surprising to see how easily Thomas shifts to a sacramental emphasis as he begins to consider the reference to baptism in the text. What is surprising, however, is that this is the first place that he does so; besides a short *excursus* on the nature of baptism in his comments on 4:5, Thomas has refrained from discussing the seven sacraments at all. Instead, he has taken all references to mystery and sacrament in the text

---

[66] "*...hoc non ad utilitatem suam, sed ecclesiae, **quia ipse est salvator corporis eius**"* [Ibid., 5.8.318].

[67] "*Effectus autem sanctificationis est mundatio eius a maculis peccatorum. Ideo subdit dicens **mundans eam lavacro aquae**. Quod quidem lavacrum habet virtutem a passione Christi. Rom. VI, 3: 'Quicumque baptizati sumus in Christo Iesu, in morte ipsius baptizati sumus, consepulti enim sumus cum illo per baptismum in mortem. Ez. XXXIX: 'Effundam super vos aquam mundam, etc.' Zac. XIII, 1: 'Erit fons patens domui David, etc.' Et hoc **in verbo vitae**, quod adveniens aquae dat ei virtutem abluendi. Matth. c. ult.: 'Euntes ergo docete omnes gentes, baptizantes eos in nomine Patris, et Filii, et Spiritus Sancti*" [Ibid., 5.8.323].

[68] SABRA, 88-90.

in a way much more compatible with the text itself, his own overwhelming interest in the sacramental system notwithstanding.

At this point, Thomas encounters a verse (27) which offers him the real (albeit weak) possibility to return to an earlier ecclesiological emphasis; namely, the Church as the manifestation of God. The reference to a "glorious Church" (*gloriosam ecclesiam*), however, occurs in the context of Christ's presentation of the Church to himself; therefore, Thomas turns his exegesis heavenward:

> The goal of this sanctifying action is the Church's purity. Thus he states **that he might present it to himself, a glorious Church**; as if the Apostle said: It would be highly improper for the immaculate bridegroom to wed a soiled bride. This is why he presents her to himself in an immaculate state, now through grace and in the future through glory.
>
> Regarding the latter, he says **glorious** by the clarity of both body and soul. For "he will reform the body of our lowliness, made like to the body of his glory" (Phil 3:21). Hence he adds **not having spot**. "The man that walked in the perfect way, he served me" (Ps 100:6). **Or wrinkle** refers to the lack of suffering since, as the Apocalypse 7 (16) remarks: "they shall no more hunger nor thirst," **or any such thing, but that it should be holy** through its confirmation in grace, **and without** the **blemish** of any defilement. Thus all of these characteristics can be understood of the [presentation] of the Church in the future through glory.[69]

This is strongly reminiscent of Thomas' exegesis of Eph 1:6, and even employs the same grace/glory distinction found there. It seems clear that

---

[69] "*Finis autem sanctificationis est puritas ecclesiae. Ideo dicit* **ut exhiberet sibi gloriosam ecclesiam**; *quasi dicat Apostolus: Indecens est quod immaculatus sponsus sponsam duceret maculatam. Et ideo sibi exhibet eam immaculatam: hic per gratiam sed in futuro per gloriam. Unde dicit* **gloriosam**, *scilicet per claritatem animae et corporis. Phil. III, v. 21: 'Reformabit corpus humilitatis nostrae, etc.' Et ideo addit* **non habentem maculam**. *- Ps. c, 6: 'Ambulans in via immaculata, etc.' Ps. C, 6: 'Beati immaculati in via, etc.' -* **Neque rugam**, *id est, sine defectu passibilitatis; quia, ut dicitur Apoc. VII, 16: 'Non esurient, neque sitient amplius.' -* **Aut aliquid huiusmodi, sed ut sit sancta**, *per confirmationem gratiae,* **et immaculata ab omni immunditia**. *Et haec omnia intelligi possunt de exhibitione, quae erit in futuro per gloriam*" [*In Eph.*, 5.8.323]. LAMB, 219, translates "*exhibitione*" as "appearance," although related terms are translated differently (e.g. "*exhiberet*" as "he might *present*"). I have changed "appearance" to "presentation" above in order to maintain both consistency and the best possible translation.

Thomas is ending as he began, his emphasis placed now as then on the Church as destined for glory through the work of Christ.

In Lecture 9 Thomas pauses from his overwhelmingly Christocentric interpretation of the passage to consider matrimony more exclusively. This is occasioned by the reference to the man's love for himself in vv 28-29. The passage brings Thomas back to the issue of human unity briefly, an emphasis which he can hardly avoid because of its direct involvement in the literal sense of the text:

> A husband and wife are somehow one; hence, as the flesh is subject to the soul, so is the wife to the husband; but no one ever held his own flesh in contempt, therefore, neither should anyone his wife. Whence he states **He that loveth his wife loveth himself.** "Therefore, now they are not two, but one flesh" (Mt 19:6). Just as a man sins against nature in hating himself, so does he who hates his wife. "With three things my spirit is pleased, which are approved before God and men: the concord of brethren, and the love of neighbors, and man and wife that agree well together" (Sir 25:1-2).
>
> He proves that they ought to love one another in saying **For no man ever hated his own flesh.** This love is evident in what happens since "love is verified when it is expressed in action." [For we love what we preserve with all our strength]. **But** everyone **nourishes and cherishes his own flesh** in order to sustain it.[70]

Thus Thomas begins to speak once again the language of unity. His focus is love in the face of the many temptations in marriage to estrangement and disharmony. For this action-oriented love, Christ is the exemplar; though

---

[70] "*Vir et mulier sunt quodammodo unum; unde sicut caro subditur animae, ita mulier viro; sed nullus unquam habuit carnem suam odio: ergo nec uxorem. Dicit ergo* **qui suam uxorem diligit, seipsum diligit**. *Matth. XIX, 6: 'Itaque non sunt duo, sed una caro.' Et ideo sicut peccaret contra naturam qui seipsum odio haberet, ita qui uxorem. Eccli. XXV, 1 s: 'In tribus beneplacitum est spiritui meo, quae sunt probata coram Deo et hominibus: concordia fratrum, amor proximorum, et vir et mulier bene sibi consentientes. Quod autem sic debeant se diligere, probat dicens,* **nemo enim carnem suam unquam odio habuit***; quod patet per effectum, quia 'probatio dilectionis exhibitio est operis.' Nam id quod pro viribus conservamus, diligimus.* **Sed** *quilibet* **nutrit et fovet carnem suam** *propter conservationem*" [Ibid., 5.9.326]. The unidentified quotation is from GREGORY THE GREAT, *Homilia 30 in Evangelia, PL* 76, col. 1220; cf. LAMB, 303 n. 152. Lamb translates "Nam id quod pro viribus conservamus, diligimus" as "For we love anything whose powers we sustain." A better translation is "For we love what we preserve with all our strength," which I have added above in brackets.

Thomas does not directly recall it himself, one remembers the picture of Christ as savior/peacegiver in the exegesis of Ephesians 2:

> Then he [Paul] indicates that a man must love his wife through an example. Thus he says, **Christ also** loved **the Church** as something of his very self **because we are members of his body**. 'For we are members one of another' (Eph 4:25). He mentions **of his flesh** on account of his sharing the same nature with us.[71]

The man's love for his wife expresses beautifully the kind of unity which is the goal of all the members of the Church, at least in degree if not in kind. Thomas' reference to Eph 4:25 gives little doubt that Thomas sees the connection between such a conception of spousal love and the interrelation of all the Church's members.[72]

He returns to a more Christocentric and ecclesiologically-oriented interpretation with Lecture 10. After giving the plain sense of the quote from Gn 2:24 in v. 31 (i.e. its meaning for marriage), Thomas considers Paul's mystical interpretation of it, which (as we have noted) he considers to be its primary meaning. There are two aspects to the interpretation of this passage. The first regards Paul's [i.e. the Vulgate text's] reference to marriage as a "*sacramentum magnum*"; the second regards the manner in which the actions of matrimony apply to Christ. It is worth quoting in full:

> He goes on to interpret this mystically, and he says **This is a great sacrament**, it is the symbol of a sacred reality, namely the union of Christ and the church. "I will not hide from you the mysteries of God" (Wis 6:24).
>
> Notice here that four Sacraments are termed great. Baptism by reason of its effect, since it blots out sin and opens the gate of paradise; Confirmation by reason of its minister, it is conferred only by bishops and not by others; the Eucharist because of what it contains, the Whole Christ; and Matrimony by reason of its signification, for it symbolizes the union of Christ and the

---

[71] "*Deinde ostendit quod virum oportet uxorem diligere, et hoc per exemplum. Unde dicit* **sicut et Christus ecclesiam***, scilicet dilexit, sicut aliquid sui, quia membra sumus corporis. Supra IV, 25: 'Sumus enim invicem membra.' Dicit autem* **de carne eius** *propter eamdem participationem naturae*" [Ibid., 5.9.330].

[72] Coincidentally, this emphasis also serves as an important counterbalance to the rather heavy-handed notion of headship in marriage (from a contemporary perspective, at least) which Thomas has suggested in 5.8.317.

Church. If, therefore, the text is mystically interpreted, the preceding passage should be explained as follows: **For this cause shall a man**, namely, Christ, **leave his father and mother**. I say **leave his father**, because he was sent into the world and became incarnate - "I came forth from the Father and am come into the world" (Jn 16:28) - **and his mother** who was the synagogue - "I have forsaken my house, I have left my inheritance, I have given my dear soul into the hands of her enemies" (Jer 12:7). **And he shall cleave to his wife**, the Church. "Behold I am with you all days, even to the consummation of the world" (Mt 28:20).[73]

A number of important elements stand out from this passage, which is the last reference to the Church contained in the *lectura*. The first is the ecclesiological interpretation of the Sacraments of Eucharist and Matrimony - their greatness derives from the fact that both signify not only Christ but also the Church in relation to him. Here we encounter what Congar has described as the "complex reality" of Thomas' vision of the Church[74] - it is a subject not so much taken up by Thomas in this or that place but rather one which he never "puts down," so to speak. Its place is everywhere that "the return of rational creatures to God" occupies Thomas' mind.

The second element of note is the unusual and beautiful interpretation of Christ's movement toward the Church. This movement has two moments or stages. The first of these, the Incarnation, is a well-explored feature of Thomas' christology. But the second, in which Christ is identified as the child of the synagogue, a mother whom he leaves to cleave to the Church, is a rare if not truly unique feature of the same. There is none of the usual ambiguity that is present in other places where Thomas treats of things Jewish; the

---

[73] *"Consequentur exponit eam mystice, et dicit **Sacramentum hoc magnum est**, id est sacrae rei signum, scilicet coniunctionis Christi et ecclesiae. Sup. VI, 24: 'Non abscondam a vobis sacramentum Dei.' Notandum est hic, quod quatuor sacramenta dicitur magna, scilicet Baptismus ratione effectus, quia delet culpam et aperit ianuam paradisi; Confirmatio ratione ministri, quia solum a pontificibus et non ab aliis confertur; Eucharistia ratione continentiae, quia totum Christum continet; item Matrimonium ratione significationis, quia significat coniunctionem Christi et Ecclesiae. Et ideo si mystice exponatur, debet sic exponi littera praecedens: **Propter hoc relinquet homo**, scilicet Christus, **patrem et matrem**. **Reliquit**, inquam, **Patrem**, inquantum, est missus in mundum et incarnatus. Io. XVI, v. 28: 'Exivi a Patre, et veni in mundum, etc.' Et matrem, scilicet synagogam. Ier. XII, 7: 'Reliqui domum meam, et dimisi haereditatem meam, etc.' Et adhaerebit uxori suae, Ecclesiae. Matth. ult.: Ecce vobiscum sum omnibus diebus, etc.'"* [*In Eph.*, 5.10.334].

[74] CONGAR, "Vision de l'Eglise chez S. Thomas d'Aquin," *Revue des sciences philosophiques et théologiques* 62 (1978) : 524.

supporting citation from Jeremiah describes the synagogue as Christ's home, his inheritance, and as standing in contrast to his enemies. The concept is certainly not well-developed in Thomas' mind, especially when we consider that elsewhere Thomas calls the "college of the Pharisees" (*collegium Pharisaeorum*) the "womb" (*uterus*) of the synagogue[75] - hence its most vital place for its children is also the place of Christ's enemies themselves! But when applied to Christ its potential ramifications are fascinating. The synagogue, the heart of the practice of Judaism, would be the very locus of Christ's preparation for his mission, preparing him to go forth and gather to himself the Church, his bride. The two testaments could hardly be more firmly united than in this image, where their unity is located in the love of Christ for both. Once again, Christ unites.

Yet even with this unique feature Thomas' final consideration of the Church is more clearly a reflection of his larger ecclesiological vision than of the theological model which he has constructed in the first four chapters of the *lectura*. This in no way decreases its value, however, nor even its fittingness. The intimate relationship which it portrays between Christ and the Church is an excellent theological *dénouement* to the horizontal model that dominates the commentary on Ephesians 2 but also elsewhere. As Thomas noted in commenting on 2:14-18, the two peoples are drawn into unity so that they may be drawn closer to God. The last picture of the Church in the *lectura* is descriptive of the second union, and with it Thomas concludes his analysis with the main theme of the majority of his ecclesiological writings - the Church as the reconciliation of God and humanity. Thus, Thomas completes his commentary by returning to his starting-point, focusing on the "*reditus creaturae rationalis in Deum*."[76] In this way he ties the picture of the Church within it into the mighty theological edifice that consists of the whole of his theology. The former is distinct, but not separate, from the latter.

C) *Chapter 6: Conclusion*

As we reach the final chapter of Thomas' *lectura* and of the Epistle itself, it is clear from the outset that Thomas considers the majority of the chapter (6:10-22) to be a long conclusion. The final subject, which regards the way to receive grace for the fulfillment of the many precepts given in the latter half of the Epistle, caps the treatment of the paraenetic section and brings Thomas finally to Paul's example, prayers and requests for prayers

---

[75] *In Gal.*, 1.4.41, where the synagogue is also identified as Paul's mother.
[76] CONGAR, "The Idea of the Church," 103.

which end the Epistle. Thomas himself is winding down; this chapter is the shortest of the commentary, and does not introduce any new themes. Instead, he completes his consideration of particular classes in the Church with 6:1-9, and then considers (in his own words): "the power by which we must carry out these precepts, for we must trust in divine assistance" (*qua virtute debent uti ad praecepta haec implenda, quia fiducia auxilii divini*).[77]   The topic is what each individual must do if he/she is to succeed in fulfilling all of the commands of the Epistle and live up to the glorious example of Christ - it is entirely concerned with issues of struggling against demonic temptation and aggressively pursuing God and salvation. The spiritual soldier which each Christian is called to be is summed up by Thomas in Lecture 4, and clearly resembles the ideal Christian, a courageous and steadfast ascetic, detached from the world:

> Therefore, we possess weapons to defend ourselves against carnal adversaries, namely, gluttony and sensuality, through temperance: **Stand therefore, having your loins girt about with truth**. By the arms of justice, which make us refrain from what is unlawful, we can conquer also earthly greed: **and having on the breastplate of justice**. This is aided by purity of heart or poverty which withdraw us even from things that are lawful: **and your feet shod with the preparation of the gospel of peace**. Moreover, we have weapons by which we are guarded from error, the armour of faith: **in all things taking the shield of faith**; and also protected from the enemies of the human race: **wherewith**, meaning the shield of faith, **you may be able to extinguish all the fiery darts of the most wicked one**. We likewise possess armour by which we are strengthened in spiritual blessings, the armour of hope: **and take unto you the helmet of salvation**. A helmet rests on the head, and so does hope in its end. Now the head of the moral virtues is the very end with which hope is concerned. Thus, to take up the helmet of salvation is nothing less than to have hope in the ultimate end. Finally, we have weapons to assault the demons themselves: **the sword of the Spirit, which is the word of God**. This happens frequently during sermons when the word of God, penetrating into the hearts of sinners, thrusts out the chaos of sin and demons.[78]

---

[77] *In Eph.*, 6.3.351.

[78]"*Sic ergo habemus arma quibus defendamur a carnalibus hostibus, scilicet a gula et luxuria, quod fit per temperantiam, ibi* **state ergo succinti lumbos vestros**, *etc. Item, quibus vincamus cupiditates terrenas, scilicet arma iustitiae, quae abstinere nos faciunt ab illicitis, ibi* **induti loricam iustitiae**. *Et puritatem affectus seu paupertatem, quae nos retrahit etiam a*

Thomas, with the Epistle,[79] is once again concerned with conduct, but now not so much with basic moral behavior as with how one is to set out to fulfill the moral imperatives given by Paul. This is another case where the main theme takes a secondary position in favor of the more direct meaning of the text.

It is only when we reach the very end of the *lectura* that we see the main theme once again, where it appears in the somewhat subtle yet powerful way Thomas interprets the ordering of the final salutation in vv 23-24. One feature of Thomas' general exegetical practice is his concern for the prioritizing of various elements within the text. This can be seen in his earlier discussion of anger in reference to 4:31 - according to Thomas, bitterness is listed first because it is the interior root of anger, then anger itself, then indignance, then clamor, in that order because, in his opinion, each follows on the one preceding it.[80] In this final case, Paul wishes the Ephesians peace before he wishes them grace, and Thomas interprets this in a way significant to the main theme of the Epistle:

> Next, when he says **Peace be to the brethren** the Apostle writes his usual greeting. And notice that although bestowal of grace precedes peace and the mutual love of men among themselves and with God since "there is no peace to the wicked, says the Lord" (Is 57:21), nevertheless, in its own way peace does precede the putting of grace into practice and the preservation of truth and charity. Hence, he first wishes that they have peace with one another and charity toward God - **peace be to the brethren and charity with faith.**

---

licitis, ibi **calceati pedes,** *etc. Item, habemus arma quibus protegamur ab erroribus, scilicet arma fidei, ibi* **in omnibus sumentes scutum fidei**; *et etiam ab hostibus generis humani, ibi* **quo**, *scilicet scuto fidei,* **possitis omnia tela nequissimi ignea extinguere**. *Item, habemus arma quibus in bonis spiritualibus confirmamur, scilicet arma spei, ibi* **et galeam salutis assumite**. *Galea ponitur in capite, sic spes in fine. Nunc autem caput virtutum moralium est ipse finis, de quo est spes. Unde nihil est aliud galeam salutis assumere, quam spem de ultimo fine habere. Item, habemus arma ad impugnandum ipsos daemones, scilicet* **gladium spiritus, quod est verbum Dei**: *quod frequenter in sermonibus, in quibus verbum Dei penetrans corda peccatorum expellit congeriem peccatorum et daemonum*" [Ibid., 6.4.367].

[79] BEST, 585, notes the clear difference between this passage, the "most original" of the Epistle, and the moral imperatives treated earlier.

[80] *In Eph.*, 4.10.264. Coincidentally, some modern exegetes would agree that the author's intention is to demonstrate a certain causal connection in 4:31 similar to the one Thomas posits; for example, see BARTH, 521.

Peace and charity contribute greatly toward the preservation of grace; yet, since they always presuppose grace - they could not be had without it - on this account he prays that they receive grace. **Grace be with all them that love our Lord Jesus Christ in incorruption. Amen.**[81]

Thomas is not constrained to interpret the text in this way; he does not always give the order of presentation the significance that he gives it here.[82] His insistence on the priority of grace confirms this - Thomas is venturing out while remaining wary of giving an interpretation that will be taken to suggest certain Pelagian undertones. Yet at the same time, he faces an Epistle which has given priority to peace and human reconciliation, making it the basis of the existence of the Church and a mandate for Christian behavior, as well as a fundamental aspect of Christ's salvific work. His creative interpretation of this passage demonstrates to what degree he has taken this message seriously; the reverberations of Ephesians 2 are obviously still echoing through his mind as he gives a place to human reconciliation in the dispensation of grace.

This final passage demonstrates that Thomas has by no means forgotten the basic insight that his reading of Ephesians has afforded him; that the Church must always remain the principal locus of human unity if it is to be informed with the power and presence of God. The origination of ecclesial unity, in Thomas' mind a salvific, historical event, breeds a conception of the

---

[81] "*Deinde cum dicit* **Pax fratribus**, *etc., ponit Apostolus consuetam salutationem. Et advertendum est, quod licet gratia praecedat pacem et charitatem mutuam hominum ad se invicem, et ad Deum quo ad collationem (quia non est pax impiis, dicit Dominus), tamen quo ad executionem gratiae et veritatis et charitatis conservationem, pax praecedit suo modo. Et ideo primo optat eis pacem ad se invicem et charitatem ad Deum, dicens:* **Pax fratribus, et charitas cum fide.** *Et quia licet pax et charitas multum faciant ad gratiae conservationem, tamen quia semper supponunt ipsam gratiam, sine qua haberi non possunt, ideo optat eis gratiam. Unde dicit:* **Gratia cum omnibus, qui diligunt Dominum nostrum Iesum Christum in incorruptione. Amen**" [Ibid., 6.5.377].

[82] For example, at the end of the Galatians *lectura* (in commenting on Gal 6:16) Thomas is confronted with a similar construction: "And whosoever shall follow this rule, peace on them and mercy..." As he comments: "...**peace on them**, namely, on those who glory, because they glory in Christ alone: peace, I say, by which they are set at rest and made perfect in good. For peace is tranquility of mind... **and mercy**, by which they are set free from sin" (**Pax super illos**, *scilicet gloriantes quia nonnisi in Christo gloriantur. Pax, inquam, qua quietentur et perficiantur in bono. Pax enim est tranquillitas mentis.... **Et misericordia**, per quam liberentur a peccatis*) [*In Gal.*, 6.5.376]. Although peace is mentioned first here just as it is in Eph 6:23-24, and although the two are both phrased as wishes by Paul for his correspondents as part of a final greeting, in the case of Galatians Thomas attributes no significance to the fact that peace is mentioned first, whereas in the case of Ephesians he does.

Church's unity that posits peace between fellows as the basis for the Church's witness, increase, and final destination, not just at its beginning but at every stage of its pilgrimage through history.

The comments of J.-M.R. Tillard in regard to the Epistle itself can be also asserted of the theological model which Thomas has constructed on it, and serves as a fitting encapsulation of the vision of the Church which Thomas has developed:

> The mystery whose fulfillment is the Church, in Christ, produces, therefore, the joining together again of humanity by the destruction and abolition of hatred. It comes about historically on the Cross: "He reconciled them both in a single Body with God, through the Cross. In his own person he killed the hatred" (2:16). Of what was divided, Christ on the Cross "makes the two into one" (2:14); of what was a humanity torn apart, he "creates one single New Man" (2:15). What was separated, he "reconciles" (2:16); what was burning with hostility, he "pacifies" (2:17). From the humanity which is living out its drama he makes the humanity-which-God-wills; a People in which we no longer speak of aliens or foreign visitors, a city in which all are fellow-citizens, a family of God which is no longer broken, a structure in which "all form one house of God in the Spirit" (2:22), one single Body. What is the Church of God? The extent of humanity where, by the Blood of Christ [that] which was *far apart* - in the strong sense... which hatred gives to this term - has become *very close* (2:13).[83]

---

[83] J.-M.R. TILLARD, *Church of Churches: The Ecclesiology of Communion*, trans. by R.C. De Peaux (Collegeville, MN: Liturgical Press, 1992), 47-48.

CHAPTER VII

THE EPHESIANS *LECTURA*
AND ITS POTENTIAL CONTRIBUTION

In his commentary on Ephesians, Thomas has provided us with a rich feast of ecclesiological images, concepts and principles. However, if such a complex and intricate theological model as the one he provides remains unappreciated in our day, perhaps this is because it is historically far removed from present-day concerns and points-of-view; the great medieval Dominican friar, expounding the Epistle for his student-friars, does so at a great distance from the contemporary theological scene. His positions, concerns and insights are dated in much the same way as are the exegetical principles which he relies on to interpret the Epistle.

Yet as we have noted in Part I, the great benefit of Thomas' Ephesians *lectura* is that he engages a text the non-narrative character of which removes him in large part from the more radical excesses of the medieval exegetical framework and places him in a much more "coin-habitable" abode with contemporary scholarship. The modern commentators whose work has supported our inquiry into the *lectura* have demonstrated Thomas' basic acuity at Pauline exegesis, and have revealed at least a basic accuracy on his behalf in interpretation. In many ways, the contemporary biblical scholar and the contemporary systematic theologian who stand before the same text, considering the same message it communicates about Church unity, have a solid and reliable point of contact with the insights Thomas offers.

With this, as well as an appreciative regard for Thomas' theological genius in mind, we can approach the *lectura* with confidence not only in our ability to understand it, but also in its benefits for contemporary theology. We have now reached **Part III** of the Genre-Identification Approach; the present chapter will employ all three of the steps listed there. In the first part (corresponding to **III.a** of our approach), we will endeavor to show the distinctiveness of the theological model contained in the *lectura* in relation to Thomas' other writings on the Church. This will provide a foundation for the second part (which corresponds to **III.b** of our approach), where we will consider the theological model of the *lectura* in relation to its predesignated theme, the origination of ecclesial unity, considering it first in itself and then in relation to contemporary ecclesiology: the 20th century Catholic magisterial teaching on the Church (as represented by Pius XII's *Mystici Corporis* and *Lumen Gentium*, the Dogmatic Constitution on the Church of Vatican II); and finally the concerns of contemporary ecclesiology (especially the ecclesiology of communion, ecumenism, and missiology). In our final section (corresponding to part **III.c** of our approach), we will return to the issue of Thomas' exegesis and attempt to draw some insights from the Ephesians commentary regarding his general exegetical practice. With this we will conclude.

A) *Thomas' Theological Model in Relation to His Other Writings on the Church*

G. Sabra has noted that very little has been written regarding Thomas' ecclesiology considered comprehensively.[1] To this should be added another significant observation which he offers concomitant with this one; that most treatments of Thomas' thought on the Church have been of service to this or that larger trend in Catholic ecclesiology, for instance, the mystical body movement of the early- to mid-twentieth century and the more perennial Catholic interest in the juridical aspects of his vision of the Church.[2]   As such, the contemporary scholar seeking a comprehensive Thomistic ecclesiology has few places to turn, as the question has been largely ignored by all but a few, among whom Sabra stands out as the most recent as well as the most balanced and insightful. Therefore, he remains the most reliable source for understanding Thomas' vision of the Church, and so will be helpful in our present task of comparing and contrasting the specific theological model of the Ephesians *lectura* with the more general ecclesiological model which Thomas provides throughout his works. In particular, Sabra's breakdown of Thomas' ecclesiology into three categories provides a useful structure for this endeavor; these are: Thomas' designations of the Church, his constitutive ecclesiological principles, and his understanding of the Church in its earthly, "constituted" reality as an institution.[3]

---

[1] SABRA, 15.

[2] Ibid., 15 n. 2-4.

[3] Ibid., 33.

In the case of Thomas' designations of the Church, we find several points of intersection between the *lectura* and his larger ecclesiological vision. The first and most central would be his use of several exclusively biblical images to describe the Church,[4] all of which (excepting the image of flock[5]) are explicitly found in Ephesians itself - body, city, house, bride and, of course, temple. And just as in his regular practice, the idea of unity predominates in his use of these images. Sabra's description of Thomas' general use of ecclesial metaphors in this regard could easily (as would be expected) be attested of the Ephesians *lectura* specifically: "Whether, the Church is referred to as a city, a house, a people, a congregation of believers, or the mystical body of Christ, the notion of unity runs through all."[6]

Along with this, Thomas' development of the images in the *lectura*, as in the case of his general use of these metaphors, is by no means univocally focused on the Church in its juridical reality as a well-defined organization.[7] The Church is described by Thomas in the broadest possible terms when he utilizes these images, which refer to the Church militant as well as the heavenly Church, not to mention in certain cases the Church in the Old Testament. The post-Tridentine juridicalism which would exclude the extension of these descriptive designations for the Church to Protestant churches is not present in the *lectura*, and if anything is even more alien to it than it is to other places in the Thomistic corpus. At the very least, the *lectura* shares with Thomas' larger theological vision "a manifold, non-univocal and primarily theological notion of the church."[8]

However, it is when we consider the designations in themselves that we see the distinctive way that they are employed by Thomas in his commentary. Nowhere is this clearer than in the case of the *corpus* designation. Sabra has noted that it is (along with *congregatio fidelium*), "the most characteristic and prevalent among all the [ecclesial] designations."[9]

---

[4] Ibid., 69.

[5] I do not mention *congregatio fidelium* and *populus*, although Thomas does use these designations in the *lectura*, because their use is such that they are never developed but act rather as basic synonyms for the Church. The only exception would be the appearance of *populus* in close connection to the imagery of the *grex Domini*, which we have already investigated.

[6] SABRA, 69-70.

[7] Ibid., 70-71.

[8] Ibid., 33.

[9] Ibid., 71.

Yet this is not the case in the *lectura*; even though it is the most frequently mentioned image in the Epistle, Thomas only expounds it in those places where it arises, and in each case very briefly. There are only two instances where he gives it more than cursory attention, and of these two only one where it is interpreted in connection with the main theme of Church unity.[10] In the majority of cases it is passed by with barely a comment, and never does it develop into an ecclesial designation which Thomas feels emboldened to apply outside of the context of its direct mention in the text. This is a bewildering phenomenon at first glance, because it would seem that this image more than any other lends itself to the theme of unity, and in fact it is employed for that purpose by Paul.[11] Yet here (unlike its use in the larger Thomistic corpus) it is a secondary image; Thomas has two other designations which surpass it.

The first of these images is that of the *templum*, the dominant image and the only one which actually receives sustained consideration, beginning with its mention in the third lecture of Chapter 2 and receiving its fullest treatment in the last two lectures of the same (5-6). We have already identified it as the hinge metaphor for the *lectura* because of its involvement in Thomas' explication of the heart of the Epistle, Ephesians 2. Thomas does not refer to it in as many places as the body metaphor, but this is only because the text does not refer to it as often either. In light of the fact that Thomas is very much a minimalist when it comes to the use of ecclesial metaphors,[12] the fact that he follows this one through such a sustained treatment and even amplifies it through the use of a moral sense[13] affirms our conclusion that Thomas gives it pride-of-place. We can recall how he uses it as well: to describe the incorporation of the Jews and Gentiles into one spiritual edifice by Christ, who is designated by God, the builder, to be its chief foundation and cornerstone. Thus the designation is a profoundly theocentric and Christocentric metaphor for the Church's unity, as it relies most essentially on the centrality of both God and Christ - without a builder or a cornerstone there is no temple.

Another image which surpasses the image of *corpus mysticum* is that of the Church as *civitas*. This is a fact that is both significant and surprising,

---

[10] *In Eph.*, 1.8.69-70; 4.5.223-229.

[11] G. HOWARD, "The Head/Body Metaphors of Ephesians," 356.

[12] SABRA, 68-69.

[13] *In Eph.*, 2.6.131.

due to Thomas' use of it outside of its direct mention in the text.[14] It is an image closely connected to the temple metaphor, and Thomas even makes them synonymous at one point (in reference to 2:20) when he discusses the heavenly foundations of the Church: "A spiritual *structure*... has its foundation in heaven... Thus we could imagine a *city*... coming down from heaven with its foundation in heaven."[15] Its first mention in Chapter 2 of the *lectura* sets the stage for Thomas' use of it - the Church is a city since its subjects share in the same public acts of faith, hope and charity.[16] The same principle characteristic is emphasized in reference to Eph 4:5-6, where the *common* elements of governorship, law, symbols and goal are considered by Thomas to be the ecclesial characteristics which render the *civitas* image an appropriate one for designating the Church.[17] In both cases the idea of members joined by common activities (those of the theological virtues) as well as common allegiances distinguishes this image as one which emphasizes human participation, a chosen communion with God and one's fellow "citizens." Thus the image is decidedly anthropocentric. Its emphasis is on the response of human beings to the work of God, although not exclusively, for God's work is also of crucial importance.

It is when these two dominant images are considered in tandem that it becomes clear why Thomas favors them in the *lectura* over his usual favorite, i.e. the image of *corpus mysticum*. Their interchangeability (both have structures and foundations, both can be built, etc.), and complementarity (one being theocentric, the other being anthropocentric) allows Thomas to underline the paradox of Church unity, which is both the work of God as well as the common responsibility of its members. The two together offer the same major sub-themes that does the Epistle in Thomas' reading - the work of God in Christ forging the initial unity of the Church (as well as, through grace, its continuance), and the call for all to strive for and to maintain this unity. Thomas' use of these images diverges from his usual practice and coheres to his encounter with the text. In this he seems to anticipate and foreshadow another biblically-centered shift which will occur centuries later, the shift from Mystical Body theology to the theology of the People of God occasioned by events in Catholic theology leading up to Vatican II. We shall explore this

---

[14] Ibid., 4.2.197-201.

[15] "*Spirituale vero aedificium fundamentum habet in caelo... ut sic imaginemur civitatem quamdam descendentem de caelo*" [Ibid., 2.6.130].

[16] Ibid., 2.6.124.

[17] Ibid., 4.2.197-201.

similarity below; it suffices to note now that, in the former as in the latter, there is not enough room in the body image to allow Thomas to develop the central paradox which concerns him, i.e. the paradox of the Church's unity as both divinely instituted and preserved but also as a matter of human responsibility. Therefore, he opts for a new paradigm.

A final aspect of Thomas' use of ecclesial designations that diverges from his usual emphases regards the two designations which are unique to the *lectura* in terms of significant development - those of the Church as *grex Domini* and *plenitudo Christi*. We have already explored these metaphors to some degree, and have noticed their primary focus on the Church as the manifestation of God's love and grace to the world, on the Church's mission to be a sign. To these two metaphors must be added those instances where Thomas brings other metaphors to serve the purpose of demonstrating the sign-character of the Church; the reference to both city and temple images regarding their heavenly foundations and consequent earth-oriented position is an example, not to mention the fact that the *plenitudo Christi* designation is interpreted by Thomas as being a function of the body image,[18] drawing the latter into this emphasis. As noted, this is not a normal emphasis for Thomas in his use of ecclesial metaphors, and he must import and develop an image (i.e. *grex*) to sustain it.

These unique aspects of Thomas' use of ecclesial metaphors demonstrate Thomas' unique direction in the *lectura*, and also that he is completely aware of this direction. The fact that there is a divergence from his usual way of naming the Church points convincingly to the possibility that Thomas is also developing a new way of defining it, one that is not contrary to his other writings but that takes a different angle on the Church. As we have said, the theological model of the *lectura* is distinct from Thomas' larger vision of the Church, but it is not alien to it.

This is reinforced when we consider the second category offered by Sabra, the constitutive principles of the Church. Here we find several points of contact as well. As Sabra, notes, this category is crucial because "the nature of the church in Thomas is to be found subsumed under its sources... that which brings about the one, holy, catholic and apostolic church in the first place."[19] In the first point of contact between the *lectura* and Thomas' general understanding of these principles, we see that they both share the same "comprehensive and fundamental principle," that the Church is the

---

[18] Ibid., 1.8.71.
[19] SABRA, 72.

"*opus effectus gratiae*."[20]   This is certainly true of the theological model
found in the *lectura*; as we have noted, Thomas considers all of the Pauline
Epistles to be about the grace of Christ, with Ephesians falling under the
heading of Paul's consideration of "the work of unity it [Christ's grace]
realizes within the Church."[21]   This is without a doubt the most fundamental
point-of-contact between the *lectura* and Thomas' larger ecclesiological
vision.

        A second shared characteristic is the primacy of Christ and his
salvific work in the constitution of the Church. As we have noted, Christ's
headship is discussed in the *lectura* in the terms that characterize all of
Thomas' writings on the subject, and it is clear that of the various elements of
this headship Thomas emphasizes the conformity of nature which allows
Christ's humanity to be an instrument in effecting the salvation of humanity
and so to have an efficient causality in grace, the latter being one of the most
unique features of Thomas' soteriology.[22]   But it is here that we also
encounter a crucial difference - the essential element of this primacy in the
larger ecclesiological vision is Christ as Savior. In the *lectura*, it is Christ as
Peace-giver - although the former element is definitely present and even
emphasized, Thomas is more concerned with how the effects of Christ's
redemptive act create a situation in which the reconciliation of peoples, Jews
and Gentiles, is possible, and not redemption *per se*. This is clearest in a
passage we have recognized in our analysis of the second chapter of the
commentary - 2.5.118, where peace with neighbor is posited as the necessary
"way" (*via*) to peace with God: "Hence, he first mentions the peace among
themselves Christ brought to men and then the peace of men with God."[23]
Christ's work of human reconciliation is a function of his act of salvation - in
fact, it is a by-product of it. But in the milieu of the Ephesians commentary it
takes center-stage as the primary aspect of Christ's constitution of the Church.
It *is* the origination of ecclesial unity.

        Finally, in the *lectura* as elsewhere the pneumatological principle of
the Church's existence is an essential element, yet one that is also subordinate
to Christ's work and centered upon it. As Sabra describes it, "Christ is the
way of the return, but the Spirit is 'the power and first action' of that return...

---

[20] Ibid., 73.

[21] "...*affectum unitatis quem in Ecclesia fecit*" [*Super epist.*, Prol., 11].

[22] SABRA, 88-89.

[23] "*Primo ergo ponit pacem hominum invicem factam per Christum, et exinde pacem
hominum ad Deum*" [*In Eph.*, 2.5.118].

the Spirit is what enables men to receive and appropriate... [the] grace [of Christ]."[24] Thus the large majority of references to the Spirit in the *lectura* are to the Spirit's work in sanctification,[25] and there is at least one to the Spirit as giver of charismatic graces as well.[26]   But one major pneumatological/ ecclesiological motif that is significantly prevalent in Thomas' other writings is not prevalent in the *lectura* - that of the Spirit as the principle of unity.[27] On only three occasions does Thomas expound this notion,[28] and it is over-shadowed by an overwhelmingly Christocentric interpretation of unity which dominates the central parts of the commentary, especially Ephesians 2. This is unique; the place normally occupied by the Spirit elsewhere is occupied by Christ in the *lectura*. Sabra notes that Thomas' pneumatology is not very developed and often remains implicit.[29]   In the case of the *lectura*, not only does the pneumatological aspect remain undeveloped, but it is (at least regarding unity) largely replaced by Christ's work of reconciliation.

This final point underlines an essential feature of the *lectura* - it is an ecclesiological model, but it is not a *De ecclesia*. Thomas endeavors to explore and develop the theme he finds there, and all other things are treated only occasionally. His lack of emphasis on the Spirit's role in Church unity seems to be connected to the fact that Christ institutes ecclesial unity through a human act, and so remains an exemplar for all human activity in the Church regarding the unity of her members. To emphasize the Spirit as the principle

---

[24] SABRA, 95-96.

[25] *In Eph.*, 2.3.95; 2.6.132; 3.4.172; 3.5.179; 6.4.366; 4.7.243; 4.10.263; 5.7.308-309.

[26] Ibid., 1.6.50.

[27] SABRA, 100-105, who identifies two ways by which the Spirit is the principle of unity for the Church, which in itself is "a forceful and clear position of Thomas'" [105]: a) through his action in bestowing the theological virtues on the faithful, who then share one faith, one hope and are joined through one love; and b) through his personal indwelling "in so far as He is one and the same Spirit dwelling in the head and in the members by flowing undivided from the head to the members" [100-102]. Of the two, it is (a) which is Thomas' favorite explanation of the Spirit as principle of unity [102]. For examples of (a) in Thomas' writings (inclusive of references to the theological virtues as constitutive of the Church's unity without reference to the Holy Spirit), see: *ST* II-II.4.6; *In I Decr.*, 1182; *In II Decr.*, 1191; *C. Imp.*, II.c.2; *In III Sent.*, 23.2.4 qua 2; *In IV Sent.*, 13.2.1; *In Symb.*, 9.973-975; *In Io.*, 6.7.972-973; *In Rom.*, 12.2.974; *In II Cor.*, 13.3.539; *In Eph.*, 4.2.199. For examples of (b), see: *In III Sent.*, 13.2.1 ad 2, 13.2.2; *De Ver.*, 29.4; *In Io.*, 1.10.202

[28] *In Eph.*, 2.5.121; 2.6.123; 4.2.199. 4.1.199 does not refer to the Spirit directly, but it is clear that in his understanding of "one faith" Thomas would include the Spirit's activity in uniting the Church through the theological virtues.

[29] SABRA, 105.

of unity would be to obscure this element, which is after all what Paul is trying to teach us about in Thomas' *schema*.

It is in the final category, the Church as a constituted, visible institution, that the *lectura* differs most radically from Thomas' larger vision. However, there is one point-of-contact; the question of the Church's visibility, although it is also the place where we see another significant difference as well.

As Sabra notes, Thomas never speaks of an *ecclesia visibilis*, but does give a justification for the visibility of the Church through his discussion of the sacraments (and particularly the sacrament of Holy Orders) which for Thomas are "the main constituents of the visible organization of the church."[30] His Aristotelianism gives him a "fundamental orientation towards concrete reality, towards the sensible world;"[31] that is, towards what can be seen and heard. With this basic orientation comes a rationale for the visibility of certain aspects of the Church's life; Sabra cites the *Summa Contra Gentiles* in this regard:

> Since it is connatural for man to receive knowledge through his senses, and since it is very difficult to transcend sensible objects, divine provision has been made for man so that a reminder of divine things might be made for him, even in the order of sensible things. The purpose of this is that the intention of man might be better recalled to divine matters, even in the case of the man whose mind is not strong enough to contemplate divine things in themselves.[32]

As such, the visible elements in the Church "serve as a means for lifting... [humans] onto a realm beyond themselves."[33]

To think that the Ephesians commentary carries this same emphasis would be to miss the point at which it is most unique. Thomas does not approach the visible aspects of the Church regarded as such in the *lectura*. Instead, he develops a clear and compelling conception of the Church itself as being visible. The image of the flock, of the Church as the fullness of Christ,

---

[30] Ibid., 111.

[31] Ibid., 110.

[32] As cited in SABRA, 110, with English translation originally from Thomas Aquinas, *Summa Contra Gentiles*, Book 3, trans by Vernon J. Bourke (South Bend, IN: Univ. of Notre Dame Press, 1956).

[33] SABRA, 111.

of the temple/city pointed towards earth out of heaven, even the teaching of the heavenly powers through the Church[34] are all focused on the nature of the Church as something seen and experienced, as well as on the issue of the content of its visibility as an essential part of its definition and structure. And what does the Church make visible? To answer this, Paul offers Thomas the notion of a mystery revealed (see especially Eph 3:3-6) in the Church, that of the "copartnership" (3:6) of Jews and Gentiles. The glory of the Church is this fascinating and ineluctable reconciliation that makes the church a visible sign of God's love. The Church witnesses this divine love by its very existence, for it could not exist without this original unification of two into one. It also witnesses it by continuing forward in that unity through all generations.

With this in mind, it is not surprising that Thomas does not follow familiar avenues in describing the institutional Church; in fact, the usual elements involved in discussing the Church's institutional reality are all but absent in the *lectura*, with the exception of some general references to ministries,[35] and of course the strong emphasis on the Apostles that the nature of the Epistle, a Letter written by an Apostle, affords. Thomas only refers to the Christian sacraments three times,[36] the episcopacy only once and indirectly,[37] and the papacy not at all.

Of all the functions of the institutional Church, Thomas' decided emphasis is on the ministry of the word. We have already noted Sabra's observation that Thomas nowhere offers a systematic treatment of the ministry of the word (i.e. preaching and teaching).[38] He also observes that Thomas' reflections on this aspect of the Church's institutional character are contained mainly in his biblical commentaries.[39] Of all the powerful effects attributed to the word of God in these reflections, one in particular stands out in the Ephesians *lectura*: the power of preaching and teaching to sanctify. We have seen throughout the *lectura* (but especially in 1.1 and the Prologue) that Paul himself is portrayed as preaching (in a sense) towards the good of the spiritual

---

[34] *In Eph.*, 3.3.159-162.

[35] For instance, teachers (1.6.55) and pastors (4.4.212).

[36] Ibid., 4.2.200; 5.8.323; 5.10.334.

[37] Ibid., 1.4.43.

[38] SABRA, 146.

[39] Ibid., 147. To this he could add that of the biblical commentaries within which these reflections on the ministry of the word are found, the commentaries on John and on the Pauline corpus stand out. One need only consider Sabra's own citations in this regard; he cites from these commentaries exclusively, with the exception of a single reference to the Matthew commentary.

strengthening of the Ephesians in the act of writing the Epistle, corresponding
to his emphasis on the revelation of the mystery of the Church's unity. In
fact, the very theme of the Epistle, the unity of the two peoples in the genesis
of the Church, is mediated to them not through sacramental means primarily
but through its proclamation by Christ and the apostles.[40] Here is where the
major difference between the *lectura* and Thomas' larger vision can be most
clearly seen in regard to the ministry of the word; rather than being reduced to
a mere dispositive function (as it is elsewhere),[41] the preaching of the word is
presented as a real cause of grace, as actually effecting the sanctification of
those who receive it. Interestingly, it is the sacraments, not preaching and
teaching, that receive only minor attention by Thomas, and in one case even
seem to be given the task of "preaching" as well, through their role as the
insignia, the common symbols, of the *civitate Dei*.[42]

The fact of this preeminence creates a picture of the institutional
Church as a missionary, proclaiming body, a picture in which the effective
annunciation of the Gospel takes precedence over order and administration,
even over sacraments. This is not to assert that Thomas would relativize the
sacraments in any way; their importance in his larger vision cautions against
any claim that their relative absence in the commentary implies any
insignificance. But surely when the ecclesiology of the *lectura* is considered
in itself we see a model much closer, for instance, to the evangelical ideals of
the Reformation than it is to any post-Tridentine model that would remove the
sacraments from their necessary symbiosis with the ministry of the word.
Indeed, what Sabra posits about Thomas' ecclesiology in general is even more
decidedly true about the *lectura*: "There are… clear indications in Thomas'
writings that he assigns greater importance to the role of the word and a
higher status to its ministry than he does to the sacraments and their
ministry."[43]

With these elements of similarity as well as difference in mind, we
can now proceed to consider the message of the *lectura* in a more systematic
fashion, applying step **III.b** of our approach.

---

[40] *In Eph.*, 2.9.119-120.
[41] SABRA, 148.
[42] *In Eph.*, 4.2.200.
[43] SABRA, 152.

B) *The Origination of Ecclesial Unity: A Systematic Consideration of the Theological Model of the Church in the Ephesians* **Lectura** *in its Potential Contribution to Contemporary Theology*

B1) *The Origination of Ecclesial Unity in the Ephesians* lectura

It would be difficult, if not impossible, to out-systematize Thomas Aquinas, who is perhaps the greatest system-builder in Christian history. However, in the present case Thomas is not designing a comprehensive system but rather a theological model, while also laboring to discern a structure in the concepts and commands of the Epistle itself. In fact, these are two moments of the same action; because of his close attention to the text combined with his own exegetical presuppositions, Thomas' own constructive activity remains a largely unconscious one. For instance, he certainly would not place his work of biblical exegesis in the same category with the elaboration of the *Summa*. Because of this, many of the finer details of his theological model remain implicit. An attempt at summarization is necessary if these finer details are to be identified and understood. It is only once this is achieved that the contemporary theological ramifications of the *lectura* can be considered adequately.[44]

We begin this summarization in the same place where we began our analysis - the dynamic, eschatologically-oriented vision of the Church in Thomas that Congar has encapsulated in his well-accepted definition of that vision: "The Church is the economy of the return of rational creatures to God, *reditus creaturae rationalis in Deum*."[45] In the *lectura* this way of thinking about the Church is Thomas' starting-point of analysis. His enumeration of the six blessings in the first seven verses of Ephesians 1 is fixed on the eternal destiny of the Church, concerning predestination to glory, redemption, purification, and liberation from diabolical slavery.[46] Thomas is on very familiar ground here; this is his "bottom-line," so to speak, the saving reality to which every aspect of the Church's existence is ultimately connected. His engagement with these first verses reaches its peak with 1:6a, where the terms "grace" and "glory" in their interconnection serve as the two poles of ecclesial reality that are actually one: "the greatness of grace is revealed in that it

---

[44] Any work of summarization risks being repetitive. We will attempt not to belabor any points already considered in the analysis, nor unnecessarily draw attention to aspects that are not central. In particular, those elements which can best be discerned through hindsight will be given the closest consideration.

[45] CONGAR, "The Idea of the Church in St. Thomas Aquinas," 103.

[46] *In Eph.*, 1.1.5.

consists in the greatness of glory."[47]   This point and many others allow us to discern that Thomas is establishing a basic conceptual *milieu* for what is to come, which will be a more directly ecclesiological exposition.   Although he never mentions the Church *per se*, for him the Ephesian congregation re-presents the Church in microcosm, and the words of Paul represent God's plan for the Church considered universally.   It is a decidedly theocentric beginning.

But it is only the beginning, not the main part of his reading of Ephesians nor the heart of its message.   Thomas does spend four lectures on this foundational "blueprint," and then takes a turn towards a new direction which he labors to demonstrate as a function of it.   This is clear at the beginning of Lecture 5; Thomas interprets 1:13-14 as being about conversion and justification, but he no longer focuses on the mechanics of these (such as he did in 1.4.12 regarding predestination).   Rather, he focuses on the effects of conversion in constituting the Church as a visible sign of charity.   The *grex Domini* image is Thomas' vehicle for this new direction, which is focused on the glory of the Church as a community of persons filled with love for God and neighbor.[48] Already in this case we see Thomas being captured by the spirit of the Epistle, which is concerned with the revelation of a mystery of love that is both glorious and compelling.   This idea of the Church as a manifestation of love will be taken up again and again.   In fact, illustrating the Church in its sign-character will remain one of the chief ways that Thomas employs ecclesiological metaphors throughout the *lectura*.

As he begins to develop this new emphasis, Thomas also begins to lay a foundation for his interpretation of the main theme.   As he puts it: "Christ has purchased a people from the Gentiles... not because they never were his, but because they previously belonged to him and yet, by sinning, had sold themselves into a diabolical slavery which oppressed them."[49]   He does not elaborate the issue any further at this point, but we can already see the paradox in the implicit necessity of merging two flocks - the Jews, who carry an outdated brand (circumcision),[50] and the Gentiles, who now have a new shepherd.   The quote from Jn 10:16, which will be repeated three more times,

---

[47] "...*magnitudo gratiae, quae consistit etiam in magnitudine gloriae*" [Ibid., 1.1.13].

[48] Ibid., 1.5.41.

[49] "*Christus autem acquisivit populum ex Gentibus... non sic quod nunquam fuerit suus, sed quia aliquando fuerat suus, sed opprimebatur a servitute diaboli, in quam peccando se redegit*" [Ibid., 1.5.44].

[50] Ibid., 1.5.41.

is interesting in this context because of the many Pauline passages which
Thomas could have used instead regarding the plan of God to bring salvation
to those born outside Judaism. Instead of opting for another Pauline source,
Thomas goes instead to Christ's discourse in Jn 10:1-18. This offers him a
higher authority, coming as it does from the lips of Christ, but also the value
of drawing into sharp focus the question of this new unity through the words
"one fold and one shepherd." In other words, this is a mutual change for both
Jews and Gentiles; not one shepherd, two folds, but a new fold to come from
the two.

As Congar has noted, Thomas generally brings in the Christocentric
aspect of his ecclesiology only subsequent to the clarification of the
theocentric aspect,[51] and this is true of the Ephesians *lectura* as well.
Lectures 7-8 consider Christ in his ecclesiological reality; the exalted One
who is Lord of all creation at the Father's right hand,[52] shares his exaltation as
"form and exemplar" with the Church. In Thomas' reading, the fact that the
Church's members share his nature makes it possible for Christ to effect a
union with them so intimate that - and here the idea of manifestation appears
once again - they as Church can be his fullness, filling out Christ and allowing
him as soul (another designation unique to the *lectura*, albeit christological) to
perform his activities through them.[53] With this passage Thomas seamlessly
merges his more general ecclesiological vision with the new one that he is
developing - the Church's exaltation is manifested by its ability to be present
in the world as Christ's instrument, his body. Thomas moves easily back and
forth from the idea of the Church as wayfarer to the idea of the Church as a
saving presence. In summary, he demonstrates that the decidedly
anthropocentric message he reads in Ephesians is a function of his larger
vision, and not a departure from it. The Church's pilgrimage to glory is also a
mission to reflect this glory, which in grace it has already realized.

With this paradox Thomas enters into the true heart of the Epistle, the
second chapter, where its main theme is to be found. He refers to it early on
as a narrative,[54] and in a certain minimal sense it is - the telling of a story of
reconciliation between estranged peoples. He has already demonstrated the
fact that both Jews and Gentiles originally belonged to Christ. Now, he shows
how they are reunited.

---

[51] CONGAR, "The Idea of the Church," 104.

[52] *In Eph.*, 1.7.60.

[53] Ibid., 1.8.69-71.

[54] Ibid., 1.1.3.

The first step is to demonstrate the problem, their mutual alienation in sin. The first two lectures of Chapter 2 are dedicated to this. Thomas uses the first verses of Ephesians 2 (vv 1-3) to demonstrate that in terms of sin, both peoples dwell on a level field before God. In sin, they are the same[55] - this demonstrates the absurdity of any notion of disunity due to the fault of either side. All are "children of wrath," even those (i.e. the Jews) who might think of themselves as chosen and blessed.[56]   Here Thomas returns again to his fundamental vision; in Lecture 2, he emphasizes Christ as Savior in a universal and non-qualified sense as a remedy to this situation.[57] He maintains this mode of exposition through the end of Lecture 3. These lectures, like the first four of Chapter 1, expound these themes in ways identical to Thomas' other writings. In short, all are saved in the same way, for all are stricken by the same disease.

The difference becomes evident in Lecture 4. Here the benefit of Judaism and its *sacramenta* serve as a point-of-contrast between the peoples. In this Thomas emphasizes the theocentric and messianic aspects of the Old Testament; the Gentiles were without the promise of a Messiah and also without the "testaments," namely the offer of the Old and the promise of the New.[58] They were also without knowledge of God, "the greatest injury from which they suffered" (*summam damnificationem qua damnificantur*).[59] Yet none of these receives the close analysis given to the one aspect which underlines the element of interpersonal alienation - the Gentiles were outside the "*societatem sanctorum*," "the society of the saints." Thomas probes the details - there was no mixing allowed, no intermarriages (he cites Dt 7:2-3 to draw this out). Even proselytes were accepted "as strangers rather than citizens" (*non sicut cives sed sicut hospites*), and so were regarded as contemptible.[60] He seems to be offended by this fact; yet does not judge it; it is somehow a part of God's plan for unity, as we shall see.

This fact of alienation and its remedy will be the thread that runs through the analysis of 2:14-22. Jn 10:16 will be repeated again in Lecture 5, this time to reinforce the assertion (in reference to v 14) that the two peoples

---

[55] Ibid., 2.1.80.

[56] Ibid., 2.1.83.

[57] Ibid., 2.2.88.

[58] Ibid., 2.4.106.

[59] Ibid., 2.4.107.

[60] Ibid., 2.4.106.

have been joined.[61] Their anger and jealousy have been removed,[62] for its cause has been taken away - the ceremonial law, a subject to which Thomas devotes most of Lecture 5.[63] Through a remarkable transformation they become one body, and only then are reconciled to God.[64] On this basis he goes on to treat Paul's equally remarkable assertion: "that in these blessings the Gentiles are not of less eminence than the Jews themselves; they enjoy a completely equal access to Christ's blessings."[65] Here we reach the absolute center - for Thomas this is the crucial foundation for all important assertions to come. We have already considered it in detail, but must continue to reflect on the essential characteristics which make it most unique. In particular, four characteristics of the convergence of the two peoples must be noticed if it is to be fully appreciated: it is Christocentric, dialectical, anthropocentric, and communocentric.

That it is a Christocentric model of reconciliation is obvious to even the most cursory reading. Thomas sums it up at the very beginning of Lecture 5; just as whatever salvation we have is caused by God, so 'whatever peace we possess is caused by Christ and, as a result, whatever convergence" (*quidquid pacis est in nobis causatur a Christo, et per consequens quidquid appropinquationis*).[66] In this Christ effectively replaces the Holy Spirit as the principal subject in the work of unity. Throughout it is Christ who is peacemaker; he is the one who removes the barrier of ceremony and makes an open field on which the two peoples can unite. This differs from his understanding of Christ as the source of grace, although the two are closely related. Here Thomas takes seriously the claim in v 14 that the enmities are put to death "in his flesh": his promise (in Jn 10:16) foretells it,[67] his sacrifice brings it about,[68] even his preaching proclaims it.[69] In very few places in Thomas' writings is Christ's humanity treated more in itself than here, or given a greater role. But Thomas does not have to assert any extraordinary activity of God for this reconciliation, except of course in the basic sense in which it is

---

[61] Ibid., 2.5.111.

[62] Ibid., 2.5.114.

[63] Ibid., 2.5.112-116.

[64] Ibid., 2.5.118.

[65] "*quod in illis beneficiis Gentiles non sunt minoris dignitatis quam sunt ipsi Iudaei, sed aeque plenarie ad Christi beneficia sint admissi*" [Ibid., 2.6.122].

[66] Ibid., 2.5.112.

[67] Ibid., 2.5.111.

[68] Ibid., 2.5.114.

[69] Ibid., 2.5.120.

the God-man who is performing it. In many ways it is as simple as a solution to a schoolyard quarrel: "Whatever is to be united must come together in some unity, and since the law divided they could not be united in that law. But Christ took the place of the law, and faith in him, as the truth of those symbols, made them one in himself."[70] Christ has the central place as he does in Thomas' larger ecclesiological vision, but here he inhabits it in a much different way. It bears repeating that this reconciliation is different from salvation, although the two are both moments of the same action. But Thomas separates them, and does so precisely to place the reconciliation first as a necessary precondition to sanctification.

The convergence itself is presented in dialectical terms. The synthesis is the original unity of the human race, which Thomas discusses only briefly.[71] Yet it remains the fundamental rationale for reconciliation. Thomas assumes that in the original order of creation, the human race was created to be a family united by a common origin in, and also a common obedience to, God. We see here the unspoken but real effect of the biblical picture of unity contained in the first chapters of Genesis on Thomas' thought. This is a unity forfeited by sin; Thomas knows the Babel story, and although he does not mention it, it is clear that one of the effects of sin is the scattering and enmity of peoples.

The antithesis, however, is not sin, but its initial remedy. In sin the peoples are still united, as Thomas makes clear in Lecture 2 of Chapter 2. God's gift of the Law to his people creates a situation where the new and negative unity in sin is disrupted by the presence of divine truth and the concomitant obligation of ceremonial worship. It is this latter aspect, the "carnal observances" (*carnales observantias*) of the Old Testament Law, which keeps the Jews separate from the Gentiles.[72] There is no doubt that this is the will of God in Thomas' view, but not in the permanent sense; it is a necessary evil, not meant to last forever but only for "a definite time" (*tempus praefinitum*).[73] There is no doubt that Thomas views it as a problem - his many references to its negative effects and to the sad circumstances of

---

[70] "*Quae autem uniuntur, oportet uniri in aliquo uno, et quia lex dividebat, non poterant in lege uniri; Christus autem in lege succeden, et fides eius (sicut veritas figurae) eos in semetipso condidit*" {Ibid., 2.5.116].

[71] Ibid., 1.5.44.

[72] Ibid., 2.5.112.

[73] Ibid., 2.5.113.

disunity permeate this section of the *lectura*, as our analysis has shown. Thus the solution is inadequate.

The synthesis is the act of Christ in which he changes the very definitions of the Law and creates a new situation wherein its ceremonial precepts are no longer valid. The point-of-contention is removed - the Gentiles no longer stand before a heavy weight of obligation which they are unwilling to shoulder, the Jews no longer need carry that weight (nor have it as an excuse for exclusion).[74] It should be noted that all of this presupposes faith in Christ on both sides, and so grace does in this way have the priority. But a new element is added to the process of salvation. In the first place, we still see faith; Thomas calls this "the foundation of the entire spiritual edifice" (*fundamentum totius spiritualis aedificii*).[75] Here we see why - the two walls of the spiritual edifice cannot be merged unless they can perceive the removal of the barrier between them by Christ, a reality perceptible only by faith. The next step, as we have repeatedly recognized, is not sanctification properly speaking, but the convergence of the peoples in the constitution of a new reality, the Church. This interpersonal step, a necessary by-product of the recognition of Christ as Savior, is the unique element to the *lectura*. Only after this recognition can they be drawn closer to God.[76]

This is a preeminently anthropocentric refashioning of the process of salvation by Thomas. The whole movement hinges on the resolution of the crisis of disunity and hatred between the two peoples. In this sense it is in the hands of the Jewish and Gentile converts whether Church unity is instituted. Thomas recognizes this especially when he interprets Ephesians 4, which he considered as a call to respond to the marvelous revelation of the mystery of the Church's initial unity. What does this response consist of? The same kind of bridge-building, peace-cultivating activity that made up this first reunification; its maintenance requires the same cooperation as its origination. It is crucial to remember Thomas' interpretation of Paul's call to walk in the good works which God has prepared (2:10): these are given "lest anyone imagine that good works are prepared for us by God in such a way that we do not cooperate in their realization through our free will... Thus has he prepared them for us, that we might perform them for ourselves..."[77] To this we can

---

[74] Ibid., 2.5.114.

[75] Ibid., 2.3.94.

[76] Ibid., 2.5.118.

[77] "*Sed ne aliquis intelligeret bona opera sic esse nobis praeparata a Deo, ut nihil ad illa per liberum arbitrium cooperaremur... Sic nobis ea praeparavit, ut ea nos ipsi nobis per liberum arbitrium impleremus*" [Ibid., 2.3.100].

also add those places where Thomas hints (and only hints, as he is absorbed more in the work of Christ in reconciliation than he is in its enactment at this point) at the task of reunion, such as his citation of Augustine's commentary on Ps 24: "Let no one pretend he has peace with Christ... if he quarrels with another Christian,"[78] and his application of Lv 26:10, "You shall eat the oldest of the old store; and, the new coming on, you shall cast away the old," to the task set before the Jewish converts to Christ.[79] In this sense the appropriation of Christ's work of reconcilation is the same as the appropriation of faith, with the crucial difference that while faith is primarily an act of acceptance and addition, this act is one of letting go, of the subtraction of obstacles.

A final aspect of this convergence is closely connected to its anthropocentrism - it is a communocentric model, one which involves the element of fellowship among the peoples, the sorting out of differences, and the forging of a new unity in Christ. Although Thomas never gives the model this label, it is apparent throughout that he understands the reunification of the peoples to be one (once instituted by Christ), effected first through proclamation and then by a true *association*; the Gentiles are to be admitted to the *conversatione Israêl* from which they had been alienated (Eph 2:12). His use of Jn 10:16 is itself marked by this emphasis; Christ is announcing the merging of the two folds. The reference to Christ preaching peace through his Apostles to those that are at a distance in Thomas' interpretation of 2:17 has a similar emphasis. In Thomas' own word-picture, the people milling around in the field are separated by a high barrier[80] which makes mingling and association impossible. This is another element which only comes out fully in the paraenetic section, especially where Thomas contrasts the dissension of pride and vainglory to humility; the injury of anger to the mildness that "softens arguments and preserves peace" (*mitigat rixas, et pacem conservat*); the impatience that does not endure to the patience which does; and the inordinate zeal which passes judgment to the charity that tolerates.[81] All of this is connected to the unity of Jews and Gentiles, because in Thomas' understanding the unity of the Church in perpetuity is modeled after that original unity.

---

[78] Ibid., 2.5.118.
[79] Ibid., 2.5.116.
[80] Ibid., 2.5.112.
[81] Ibid., 4.1.191.

Once Thomas establishes this, he moves with the text to describe the new reality of the Church that has come from the merging of the peoples. This is Lecture 6 of Chapter 2 (on 2:19-22), where Thomas embraces the flourishing of ecclesiological metaphors in their polyphonic testimony to the miracle of the most unlikely of combinations, which is the Church itself. It is interesting that the most intimate of images, the Church as *domus*, is the one which he gives the least attention to, and the only one which he does not connect to the main theme. Perhaps this is because he wishes to emphasize that, unlike a family, the original unity of the Church was based on no ties of affection and intimacy bred by blood and long fellowship. He prefers the *civitas* when considering the Church's subjects *per se*,[82] as we have noted, because it emphasizes the reality of a willed unity, one that must be striven for and habitually protected.

But above all he offers us the temple image; with it Thomas gives us the most comprehensive picture of the Church from the perspective of unity that exists in his writings. Built upon the foundation of the revealed truth regarding Christ crucified (the doctrine of the Apostles and Prophets),[83] the Church takes as its cornerstone Christ himself, not on account of his saving work considered in itself but rather "on account of the convergence of both [Jews and Gentiles]" (*propter utriusque coniunctionem*). As Thomas explains, "As two walls are joined at the corner, so in Christ the Jewish and Pagan peoples are united."[84] No statement in the commentary demonstrates as well as this one how absolutely essential this unity is in Thomas' vision of the Church. Christ founds the Church by virtue of his reconciliatory work - not only the work of reconciling God and humanity, but also of reconciling the human members themselves.

And with this revolutionary statement, Thomas returns to the issue of the Church as manifestation: "Thus we could imagine a city, as it were, coming down from heaven... the building itself appearing to come downwards towards us below."[85] It is possible to imagine his enthusiasm as he draws this picture, and the intention in his mind for his students - he wants them to imagine a glory that is inextricably intertwined with the love necessary for unity. This may be why he quickly moves to discuss the building's construc-

---

[82] Ibid., 2.6.124.

[83] Ibid., 2.6.127.

[84] "*nam ut in angulo duo parietes uniuntur, sic in Christo populus Iudaeorum et Gentium uniti sunt*" [Ibid., 2.6.129].

[85] "*sic imaginemur civitatem quamdam descendentem de caelo... aedificium demissum ad nos videatur inferius*" [Ibid., 2.6.130].

tion, and adds the element of the moral sense of the passage regarding the
sanctified soul.[86]   To contemplate the glory of the Church, now revealed as a
unity despite all odds, is to search one's self and one's part in that unity.   In
Thomas' mind, to know the Church as Church means to believe in it as an
article of faith;[87] thus to know it means to be a part of it, and to come under its
obligation of unity.   This is the foundation for Thomas' interpretation of the
paraenetic section of Ephesians.

Thus the growth of the temple is a function of the original gathering
together of the two peoples into it; "this happens when the number of those
saved increases."[88]   But concomitant with this, it also alludes (in Thomas'
reading) to the growth of the sanctified soul when it "makes progress in good
works" (*crescit in bonis operibus*).   Through these God dwells in the temple,
sanctifying its unity by his presence.[89]   It is a habitation of God that he dwells
in through faith - here again Thomas recalls his larger vision.   But this is not
his last word - the temple is primarily an edifice of love:

> Yet this [indwelling] cannot happen without charity since "he that
> abides in charity abides in God, and God in him" (1 Jn 4:16). And
> charity is bestowed on us through the Holy Spirit: "The charity of
> God is poured forth in our hearts by the Holy Spirit who is given to
> us" (Rom 5:5). Thus he adds **in the Spirit**.[90]

Thomas will add many aspects to this basic picture: the primary
virtues necessary if unity is to be preserved;[91] the elements of common
allegiance in the Church;[92] the relationship between diversity and unity;[93] the
many imperatives of harmony (considered throughout his exegesis of Eph 4-
6), etc.   We have already analyzed these in detail, and need not belabor them.
It is fitting to end our summary here at the most crucial center of the *lectura* in

---

[86] Ibid., 2.6.131.

[87] *In Symb.*, 9.2.

[88] "*quod quidem fit quando multiplicantur qui salvi fiunt*" [Ibid., 2.6.131].

[89] Ibid., 2.6.131.

[90] "*Hoc autem non potest fieri sine charitate, quia qui manet in charitate, in Deo manet,
etc. 1 Io. IV, 16. Charitas autem datur nobis per Spiritum Sanctum. Rom. V, 5: 'Charitas Dei
diffusa est in cordibus nostris per Spiritum Sanctum qui datus est nobis.' Ideo subdit in Spiritu
Sancto*" [Ibid., 2.6.132].

[91] Ibid., 4.1.191

[92] Ibid., 4.2.198-201.

[93] Ibid., 4.4-5.

order to draw out its relevance for contemporary theology from the place at which its main message and theme is most clearly evident.

B2) *The Ephesians* lectura *in Relation to 20th Century Magisterial Teaching on the Church.*

To discuss Roman Catholic magisterial teaching on the Church in the twentieth century is to focus on a relatively rapid proliferation of documents that witness two profound shifts in the Church's self-understanding, the first occurring in the period between the World Wars and the second between World War II and the Second Vatican Council. In the first case, there is a change in emphasis from the presentation of the Church primarily as a perfect society, a characterization which had marked the Church's self-understanding since the Council of Trent,[94] to "a new and decisive orientation" on the idea of the Church as a communion characterized by the image of the Mystical Body of Christ and culminating in the encyclical of Pius XII, *Mystici Corporis Christi*.[95] The second shift is characterized by the change of primary ecclesial self-designations from Mystical Body to People of God due to the various limitations of the former, and culminating in *Lumen Gentium*, the Dogmatic Constitution on the Church offered by the fathers of Vatican II.[96] We have noted that the image of the Church as an organized, juridical and hierarchical society is far from Thomas' own emphasis in the *lectura*; thus the first paradigm shift is obviously one that, with its new emphasis on communion, moves in a similar direction as the Ephesians commentary. But in the case of the second shift, we see on both sides of the change concerns and emphases which resemble Thomas' own. Considering which side of this change the *lectura* falls on from a conceptual perspective will help demonstrate its relevance to the way the Church understands itself today.

We begin with *Mystici Corporis* [97] (hereafter referred to as *MC*), Pius XII's encyclical of 1943, which legitimized the revival of the mystical body paradigm that had been gaining acceptance and influence in Catholic

---

[94] Ernest KOENKER, *The Liturgical Renaissance in the Roman Catholic Church* (St. Louis: Concordia, 1966), 36.

[95] Jerome HAMER, *The Church is a Communion* (NY: Sheed & Ward, 1965), 13.

[96] Avery DULLES, "A Half Century of Ecclesiology," *Theological Studies* 50 (1989), 423-429.

[97] All quotations of this document are taken from *Mystici Corporis Christi* in *The Papal Encyclicals: 1939-1958*, ed Claudia Carlen (NY: McGrath Publishing, 1981), 37-62.

magisterial teaching as far back as the turn of the century.[98] Interestingly, the encyclical relies more on Thomas than on any other non-biblical source. In fact, among the thirteen citations from Thomas, three come from the Ephesians *lectura*. It is clear that Thomas' thought on the Church is a decisive influence on *MC*; there are several points of contact between the two.

In the first place, there is a strong contrast at the beginning of the encyclical between the chaos and disunity of the world (at that time, a world at war) and the unity of the Church,[99] in which the Church is given a certain sign-value for those outside its boundaries: "If they turn their gaze to the Church, if they contemplate her divinely-given unity - by which all men of every race are united to Christ in the bond of brotherhood - they will be forced to admire this fellowship in charity, and... will long to share in the same union of charity."[100] Here Pius XII emphasizes the unity of the Church as its glory in much the same way as Thomas develops the same idea through the images of the *grex Domini* and the heavenly temple in the *lectura*. In both cases, unity is attributed an attractive power which draws the contemplation of a sinful and divided world.

Both the *lectura* and *MC* also share the same starting-point regarding sin and division; in fact, the words of Pius XII could be Thomas' own, especially his use of Eph 2:3: "But after the unhappy fall of Adam, the whole human race, infected by the hereditary stain, lost their participation in the divine nature, and were all 'children of wrath.'"[101] When one compares this statement to *In Eph.*, 2.2.83, one finds the identical element of solidarity in sin as the human reality to be replaced by a new solidarity in redemption in the Church. The forging of this new solidarity through the reconciliation of the two peoples by the abolition of the ceremonial law through the sacrifice of Christ also figures into *MC*,[102] although not with the same force and singularity as it does in the *lectura* - Pius XII is more concerned with the soteriological element of Christ's sacrifice. In fact, in this way the encyclical and the *lectura* are mirror-images; the latter mentions soteriology in relation to its main theme but emphasizes convergence, while the former mentions

---

[98] Many have studied this history, though very few in detail. The best treatment I have encountered is Gregory BOQUET, "Mystical Body Theology: Nineteenth-Century Revival and Twentieth-Century Development," (M.A. Thesis, Notre Dame Seminary, 1989), 39-83.

[99] *MC*, 4-5.

[100] Ibid., 5.

[101] Ibid., 14.

[102] Ibid., 29; 32.

convergence and emphasizes soteriology. As we shall see, it is a key difference.

Finally, both carry the mystical body image as part of their message; and of course, for *MC* it is the predominant image, the very heart of the encyclical. We know that this is not the case with the *lectura*, but must recognize the similarity nonetheless. The fact that no other Thomistic commentary on the Pauline corpus is mentioned in *MC* while the Ephesians *lectura* is cited three times demonstrates the latter as a primary (if not *the* primary) source for Pius XII's teaching on the Mystical Body. All of the aspects of the Church recognized by Thomas in the references to the Church as the Body of Christ in Ephesians are present in *MC*: unity in diversity[103]; the parameters of Christ's headship,[104] including his headship of the angels[105]; and, in a section that relies directly on the Ephesians *lectura*, the Church as Christ's fullness.[106]

Yet the question remains: does *MC* reflect the influence of the *lectura* in the sense of carrying an identical or even similar emphasis? While the message of *MC* certainly does not contradict the message of the *lectura*, we must answer in the negative. In fact, the ecclesiological orientations of *MC* and the *lectura* are in an inverse relationship; each begins where the other ends. As we have noted, *MC* does begin with a picture of a divided world in which the Church stands as a sign of unity. But from there it moves in the direction of what we have termed the larger Thomistic vision of the Church - the Church considered in its relationship to God rather than in its human reality as the locus of human reconciliation. This is opposite to the *lectura*, which begins with the Church's theocentric reality and then demonstrates human unity as a part of this theocentric emphasis, making it the decisive element. In composing a list of topics in the encyclical, we see that the supernatural element considered in itself rather than in its relationship to human harmony is the decisive element in *MC*: the nature of the Church's unity as organic and hierarchically instituted rather than humanly willed and maintained[107]; the sacraments as means of sanctification rather than as common symbols of allegiance[108]; the emphasis on Christ as Savior rather

---

[103] Ibid., 15-17.
[104] Ibid., 37-39.
[105] Ibid., 46.
[106] Ibid., 48.
[107] Ibid., 16-17; 40-43; 54.
[108] Ibid., 18-21.

than as peace-giver.[109]   Nowhere is the difference more clear than in the encyclical's paraenetic section, where the faithful are exhorted to love the Church itself:

> Our pastoral office now requires that We provide an incentive for the heart to love this Mystical Body with that ardor of charity which is not confined to thoughts and words, but which issues in deeds... for nothing more glorious, nothing nobler, nothing surely more honorable can be imagined than to belong to the One, Holy, Catholic, Apostolic and Roman Church.[110]

For Thomas in the *lectura*, it is the fact of mutual love between the members which makes the Church glorious; for *MC*, it is the Church's supernatural origin considered in itself, as seen in the fact that this is highlighted here as the reason to love it.

Also, the visibility of the Church which is emphasized by *MC* is not that of being a sign of love (although as we have noted, its first mention does carry this emphasis), but rather its "external, visible, social, hierarchic and juridical reality" as a value in itself.[111]   For the *lectura*, the value of the Church's visibility is entirely connected to the reality of love which is made manifest through that visibility.   In *MC*, any dichotomy between the "Juridical Church and the Church of Charity" is denied,[112] but never is the positive element of the visible Church's sign-character developed.   Rather, the visibility of the Church is tied to its necessity for recognizing the Church's government, especially the primacy of the Pope.[113]

The approach of *MC* has been observed by a number of authors to be ecumenically underdeveloped,[114] and the *lectura* is certainly more amenable

---

[109] Ibid., 25-53.

[110] Ibid., 91.

[111] Bonaventure KLOPPENBURG, *The Ecclesiology of Vatican II* (Chicago: Franciscan Herald Press, 1974), 44, who notes this as the difference between the definition of the Church offered by St. Robert Bellarmine and the more sacramental understanding of Vatican II.

[112] *MC*, 64-66.

[113] Ibid., 40-41.

[114] DULLES, "A Half-Century of Ecclesiology," 423. Cf. J. Robert DIONNE, *The Papacy and the Church* (New York: Philosophical Library, 1987), 195-236, for his treatment of the dissatisfaction among many theologians of the period in this regard. This dissatisfaction is best expressed by Augustin BEA, *The Unity of Christians* (New York: Herder & Herder, 1963), 32-34.

to an ecclesiological perspective which gives weight to compromise and the reconciliation of differences as a primary element of the Church's mission. The difference is made clear in the definition of the Church offered by *MC*: "if we would define and describe this true Church of Jesus Christ - which is the One, Holy Catholic, Apostolic and Roman Church - we shall find nothing more noble, more sublime, or more divine than the expression 'the Mystical Body of Christ.'"[115] Here it is clear that Pius XII defines the Mystical Body according to its visibility as the Roman Catholic Church, and juridically, a fact augmented by a qualification regarding its members: "Actually, only those are to be included as members of the Church who have been baptized and profess the true faith... it follows that those who are divided in faith *or government* [emphasis mine] cannot belong to the unity of such a Body, nor can they be living the life of its one Divine Spirit."[116] Such a definition actually seems to caution against dialogue and compromise, since any change might result in an alteration of the perfect formula of membership.

This is not meant to be an indictment of *MC*, an encyclical that is so decidedly Thomistic in its approach that to reject it outright would be to reject Thomas' larger vision of the Church which is so clearly reflected in it. This could only be done to the detriment of the *lectura* itself, which is clearly grounded in that larger vision as well. We must also remember the revolutionary character of this encyclical and the communion-oriented presentation of the Church that is so intrinsic to it. In fact, Pius XII himself will correct some of its one-sidedeness in *Mediator Dei*, where he broadens his definition of the Mystical Body to include all of the baptized.[117] Yet at the same time we must note that Thomas goes further than the encyclical when he makes the theme of reconciliation and the merging of the two peoples to be synonymous with the very origination of the Church itself and the enduring paradigm of its unity. *MC* does not lend itself to such a conclusion about the Church, which in the encyclical is still founded by Christ as a perfect society[118] without the need for humanly-willed unity. In fact, the latter is a non-consideration, as the sin which produces division merely divides one from the body itself, leaving its unity intact.[119] While Thomas shares this

---

[115] *MC*, 13.

[116] Ibid., 22.

[117] DULLES, "A Half Century of Ecclesiology," 423.

[118] *MC*, 65.

[119] Ibid., 22.

perspective to a certain degree,[120] he nonetheless gives a real role to the Church's members in its unity by making the convergence of its first members concomitant with its very existence; their reconciliation is the *ecclesiogenesis*, the birth of the Church.

When we turn our attention to the new paradigm offered by *Lumen Gentium*[121] (hereafter referred to as *LG*), we encounter a work which not only has similarities to the *lectura*, but also shares its direction and most essential characteristics. The two are not identical, however. Some of the differences that exist between *MC* and the *lectura* also exist between *lectura* and *LG*. For instance, the Ephesians commentary contains no developed consideration of the sacraments, while *LG* offers a treatment of each one.[122] Also, *L G* emphasizes the juridical, hierarchical aspect of the Church,[123] while the *lectura* makes hardly any distinctions between the Church's members (with the notable exception of the Apostles and, perhaps, Thomas' pedagogical focus on the duties and moral obligations of the friars in his classroom). Finally, there is no emphasis in the *lectura* on the Blessed Virgin, while *LG* contains an entire chapter on Mary's role in the Church.[124]

These differences, however, are far outshadowed by the similarities. In the first place, there is, in both *L G* and the *lectura*, a plurality of ecclesiological images and designations that (unlike in *MC*) allows the tension and ambiguity necessary to describe the Church in its vastness and mystery with an "open-approach."[125] As in the *lectura*, this plurality of images allows a vision of the Church in *LG* that is non-univocal in ways that a work focused entirely on one image cannot escape. Within the document we find all of the images that Thomas employs himself in the *lectura*: flock, temple, house, city, bride, body and fullness.[126]

In the second place, *LG* gives the same primary emphasis as the *lectura* to the ministry of the word as an essential aspect of the Church's life.

---

[120] *In Eph.*, 4.1.187.

[121] All quotations of this document are taken from "*Lumen Gentium*: The Dogmatic Constitution on the Church" in *Vatican Council II: The Conciliar and Post Conciliar Documents*, ed. Austin Flannery, 350-426 (Boston: Daughters of St. Paul, 1988).

[122] *LG*, 2.11.

[123] Ibid., 3.18-29.

[124] Ibid., 7.52-69.

[125] H. RIKHOF, *The Concept of Church: A Methodological Inquiry into the Use of Metaphors in Ecclesiology* (London/Shepherdstown: Sheed & Ward/Patmos Press, 1981), 3.

[126] *LG*, 1.6.

The importance of the proclamation of the Gospel is demonstrated in *LG* by its consideration not only of the priestly dimension of the People of God, but also the prophetic office.[127] Thomas' stress on the teaching of the Apostles as foundational to the Church is echoed in *LG*,[128] as is his emphasis on preaching.[129]

Yet when compared to the central emphasis of the *lectura* these are only superficial resemblances. The more crucial similarities are demonstrated in those aspects of *LG* that are truly innovative and signal a new direction in the Church's self-understanding. In the first place, the central designation for the Church in *LG*, the People of God, is one that carries the same connotations as Thomas' metaphor of the city-temple, especially the city aspect of the same. Both underline the human aspect of the Church, "indicating the importance of the collective aspect of the human contribution, i.e. the role of mankind in God's plan and the importance of the response by man."[130] Both also give pride-of-place to the idea of the Church as a community of basic equality in faith. In the case of *LG*, we encounter an ecclesiology which does not exclude structure but which does not emphasize it either.[131] In the case of the *lectura*, we have seen this same emphasis in Thomas' preference for the image of *civitas* over *domus*.

The People of God designation also allows for an emphasis on unity which eludes *MC* but is the most important element of the *lectura*. The Church is not only one herself, but is "a most sure seed of unity... for the whole human race"[132]; "all men are called to belong to the new People of God,"[133] whose unity "prefigures and promotes universal peace."[134] Such an emphasis is nearly identical to the vision in the *lectura* of the Church as the herald and sign of unity in love. In fact, in *LG* as in the *lectura* the Church is visible *as* the sacrament of unity, a unity which is her glory. This aspect is set forth as the very reason for the document: "Since the Church, in Christ, is in the nature of sacrament - a sign and instrument, that is, of communion with

---

[127] Ibid., 2.12.

[128] Ibid., 3.19-20.

[129] For example, see Ibid., 2.16-17.

[130] RIKHOF, *The Concept of the Church*, 53.

[131] Ibid., 53. See A. LUNEAU and M. BOBICHON, *Église ou Troupeau? De Troupeau fidèle au peuple de l'Alliance: II. Une Volonté de Renouveau* (Paris: Les Éditions Ouvrières, 1972), 13-17, for the origins of Rikhof's remarks.

[132] *LG*, 2.9.

[133] Ibid., 2.13.

[134] Ibid., 2.14.

God and of unity among all men - she here purposes... to set forth... her own nature and universal mission."[135] This is not so different from the way Pius XII begins *MC*. However, unlike in *MC* and like the *lectura* such a conception will take a central place throughout. Indeed, the very gathering of the Church's members together in faith is for this purpose: "All those, who in faith look towards Jesus, the author of salvation and the principle of unity and peace, God has gathered together and established as the Church, that it may be for each and everyone the visible sacrament of this saving unity."[136]

In the Ephesians *lectura* the Church is portrayed as an unlikely reconciliation of the estranged and alienated elements of humanity through the putting aside of the differences of religious custom and the coming together of these elements in faith and love, and nowhere is the message of the *lectura* and *LG* more closely united than in this aspect. Such a reconciliation is in both of these works the enduring paradigm of the Church, as can be seen in *LG* especially in its ecumenical emphasis. The stress is laid not on the Church as distinct from the world and other churches, but as the place for all where all truth is welcome: "This Church, constituted and organized as a society in the present world, subsists in the Catholic Church... Nevertheless, many elements of sanctification and truth are found outside its visible confines."[137] As such the Church is not portrayed as clutching her own customs and outlook but as reaching past herself:

> ...she fosters and takes to herself, in so far as they are good, the abilities, the resources and customs of peoples... This character of universality which adorns the People of God is a gift from the Lord himself whereby the Catholic Church ceaselessly and efficaciously seeks for the return of all humanity and all its goods under Christ the Head in the unity of his Spirit.[138]

Such an understanding of the Church's mission locates its outreach to the world as one of embrace, the coming together in love of the many diverse cultures which make up the human family. In the *lectura*, Christ recognizes the unwillingness of the Gentiles to embrace the laborious observances of the ceremonial law and actually legitimizes this unwillingness through his nulli-

---

[135] Ibid., 1.1.
[136] Ibid., 2.9.
[137] Ibid., 1.8.
[138] Ibid., 2.13.

fication of that law.[139] In the same way, *LG* takes the posture of openness and affirmation rather than heavy-handedness and rigidity, recognizing the elements of truth and sanctification among those who are on the outside of the Church and even of Christianity in a willingness to embrace these elements, to make them part of her own tradition to the degree that they are compatible with revelation.[140] It is interesting that all of this is dealt with in *LG* before the hierarchical aspect; as in the *lectura* it is prior to such considerations. The openness of reconciliation is more decisively constitutive of the Church than is its governance.

Ironically, it is here that we also come across a crucial difference between the two works. *LG* never founds its openness on the work of Christ as does the *lectura*. In Thomas, the rationale for the posture of openness among the converts from the two peoples to each other is based on Christ's own concession to the Gentiles in the work of salvation. That the way to unity be open to them is given as one of the reasons why Christ undertakes his salvific work, and is therefore an essential part of why the carnal observances are abolished. In this sense the *lectura*, in its own assertions regarding the Church's unity, is even more developed than is *LG*. It is true that *L G* proclaims Christ as "the principle of unity and peace,"[141] but in the *lectura* it is actually demonstrated how and why Christ achieves this role.

Yet this in no way subtracts from the fact that of the two magisterial documents considered, *MC* and *L G*, and the paradigm-shift that the latter represents, the *lectura* falls clearly on the side of *LG*. As such it is demonstrated to be close to the heart of the post-Vatican II Church's understanding of itself and its mission. It is not surprising therefore, that in the ecclesiological reflection which has occurred in the almost thirty-five years since the close of the Council, various concerns have developed which resound with the *lectura* in ways similar to its resonances with *LG*. It is to these that we now turn.

B3) *The Ephesians* lectura *in Relation to Post-Vatican II Ecclesiological Reflection.*

Roch Kereszty has remarked that the success of a christological synthesis depends on two criteria: on the one hand, it requires the objective element of revelation, and on the other, the subjective element determined by

---

[139] *In Eph.*, 2.5.114.
[140] *LG*, 2.15-17.
[141] Ibid., 2.9.

"the needs and questions" of the contemporary audience.[142] The same could be said of any theological synthesis, including those in which the Church is the primary object of consideration. In the case of the Ephesians *lectura*, the objective element has already been provided for in Thomas' own encounter with God's Word in the Epistle. We have added a second level to this objective criteria in the comparison of the *lectura* to Catholic magisterial teaching on the Church, a source which is authoritative in the Catholic tradition as the development and application of God's revelation. What remains is to place the theological model of the *lectura* in relation to the present-day "needs and questions" of ecclesiological inquiry. We will focus on the areas of connection and similarity between the two, particularly on the ways that the *lectura* provides impetus and reinforcement to contemporary ecclesiology.

In the first place, the communocentric focus of the *lectura* is particularly relevant. Tillard has noted the notion of communion "represents the horizontal line on which the major affirmations [of Vatican II] about the Church and its mission stand out clearly." Although he posits that insufficient work has been done towards the end of reviving the vision of the Church as a communion since the Council,[143] it is also true that many excellent insights have been made into this overarching principle for ecclesiology. That such development continues is crucial not only for the Church's self-understanding but for its very existence in a world where division and alienation are the hallmarks of human life. We will rely on the insights of Walter Kasper to demonstrate how the *lectura* complements a vision of the Church that is centered on communion.

Kasper's main assertion is that, in light of the vision of the Church offered by *LG*, the Church must be "a unity in communion"; by this is meant that the primary aspects of communion which are by nature theocentric (i.e. fellowship with God, participation in God's life through word and sacrament) find their culmination in "fellowship between Christians."[144] As he puts it: "The church is essentially the one, holy, catholic and apostolic church, in which all differences of nation, culture, race, class and sex are ultimately speaking *aufgehoben*.... that is, they are abolished in the sense of being gathered up and preserved in something higher." Such a perspective involves

---

[142] Roch KERESZTY, *Jesus Christ: Fundamentals of Christology* (NY: Alba House, 1991), 277-278.

[143] TILLARD, *Church of Churches*, xi.

[144] Walter KASPER, *Theology & Church* (New York: Crossroad, 1989), 156.

the recognition that divisive factors must be relativized, as they "can play no really decisive role in this unity."[145]   However, this is not "a bloodless, abstract, uniform and ultimately totalitarian system"; the Church must be "a unity in plenitude."[146] Such a perspective has been all but lost on the present-day members of the Church. As such, "the first task of the Church's ministry and its service for unity seems... to be to restore dialogue and communication"; in this regard he uses the felicitous term *communicatio fidelium* to describe the ideal for which the Church must strive - "communion and communication among the faithful."[147]

The need for dialogue within the Church which Kasper underscores can be seen especially within the Church in the United States and Western Europe. One of the most significant projects in the Catholic Church in the past decade has been the Catholic Common Ground Project,[148] which seeks dialogue not between Catholics and other Christians primarily but among Catholics themselves. Despite the best hopes of the Council, the Church of the West has ceased to be a sign of unity and has become instead an uneasy gathering of both covertly and openly hostile tribes, mirroring the growing tribalism and fragmentation of Western society in general.[149] It is here that the *lectura* offers a powerful challenge to our understanding of the Church, which has in many ways come to be conceived as a battle-ground, the locus of a power-struggle resulting in victories and defeats but not fellowship. For Thomas, mutual compromise resulting in a unity of charity is the very way in which we cooperate with Christ in his institution and maintenance of the reality called Church. In the *lectura*, especially in the paraenetic section, the precise moment that the Church ceases to be a place of dialogue, mutual acceptance and the abolition of hostility, it ceases to be Church. Thus communion is decisive, and it must be placed before any other consideration short of faith. This is a call to self-knowledge as well as knowledge of the other. The liturgical, theological, sociocultural and ethnic divides which currently tear the Church into separate compartments even at times on legitimate terms

---

[145] Ibid., 159.

[146] Ibid., 160.

[147] Ibid., 163.

[148] This initiative by the late Joseph Cardinal Bernardin aims to sponsor conferences and papers devoted to promoting dialogue on critical issues in the Church. See the Archdiocese of Chicago's web page (http://www.archdiocese-chgo.org/ccgi.html) for the project's Statement-of-Purpose.

[149] Jimmy LONG, *generating hope: a strategy for reaching THE POSTMODERN GENERATION* (Downers Grove, IL: Intervarsity Press, 1997), 70-73.

are of secondary value to the crucial unity which is itself an article of faith. For Thomas, to profess to believe in one Church is also to pledge to bridge all divides.

This brings us to the theocentric and christocentric aspects of the *lectura*, aspects which Kasper points out as essential to true communion. In the picture given us of the Jews and the Gentiles, Thomas is careful to re-present both as being beholden to equally true but incompatible points-of-view. In the case of the Jews, no one would contest their respect for the divinely-instituted obligation of worship and sacrifice; in the case of the Gentiles, Thomas does not contest their unwillingness to observe a law not given to them. Only Christ is able to unite the two in a unity which respects both truths. In the same way, deeper unity will not come so much at the price of truth as through a deeper understanding of and appreciation for God's truth in which seemingly contradictory positions can be brought into a higher unity. The *lectura* demonstrates that only rigidity and an unwillingness to change can be obstacles to God's work in bringing forth unity in communion - a willingness to change being the essential cooperation given by the first Christians to Christ in his formation of the Church.

It is with a sense of irony that we turn to another area of ecclesiological concern in theology today, and that is the issue of ecumenism. In the face of such divisions and ideological *coteries* which have resulted in the fragmentation of the Catholic Church in the West, it is difficult to broach the issue of dialogue with other Christian churches without a sense of hopelessness. Yet the self-conception of the Church forged at Vatican II is one that is deeply ecumenical,[150] and so has led to much discussion of this aspect of the Church's mission which retains its importance in spite of the lack of preparedness which exists to undertake it. It must suffice to say that the principles of the ecumenical movement must now be turned "inward" as well as "outward." The *lectura* has much to offer in this regard as well.

Perhaps the most promising vision of an ecumenical ecclesiology since Vatican II has been the understanding of the situation of ecclesial separation offered by Louis Bouyer. Contrasting the situation of heresy and schism in the early Church with the divisions among the Christian churches today, he notes that unlike the brief crises of the patristic period in which satisfactory solutions resulted in the "automatic" extinction of misunderstandings in the span of one or two generations, the present situation has

---

[150] KLOPPENBURG, 129.

arisen under much different circumstances. This is because the initial faults were shared widely on both sides. As such, the ever-growing number of centuries which have passed without reunion have only deepened and broadened the chasms which separate Christians. Yet the hindsight offered by these many centuries also offers a fresh perspective as well:

> ...those who separated from us, and remain separated, have produced results of undeniable holiness. They are quite capable of positive missionary endeavor. In fact, they continue to develop essential elements of the Catholic tradition which today, with Catholics themselves, have only a dwarfish existence or a barely visible survival. In such cases, it is clear that comparison of the schismatic or the heretic with a detached branch of the trunk, condemned to a swift death if its connection with the stock is not quickly restored... has no or hardly any application.[151]

With this in mind, Bouyer draws a bold conclusion which is in every way identical to the standpoint of the *lectura*, although it is much more radical under the present circumstances of separation - namely, that unity is so essential that the Church could not and would not exist if it did not possess it:

> ...this unity is so constitutive that to say that the Church has ceased to be one, to be *the* one Church of Jesus Christ, would come down to saying there is no longer *any* Church in the New Testament sense and that Jesus' work in history has therefore failed... Consequently, we must believe that, despite all contestations, the Church still subsists, is still one and unique.[152]

In other words, the question of the basic legitimacy of the ecclesial reality of Protestant denominations (given they remain within the basic Christian confession of faith) cannot ever be raised without also raising the question of whether the Church exists at all - to answer the former in the negative would also be to answer the latter negatively. This picture of unity, "the greatest gift of God,"[153] resonates entirely with the *lectura*. Indeed, Thomas' larger vision of the Church itself has been demonstrated as having a

---

[151] Louis BOUYER, *The Church of God: Body of Christ and Temple of the Holy Spirit*, trans by Charles Underhill Quinn (Chicago: Franciscan Herald Press, 1982), 510-511.
[152] Ibid., 511.
[153] Ibid., 512.

strong compatibility with an ecumenically-oriented ecclesiological vision,[154] though this compatibility remains entirely accidental - nowhere does Thomas ever envision an ecumenical movement. Yet the *lectura* comes closer than this larger vision to being positively ecumenical, particularly in two crucial ways.

In the first place, the *lectura* takes as its fundamental theme the union of peoples alienated by differences of creed and cult through their initial coming together in faith. Such a movement would seem to be an excellent paradigm for all interdenominational dialogue. The fact that the most basic aspect of Christian life, i.e. faith in Christ, is emphasized by Thomas as the foundation of the whole spiritual edifice which is the Church[155] clearly underlines the basic starting-point for all ecumenical efforts among Christians, which is commonality of faith in Christ. Indeed, no other element of commonality is offered by Thomas as part of this initial reconciliation; they become temple and city and body on this sole basis, with no common history or any other points-of-contact, except perhaps the Natural Law, which is only mentioned briefly and is not offered as a decisive element.[156] If it is in faith alone that the two peoples are joined (at least initially), then surely we can conclude that the *lectura* offers a mandate to Christians of all denominations to do the same.

The second element is closely related to this one. Thomas' use of Augustine's maxim, "Let no one pretend that he has peace with Christ if he quarrels with another Christian," is such that it makes brotherly and sisterly goodwill the first step towards peace with God, in not only an individual but also in an ecclesial sense. Thomas is speaking not of individuals but of the Church as Church when he asserts that the two peoples are united "in one body of the Church" before they are reconciled to God "through faith and charity."[157] This radical emphasis on communion among the Church's members when applied to the issue of ecumenism results inescapably in the conclusion that the Church's growth in sanctity (which is in itself always first and foremost an individual reality) is hindered by the separations that exists within it. Thus the *lectura* presents a dilemma to the present situation, as it would vitiate any attempts at holiness in exclusion and non-consideration of

---

[154] SABRA, 197.
[155] *In Eph.*, 2.3.94.
[156] Ibid., 2.5.115.
[157] Ibid., 2.5.118.

the Church's unity. In this sense, the *lectura* would even dictate that all spirituality must be "ecumenical" in nature. The soul must seek union with neighbor prior to seeking union with God, and with one's separated brother or sister in Christ even more so.

A final aspect of post-conciliar ecclesiology that resonates with the *lectura* is the issue of missiology. It should be noted that the present situation of the Church in the West is no longer primarily about evangelization in distant lands. As the Catholic novelist and philosopher Walker Percy has noted, contemporary Western society and culture is itself post-Christian[158]; and as such the issue of missiology now involves the overwhelming task of a new outreach to the West itself. As Richard Cote puts it, mission must now have a "homing perspective... reimagined within our own culture first."[159] This places a new stress on the importance of a proper understanding of culture to missionary activity, as present-day missiology must necessarily involve not only reflection on faith as related to cultures foreign to one's own, but also on the way faith relates to life in the very society in which we live, which in the case of the U.S. is itself "a pluralistic, multiracial and multicultural society."[160]

In his study of the theology of mission, Richard Cote offers a new paradigm for missionary activity that is as relevant to outreach in our post-Christian culture as it is to outreach in other cultures. He isolates a crucial mistake in much missionary outreach; a surface approach to culture with the concomitant tendency to pick-and-choose those elements of a culture that seem compatible with the Gospel and the consequent rejection of those that are unacceptable from a Christian perspective. Actually, the evangelization of a culture must arise from within it. As he notes:

> The basic mistake here is due to a faulty notion of culture, namely, to think of culture as though it were a loose collection of variegated marbles (values) and that one could arbitrarily select some and discard others... If anything, culture should be viewed more like an

---

[158] Walker PERCY, "Why are You a Catholic?," in *Sign-posts in a Strange Land*, ed. with an introduction by Patrick Samway (NY: Farrar, Straus & Giroux, 1991), 309.

[159] Richard G. COTE, *Revisioning Mission: The Catholic Church and Culture in Postmodern America*, Isaac Hecker Studies in Religion and American Culture, ed. John A. Coleman (New York/Mahwah: Paulist Press, 1996), 20-21.

[160] Francis E. GEORGE, *Inculturation and Ecclesial Communion: Culture and Church in the Teaching of Pope John Paul II* (Rome: Urbaniana University Press, 1990), 26.

invisible spider's web where every strand hangs together and forms
a *whole* filigree of meaning.[161]

As such, the challenge for Christians involved in missionary work is
to be willing "to seek out and fathom the deepest level of a culture" in a
process by which the faith "proceeds from inside culture outward."[162] This
process is inculturation, for which Cote offers a helpful "root-metaphor":
marriage. His reasons for drawing this connection are worth considering
more closely.

In the first place, marriage (in the words of Eph 5:32) is a "profound
mystery," and therefore must be initially regarded not as a problem but rather
as a grace, a divine "happening, before which one stands in reverence and
wonder."[163] Yet at the same time it is also a natural reality, "immediately
derived from nature itself."[164] In the same way inculturation is both a work of
God and a natural occurrence, one which flows naturally from the nature of
human interpersonal relationships but also one in which we are enabled to
perceive God's work in the world. It is also a process, a long journey involving stages and "that must be recognized, ritualized and celebrated throughout
the process."[165] Finally, along with this is included the ever-present possibility of breakdown, of a divorce between faith and culture, involving risk and
a certain vulnerability for both. Thus it is, like marriage, revealed by the
metaphor to be dialogical, egalitarian, intimate, inclusive and affective.[166]

How does the *lectura* contribute to such a vision of mission? In the
first place, by envisioning the formation of the Church itself as a union of
disparate peoples who must learn to love each other if love for God is to be
possible for them. The convergence of the two peoples, itself the most unlikely of marriages, is understood by Thomas as a great mystery, an act of
God, while also involving the basic elements of any encounter between

---

[161] COTE, 30.

[162] Ibid, 41. Cote's point, while timely and insightful, is not balanced by any assertion of
the necessity of judging those aspects of a culture which may be entirely antithetical to the
Gospel, for instance as Paul does regarding Greco-Roman culture in 1 Cor 5:11-13 and 6:9-10.
There is certainly a difference between embracing a culture as a whole and trying to "seek out
and fathom" its deepest level which he does not recognize; in the former case, one would have
to be willing to relativize or even contradict the Gospel in the process of sharing it.

[163] Ibid., 46.

[164] Ibid., 44.

[165] Ibid., 47.

[166] Ibid., 47-49.

cultures and faith. Although Thomas downplays the process element (as he does not elaborate the interpersonal mechanics of the convergence in any sustained fashion), the other elements emphasized by Cote through his nuptial root-metaphor are all present. We have already recognized the communo-centric nature of Thomas' understanding of the origination of ecclesial unity; the intimacy suggested by his interpretation of the paraenetic section and also by the image of an integrated building and a unified city; the inclusivity which embraces even those outside the original fold (i.e. the Gentiles); and the charity dictated by this integration throughout the *lectura*. In this way the Church is depicted as an encounter between cultures and between God and these cultures, challenging the faithful of all ages to reach past the boundaries which still mark the field of the world.

Therefore, the present-day inquiry into the nature of the Church, its reunification, its mission, can all benefit greatly from the vision of unity contained in the *lectura*. It represents a crucial place of creativity, challenge and positive theological direction that spans the many centuries which separate it from the contemporary Church and reaches the heart of that Church's quest for self-understanding with the dual elements of the original message of the Epistle and the theological genius of Thomas Aquinas. As the Church enters a new millenium, the *lectura* represents a crucial part of its past that challenges its direction for the future. We do well to answer the challenge it offers in the same way that Thomas answered the challenge of faithful interpretation and allowed Ephesians to forge a new element in his ecclesiology. May all sectors of the Holy Temple be fortified and given cohesion by this unique gift.

C) *Thomas' Exegetical Practice in the Ephesians Lectura: Towards a New Collaboration in Understanding His Exegetical Corpus*

In Chapter III we noted that an in-depth encounter with Thomas' exegesis should culminate in a consideration of those observations which have the most potential value to the general and comparative analysis of Thomas' biblical commentaries (step **III.c** of our approach). The search for patterns in Thomas' exegetical practice will ultimately not only serve other analysts, but also increase the general accessibility of his exegetical corpus. As we have also noted, these are not to be taken as unquestionable and axiomatic but rather as limited observations, careful steps in a direction that will further deepen our knowledge of Thomas' exegetical practice in a way that only direct study can. In particular, the present study of the Ephesians *lectura* has uncovered certain heretofore unrecognized features of Thomas' practice that may be helpful in the future for developing a truly comprehensive model of that practice, as opposed to merely cataloguing its characteristics. Our analysis has uncovered three features that deserve attention in this regard.

In the first place, our analysis of the *lectura* has reinforced our initial hypothesis that Thomas' is best at exegeting texts that are more expository than narrative in nature, and that he is able to give the literal sense the fullest and most penetrative consideration when he encounters texts which are non-narrative. Yet it has also demonstrated that this type of text does not entirely remove the possibility of what we have heretofore described as a warning-signal that Thomas is on difficult (albeit sometimes fruitful) hermeneutical terrain, i.e. the presence of spiritual senses. In the case of 2.6.131, we observed that, in spite the clearly non-narrative nature of the text, Thomas still chooses to posit a moral sense for Eph 2:21 (i.e. the temple as the sanctified soul), taking the temple image and adding a deeper meaning to the obvious sense of the text which regards the Church. Yet this addition differs in important ways from Thomas' usual practice regarding narrative texts, and demonstrates a unique use for this exegetical technique.

We have already explored the fact that this moral sense is one that is linked to the literal sense as a reflective measure, i.e. as a way of drawing his audience into a self-examination regarding the nature of the Church as the locus of reconciliation. This is accomplished particularly by the references to charity and holiness and their increase in the soul as the necessary concomitant to the growth of the Church. The soul and the origination of ecclesial unity are placed side-by-side, and the reader (or listener) is drawn to consider his/her own role in the reality of the Church as an interpersonal communion. To use the analogy of the *lectura*, it is the temple's magnificence questioning the integrity of the individual stone and its suitability for the building - it ether augments the temple's holiness or detracts from it.

We have already included a step in our approach (**II.c.2**) that involves the consideration of the spiritual senses posited by Thomas from the angle of their use by him; that is, whether they are illuminative or non-illuminative in relation to the literal sense. In this case, the moral sense of Eph 2:21 is not so much illuminative as it is applicative. It takes a literal sense which is primarily theological and, in explaining its theological ramifications regarding the soul in grace, challenges the recipient through an invitation to comparison. The fact that Thomas endeavors to give a spiritual sense here may signal an element of his exegesis of non-narrative texts that has remained unnoticed: the use of an unexpected spiritual interpretation to provoke self-examination, the use of an expository text for exhortatory purposes. This may be the only place where he does this, an anomaly in his normally uniform approach. But it is worth recognition precisely because of the possibility that it is more than that.

The second element of note is Thomas' use of Jn 10:16. In Chapter IV we considered Thomas' announced scriptural *accessus* for Ephesians, Ps 74:4. Yet this latter verse is used more as a description of Paul's pastoral practice in writing the Epistle than it is a description of the Epistle itself; it presents Thomas' own enthusiasm for Ephesians and his high regard for the effect he believes it to have had on the Ephesian congregation. It also has no real connection to the main theme, except perhaps through an allusion to the temple image in its mention of "pillars." Yet in Jn 10:16, we have a verse that refers directly to the subject of convergence in Christ's promise of the inclusion of the Gentiles in the one fold of the Church, drawing the important *grex* metaphor into a closer connection to the main theme of the Epistle. The verse appears four times in the commentary, twice more than any other verse. And in each case Jn 10:16 is mentioned, it is always in places that are crucial to the main theme, either within the central chapter of the *lectura* or in other areas closely connected to it.

Is it possible that this verse serves as Thomas' unofficial motif, a "theme-verse" which he can rely on to tie the various emphases of Ephesians to each other? If so, it was certainly not chosen beforehand by Thomas to be so; if he had chosen it for this purpose, in all likelihood it would have served as the official *accessus* instead of Ps 74:4. It seems much more likely that it is a verse which gains importance in Thomas' mind as he employs it. In any case, the fact that its interpretive value far outweighs that of Ps 74:4 in Thomas' actual exegesis cannot be doubted. Hence, it behooves the analyst of Thomas' exegetical works to observe carefully the repetition of scriptural *auctoritates*. We have already noted the importance of biblical citation as part of the proposed approach, where frequency of citation is quantified for the purpose of discerning patterns and emphases. In hindsight, it may be even more helpful to focus this quantification on specific verses. Given the fact that he is lecturing, it would not be surprising to find that in his search for illuminating scriptural citations with which to reinforce his exegesis, he fastens his exposition to passages from other texts which not only lend support but also allow him to draw out particular emphases from the text.

This leads to a final element our consideration of the *lectura* has uncovered which, although not decisive for Thomas, played an important part in shaping his exegesis (especially his exegesis of the paraenetic section), and that is its nature as a pedagogical exercise. We have noted that in a number of places in the *lectura* Thomas' attempts to gear his presentation toward the formation of his student-friars seems to affect the way he interprets the text. This is a factor which could easily become decisive in other exegetical arenas. In fact, if Thomas had viewed Ephesians as being primarily paraenetic rather than theological, there is no doubt that the pedagogical factor would have been even more decisive in this case as well, given the fact that he was teaching moral theology in tandem with the course on Ephesians. Attention should be paid to the influence of pedagogical concerns other than content which may factor into how that content is assessed and elaborated. Thomas was not a rhetorician; one should not expect the oratorical flourishes of an Augustine or a Chrysostom. But at the very least, an awareness of the context of the commentary - the classroom - should be brought to any in-depth analysis of Thomas' work as an exegete. In hindsight, such an atmosphere may be the reason why Thomas emphasizes preaching over sacraments in the *lectura*. Circumstances where his pedagogical concerns cohere closely to the text he is analyzing may touch the model he produces.

D) *Conclusion*

The present study would be incomplete without a brief return to its early chapters, in which the groundwork was laid for the analysis of the Ephesians *lectura*. Has this analysis confirmed the fundamental principles with which it was undertaken? Is it possible to assert that the decision to take a new approach has been a fruitful one?

In our first chapter, we observed that the Pauline commentaries of Thomas rank highly among his exegetical works in scholarly estimation, and that the general approach which has characterized inquiry into Thomas' exegesis since the time of Hugh Pope does not offer any significant rationale for why this is so. In-depth analysis of the Ephesians *lectura* from the standpoint of the expository, non-narrative character of the Pauline corpus has revealed that it is not possible to consider Thomas' exegetical corpus as homogenous and yet continue to appreciate its significance. At the same time, the observations of Pope and others have provided many of the important features of the approach that has been proposed and utilized in the present study. Thus our analysis of the *lectura* has revealed that a new avenue of approach is possible without overturning decades of inquiry or minimizing the older approach with its attention to Thomas' exegetical presuppositions and techniques. Instead, our approach offers another necessary element – attention to the nature of the text under comment itself, and how it affects Thomas as commentator.

In regard to Chapter II, the present inquiry into the Ephesians *lectura* has confirmed two essential points. In the first place, it has revealed the benefit of approaching Thomas' biblical commentaries as theological models of their respective themes. Thomas' development of the notion of ecclesial unity gives rise to a certain vision of the Church in which unity is the most fundamental element. It becomes the concept by which most ecclesiological assertions, images and ethical imperatives are evaluated. Therefore, while not contradicting Thomas' larger vision, it stands on its own, and is able to be considered in its own right.

Secondly, our espousal of Pesch's assertion that Thomas allows Paul to challenge him "to adjust his entire thinking to the text and feel stimulated by it to a completely new speculative conception"[167] has proven to be justified. In the *lectura* Thomas is willing to "go the distance" with Paul, even to the point that he reverses his usual order of theological priority so as to allow human reconciliation and unity pride-of-place, even over sanctification. He also reverses this order in regard to the superiority of preaching over sacraments. In these ways Thomas places the text before his own theological vision, allowing the former to give rise to the latter.

Finally, the Genre-Identification Approach proposed in Chapter III has proven to be useful in the analysis of the *lectura*. While by no means perfect or even complete, it has proven to be a comprehensive approach that has allowed a certain precision in pinpointing important concepts and directions within the *lectura*. In this way it can be a starting-point for inquiry into any of Thomas' exegetical works, and perhaps a small step towards a common scholarly venture into Thomas' exegetical corpus through which his massive contribution can be better assessed and appreciated.

In his classic work on the life and thought of Thomas entitled *St. Thomas Aquinas: "The Dumb Ox,"* G.K. Chesterton makes the following remark about Thomas' philosophy which is also *apropos* to the Ephesians *lectura*:

> The Thomist philosophy began with the lowest roots of thought, the senses and the truisms of the reason; and a pagan sage might have scorned such things as he scorned the servile arts. But the materialism, which is merely cynicism in a Pagan can be Christian

---

[167] PESCH, "Paul as Professor of Theology," 597.

humility in a Christian. St. Thomas was willing to begin by record-
ing the facts and sensations of the material world, just as he would
have been willing to begin by washing up the plates and dishes in
the monastery. The point of his Aristotelianism was that even if
common sense about concrete things really was a sort of servile
labor, he must not be ashamed to be *servus servorum Dei*.[168]

In considering the Ephesians *lectura*, certainly the same insight into
Thomas' philosophy asserted by Chesterton can be asserted of Thomas'
ingenuity at biblical exegesis. He was not afraid to find what he would find;
confident assurance, brilliance of insight and a close attention to even the
most minute details of the revealed Word before him allowed him to consider
the Epistle not first for what it could be used to illustrate but rather for what it
illustrated itself - a vision of the Holy Temple that is the Church. Even
without the techniques of modern scriptural inquiry, Thomas' approach has
paid great dividends.

---

[168] G.K. CHESTERTON, *St. Thomas Aquinas: "The Dumb Ox"* (New York: Image Books,
1956), 117.

BIBLIOGRAPHY

Works by Thomas Aquinas
Latin/Polyglot Editions

AQUINAS, St. Thomas. *Compendium Theologiae*. In Vol. I, *Opuscula theologica*, ed. by R. Verardo, 13-138. Turin: Marietti, 1954.

_____. "*De commendatione et partitione sacrae scripturae.*" In Vol. I, *Opuscula theologica*, ed. by R. Verardi, 435-443. Turin: Marietti, 1954.

_____. *De Potentia*. In Vol. XXII, *Quaestiones Disputatae*, ed. by P. Bazzi, et al., 7-276. Turin: Marietti, 1965.

_____. *De Veritate*. Vol. I, *Quaestiones disputatae*, ed. by R. Spiazzi. Turin: Marietti, 1964.

_____. *Expositio super Iob ad litteram*. Vol. XXVI, Leonine Edition. Rome: 1965.

_____. *Expositio super librum Boethii De trinitate*. In Vol. II, *Opuscula theologica*, ed. by R. Spiazzi and M. Calcaterra, 313-389. Turin: Marietti, 1954.

_____. *Expositio super Symbolum*. In *Opuscula theologica*, ed. by R. Spiazzi and M. Calcaterra, 193-241. Turin: Marietti, 1954.

_____. *Expositio super Isaiam ad litteram*. Vol. XXVIII, Leonine Edition. Rome: 1974.

_____. "Aquinas' Commentary on the Psalms: In Latin with an English Translation." Trans. online by Hugh McDonald (http://www.vaxxine.com/hyoomik/aquinas/ps000000.htm).

_____. *Quaestiones quodlibetales*. Edited by R. Spiazzi. Turin: Marietti, 1956.

_____. *Sententia super Peri Hermenias*. Edited by R. Spiazzi. Turin: Marietti, 1955.

_____. *Sententia super Physicam*. Edited by M. Maggiòlo. Turin: Marietti, 1965.

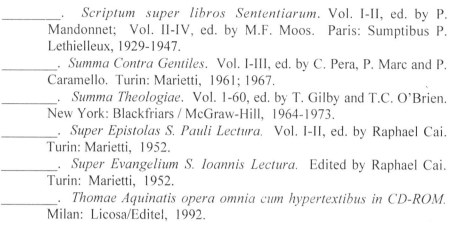

_____. *Scriptum super libros Sententiarum.* Vol. I-II, ed. by P. Mandonnet; Vol. II-IV, ed. by M.F. Moos. Paris: Sumptibus P. Lethielleux, 1929-1947.

_____. *Summa Contra Gentiles.* Vol. I-III, ed. by C. Pera, P. Marc and P. Caramello. Turin: Marietti, 1961; 1967.

_____. *Summa Theologiae.* Vol. 1-60, ed. by T. Gilby and T.C. O'Brien. New York: Blackfriars / McGraw-Hill, 1964-1973.

_____. *Super Epistolas S. Pauli Lectura.* Vol. I-II, ed. by Raphael Cai. Turin: Marietti, 1952.

_____. *Super Evangelium S. Ioannis Lectura.* Edited by Raphael Cai. Turin: Marietti, 1952.

_____. *Thomae Aquinatis opera omnia cum hypertextibus in CD-ROM.* Milan: Licosa/Editel, 1992.

Modern Translations of Thomas' Works

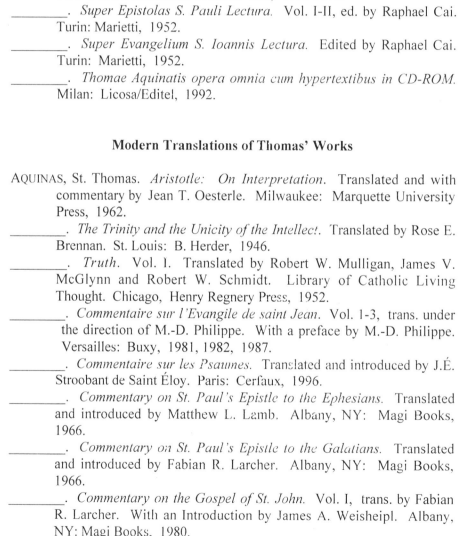

AQUINAS, St. Thomas. *Aristotle: On Interpretation.* Translated and with commentary by Jean T. Oesterle. Milwaukee: Marquette University Press, 1962.

_____. *The Trinity and the Unicity of the Intellect.* Translated by Rose E. Brennan. St. Louis: B. Herder, 1946.

_____. *Truth.* Vol. 1. Translated by Robert W. Mulligan, James V. McGlynn and Robert W. Schmidt. Library of Catholic Living Thought. Chicago, Henry Regnery Press, 1952.

_____. *Commentaire sur l'Evangile de saint Jean.* Vol. 1-3, trans. under the direction of M.-D. Philippe. With a preface by M.-D. Philippe. Versailles: Buxy, 1981, 1982, 1987.

_____. *Commentaire sur les Psaumes.* Translated and introduced by J.É. Stroobant de Saint Éloy. Paris: Cerfaux, 1996.

_____. *Commentary on St. Paul's Epistle to the Ephesians.* Translated and introduced by Matthew L. Lamb. Albany, NY: Magi Books, 1966.

_____. *Commentary on St. Paul's Epistle to the Galatians.* Translated and introduced by Fabian R. Larcher. Albany, NY: Magi Books, 1966.

_____. *Commentary on the Gospel of St. John.* Vol. I, trans. by Fabian R. Larcher. With an Introduction by James A. Weisheipl. Albany, NY: Magi Books, 1980.

_____. "The Inaugural Sermons." Translated by Ralph McInerny. In Thomas Aquinas, *Selected Writings*, trans. and ed. by Ralph McInerny, 5-17. Harmondsworth: Penguin, 1998.

_____. *The Literal Exposition on Job: A Scriptural Commentary Concerning Providence.* Translated by Anthony Damico. Interpretive Essay and Notes by Martin D. Yaffe. Classics in Religious Studies, ed.Carl A. Raschke. Atlanta: Scholars Press, 1989.

_____. *On the Power of God.* Translated by Laurence Shapcote. Vol. I-III. London: Burns, Oates and Washbourne, 1932-1934; reprint in 1 vol., Westminster, MD: Newman, 1952.

_____. *On the Truth of the Catholic Faith (Summa Contra Gentiles).* Vol. I-V. New York: Doubleday, 1955-1957; reprinted as *Summa Contra Gentiles*, Notre Dame, IN: Univ. of Notre Dame Press, 1975.

_____. *Summa Contra Gentiles.* Translated by Vernon J. Bourke. South Bend, IN: Univ. of Notre Dame Press, 1956.

Works by Other Authors

ARISTOTLE. *Nicomachean Ethics.* Translation with commentaries and glossary by Hippocrates G. Apostle. Grinnell: Peripatetic Press, 1984.

_____. *Politics.* Translation with commentaries and glossary by Hippocrates G. Apostle. Grinnell: Peripatetic Press, 1986.

AUGUSTINE. *The City of God.* Translated by Henry Bettenson with an introduction by John O'Meara. New York: Penguin Books, 1984.

_____. *De Doctrina Christiana.* Ed. And Trans. by R.P.H. Green. Oxford/New York: Clarendon Press, 1995.

_____. *De Natura Boni.* Trans. with an introduction and commentary by A. Anthony Moon. Washington D.C.: Catholic University of America Press, 1955.

BAGLOW, Christopher T. "The Doctrine of the Eucharist in St. Thomas Aquinas' *Commentary on the Gospel of St. John.*" M.A. Thesis, University of Dallas, 1996.

BARTH, Markus. *Ephesians.* Vol. I-II. Anchor Bible Series 34-34A. Garden City, NY: Doubleday, 1974.

BEA, Augustin. *The Unity of Christians*. New York: Herder & Herder, 1963.

BENOIT, P. "Corps, tête et plérôme dans les Épîtres de la captivité." *Revue biblique* 63 (1956) : 5-54.

_____. *Inspiration and the Bible*. Translated by Jerome Murphy-O'Connor and M. Keverne. London; Melbourne; New York: Sheed and Ward, 1965.

BEST, E. *A Critical and Exegetical Commentary on Ephesians*. Edinburgh: T&T Clark, 1998.

BILLY, Denis J. "Grace and Natural Law in the *Super epistola ad Romanos lectura*: A Study in Thomas' Commentary on Romans 2:14-16." *Studia Moralia* 26 (1988): 15-37.

BLACK, C. Clifton. "St. Thomas' Commentary on the Johannine Prologue: Some Reflections on Its Character and Implications." *Catholic Biblical Quarterly* 48 (1986) : 681-698.

BLANCHE, F.-A. "Le sens littéral des Écritures d'après saint Thomas d'Aquin." *Revue Thomiste* 14 (1906) : 192-212.

BLANCO, A. "Word and Truth in Divine Revelation. A study of the Commentary of St.Thomas Aquinas on John 14,6." In *La doctrine de la révélation divine de saint Thomas d'Aquin. Actes du Symposium sur la pensée de saint Thomas d'Aquin tenu à Rolduc, les 4 et 5 Novembre 1989,* ed. Leo Elders, 27-48. Cittá del Vaticano: Libreria Editrice Vaticana, 1990.

BOADT, Lawrence. "St. Thomas Aquinas and the Biblical Wisdom Tradition." *The Thomist* 49 (1985) : 575-611.

BOQUET, Gregory. "Mystical Body Theology: Nineteenth-Century Revival and Twentieth-Century Development." M.A. Thesis, Notre Dame Seminary, 1989.

BOUILLARD, Henri. *Conversion et grâce chez saint Thomas d'Aquin.* Paris: Aubier, 1944.

BOURKE, Vernon . *Thomistic Bibliography: 1920-1940.* St. Louis: Modern Schoolman, 1945.

BOUYER, Louis. *The Church of God: Body of Christ and Temple of the Holy Spirit*. Translated by Charles Underhill Quinn. Chicago: Franciscan Herald Press, 1982.

BOYLE, John F. "St. Thomas Aquinas and Sacred Scripture." *Pro Ecclesia* 4 (1996) : 92-104.

BOYLE, L. "Notes on the Education of the *Fratres communes* in the Dominican Order in the Thirteenth Century." In *Xenia medii aevi historiam illustrantia oblata Th. Käppeli O.P.*, ed. R. Creytens and P. Künzle, 249-267. Vol. 1, Storia e Letteratura, Raccolta di Studie Testi 141. Rome: Edizioni di storia e letteratura, 1978.

_____. *The Setting of the Summa Theologiae of Saint Thomas.* Etienne Gilson Series 5. Toronto: Pontifical Institute of Medieval Studies, 1982.

BUSA, Roberto. *Index Thomisticus S. Thomae Aquinatis Operum Omnium Indices et Concordantiae*, 50 vols. Stuttgart-Bad Cannstatt: Fromman-Holzboog, 1974-1980.

CAHILL, Michael. "Not a Cornerstone! Translating Ps 118, 22 in the Jewish and Christian Scriptures." *Revue Biblique* 106 (1999) : 345-357.

CALLAN, Charles J. "The Bible in the Summa Theologica of St. Thomas Aquinas." *Catholic Biblical Quarterly* 9 (1947) : 33-47.

CARAGOUNIS, C. *The Ephesian Mysterion: Meaning and Content.* Lund: CWK Gleerup, 1977.

CASSIODORUS. *Explanation of the Psalms.* Trans. and annotated by P.G. Walsh. New York: Paulist Press, 1991.

CESSARIO, Romanus. *The Godly Image: Christ and Salvation in Catholic Thought from Anselm to Aquinas.* Studies in Historical Theology 6. Petersham, MA: St. Bede's, 1990.

CHADWICK, H. "Die Absicht des Epheserbriefes." *Zeitschrift für die neutestamentliche Wissenschaft und die Kunde der älteren Kirche* 51 (1960) : 145-154.

CHENU, M.D. *La Théologie comme science au XIIIe siècle.* 3rd ed., vol. 33, Bibliothèque Thomiste (Paris: J. Vrin, 1957).

_____. "La loi ancienne selon S. Thomas." *Revue Thomiste* 61 (1961) : 485-497.

_____. *Toward Understanding St. Thomas.* Translated by A.-M. Landry and D. Hughes.Chicago: Henry Regnery Press, 1964.

CHESTERTON, G.K. *St. Thomas Aquinas: The Dumb Ox.* New York: Image Books, 1956.

CHILDS, Brevard S. *The New Testament as Canon: An Introduction.* Philadelphia: Fortress, 1985.

_____. *Biblical Theology of the Old and New Testaments: Theological Reflection on the Christian Bible.* Minneapolis: Fortress, 1992.

COLISH, Marcia L. *Peter Lombard.* Vol. I. Leiden, New York, Köln : E.J. Brill, 1994.

CONGAR, Yves. "Le sens de l'économie salutaire dans la théologie de S. Thomas." In *Festgabe Joseph Lortz*. Vol. I, 73-122. Baden-Baden: B. Grimm, 1957.

_____. "The Idea of the Church in St. Thomas Aquinas." In *The Mystery of the Church*. Translated by A.V. Littledale, 97-117. Baltimore: Helicon Press, 1960.

_____. "L'apostolicité de l'Eglise chez S. Thomas d'Aquin." *Revue des sciences philosophiques et théologiques* 44 (1960) : 209-224.

_____. "'Ecclesia' et 'populus (fideles)' dans l'ecclésiologie de S. Thomas." In vol. I, *St. Thomas Aquinas, 1274-1974, Commemorative Studies*, ed. A. Maurer, et al, 159-173. Toronto: Pontifical Institute of Medieval Studies, 1974.

_____. "Vision de l'Eglise chez S. Thomas d'Aquin." *Revue des sciences philosophiques et théologiques* 62 (1978) : 523-541.

_____. "'In dulcedine societatis quaerere veritatem.' Notes sur le travail en équipe chez S. Albert et chez les Prêcheurs au XIIIᵉ siècle." In *Albertus Magnus, Doctor Universalis, 1280/1980*, ed. G. Meyer, A. Zimmerman and P.-B. Lüttringhaus, 47-57. Mayence: Matthias Grünewald Verlag, 1980.

_____. *Thomas Aquinas: sa vision de la théologie et de l'Eglise*. London: Variorum Reprints, 1984.

CORBIN, Michel. *Le chemin de la théologie chez Thomas d'Aquin*. Vol. 16, Bibliothèque des Archives de Philosophie, Nouv. Ser. Paris: Beauchesne, 1974.

_____. "Le Pain de Vie. La Lecture de Jn 6 par S. Thomas d'Aquin." *Recherches de Science Religieuse* 65 (1977) : 107-138.

COTE, Richard G. *Revisioning Mission: The Catholic Church and Culture in Postmodern America*. Isaac Hecker Studies in Religion and American Culture, ed. John A. Coleman. New York/Mahwah: Paulist Press, 1996.

CUÉLLAR, Miguel Ponce. *La Naturaleza de la Iglesia según Santo Tomas. Estudio del Tema en el Comentario al "Corpus Paulinum."* Pamplona: Ediciones Universidad de Navarra, 1979.

DALY, Mary S. "The Notion of Justification in the Commentary of St. Thomas Aquinas on the Epistle to the Romans." Ph. D. diss., Marquette University, 1971.

DAVIES, Brian. *The Thought of Thomas Aquinas*. Oxford: Clarendon Press, 1992.

DEFERRARI, Roy J. *A Latin-English Dictionary of St. Thomas Aquinas.* Boston: Daughters of St. Paul, 1960.

DENIFLE, Heinrich. "Quel livre servait de base à l'enseignement des Maîtres en Théologie dans l'Université de Paris?" *Revue Thomiste* 2 (1894) : 129-161.

DIONNE, J. Robert. *The Papacy and the Church.* New York: Philosophical Library, 1967.

DOMÍNGUEZ, O. "La fé, fundamento del Cuerpo Místico en la doctrina del Angélico." *Ciencia Tomista* 76 (1949) : 550-586.

DONDAINE, A. Preface to *Expositio super Job. Tom. XXVI, Opera Omnia,* by Thomas Aquinas, 420-430.

_____. "Les *Opuscula fratris Thomae* chez Ptolémée de Lucques" *Archivum fratrum praedicatorum* 31 (1961), 142-203.

DUBOIS, M. "Mystical and Realistic Elements in the Exegesis and Hermeneutics of St.Thomas Aquinas." In *Creative Biblical Exegesis: Christian and Jewish Hermeneutics through the Centuries,* ed. Benjamin Uffenheimer and H.G. Reventlow, 39-54. Vol. 59, Journal for the Study of the Old Testament Supplement Series. Sheffield, England: JSOT Press, 1988.

DULLES, Avery. "The Church according to St. Thomas Aquinas. In *A Church to Believe In*, 149-169. NY: Crossroad, 1982.

_____. "A Half Century of Ecclesiology." *Theological Studies* 50 (1989) : 419-442.

ELDERS, Leo J. "Aquinas on Holy Scripture as the Medium of Divine Revelation." In *La doctrine de la révélation divine de saint Thomas d'Aquin. Actes du Symposium sur la pensée de saint Thomas d'Aquin tenu à Rolduc, les 4 et 5 Novembre 1989,* ed. Leo Elders, 132-152. Cittá del Vaticano: Libreria Editrice Vaticana, 1990.

_____. "Thomas Aquinas and the Fathers of the Church." In *The Reception of the Church Fathers in the West,* ed. Irena Backus, vol. I, 337-366. Leiden; N.Y.: E.J. Brill, 1997.

ESCHMANN, I.T. "A Catalogue of St. Thomas' Works." In Etienne Gilson, *The Christian Philosophy of St. Thomas Aquinas,* trans. L.K. Shook, 381-430. London: Victor Gollancz, 1957.

FERNANDEZ, A. "Système exégétiques de saint Thomas." *España y America* 10 (1909).

FROEHLICH, Karl. "Aquinas, Thomas." In *Historical Handbook of Major Biblical Interpreters,* ed. Donald K. McKim, 85-91. Downers Grove, IL/Leicester, England: InterVarsity Press, 1998.

GADAMER, Hans-Georg. *Truth and Method.* New York: Seabury, 1975.

GARDEIL, A. "Les procédés exégétiques de S. Thomas." *Revue Thomiste* 11 (1903) : 428-457.

GARLAND, Peter B. *The Definition of Sacrament according to Saint Thomas.* Ottawa: Univ. of Ottawa Press, 1959.

GEORGE, Francis E. *Inculturation and Ecclesial Communion: Culture and Church in the Teaching of Pope John Paul II.* Rome: Urbaniana University Press, 1990.

GILBY, T. Appendix to *Summa Theologica.* Vol. 1, ed. by T. Gilby. New York: Blackfriars / McGraw -Hill, 1964-1973.

GLORIEUX, P. "Essai sur les commentaires scripturaires de saint Thomas et leur chronologie." *Recherches de théologie ancienne et médiévale* 17 (1950) : 237-266.

GRABMANN, M. *Die lehre des heiligen Thomas von Aquin von der Kirche als Gotteswerk. Ihre Stellung im thomistischen System und in der Geschichte der mitteralterlichen Theologie.* Regensburg : C.J. Manz, 1903.

GREGORY THE GREAT. *The Homilies of St. Gregory the Great on the Book of the Prophet Ezekiel.* Trans by Theodosia Gray, intro. by Bishop Chrysostomos, ed. by Juliana Cownie. Etna, CA: Center for Traditionalist Orthodox Studies, 1990.

HAGGARD, Frank Powell. "An Interpretation of Thomas Aquinas as a Biblical Theologian with Special Reference to his Systematizing of the Economy of Salvation." Ph.D. Thesis, Drew University, 1972.

HALLIGAN, Nicholas. "The Teaching of St. Thomas Aquinas in regard to the Apostles." *American Ecclesiastical Review* 144 (1961) : 32-47.

HAMER, Jerome. *The Church is a Communion.* NY: Sheed & Ward, 1965.

HANSON, S. *The Unity of the Church in the New Testament, Colossians and Ephesians.* Acta seminarii neotestamentici upsaliensis. Uppsala: Almquist, 1946.

HARTMANN, Louis N. "Jerome as an Exegete." In *A Monument to St. Jerome,* ed. Francis Xavier Murphy. New York: Sheed & Ward, 1952.

HOOD, J. Y.B. *Aquinas and the Jews.* The Middle Ages Series. Philadelphia: Univ. of Philadelphia Press, 1995.

HOWARD, G. "The Head/Body Metaphors of Ephesians." *New Testament Studies* 20 (1974) : 350-356.

JOHNSON, John F. "Biblical Authority and Scholastic Theology." In *Inerrancy and the Church,* ed. John D. Hannah, 67-97. Chicago:

Moody Press, 1984.

JORDAN, M.D. "Thomas Aquinas." In *Dictionary of Biblical Interpretation: K-Z*, ed. John H. Hayes, 573-575. Nashville: Abingdon Press, 1999.

KÄSEMANN, E. "Ephesians and Acts." In *Studies in Luke-Acts,* ed. L.E Keck and J.E. Martyn, 288-297. London: S.P.C.K., 1968.

KASPER, Walter. *Theology and Church.* New York: Crossroad, 1989.

KEALY, Sean P. *Matthew's Gospel and the History of Biblical Interpretation.* Mellen Biblical Press Series 55A. Lewiston: Edwin Mellen Press, 1997.

KECK, L.E. and V.P. FURNISH, *The Pauline Letters.* Atlanta: John Knox, 1975.

KENNEDY, Robert G. "Thomas Aquinas and the Literal Sense of Sacred Scripture." Ph. D. diss., University of Notre Dame, 1985.

KERESZTY, Roch. *Jesus Christ: Fundamentals of Christology.* NY: Alba House, 1991.

KLEIN, William W. *The Book of Ephesians : An Annotated Bibliography.* Vol. 8, Books of the Bible Series. NY, London : Garland, 1998.

KLOPPENBURG, Bonaventure. *The Ecclesiology of Vatican II.* Chicago: Franciscan Herald Press, 1974.

KOENKER, Ernest. *The Liturgical Renaissance in the Roman Catholic Church.* St. Louis: Concordia, 1966.

LABEAGA, José A. Izquierdo. "San Tommaso nell'ambiente informatico." *Angelicum* 75 (1998) : 459-475.

LAMB, Matthew. Foreword to *Commentary on St. Paul's Epistle to the Ephesians* by St. Thomas Aquinas. Albany, NY: Magi Books, 1966.

LIGHTFOOT, J.B. *Colossians and Ephesians.* London: Macmillan, 1912.

LINCOLN, A.T. *Ephesians.* Word Bible Commentary. Dallas : Word, 1990.

LOEWE, Raphael. "The Medieval History of the Latin Vulgate." In *The Cambridge History of the Bible.* Volume 2, *The West from the Fathers to the Reformation*, ed. G.W.H. Lampe, 102-154. Cambridge: Cambridge University Press, 1969.

LONERGAN, Bernard. *Verbum: Word and Idea in Aquinas.* Edited by David B. Burrell. Notre Dame: University of Notre Dame Press, 1967.

LONG, Jimmy. *generating hope: a strategy for reaching THE POST-MODERN GENERATION.* Downers Grove, IL: Intervarsity Press, 1997.

LUBAC, Henri de. *Exégèse Médiévale: Les Quatre Sens de l'Écriture.* Vol. I-IV. Paris: Aubier, 1964.

LUNEAU, A. and M. BOBICHON. *Eglise ou Troupeau? De Troupeau fidèle au peuple de l'Alliance: II. Une Volonté de Renouveau.* Paris: Les Éditions Ouvrières, 1972.

MAHONEY, J. "The Church and the Holy Spirit in Aquinas." *Heythrop Journal* 15 (1974) : 18-36.

MALHOIT, M.D. "La pensée de saint Thomas sur le sens spirituel." *Revue Thomiste* 59 (1959) : 613-663.

MANDONNET, P. "Chronologie des écrits scripturaires de s. Thomas d'Aquin." *Revue Thomiste* 33 (1928) : 222-245.

MARGERIE, Bertrand de. "Mort sacrificielle du Christ et peine de mort chez Thomas d'Aquin, commentateur de Saint Paul." *Revue Thomiste* 83 (1983) : 394-417.

MARTÍNEZ, F. "La Eucaristía y la Iglesia en Santo Tomás de Aquino." *Studium* 9 (1969) : 377-404.

MCCARTHY, Brian. "El modo del conocimiento profético y escriturístico según Sto. Tomás de Aquino." *Scripta Theologica* 9 (1977) : 425-484.

MCGLASHAN, A.R. "Ephesians 1:23." *Expository Times* 76 (1964-1965) : 132-133.

MCGUCKIN, Terence. "St. Thomas Aquinas and Theological Exegesis of Sacred Scripture." *New Blackfriars* 74 (1993) : 197-213.

MÉNARD, Etienne. *La Tradition: révélation, écriture, Église selon s. Thomas d'Aquin.* Bruges: Desclée de Brouwer, 1964.

MERKLINGER, H.A. "Pleroma and Christianity." *Concordia Theological Monthly* 36 (1965) : 739-743.

MOULE, C.F.D. "'Fullness' and 'Fill' in the New Testament." *Scottish Journal of Theology* 4 (1951) : 79-86.

MURPHY, Roland. "Patristic and Medieval Exegesis - Help or Hindrance?" *Catholic Biblical Quarterly* 43 (1981) : 505-510.

O'CONNOR, Donal J. "The Concept of Mystery in Aquinas' Exegesis, Pt. I-II." *Irish Theological Quarterly* 36 (1969) : 183-210, 261-282.

O'HARA, Mary L. "Truth in Spirit and in Letter: Gregory the Great, Thomas Aquinas and Maimonides on the Book of Job." In *From Cloister to Classroom : Monastic and Scholastic Approaches to Truth,* ed. E. Rozanne Elder, 47-79. Vol. III, The Spirituality of Western Christendom. Kalamazoo, MI: Cistercian, 1986.

O'NEILL, Colman. "St. Thomas on Membership of the Church." *Thomist* 27 (1963) : 88-140.

ORIGEN. *On First Principles: Being Koetschau's text of the De Principiis.*

Trans. with an introduction and notes by G.W. Butterworth. New York: Harper & Row, 1966.

PATZIA, A.G. *Colossians, Philemon, Ephesians.* New York: Harper & Row, 1984.

PERCY, Walker. "Why are You a Catholic?" In *Signposts in a Strange Land*, ed. with an introduction by Patrick Samway, 304-315. New York: Farrar, Straus & Giroux, 1991.

PERSSON, Erik. *Sacra Doctrina: Reason and Revelation in Aquinas.* Translated by Ross Mackenzie. Philadelphia, Fortress Press, 1970.

PESCH, Otto Herman. "Paul as Professor of Theology: The Image of the Apostle in St. Thomas' Theology." *Thomist* 38 (1974) : 584-605.

PIUS XII. *Mystici Corporis Christi.* In *The Papal Encyclicals: 1939-1958,* ed. Claudia Carlen, 37-62. New York: McGrath Publishing, 1981.

_____. "An Address to the Faculty and Students of the Roman Athenaeum Angelicum," (January 14, 1958). *The Pope Speaks* 5 (1958) : 91-95.

PLASSMAN, J. and J. VANN, ed. *Lives of Saints: With Excerpts from Their Writings.* New York: J.J. Crawley, 1954.

PLOEG, J. van der. "The Place of Holy Scripture in the Theology of St. Thomas." *The Thomist* 10 (1947) : 398-422.

POKORNY, P. *Der Epheserbrief und die Gnosis.* Berlin: Evangelische Verlagsanstalt, 1965.

PONTIFICAL BIBLICAL COMMISSION, "The Interpretation of the Bible in the Church." April 23, 1993.

POPE, Hugh. *St. Thomas as Interpreter of Holy Scripture.* Oxford : Basil Blackwell, 1924.

POTTERIE, I. de la. "Le Christ, Plérôme de l'Église (Ep 1,22-23)." *Biblica* 58 (1977) : 500-524.

REVUELTA, Jose M. "Los Comentarios Bíblicos de Santo Tómas." *Scripta Theologica* 3 (1971) : 539-579.

RICOEUR, Paul. *Interpretation Theory: Discourse and the Surplus of Meaning.* Fort Worth, TX: Texas Christian University Press, 1976.

RIKHOF, Herwi. *The Concept of Church: A Methodological Inquiry into the Use of Metaphors in Ecclesiology.* London/Shepherdstown: Sheed & Ward/Patmos Press, 1981.

RUBEIS, B. de. "Dissertatio II: De Vetustis opera sancti Thomae Indicibus: deque genuinis commentariis eius in Iobum, in Psalmos, in Cantica Canticorum: suppositisque in Genesim, in totum Pentateuchum, in

Ecclesiasticem," in Thomae Aquinatis, *Opera Omnia*, lxxvi-lxxxviii. Vol. I, Leonine edition. Rome: 1932.

RYKEN, Leland. *Words of Delight:A Literary Introduction to the Bible.* 2d ed. Grand Rapids: Baker Book House, 1992.

SABRA, George. *Thomas Aquinas' Vision of the Church: Fundamentals of an Ecumenical Ecclesiology.* Mainz : Matthias Grünewald, 1987.

SAUL, D. "Thomas von Aquino als Ausleger des A.T." *Zeitschrift für wissenschaftliche Theologie* (1895) : 603-625.

SAWATSKY, S. "Pleroma in Ephesians 1:23." *Taiwan Journal of Theology* 11 (1989) : 107-115.

SCALISE, Charles J. "The '*Sensus Litteralis*' : A Hermeneutical Key to Biblical Exegesis." *Scottish Journal of Theology* 42 (1989) : 45-65.

SELDEN, J. "Aquinas, Luther, Melancthon and Biblical Apologetics." *Grace Theological Journal* 5 (1984) : 181-195.

SHEETS, John. "The Scriptural Dimension of St. Thomas." *American Ecclesiastical Review* 144 (1961) : 154-173.

SMALLEY, Beryl. *The Study of the Bible in the Middle Ages,* 2d rev. ed. Oxford: Basil Blackwell, 1952.

_____. *The Gospels in the Schools: c.1100-c.1280.* Vol. 41, Hambledon History Series. London: The Hambledon Press, 1985.

SPICQ, Ceslas. "*Saint Thomas d'Aquin Exégète.*" In vol. 15, *Dictionnaire de Théologie Catholique*, ed. A. Vacant, E. Mangenot and E. Amann, col. 694-738. Paris: Libraire Letouzey et Ané, 1946.

STUMP, Eleonore. "(Aquinas') Biblical Commentary and Philosophy." In *The Cambridge Companion to Aquinas*, ed. Norman Kretzmann and Eleonore Stump. Cambridge: Cambridge University Press, 1993.

SWIERZAWSKI, Waclaw. "God and the Mystery of his Wisdom in the Pauline Commentaries of St. Thomas Aquinas." *Divus Thomas* 74 (1971) : 466-500.

_____. "Faith and Worship in the Pauline Commentaries of St. Thomas Aquinas." *Divus Thomas* 75 (1972) : 389-412.

_____. "L' exégèse biblique et la théologie spéculative de s. Thomas d'Aquin." *Divinitas* 18 (1974) : 138-153.

_____. "Christ and the Church : *Una Mystica Persona* in the Pauline Commentaries of St. Thomas Aquinas." In *S. Tommaso Teologo,* ed. A. Piolanti, 239-250. Rome: Libreria Editrice Vaticana, 1995.

SYNAVE, P. "Les Commentaires scripturaires de saint Thomas d'Aquin." *Vie Spirituelle* 8 (1923) : 455-469.

_____ and Pierre BENOIT. *Prophecy and Revelation. A Commentary on the Summa Theologica II-II, Questions 171-178.* Translated by Avery Dulles and Thomas L. Sheridan. New York: Desclée, 1961.

THOLUCK, A. *De Thoma Aquino et Abaelardo S. Scripturae interpretibus.* Halle: E. Anton, 1842.

TI-TI CHEN, J. "La unidad de la Iglesia según el Comentario de Santo Tomás a la Epístola a los Efesios." *Scripta Theologica* 8 (1976) : 111-230.

TILLARD, J.-M.R. *Church of Churches: The Ecclesiology of Communion.* Translated by R.C. De Peaux. Collegeville, MN: Liturgical Press, 1992.

TOLOMEO OF LUCCA, *Ptolomaei Lucensis Historia ecclesiastica nova,* Lib. XXII17-XXIII16. In L.A. Muratori, *Rerum italicarum scriptores,* vol. 11. Milan: 1724. As found in the partial critical edition by A. Dondaine, "Les *Opuscula fratris Thomae* chez Ptolémée de Lucques," *Archivum fratrum praedicatorum* 31 [1961] : 142-203.

TORRANCE, Iain R. "A Bibliography of the Writings of T.F. Torrance : 1941-1989." *Scottish Journal of Theology* 43 (1990) : 225-262

TORRANCE, T.F. "Scientific Hermeneutics according to St. Thomas Aquinas." *Journal of Theological Studies* 13 (1962) : 259-289.

TORRELL, J.P. "La question disputée De prophétie de saint Albert le Grand. Edition critique et commentaire." *Revue des sciences philosophiques et théologiques* 65 (1981) : 5-53; 197-232.

_____ and D. BOUTHILLIER. "Quand saint Thomas méditait sur le prophète Isaïe." *Revue Thomiste* 90 (1990) : 5-47.

_____. "Le traité de la prophétie de s. Thomas d'Aquin et la théologie de la révélation." In *La doctrine de la révélation divine de saint Thomas d'Aquin. Actes du Symposium sur la pensée de saint Thomas d'Aquin tenu à Rolduc, les 4 et 5 Novembre 1989,* ed. Leo Elders, 171-195. Città del Vaticano: Libreria Editrice Vaticana, 1990.

_____. *Saint Thomas Aquinas : The Person and His Work.* Vol. 1, trans. by Robert Royal. Washington, D.C.: Catholic University of America Press, 1996.

TURNER, D.L. "Ephesians 2:3c and peccatum originale." *Grace Theological Journal* 1/2 (1980) : 195-219.

VAN ACKEREN, Gerald F. *Sacra Doctrina: The Subject of the First Question of the Summa Theologica of St. Thomas Aquinas.* Rome: Catholic Book Agency, 1952.

VALKENBURG, Wilhelmus G.B.M. "'Did not our Hearts Burn?' Place and Function of Holy Scripture in the Theology of St. Thomas." Ph.D. diss., Katholieke Theologische Universiteit Utrecht, 1990.

VATICAN COUNCIL II. *Lumen Gentium*: *The Dogmatic Constitution on the Church*. In *Vatican Council II: The Conciliar and Post-Conciliar Documents*, ed. Austin Flannery, 350-426. Boston: Daughters of St. Paul, 1988.

VAUTHIER, E. "Le Saint Esprit principe d'unité de l'Église d'après Saint Thomas d'Aquin." *Mélanges de science religieuse*. 5 (1948) : 175-196; 6 (1949) : 54-80.

VOSTÉ, J.-M. "S. Thomas epistularum S. Pauli interpres." *Angelicum* 19 (1942) : 256-276.

WEISHEIPL, James A. *Friar Thomas D'Aquino: His Life, Thought, and Works*. Washington, D.C.: Catholic University of America Press, 1974.

_____. "The Johannine Commentary of Friar Thomas." *Church History* 45 (June 1976) : 185-195.

_____. Introduction to *Commentary on the Gospel of St. John*, by Thomas Aquinas. Vol. 1, trans. by Fabian R. Larcher. Albany: Magi Books, 1980.

WIESMAN, H. "Der Kommentar des hl. Thomas von Aquin zu den Klageliedern des Jeremias." *Scholastik* 4 (1929) : 82-86.

WILD, R. "'Be Imitators of God': Discipleship in the Letter to the Ephesians." In *Discipleship in the New Testament*, ed. F.F. Segovia. Philadelphia: Fortress Press, 1985.

YATES, R. "A Re-examination of Ephesians 1:23." *Expository Times* 83 (1972) : 146-151.

Finito di stampare
nel mese di gennaio 2002

presso la tipografia
"Giovanni Olivieri" di E. Montefoschi
00187 Roma - Via dell'Archetto, 10,11,12